THE APOSTLE OF GOD

PAUL AND THE PROMISE OF ABRAHAM

JOHN L. WHITE

HENDRICKSON
PUBLISHERS

Hendrickson Publishers, Inc.
P. O. Box 3473
Peabody, Massachusetts 01961–3473

Printed in the United States of America

ISBN 1–56563–283–4

First Printing — July 1999

Library of Congress Cataloging-in-Publication Data

White, John Lee.
   The Apostle of God: Paul and the promise of Abraham   /   John L. White.
   Includes bibliographical references and index.
   ISBN 1–56563–283–4 (hardcover)
   1. Bible.   N.T.   Epistles of Paul—Theology.   2. Adoption (Theology)—Biblical teaching.   3. God—Fatherhood—Biblical teaching.   I. Title.
BS2655.A35W45   1999
227'.06—dc21
                                                                98-54746
                                                                        CIP

THE APOSTLE
OF GOD

In Memory

of

Julie Dorin, a friend
Sophia Wacker, my mother-in-law
Clarice White, my mother

TABLE OF CONTENTS

Part One:
God's Character as Creator
in Paul's Rhetoric

Part Three:
God Our Father, Christ the Lord,
and the Household of Faith

ILLUSTRATIONS

ACKNOWLEDGEMENTS

I want to thank my editor at Hendrickson Publishers, Patrick Alexander, for his initial receptivity to the way that I was conceiving Paul's theology. I want to thank Patrick for several other things, but particularly for his help in suggesting ways to present material so that it would enhance the book's main thesis.

Near the start of research on this book, William Thompson, S.J., and Joep van Beeck, S.J., were good conversation partners, who directed me around some pitfalls. Joep was especially helpful in removing Protestant blinders so that I could have a more analogical view of Paul's theology.

Two New Testament scholars and friends, Brandon Scott and Wendy Cotter, C.S.J., seemed to understand where the research was headed almost from the beginning and have been sources of encouragement and practical advice throughout. In addition to Wendy, other biblical colleagues in Loyola's Theology Department have rendered valuable service along the way. Thomas Tobin, S.J., has been a good theological companion for years and I am grateful for the many things learned in his graduate course on Hellenistic Judaism that he allowed me to audit. Tom's own research on the rhetoric of Romans is congruent with my work. David Aune likewise has assisted me in several ways over the years. Finally, conversations with Pauline Viviano have added to my sense of having a right understanding of Paul's theology.

Three Loyola University administrators stand out as contributors to my study of Paul: John McCarthy, Chair of the Theology Department; Mary Peter McGinty, C.S.J., Assistant Chair of the Theology Department; and Kathleen McCourt, recently Dean of the College of Arts and Sciences. All three facilitated my teaching two years at Loyola's Rome Center in Rome, Italy. That experience confirmed my view that Roman culture was a major influence on Christian beginnings.

Numerous people at the Rome Center made access to ancient culture enjoyable. John and Kate Felice first introduced my wife Myrna and me to Etruscan culture by driving us to several sites. Such hospitality was not part of John's or Kate's duties as Director and Registrar, but they willingly shared their time with us. My onsite classes and field trips with Rome Center faculty were especially educational. John Nicholson, Valerie Higgins, and Giovanni Scichilone were all excellent teachers and I consider myself fortunate to have been their student.

I also want to thank Ronald Strom, who was a good host to us in Rome on many occasions. Ronald was a helpful critic, both in conversation and in reading things I had written. Not being a scholar of religion, he brought a scholarly but outside perspective that proved useful.

Finally, my family needs to be acknowledged one more time for putting up with a husband's and father's excessive tossing and turning in research. Thanks to my wife, Myrna, and to our children and their mates, Barak, Krista, Karis, Eric, Kristen, and Ibrahim. Old "crab claw" may as well acknowledge his grandchildren as well. Thanks to Jonathan, Nicolas, and Amy. Maybe now we will have more time to play together.

ABBREVIATIONS

Secondary Sources

ABR	*Australian Biblical Review*
ANRW	*Aufstieg und Niedergang der römischen Welt: Geschichte und Kultur Roms im Spiegel der neueren Forschung.* Ed. H. Temporini, W. Hasse. Berlin, 1972
BR	*Biblical Research*
BZNW	Beihefte zur ZNW
CAMGR	*Civilization of the Ancient Mediterranean: Greece and Rome.* Ed. M. Grant and R. Kitzinger. 3 vols. New York, 1988
CBQ	*Catholic Biblical Quarterly*
FRLANT	Forsuchungen zur Religion und Literatur des Alten und Neuen Testaments
HBC	*Harper's Bible Commentary.* Ed. J. L. Mays et al. San Francisco, 1988
HBD	*Harper's Bible Dictionary.* Ed. P. J. Achtemeier. San Francisco, 1985
HDR	Harvard Dissertations in Religion
HNT	Handbuch zum Neuen Testament
HTR	*Harvard Theological Review*
IDB	*Interpreter's Dictionary of the Bible.* Ed. G. A. Buttrick et al. Nashville, 1962
IDBSup	*Interpreter's Dictionary of the Bible: Supplementary Volume.* Ed. K. Crim. Nashville, 1976
Int	*Interpretation*
JAC	Jahrbuch für Antike und Christentum
JBL	*Journal of Biblical Literature*
JHS	*Journal of Hellenic Studies*

JRH	*Journal of Religious History*
LCL	Loeb Classical Library
MNTC	Moffatt New Testament Commentary
NovT	*Novum Testamentum*
OCD	*The Oxford Classical Dictionary.* Ed. N. G. L. Hammond and H. H. Scullard. Repr. of 2d ed. Oxford, 1973
SBLDS	Society of Biblical Literature Dissertation Series
Str-B	Strack, H. L., and P. Billerbeck. *Kommentar zum Neuen Testament aus Talmud und Midrasch.* 6 vols. Munich, 1922–1961
TDNT	*Theological Dictionary of the New Testament.* Ed. G. Kittel and G. Friedrich. Trans. G. W. Bromiley. 10 vols. Grand Rapids, 1964–1976
ZNW	*Zeitschrift für die neutestamentliche Wissenschaft*

Primary Sources

Dio Chrysostom
    Or. [Cor.] *Oration 37 (Corinthiaca)*
Josephus
    Ant.   *Jewish Antiquities*
    Ag. Ap.   *Against Apion*
Juvenal
    Sat.   *Satirae*
Martial
    Ep.   *Epigrammata*
Philo
    Abr.   *De Abrahamo*
    Conf.   *De confusione linguarum*
    Decal.   *De decalogo*
    Ios.   *De Iosepho*
    Leg.   *Legatio ad Gaium*
    Mos.   *De vita Mosis*
    Mut.   *De mutatione nominum*
    Praem.   *De praemiis et poenis*
    Sobr.   *De sobrietate*
    Spec.   *De specialibus legibus*
    Virt.   *De virtutibus*
Pindar
    Isthm.   *Isthmian Odes*

Pliny the Younger
    Ep.   *Epistulae*
    Pan.   *Panegyricus*
Suetonius
    Augustus *Divus Augustus*
    Julius   *Divus Julius*
    Tiberius   *Tiberius*
4QFlor   *Florilegium*
Jub.   *Jubilees*
Let. Aris.   *Letter of Aristeas*
T. Jud.   *Testament of Judah*

Papyri

P.Oxy.   *Oxyrhynchus Papyri*
P.Mert.   *Merton Papyrus (A Descriptive Catalogue of the Greek Papyri in the Collection of Wilfred Merton)*
P.Mich.   *Michigan Papyri*

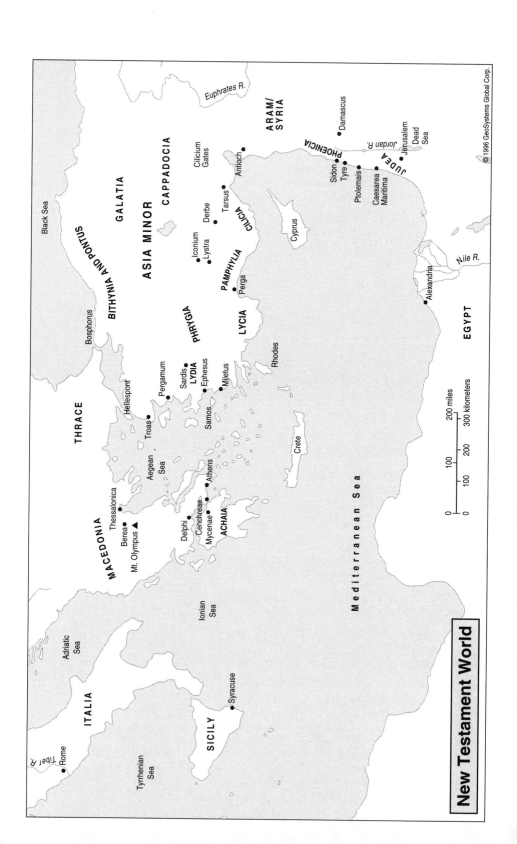

New Testament World

You have heard, no doubt, of my earlier life in Judaism. I was violently persecuting the church of God and was trying to destroy it. I advanced in Judaism beyond many among my people of the same age, for I was far more zealous for the traditions of my ancestors. But when God, who had set me apart before I was born and called me through his grace, was pleased to reveal his Son to me, so that I might proclaim him among the Gentiles, I did not confer with any human being. (Gal 1:13–16)

INTRODUCTION: PAUL'S VISIONARY EXPERIENCE OF GOD

Despite a dearth of evidence moderns are wont to demand, without question something transformed Saul the persecutor into Paul the Apostle. What caused one "advanced in Judaism, . . . zealous for the traditions of [his] ancestors" to proclaim the crucified Jesus, cursed according to Jewish Law, as the Messiah of the entire world? What prompted Paul's radical new understanding of the God of Abraham, and what was that understanding?

In the pages that follow I answer these and related questions in light of my proposal that Paul's idea of God changed radically because of a personal vision of the resurrected Jesus. Chiefly Jesus' resurrection proved he was vindicated by God, not cursed, and that, indeed, he was God's Messianic Son as persecuted Christians were claiming. The unexpected resurrection of the crucified Jesus caused Paul to form a new understanding of God. No longer was he primarily lawgiver and judge, but creator of spiritual offspring: one who generated life out of Jesus' sterile-like death and a power who made "lawless" non-Jews his offspring and members of the family of God. In subsequent chapters we will explore how Paul came to hold creator as his chief metaphor for understanding God. Further, we will investigate the potentiality of the metaphor of adoption to convey Paul's new system of belief. Naturally we must pay attention to how Paul's new understanding fits within the context of his

Greco-Roman environment, particularly the ruler cult, and finally we will see how other images, especially those drawn from the household, allow Paul to proclaim his radical message.

THE RADICALITY OF PAUL'S IDEA OF GOD

Paul's conception of God is less radical in an absolute sense than it is radical in comparison with his own ideas about God prior to becoming an apostle. Unfortunately, although Paul himself contrasts his viewpoint as an apostle with his former values as a Pharisee, some scholars infer that Paul never really moved outside his former commitment to God's identity as lawgiver and judge.[1] That is *not* the viewpoint of this book. I take quite seriously Paul's statement that his former way of defining Jewish identity by means of adherence to Mosaic law was something he came to consider no better than garbage (see Phil 3:3–11; esp. 3:8).

What new basis of relationship with God did Paul come to advocate? Paul believed that no amount of natural birth status or of community recognition could make someone God's offspring. Instead, for Paul, people must have the mindset of Christ. Christ looked not to his own interests but to the interests of others, and he did not put himself forward but, even in the face of death, submitted and trusted himself to God (Phil 2:1–8). Therefore, true status comes only from God and what God is able to make of one's life, not from nobility of birth or recognition of accomplishment within the community (see 1 Cor 1:26–31).

In addition to this reversal in Paul's own idea of the basis of relationship with God, Paul came to believe that non-Jews also were members of God's elect community. The idea that Gentiles were among God's people was not novel; Judaism had admitted non-Jews into its community virtually from the beginning. What was radically distinctive was Paul's idea that Gentile converts did not have second-class status within the community. To be sure, even Paul's thinking was not unique, since certain Jewish leaders, such as Philo of Alexandria, had also given special recognition to Jewish proselytes. Philo says that like Abraham, who was a model for Jewish proselytes, Gentile converts had made the tremendous

---

[1]Regarding Paul's autobiographical contrast between his former values as a Pharisee and his present commitments as an apostle of Christ, see Gal 1:11–17; Phil 3:3–11; and 2 Cor 11:1–12:10. Note 3 below lists some of the scholars who suggest that Paul remained committed to his former Pharisaic values.

sacrifice of giving up family, friends, and homeland in order to become God's people.[2]

Paul exceeded Philo and almost all members of the Jewish community, however, when he allowed non-Jews to be equal members of God's people *without* traditional admittance requirements, namely, circumcision, observance of Jewish dietary laws, and other Mosaic prescriptions. Only Greek-speaking Jewish Christians, like the ones Paul had formerly persecuted, had gone this far in lowering standards for Gentiles. Even in relation to Greek-speaking Jewish Christians, Paul stands out. He produced thoroughly positive argumentation demonstrating that God required that Gentiles be admitted to the community on such terms.

To the extent that Jews placed confidence in themselves rather than in God as the means of effecting something positive out of human action, to that extent Paul argued that Gentile converts were *superior* to Jews even in being Abraham's descendants. Thus, because of the priority of trust in God over obedience to Mosaic law in Paul's system of belief, I am opposed to modern interpretations of Paul that make him into a kind of closet rabbi and make his communities of converts into synagogues.[3]

Even Krister Stendahl, who rightly proposed that Paul's idea of salvation must be interpreted not in terms of personal liberation from the law but as a social liberation whereby Gentiles become God's people without becoming Jews, finally fails to grant Paul the cultural elasticity he deserves. By insisting on Gentile converts' release from Mosaic law, Paul continued to have a legalistic mind-set. Namely, *justification by faith* was itself a commitment to legalism. Thus, out of excessive concern with the principle of liberation from the law, Stendahl says that Paul's ministry was divisive and ineffective (see "The Apostle Paul," 70–77).

Later in the book, I cite data in Paul's letters and various scholarly explanations indicating that Paul did not model his congregations after synagogue communities. The synagogue is the wrong institutional

---

[2]Philo and certain other Greek-speaking Jewish representatives state that Abraham himself was a proselyte and had to be "adopted" as God's son. As founder of the Jewish race and as someone who had to break his own traditional and hereditary ties to family in order to father a new people, Abraham was not himself a Jew. Nor was he an adherent of prescribed Jewish customs, since they did not yet exist. See Philo, *Sobr.* 56–57; *Abr.* 75; and *Virt.* 219. See also John Collins's treatment of Jewish authors in *Between Athens and Jerusalem,* where he discusses the universalist tendency associated with the figure of Abraham in Jewish Diaspora authors of the Hellenistic and Roman periods (see pp. 35–46 and 204–7).

[3]E.g., Peter Tomson says that Paul conducted himself like a Hellenistic Pharisee who taught halakic instruction to his congregations (see *Halakha in the*

model for understanding Paul's theological viewpoint. Modern advocates of this viewpoint depend entirely too much on the picture of the apostle's ministry in the Acts of the Apostles and not enough on data within Paul's own letters.[4]

I am not suggesting that Paul abandoned Jewish tradition; nevertheless, it is significant that he did not require Gentiles to become Jews in order to be God's people. He clearly advocated a different basis of communal identity. Therefore, we must ask whether Paul's theological differences with the Jewish community, including some Jewish-Christian churches, amounted to anti-Semitism.

At least three reasons exist why Paul's representation of God should not be described as anti-Jewish. First, at the time he was writing, he thought of his converts not as adherents of a separate religion but as a reform movement within Judaism itself. Second, Paul was not opposed just to the priority of law as a way of defining the Jewish relationship with God. He was equally opposed to analogous Gentile principles and emphases within his own communities. Third, his idea of God did not derive from some alien quarter but was modeled on alternative traditions and emphases within Judaism itself. The unfolding argument of the book will make clear that antagonism to Judaism is not the center of Paul's theology. Both what he argued for and what he argued against applied to non-Jews as much as to Jews.

ADOPTION AS THE TRUE BASIS OF BEING GOD'S FAMILY

Paul considered Gentile converts as much God's people as the Jews. But since Gentiles were clearly not God's race through physical descent from Abraham, Paul had to use the metaphor of adoption to justify their status as Abraham's children (see Gal 4:1–7).

Letters of the Apostle, 51–53). Paul's instruction, both theological and practical, derived continually from Scripture (see ibid., 58).

[4]Acts says that Paul began each new stage of missionary activity in the synagogue(s) of the city he was visiting (e.g., see Acts 13:5ff.; 13:14ff.; 14:1ff.; 17:1ff.). By contrast, Paul's own letters suggest that the founding of Paul's churches resulted not from working in the synagogues but from working directly with Gentiles. E.g., whereas Acts 17:1ff. says that persecution of the church at Thessalonica arose from Jewish jealousy, Paul indicates in 1 Thess 1–2 that his converts were formerly not Gentile "Godfearers" (i.e., Gentiles attracted to the synagogue) but worshippers of pagan gods and were persecuted by fellow Gentiles after conversion.

It might appear, then, that Gentile converts constituted an anomaly within the Jewish community. Paul, however, argued just the opposite. He asserted paradoxically that all of God's "legitimate" offspring are adopted, including the founder of the race, Abraham! Even Christ, Abraham's promised offspring, was empowered to effect the Gentiles' inclusion only by means of his own resurrection and anointing at God's hands (spiritual adoption).

Where Did Paul Get His Idea of Spiritual Adoption?

Paul emphasized trust in God, rather than confidence in conventional ways of status definition (noble birth and recognition of one's achievements by members of the community), as the true basis for being God's people. Unfortunately, this emphasis on the subjective disposition of trust, often described as "justification by faith" by Pauline scholars, fails to capture the role of God in effecting salvation. Paul is more concerned with *God's* action in creating something out of our faith than with our trust as such. In fact, Paul argues that precisely God's power to effect something out of human faith was the condition for trusting him.

Returning to the key question, what led Paul to alter his former conception of God as lawgiver and turn to his new apostolic emphasis on God as spiritual procreator? Paul indicates, especially in his letter to the Galatians, that this shift came as a result of a mystical experience. Paul refers to the experience in Gal 1:12 as a "revelation of Jesus Christ," and he makes it clear here and elsewhere in Gal 1–2 that his new belief in Jesus' resurrection was in no respect the result of human persuasion. He certainly was not driven to belief in Christ's resurrection out of some personal inadequacy in his ability to obey Mosaic law.

Rather, Paul insists in Gal 1:13–14 that his adherence to Mosaic law and his own excellence in performing the law motivated him to destroy the Christian movement.[5] What fueled Paul's opposition was the lawlessness of certain liberal Hellenistic Christians in admitting to the Jewish community Gentile converts who did not meet traditional admittance requirements.

Nor was this the only reason Paul persecuted the church. For liberal Hellenistic Christian converts were advocating the view that a man

---

[5]In Gal 1:13–14 Paul connects his violent persecution of the church explicitly to his zeal for the traditions of his ancestors, i.e., the laws/customs thought to derive from Moses. Similarly, in Phil 3:5–6, Paul states that his former zeal for the law as a Pharisee motivated him to persecute the church.

condemned and executed under Mosaic law, Jesus of Nazareth, was the
Messiah. On the basis of Jewish Scripture and Mosaic law, Paul knew
that Jesus was just the opposite of God's promised agent of blessing.
Paul indicates his former line of attack on the followers of Christ in Gal
3:13: "Cursed is everyone who hangs on a tree." According to Deut
21:22–23, whenever anyone in the Jewish community committed a crime
punishable by death and was executed, the atrocity of the offense was accentuated by hanging the offender up to public view on a tree. Anyone
subjected to such a scandalous death was believed to be cursed by God
and capable of contaminating the very soil on which the community relied for its livelihood. Therefore, Mosaic law required that the corpse of
the criminal not remain on the tree overnight but be buried the same day
(see Deut 21:23).

Because Jesus was publicly "hanged on a tree" by being crucified,
Paul knew that he was accursed by God.[6] Moreover, by making something positive of this man, his followers were keeping the scandal in view
and thus spreading the contamination. Therefore Paul aspired to lay this
Jesus to rest once for all by destroying the people who kept his scandal
alive (see Gal 1:13; Phil 3:6). To Paul's utter surprise, however, God revealed the resurrected Jesus to him. Since the crucified Jesus was alive, he
therefore must have been vindicated by God and not cursed, and if vindicated, then he must be the Messiah whom his followers claimed.

And if the crucified one was vindicated and not cursed, then Mosaic law was not fully able to explain the ways of God. This revelation
about the law had to be as surprising to Paul as the fact that God had vindicated a criminal and made him an agent of blessing. He was driven
back to Jewish tradition to find something that made sense out of God's
resurrection of an executed criminal and the salvation of "lawless"
Gentiles. Although it is probably impossible to reconstruct the order in
which the pieces fell into place, the importance of the Abraham tradition
to Paul's idea of God allows us to use it as a starting point.[7]

---

[6]The scandal that Paul associated with Jesus' death by crucifixion is not
confined to Gal 3:13 and like statements in Galatians. In 1 Cor 1:18–25 Paul admits the irrationality and scandal of preaching that God effected salvation by
means of the crucified Jesus, e.g., see v. 23: "we proclaim Christ crucified, a stumbling block to Jews and foolishness to Gentiles." Philippians 2:8 accentuates the
radicality of Christ's submission to God by not stopping with the giving up of his
life but by adding "even death on a cross."

[7]As illustrated here and later in the book, in Galatians and Romans Paul
connects Jesus' status as Christ and Gentile converts' status as God's people explicitly with the Abraham tradition.

It is unlikely that Paul interpreted the crucifixion positively at the outset. More likely, he initially reflected on more obvious, negative aspects about Christ and Gentile converts.[8] He knew that Jesus had not faithfully adhered to the law, or he would not have been condemned and executed. And he knew that Gentiles were becoming God's people even without adopting traditional Jewish customs. Thus, like Christ, Gentiles were acceptable to God apart from their adherence to Mosaic law. The Jewish precedent that made sense of both oddities was God's promise to Abraham that all nations (Gentiles) would be blessed through his offspring. Somehow, the accursed Jesus must be the promised offspring through whom the Gentiles were becoming God's people.

Paul found correspondence with, and confirmation of, this idea in the fact that God had to adopt Abraham to father the Jewish race. At the time of God's promise, Abraham himself was not Jewish, neither circumcised nor obedient to Mosaic law. Therefore, Christ's and Gentile converts' lack of adherence to Mosaic law, far from making them different from the founder of the race, was analogous to Abraham's own lack of legal qualifications. At all three stages, God had adopted people by spiritual, not physical, means to be his offspring. None were qualified by birth or by their performance of the law. Only trust in God's grace constituted their basis of inclusion. Moreover, Gentiles were at no disadvantage in comparison with Abraham's actual descendants. From Paul's conversion viewpoint, *only* spiritual offspring (i.e., those whom God admitted through grace), whether Gentile or Jew, were truly Abraham's race.

Paul underscores Christ's paradoxical resurrection out of scandalous death as the event that designated him as Abraham's promised offspring in Gal 3:13ff. In turn, it formed the basis for God's further designation of Gentiles as Abraham's offspring:

> Christ redeemed us from the curse of the law by becoming a curse for us—for it is written, "Cursed is everyone who hangs on a tree"—in order that in Christ Jesus the blessing of Abraham might come to the Gentiles, so that we might receive the promise of the Spirit through faith. . . . Now the promises were made to Abraham and to his offspring; it does not say, "And to offsprings," as of many; but it says, "And to your offspring," that is, to one person, who is Christ. (Gal 3:13–14, 16)

---

[8]The manner in which Paul connects Christ, Gentile converts, and Abraham is a topic taken up on several occasions in this book, but the most sustained explanation is given in ch. 8.

The only positive qualification Abraham, Christ, and the Gentile converts shared was their dependence on God to effect something out of their present situation.

To be sure, people's faith in God's ability to do what he promised was, for Paul, the necessary attribute that qualified them to be his offspring. Nevertheless, it is not the subjective disposition of trust on which we should focus if we want to understand Paul's idea of God. Faith is only an appropriate response to what is the true source of Paul's theology, his recognition of God's benevolent power as creator to procreate life out of negative situations, even out of death itself.

More explicitly, how is God's salvific action as creator similar typologically in the cases of Abraham and Christ? What most characterized Christ's death, from Paul's former Pharisaic viewpoint, was the scandal it represented. According to Jewish law, being hung on a tree for having committed a crime punishable by death was a terrible stigma. Not only was such a person thought to be under God's curse; the criminal could mediate curse to others. Abraham, the so-called father of the race, had reached old age without procreating an offspring with Sarah. Like Christ's, their situation was scandalous and shameful. They were sterile. Metaphorically speaking, then, Paul could liken Abraham and Sarah's barrenness to (Christ's) death, and the enlivening of their procreative powers to (Christ's) resurrection (cf. Rom 4:17–21).

In reverse, Paul could liken the crucified Christ, whose accursed status could have made the very soil unproductive, to Abraham and Sarah, accursed by sterility. Correspondingly, his resurrection may be compared metaphorically to Isaac's miraculous procreation. Thus, for Paul, through Christ's resurrection God made him Abraham's promised offspring and, simultaneously, the promised Son (the Christ) who could mediate spiritual procreation to Gentiles.

Indeed, since the promised blessing to the nations was effected through Christ, Paul describes him, rather than Isaac, as Abraham's miraculously procreated son.

> Now the promises were made to Abraham and to his offspring; it does not say, "And to offsprings," as of many; but it says, "And to your offspring," that is, to one person, who is Christ. (Gal 3:16)

The similarities between Abraham, Christ, and the Gentile church as spiritual offspring, together with the analogous ways God effected their spiritual procreation, will be explained in greater detail in subsequent chapters. For the time being, this must sufficiently explain how Paul came to replace his conception of God as lawgiver with the idea of

God as creator and "Father." But what about Christ's adoption as Abraham's and God's Son, an idea many readers may regard initially as problematic?

How Did Paul Understand Jesus' Adoption?

First of all, Paul's image of adoption is a metaphor. This does not mean the idea is any less true, but it does mean the image resists simple, literalistic explanation. In addition, the images must be discussed in terms that would have made sense in Paul's own first-century setting. It is utterly wrong to describe Paul's presentation of Christ's adoption in twentieth-century terms, whether of the liberal or of the fundamentalist variety. For example, Paul did not advocate, on the one hand, the modern view that, prior to his human life on earth, Jesus had a fully conscious, personal existence in heaven. Nor, on the other hand, did he endorse the so-called adoptionistic Christology of modern liberals, who say that Christ was human, and nothing more, until God empowered him to be his agent of salvation.

Moreover, we may not identify Paul's conception of Christ with creedal statements of the fourth and fifth century CE: "true God from true God, begotten, not made, of one being with the Father," etc. Paul's representation of Christ was not so detailed, in a literalistic sense, as that of the later church fathers. Neither was it as explicit as we moderns would like. He was less concerned with Christ's metaphysical nature than with his role in the mediation of God's salvation. Paul was even less disposed to philosophical declarations than many of his Jewish and Christian contemporaries. Although he was a Greek-speaking Jew exposed to ideas about wisdom (σοφία) and reason (λόγος) as divinized agents of God, Paul does not clearly identify Christ with such figures. Unlike John's Gospel, for example, Paul's writing does not refer explicitly to Christ as the Word (Reason) of God. Nor do we find anything in Paul's letters comparable to Philo's idea of the Logos as a divine intermediary.

On the other hand, Paul does indicate that Christ had some kind of existence prior to that lived in the historical Jesus. Thus he states that Christ was the "spiritual rock" from which the water flowed that sustained Jewish forefathers in the wilderness (1 Cor 10:4). Did Paul think that Christ was literally present as a rock, allaying the Hebrews' thirst? Or was Paul indicating, metaphorically, that the same divine power of nourishment that sustained the Hebrews in the wilderness was now present in Christ's sustenance of the church? We do not know.

We find another example of Christ's prior life exhibited in the so-called Christ hymn of Phil 2:6–11. Although Paul was not the original author of this hymn, he quotes it approvingly as it speaks of Christ before his life as the historical Jesus:

> who, though he was in the form of God,
> did not regard equality with God
> as something to be exploited,
> but emptied himself,
> taking the form of a slave,
> being born in human likeness.

Despite the divinity attributed to Christ even before his life as a mortal, it is significant that Paul ascribes even greater status to Christ as a result of Jesus' scandalous suffering and death:

> And being found in human form,
> he humbled himself
> and became obedient to the point of death—
> even death on a cross.
> Therefore God also highly exalted him
> and gave him the name
> that is above every name,
> so that at the name of Jesus
> every knee should bend,
> in heaven and on earth and under the earth
> and every tongue should confess
> that Jesus Christ is Lord,
> to the glory of God the Father.

Whatever previous status Christ had, Paul says that Jesus' full empowerment as universal Lord was not effected until after God resurrected him. Moreover, the glory of his reign results in praise not of Jesus himself but of God, precisely in his capacity as Father: "Jesus Christ is Lord to the glory of God the Father."

One can hardly escape the conclusion that both Jesus' status as universal Lord and his identity as divine Son are given definitively only at the resurrection. Nor can one ignore the political overtones of Jesus' appointment as Lord. Paul's use of the title Christ (the "anointed") indicates that God has appointed Jesus as the successor to David's throne. Moreover, the universality of Christ's rule can not be fully explained by means of Jewish precedent, even if it includes the idea of Christ as God's ideal ruler in an apocalyptic sense. Later chapters of this book will show that the types of lordship Paul attributes to Christ's rule were precisely the same as those attributed to Roman emperors.

In summary, then, Jesus' various roles as promised offspring of Abraham, anointed successor to David, and divine and human being all resist simple definition. On the one hand, Christ himself had to be empowered by means of God's resurrection to be Abraham's promised seed (heir) and David's spiritual successor. In both the political and familial realms, Christ's status was generated by God at his resurrection, so that Christ himself was a fellow citizen and sibling of other recipients of God's new spiritual reality. On the other hand, Christ is the paradigm for spiritual sonship in Paul's system of belief, and he has the temporal priority of being "firstbegotten Son" and "first (leading) citizen" of the realm.[9] Even recognition of this temporal priority probably does not do justice to Paul's conception of Christ's special status. Paul never calls Christ "brother," but always "Lord." Thus, an unrelieved ambiguity lies at the heart of Paul's metaphors. Christ is coheir in a new family and fellow citizen in a new realm, but he is also Lord of both.

These comments have not resolved exactly how Christ was the spiritual recipient of God's procreative powers, but they have showed that Paul's images should not be defined too literally. The images need to resonate as metaphors. The next section considers the centrality, for Paul, of God's identity as creator. Two aspects of this idea are discussed: whether the Father as creator constituted Paul's leading idea about God, and whether there was any progressive development in Paul's idea of God during his apostolic career. Although not as important for most readers as the issue of Christ's adoption, these subjects are strategic concerns for scholars trying to reconstruct Paul's theology.

THE CENTRALITY OF GOD AS CREATOR IN PAUL'S BELIEF

Striking both in the way Paul connects Christ's saving sonship to resurrection and in the way he interprets God's adoption of Abraham to be father of a spiritual race (including God's role in Abraham and Sarah's procreation of Isaac)—is God's analogous role as creator. Paul's

---

[9]For example, see Paul's reference to Christ as "first born" of many children in Rom 8:29. A comparable emphasis is indicated in Gal 3:16 where Christ is referred to as *the* offspring promised to Abraham through whom all God's blessings would be mediated. The same idea of Christ's priority appears in Paul's metaphor of Christ as "first fruits" (1 Cor 15:20, 23). Christ's status as political head of God's new social order is suggested by such statements as 1 Cor 15:27: "God has put all things in subjection under his feet."

emphasis on the analogous nature of these acts demonstrates that God shows himself to be the creator who brings life out of death, fertility out of barrenness, and hope out of hopelessness.

Despite the importance of these correspondences in certain Pauline letters, readers might be skeptical of the centrality of spiritual adoption and of God's identity as creator in Paul's remaining letters. True, he calls attention to the parallels between Christ and Abraham only in Galatians and Romans, and admittedly explicit references to spiritual adoption are confined to these letters. Still, God's identity as creator is the most fundamental element in Paul's idea of God, as this book will show. For the time being, allow me to state the matter in the way it became personally meaningful for me. By puzzling over the correspondences Paul drew between Abraham, Christ, and Gentile converts and by attending to his regular reference to God as "Father" at the beginning of all his authentic letters, I was led increasingly to the importance, for Paul, of God's creative identity. The explicit references to spiritual adoption made the idea of God as Father (creator) come graphically alive. And once I grasped the spiritual reality behind such references, I could see like emphases in Paul's letters even when God's procreativity is not stated explicitly. The reader is invited to see these emphases in the following examples from Paul's letters.

Is "Creator" Really Paul's Central Image for God?

If the analogy of God's generative powers were confined to Abraham and Christ, we would have cause for doubting the centrality, for Paul, of God's identity as creator. Paul extends the analogy, however, to his own change from destroyer to builder, and to Gentile converts' status as Abraham's offspring. The texture of Paul's language in every letter, as well as his stock images, presupposes God's identity as creator.

Paul frequently illustrates the way God has effected life out of his Gentile converts' deathlike situations. Indeed, these statements are as important to Paul as his emphasis on what God effected in the cases of Abraham and Christ.

> Consider your own call, brothers and sisters: not many of you were wise by human standards, not many were powerful, not many were of noble birth. But God chose what is foolish in the world to shame the wise; God chose what is weak in the world to shame the strong; God chose what is low and despised in the world, things that are not, to reduce to nothing things that are, so that no one might boast in the presence of God. He is the source of your life in Christ Jesus, who became for us wisdom from God, and righteousness and sanctification and redemption. (1 Cor. 1:26–30)

> For we know, brothers and sisters beloved by God, that he has chosen you, because our message of the gospel came to you not in word only, but also in power and in the Holy Spirit and with full conviction. . . . And you became imitators of us and of the Lord, for in spite of persecution you received the word with joy inspired by the Holy Spirit. . . . For the people of those regions [Macedonia and Achaia] report about us what kind of welcome we had among you, and how you turned to God from idols, to serve a living and true God. (1 Thess. 1:4–5, 6, 9)

Paul depicts God's salvation in both instances above, just as in the case of Christ and Abraham, in terms of God's creativity. Thus, in the case of the Corinthians, Paul contrasts their former lack of status with their present identity as God's people. God's character as creator is made explicit by Paul's statements that God created something out of nothing when he chose the Corinthians and that God was their source of life. Correspondingly, in the case of the Thessalonians, Paul likens their transformation to what God effected out of Christ's crucifixion: their persecution from fellow townspeople corresponds to Christ's crucifixion, and their being lifted above adversity ("with joy inspired by the Holy Spirit") corresponds to Christ's resurrection. And when Paul adds that the Thessalonians turned from idols to serve a living and true God, he has in mind God's vivifying power to effect transformation.

Paul assumes that the same power that created the physical universe is also the creator of the new spiritual world. Moreover, the spiritual universe is not a totally new work but a regeneration and perfection of the existing order. Granted, the physical creation must be liberated from the enslaving and *de*generative effects of sin. On the other hand, God enables it to grow to its full-term, spiritual potential. Paul identifies God as the creator of both orders, physical and spiritual, on several occasions.

> For the creation waits with eager longing for the revealing of the children of God; for the creation was subjected to futility, not of its own will but by the will of the one who subjected it, in hope that the creation itself will be set free from its bondage to decay and will obtain the freedom of the glory of the children of God. We know that the whole creation has been groaning in labor pains until now; and not only the creation, but we ourselves, who have the first fruits of the Spirit, groan inwardly while we wait for adoption, the redemption of our bodies. (Rom 8:19–23).

> For it is the [same] God who said, "Let light shine out of darkness," who has shone in our hearts to give the light of the knowledge of the glory of God in the face of Jesus Christ. (2 Cor 4:6)

The most striking aspect of Paul's representation of God as the source of universal regeneration (i.e., spiritual regeneration) is the way

Paul likens God's creativity to the affectionate relationship that a father has with his offspring. Thus he describes God's special favor toward Gentile converts in terms of Jewish ideas of election (i.e., being called out from other peoples). Indeed, apart perhaps from the prophet Hosea, Paul presents the familiarity of the relationship in more intimate terms than any other biblical representative.

Nonetheless, since God is the universal creator, Paul assumes—as the above citation from Romans 8 attests—that it is only a matter of time until all creation will share, paradoxically, the same special relationship with God enjoyed by children. For the most part, the following chapters in Romans concentrate on God's role as the special Father of Gentile converts. Still, never far in the background is Paul's conviction that the same power who called the world into being will eventually regenerate it.

These examples certainly expand the number of Paul's letters in which God's identity as creator is important. Whether or not these examples are enough to demonstrate its centrality for Paul, they provide sufficient warrant for examining the subject in greater detail. Thus, we proceed to another presupposition, that God's identity as Father (procreative creator) was Paul's most foundational and organizing theological metaphor from the beginning of his apostolic career.

Was There Any Major Development in Paul's Idea of God?

Scholars often assume one of the following views about Paul: (i) his thought lacks continuity because he always was addressing situational issues in his letters; or (ii) his thought exhibits an underlying coherence, but it derives from a recurring external problem, namely, Judaizing opposition to his missionary work.

Christiaan Beker, Daniel Patte, Norman Petersen, and several other scholars have recently proposed not only that there is a coherence to Paul's thought but that it derives from the apostle's own theological convictions and not from recurring external circumstances to which he had to respond.[10] I agree with this group of scholars that Paul's own theo-

---

[10]E.g., see the following works: Beker, *The Triumph of God;* Patte, *Paul's Faith;* Petersen, *Rediscovering Paul.* In recent professors and former students at Yale University I find a similar emphasis on Paul's own theological agenda; e.g., see works by Nils Dahl, Abraham Malherbe, and Stanley Stowers. Some published essays by Wilhelm Wuellner also emphasize the importance of Paul's convictions in shaping his rhetoric. Dieter Georgi's *Theocracy* attends similarly to Paul's somewhat systematic appropriation and adaptation of Greco-Roman ruler cult ideology to his picture of God and Christ.

logical convictions give coherence to his language and theology. Although our respective emphases appear to have arisen independently of one another, our viewpoints are complementary and supportive. We share the opinion that the same system of values and convictions may be assumed in all of Paul's letters.

So far as I recall, none of these scholars says anything about evolution or development in Paul's thought. This does not mean that they think that Paul's system of convictions remained static. For example, in one way or another, Beker, Patte, and Petersen show that Paul adapted his convictions to fit the individual circumstances of each letter. Nonetheless, they do not think that Paul altered his central theological values in the course of his apostolic career.

Since most interpreters assume that Paul's authentic letters were all written within the last decade of his life, they do not find the idea of development a problem.[11] It can be assumed, in this opinion, that Paul's defense of the Christian church was fully formed by that stage. By contrast, I hold the less popular view that Paul's missionary work in Greece, as well as his correspondence with churches there, began about a decade earlier than is usually assumed.[12] In this view, Paul's letters span a period of about two decades. Although Paul's longer contact with churches on the Greek mainland is not a subject defended or even described in this book, it does make the idea of theological development more feasible. Nonetheless, because of contrary evidence in his letters, I still reject the idea of any major development in Paul's thought. The data in Paul's letters show that his fundamental idea of God as creator—though radical in view of his former ideas about God—was in place at the start of his apostolic career.

Most scholars agree that 1 Thessalonians was Paul's earliest letter, whether written in 50–51 CE or, according to the earlier chronology

---

[11]I confine the analysis of Paul's metaphors and central conception of God to the seven letters almost all agree were written by Paul: Romans, 1 and 2 Corinthians, Galatians, Philippians, 1 Thessalonians, and Philemon.

[12]This chronology, which places Paul's missionary work in Greece earlier in his career, draws on the chronological thesis first proposed by John Knox in 1936 and published in book form in 1950 (Life of Paul). Knox's teacher, Donald Riddle, used the chronology in 1940 in Paul, Man of Conflict. Since the publication of Knox's book, Donald Rowlingson has published an essay in support of the thesis ("The Jerusalem Conference"). Similarly, M. Jack Suggs has written in support of Knox's chronology ("Paul's Macedonian Ministry"). John Hurd, F. Stanley Jones, and a few other scholars have also supported Knox's viewpoint. The most recent defense, in book form, of an early Pauline chronology was written by Gerd Luedemann (Paul, Apostle to the Gentiles).

suggested above, about 40 CE. Already in this first letter Paul refers to God several times as "Father" at the outset. Moreover, by referring to the Thessalonians as "beloved" and "chosen" by God in 1 Thess 1:4, Paul clearly defines "Father" in the affectionate sense of father of the family. In turn, Paul addresses the Thessalonians as "brothers and sisters," i.e., spiritual siblings, and, in various other ways discussed later, shows that they are God's offspring. Thus, the ideas of adoption and of God's identity as spiritual procreator are assumed already in Paul's earliest letter. Although Abraham himself is not presented as a model of adoption, Christ, Paul, and the churches of Judea are evoked as analogies for the Thessalonians' experience of God's life-begetting power. In particular, Christ's death and resurrection are presented as the primary paradigm of God's creative power to generate life out of death. The idea of God as life giver is clearly present.

A foundation slab behind high altar that reads "Paul apostle martyr." St Paul's Outside-the-Walls Church, Rome, Italy. Photo courtesy of Erich Lessing/Art Resource, N.Y.

Nor is it insignificant that God is regularly identified as "Father" at the beginning of all of Paul's letters. Even more important, Paul refers to himself as the "apostle of (to) the Gentiles" (e.g., see Rom 11:13–14; 15:14–21; Gal 2:1–10; also Gal 2:8), and he indicates by other means that his apostolic status derives directly from God and not from a Jewish, institutional basis.[13] This kind of apostolic authority shows us how "Father" is to be interpreted with regard to Paul's converts. Their status as God's offspring does not derive either from physical birth status as Jews or from performance of the Jewish law. They are God's people *as* Gentiles, without becoming Jews, as a result of God's procreative grace.

Nowhere does Paul ever advocate a different gospel for the conversion of Gentiles. He simply did not evolve from Pharisaism to his "law-free" mission to Gentiles. The change was abrupt. From the start, he was a defender of the "law-free" Greek-speaking Jewish-Christian church he formerly tried to destroy. Indeed, he states explicitly that he had never been an apostolic advocate of Gentiles' circumcision or subjection to Jewish dietary laws.[14]

To what may we attribute Paul's unerring commitment to the same theological values from the beginning of his missionary career? His mystical experience of God. From the time Paul became convinced that God had resurrected a man condemned under Mosaic law, he had to reconceive his idea of God. As a result of this experience, Paul could no longer think of God as lawgiver and judge. Nor could he any longer require Gentiles to obey Mosaic law as the basis of acceptance before God. The idea he did find compatible with his mystical experience of the resurrected criminal and with the admittance of Gentiles qua Gentiles into God's community was God's identity as creator. One's status as divine offspring derived directly from confidence in God's power to make it happen and not from natural ("human") status or achievment. We shall see that Paul adapted this fundamental vision of God as creator to address several different contexts, but he never departed from the conception itself.

---

[13]E.g., see 1 Cor 1:17–25; 2 Cor 4:1–12; 5:11–21; 11:1–12:10; Phil 3:3–11; 1 Thess 2:1–16. These references indicate that Paul's authorization looks foolish and insignificant from the vantage point of conventional (human) authority structures. Thus, his authority is of a special, spiritual nature.

[14]In the first two chapters of Galatians, see Paul's discussion of his unswerving position against the circumcision of Gentiles. Also, in Gal 2:11ff. see Paul's opposition to Jewish Christians' withdrawal from table fellowship with Gentile converts at Antioch because of the Jewish Christians' ostensible support of Jewish dietary laws.

PART ONE
GOD'S CHARACTER AS CREATOR
IN PAUL'S RHETORIC

*Apse mosaic of acanthus leaves growing profusely from
the cross as evidence of God's power to bring life and
productivity out of death. San Clemente (Rome, Italy).
Photo courtesy of Alinari/Art Resource, N.Y.*

God, considering our frame, hath not only appointed that we should be told of the great things of the gospel, and of the redemption of Christ, and instructed in them by his Word; but also that they should be, as it were, exhibited to our view, in sensible representations, in the sacraments, the more to affect us with them.

Jonathan Edwards, *A Treatise Concerning Religious Affections*

1

CREATOR: PAUL'S ROOT METAPHOR FOR GOD

Part one examines how Paul's different forms of language converge to emphasize God's identity as creator. The present and next chapter focus on Paul's metaphors, a subject usually not even included in the study of his rhetoric. Why devote so much attention to the apostle's imagery? Because imagery (metaphor) allowed Paul to transcend both his former ideas about God and the limited early Christian understanding of Christ's resurrection. In order to grasp what is most important to him, we must work through his metaphors and not around them. They express his deepest convictions and are not mere ornamental trappings.

In contrast to the importance of analogy and imagery proposed here, Judaism and Christianity usually emphasize that God revealed salvation directly, through specific historical events. Thus, Jews confessed (and still confess) that God liberated them from Egyptian bondage at a critical moment in their history. Christians say that the same God effected comparable salvation through Christ's death and resurrection. Nor were Christians and Jews the only people in antiquity who believed in the direct intervention of the divine in human affairs. Greeks in the early fifth century BCE regarded the expulsion of the Persians from their country as divine confirmation of their special destiny. Similarly, the Romans regarded Scipio's legendary defeat of Carthage in the late third century BCE as a manifestation of divine intervention.

Although many ancient peoples defined themselves by means of particular events effected on their behalf, none of them did so exclusively in these terms. No event was totally self-contained in its meaning. Historical and mythical precedents helped interpret the significance of past events. For example, the Hebrew liberation from Egypt was explained by means of God's earlier relationship with Jacob and Abraham. Similarly, the Greeks' expulsion of Persian barbarism was likened to the mythical defeat of chaos by the gods' conquest of the giants and to the mythical defeat of centaurs and Amazons.

Therefore, when we differentiate revelational and analogical forms of religion, we are describing only lesser and greater gradations of analogical relationship to salvific events. A greater dependence on historical particularity is said to reflect revelational religion, and greater freedom from historical particularity, analogical religion. I propose that Paul's interpretation of God's salvation is more analogical than scholars usually assume. Specifically, Paul evidences little concern that Gentiles appropriate God's salvation in strictly Jewish categories. His way of broadening salvation may be clarified by the similar way Second Isaiah presented Jewish liberation from Babylon.

On the one hand, Second Isaiah modeled the anticipated liberation of Jews from Babylon in terms of his ancestors' exodus from Egypt.[1] On the other hand, he exceeded what could be considered the historical when he identified the God who separated the waters of the Red Sea with God's mythological division of the watery monster of chaos at the beginning of creation:

> Awake, awake, put on strength, O arm of the LORD!
> Awake, as in the days of old, the generations of long ago!
> Was it not you who cut Rahab in pieces, who pierced the dragon?
> Was it not you who dried up the sea, the waters of the great deep;
> who made the depths of the sea a way for the redeemed to cross over?
> (Isa 51:9–10)

The prophet not only reassures his people of the correspondence between God's present action and an earlier exodus event; he also juxtaposes the separation of the historical waters of the exodus with the mythological division of the chaos monster. With this he enlarges the idea of a national God into the notion of a universal redeemer and world creator.

---

[1]E.g., see Isa 43:1–7, 16–21; 51:10.

Analogy and typology play a comparable role in Paul's interpretation of God's salvation in Christ. Like Second Isaiah, Paul imagined God's salvation typologically in terms of previous historical acts. Correspondingly, however, he exceeded national models by arguing analogically that the salvation effected in Christ reveals God's character as universal creator and savior. Thus, Paul not only expanded God's procreative act of fathering Jews to include Gentiles but, like Second Isaiah, enlarged God's powers of procreation to include all creation:

> I consider that the sufferings of this present time are not worth comparing with the glory about to be revealed to us. For the creation waits with eager longing for the revealing of the children of God; for the creation was subjected to futility, not of its own will but by the will of the one who subjected it, in hope that the creation itself will be set free from its bondage to decay and will obtain the freedom of the glory of the children of God. We know that the whole creation has been groaning in labor pains until now; and not only the creation, but we ourselves, who have the first fruits of the spirit, groan inwardly while we wait for adoption, the redemption of our bodies. (Rom 8:18–23)

Up to this point only one reason for Paul's use of metaphor has been mentioned: the power of analogy to expand an earlier experience of God to an equivalent experience of meaning in a later or another context. Metaphors serve Paul well for a second reason: the power of metaphor to communicate its subject in an affective and persuasive way. Granted, early Christians such as Hippolytus and Tertullian ridiculed the mystery cults' use of affective symbols. Tertullian reports that what was revealed at the highest grade of initiation (ἐποπτεία) in cult ritual was nothing but an image of male genitalia.[2] In turn, Hippolytus reports that one of the things revealed was nothing but a grain of wheat.[3] Nonetheless, what was a commonplace image for Hippolytus and an object of disgust for Tertullian was a potent symbol for initiates participating in the mysteries.[4]

---

[2]Tertullian, *Against the Valentinians* 1.

[3]Hippolytus, *Refutation of All Heresies* 5.8.39. Initiation into the mysteries was divided into four stages: (1) preliminary fasting, sacrifice, and purification (καθαρμός); (2) communication of mystic knowledge (τελετῆς παράδοσις) *(myesis)*, which included some sort of instruction or exhortation; (3) revelation of the holy things (ἐποπτεία), which was the central point of the rite; and (4) crowning/garlanding of the initiate, who was thereby acknowledged to be a privileged person. The central revelation (ἐποπτεία) was something enacted or represented (seen) and not something spoken (or at least not merely spoken). See the comments by Farnell and Rose, "Mystery." See also Cole, "Greek Cults," 904–7.

[4]See the comments on the mysteries by Cole, "Greek Cults," 904–7.

Like the mysteries, Paul did not limit his program of persuasion to rational argumentation. For example, he reminded the Galatians that Christ's crucifixion was displayed before their very eyes. Thus Paul comfortably uses metaphor in an affective and persuasive manner. Nor is it accidental that Paul's spiritual brother, Jonathan Edwards, later emphasized the *affective* nature of Christian worship and insisted that God's liberation be celebrated with song and *sensible* sacraments.[5]

A third reason Paul enlisted metaphors to represent God concerns their ability to help people conceive reality in new ways. Metaphors function as a language of discovery.

THE ROLE OF METAPHOR IN HUMAN COMPREHENSION

The Foundational Nature of Figurative Language

Largely because of the printing press, scholars now tend to think in terms of the linear logic (the sequential order) of the printed page. Accordingly, modern argumentation engages in greater abstraction than was the case in antiquity. Thus, even when scholars use graphic images, they are careful to take them from the same metaphorical domain. By contrast, when ancient scholars engaged in rhetoric, whether orally or in writing, they thought of the spoken word's effect on the ear. They often interrupted the argument's flow with asides, they drew upon many more colorful and concrete images, and they often mixed metaphors.[6]

Unfortunately, there is a modern myth about "objectivity," which equates rational argumentation and the formal language of the scientific

---

[5]In Edwards's work, *A Treatise Concerning Religious Affections*, the following statements illustrate his emphasis on the affective nature of worship:

> . . . the duty of singing praises to God seems to be appointed wholly to excite and express religious affections. No other reason can be assigned why we should express ourselves to God in verse, rather than in prose, and do it with music, but only, that such is our nature and frame, that these things have a tendency to move our affections.
>
> The same thing appears in the nature and designs of the sacraments. . . . God, considering our frame, hath not only appointed that we should be told of the great things of the gospel, and of the redemption of Christ, and instructed in them by his Word; but also that they should be, as it were, exhibited to our view, in sensible representations, in the sacrament, the more to affect us with them. (*A Treatise*, 115)

[6]Fernandez, *Persuasions and Performances*, vii–xiv (see esp. viii).

theorem with the idea of reality. By contrast, figurative language is obviously more imprecise and approximate in the way it describes things. Nonetheless, this informal language allows us to make sense of our experiences initially and also permits us to alter our overly ossified ideas of reality. To illustrate the need for revising the "objective language" viewpoint, Owen Barfield once observed that, contrary to the widespread belief in the objectivity of science, hard sciences such as physics willingly admit that they engage in "language games" and that their theorems are only provisional.[7]

Barfield did not assume that the scientific viewpoint was made up of whole cloth. He admitted that we could not have sent men to the moon if there were nothing to it. Nonetheless, he observed that we need to remind ourselves that our language, as well as our knowledge, is never exact but always approximate.

In the same vein, James Fernandez suggests that our very perception of reality derives from the analogies that jump out at us as applicable to our experiences of it. In turn, the analogies that we choose to describe our experiences color the ongoing meaning we give them.[8] Consequently, metaphors are both essential to our comprehension of reality and revealing of our understanding of it. With such ideas in mind, we now turn to a more detailed explanation of how metaphor informs the human conception of reality.

Lakoff and Johnson's View of Metaphor

George Lakoff and Mark Johnson describe the metaphorical nature of human comprehension.[9] First of all, they note that the properties that we attribute to our experiences derive from what is most familiar to us. Although abstract concepts such as love, time, happiness, health, morality, arguments, and labor are common experiences, they are not delineated clearly enough in their own terms to satisfy the needs of ordinary communication. Thus, they need to be grounded metaphorically in more concrete experiences.[10]

---

[7]Barfield made his observations in an essay called "Language and Discovery," which he presented at the University of Missouri–Columbia about twenty-five years ago. Apparently, Barfield never published this essay, but his published works assume the same kind of perspective on language.

[8]See Fernandez, *Persuasions and Performances,* viii–x, 5–8.

[9]Lakoff and Johnson, *Metaphors.*

[10]Ibid., 118.

Lakoff and Johnson identify three broad types of conventional metaphors: structural, ontological, and orientational. Orientational metaphors derive from the orientational experiences we have with the world as beings with physical bodies.[11] Because of our own front-back orientation, we attribute like characteristics to inanimate things that have no intrinsic fronts or backs. For example, we speak metaphorically of fog being in front of a mountain. The mountain's "front" is determined relationally by the fact that it is the part of the mountain facing us as we look at it. Its "back" is that part behind the area we "face."[12]

Spatial orientations such as front-back, up-down, and near-far are useful in understanding concepts in orientational terms. But we can do only so much with spatial orientation. The circumscribed boundaries of objects and substances offer a further basis of understanding, one Lakoff and Johnson call ontological. When things are not identifiably discrete, we nonetheless describe them as if they had intrinsic, physical boundaries like ourselves.[13]

To illustrate, "*rising* prices" are often viewed as a concrete entity via the noun "inflation." Viewing inflation as an entity, we quantify it, see it as a cause, act in conformity to it, etc. We say such things as, "Inflation is *lowering* our standard of living"; "We need to *combat* inflation"; "Inflation is *backing us into a corner*."[14] Correspondingly, as physical beings who are set off from each other by the surface of our skin, we experience ourselves as containers, with a bounding surface and with an in-out orientation. Thus, we project our container-like orientation onto other physical objects. For example, the rooms of our homes are perceived as containers, with the result that we move, container-like, *out* of one room *into* another.[15]

---

[11]Ibid., 115–22.

[12]Ibid., 182–83. Regarding our own bodies, the human "front" is that part containing the physical receptors for the senses (the eyes, the nose, the ears, and the mouth). Accordingly, when we say we "face" in a certain direction, we are referring to what is in front of us, as this is determined relationally by the direction in which the face is oriented. When we say something is "behind" us, we mean it is opposite to where the face is oriented. Although our body is the most concrete means of conceptualizing orientation, the idea that a person's life has a direction is also a common experience in our culture and a source of orientational metaphor. We assume that life is structured like a story that has causal connections with a meaningful "narrative" direction.

[13]Ibid., 25–32.

[14]Ibid., 26.

[15]Ibid., 29–30.

Like ontological and orientational metaphors, so too structural metaphors are grounded in human experience. They have even greater potential for using one field of meaning to structure another experience.[16] For example, arguments are often talked about in terms of war.

He attacked *every weak point* in my argument.
His criticisms were *right on target.*
I *demolished* his argument.
If you use that *strategy,* he'll *wipe you out.*
He *shot down* all of my arguments.[17]

Lakoff and Johnson contend that we not only talk about arguments in terms of war, we think we actually win or lose arguments. We attack our opponent's positions and defend our own:

We gain and lose ground. We plan and use strategies. If we find a position indefensible, we can abandon it and take a new line of attack. . . . Though there is no physical battle, there is a verbal battle, and the structure of an argument—attack, defense, counterattack, etc.—reflects this. It is in this sense that the ARGUMENT IS WAR metaphor is one that we live by in this culture.[18]

On the other hand, the very systematization that allows us to comprehend one element of arguing, the "battling" aspect, hides and prohibits elements that are inconsistent with that metaphorical field of meaning. In the midst of heated argumentation, we lose sight of the cooperative aspects of arguing. For example, we lose sight of the fact that the "opponent" is giving us his/her time, a valuable commodity. In the same way, our use of elements from the other domain of experience is selective. For if correspondences were total, one concept would *be* the other and not merely understandable in terms of it.[19]

Although our choice of elements from one domain of experience (in this case "war") is partial, understanding does not occur strictly in terms of the isolated concepts taken from that realm of experience. To the extent that it is possible, the larger domain that we use for comparison colors our comprehension. The fact that we use metaphors such as

---

[16]Lakoff and Johnson suggest that structural metaphors have greater potential for elasticity than either orientational or ontological metaphors (ibid., 61–68).

[17]These quotations are used by Lakoff and Johnson, ibid., 4. Regarding the fuller illustration of the "Argument is war" metaphor, see ibid., 4–6, 61–65.

[18]Ibid., 4.

[19]Ibid., 10–13.

"ARGUMENT IS WAR" suggests that the definitional emphasis is on the domain in general. This is the case because we experience domains as a coherent whole.[20] Even though we tend to use certain stock elements of an idea, their emotional and conceptual associations nonetheless color their usage. Thus, although we tend to use only the foundation and the outer shell (the walls) when we use a building as a metaphor, more general nuances are at work in the particular choice of an image. If the building is a family dwelling, emotional associations from the experience of the household are at work. If the building is a temple, other associations color the usage.

Metaphor and the Creation of New Meaning

So far we have considered how metaphors structure conventional experience. Indeed, people usually think metaphors only enchance ideas, and they resist the idea that metaphors change the way they think about reality. But Lakoff and Johnson also discuss how metaphors can cause us to *reconceive* experience.[21] If a new idea is convincing enough that we begin to act in conformity to it, then it alters the conceptual system that gave rise to it in the first place.

Although words themselves do not create reality, the change in perception evoked by metaphors can alter our understanding of experience. In turn, a change in comprehension can alter our conviction about what is real. Correspondingly, we cannot literally say Paul created a *new* metaphor for God when he called him creator and Father. Such ideas were already present in antiquity. Nonetheless, the priority of "creator" to other ideas in Paul's own system of belief, as well as the way he modified existing cultural ideas about God as creator, resulted in a distinctive use of such imagery.

PAUL'S ROOT METAPHOR FOR GOD

Despite the individuality of Paul's letters and the diversity of imagery that characterizes them, all of his major metaphors belong to the same overarching field of meaning. As suggested in the introduction, Paul derived this symbolic field from an earth-shaking experience giving rise to the "master metaphor" that caused him to reconceive God as he

---

[20]Therefore, Lakoff and Johnson describe the influence of broader domains on our experience as experiential gestalts (ibid., 117–19).

[21]Ibid., 139–58.

did. To be sure, the images Paul derived from this experience are not unique. For example, "father" was a relatively common way of referring to a god's creativity in antiquity. Nonetheless, Paul's overall network of images derived from his personal experience that God was making Gentile converts his offspring by means of Christ's resurrection.

Lakoff and Johnson discuss this model of analogy under the rubric of new metaphors. In the case of Paul, as well as in Lakoff and Johnson's examples, this does not mean totally new ideas. Rather, the designation "new" refers to an unexpected adaptation of an analogy or, even more strikingly, to the juxtaposition of paradoxical correlations.[22] For example, in the case of Paul, it was unexpected, from the Jewish perspective, for him to describe Gentiles as Abraham's offspring, especially when he did not require them to be circumcised or to observe certain other major Jewish practices.[23]

Convergence in the Interpretation of Paul

Christiaan Beker, Daniel Patte and Norman Petersen agree that Paul's rhetoric was determined by his theological convictions. These internal convictions, *not* some recurring external problem such as "Judaizers," give an underlying coherence to his language.[24] Petersen proposes that an underlying symbolic world view, or "master-narrative," has to be assumed in order to make sense of Paul's use of metaphor. For example, in the case of Paul's letter to Philemon, Petersen suggests that Paul colored what happened between Philemon and his slave Onesimus by the way he reconstructed the order of events. In turn, Paul's creative editing of the individual story of Philemon reflects the theological convictions of his wider symbolic viewpoint (master narrative).[25]

Lest we fault Paul for his creative arbitrariness in reordering causal relations and conventional social structures, Petersen points out that "real" stories also construct coherence out of events that, in themselves, do not possess the specific causal relationship that historians attribute to them.[26] In any case, Paul manipulates the order of events as well as his

---

[22]See "The Creation of Similarity," in ibid., 147–55.

[23]Because of Jewish assumptions about the immorality of Gentiles, it is equally startling that Paul would describe his converts as God's temple and call them "saints" and the "sanctified."

[24]In this connection, see the comments by Petersen, *Rediscovering Paul*, 5–6.

[25]Ibid., 8–9, 14–16.

[26]Ibid., 10–11.

depiction of social relationships in order to secure a specific response from his recipients. Thus Paul believed that the fictive relationship between Philemon and Onesimus as spiritual brothers took precedence over their actual master-slave relationship.

In most cases, interpreting social relationships in Paul's letters is not a linguistic problem. In the case of Philemon, with the exception of Paul's reference to himself as ambassador, the social categories are quite conventional: fathers, children, brothers, sisters, masters, and slaves. Sociologically, the language refers to the institutions of family and slavery. Nonetheless, the interpretation of these social relationships is complicated by the fact that Paul's most important uses are symbolic rather than literal. When he transfers conventional social categories figuratively to social relationships in the church, they are no longer governed by their ordinary meaning. To complicate the situation further, Paul sometimes attributes a contradictory array of social roles to the same people. Jesus is not only Lord, Christ, Master, and Son; he is also a slave. Correspondingly, Paul is not only the father and authoritative head of the communities that he has founded; he is also a fellow sibling, and in his relationship to God (the community's definitive head) he is a slave. Although there is no lexical difference between Paul and God as fathers, between Philemon and Christ as masters, and between Jesus and other believers as slaves and sons, there are signficant levels of distinction.[27]

Because of the symbolic character of Paul's rhetoric, Petersen says that the interpreter should be concerned less with the literal lineaments of Paul's theology than with the presuppositions underlying his letters. Accordingly, theology is a kind of secondary knowledge that Paul produced in order to defend and maintain the prereflective commitments of his symbolic universe.[28]

Although Patte's language describing Paul's theological perspective differs from that of Petersen, his understanding is similar. Patte also stresses the priority of Paul's convictions to the "argumentative" logic that the apostle uses to justify his viewpoint. Thus, whereas Petersen says Paul's symbolic universe take precedence over any individual articulation of that worldview, Patte says Paul's undergirding system of convictions takes precedence over any specific justification of his belief. Conse-

---

[27]E.g., in Paul's mind, there is a significant difference between his own role as father and God's paternity, just as there is a considerable distinction between Philemon's status as master and benefactor and Christ's household mastery. See ibid., 17–30.

[28]Ibid., 28–30.

quently, without attending to Paul's theological presuppositions, we will not comprehend his intention very well.[29]

According to Patte, Paul's most fundamental convictions may be described by three adjectives: charismatic, eschatological, and typological.[30] By *charismatic*, Patte means Paul's converts actually experienced God's saving power in ways that changed their present circumstances. Salvation was *not* a mere possibility. Moreover, the reality of salvation was not limited only to Paul's converts, but its truth was confirmed *typologically* in what God effected in the lives of other believers. Converts' salvation was analogous to what believers like Paul had experienced, to what tradition reports about biblical figures like Abraham and, above all, it corresponded to what God effected in Christ's resurrection. Nonetheless, God's salvation will be effected fully only in the *future*. Present and past manifestations of power lead believers to trust in God's final ("eschatological") restoration of creation.[31]

In summary, Patte and Petersen suggest that comprehending Paul's theology depends on grasping his system of convictions. Both show that Paul adapted his convictions to the individual circumstances of each letter. Beker's emphasis on the interaction between "coherence" and "contingency" in Paul's interpretation of the gospel corresponds to Patte's and Petersen's perspectives. Although Paul had unchanging convictions about the gospel's abiding truth, the contingencies of each unique situation required specific adaptations of his gospel's coherence.[32]

Beker prefers the word *coherence* to *core* as a way of signaling the symbolic and fluid character of Paul's thought. Paul expresses his convictions as a "network of interlocking parts" rather than as inflexible doctrinal concepts. Similarly, *contingency* communicates the flexibility in how Paul adapted his convictions to the circumstances of his individual letters. Thus, the differing contours of the letters are not to be explained as Paul's arbitrary accommodation of theology to his audience.[33] Although Beker does not use Petersen's language of master-narrative, he nonetheless assumes a comparable perspective in the importance he attaches to the symbolic character of Paul's system of belief and to the

---

[29]See Daniel Patte, *Paul's Faith*, 3–27.

[30]Ibid., 233–41.

[31]Patte takes up these essential characteristics of Paul's faith under separate headings: "A Radical Charismatic Faith" (ibid., 233–36); "An Eschatological Faith" (236–38); and "A Typological Faith" (238–41).

[32]Beker, *The Triumph of God*, x–xi.

[33]Ibid., xi–xii.

network of connections within it. He argues that so long as we examine key concepts only in isolation from one another, we cannot understand Paul's real intention. Such concepts as righteousness, justification, reconciliation, and salvation cannot be played off against each other, as if any one were decisive for explaining the meaning of the others. All serve, metaphorically, to make the gospel applicable to particular situations. Therefore, Paul's theology is best comprehended by grasping the coherent center that creates the field of interlocking connections among key concepts.[34]

Detail of apse mosaic with God's hand stretching a wreath toward the crucified Christ, who has won the victor's crown. San Clemente apse mosaic (Rome, Italy). Photo courtesy of Alinari/Art Resource, N.Y.

Root Metaphor and Paul's Idea of God

Taking Beker's idea of the fluidity of coherence in Paul's letters as a basis, along with Patte's and Petersen's comparable emphases on Paul's system of convictions, I examine below how Paul's root idea of God as creator provides a means of connecting his diverse metaphors. Several aspects of Paul's idea of God as creator have already been mentioned. God is the benevolent founder and savior of a worldwide empire. God is creator of the physical universe and of a new spiritual creation that is groaning in labor pains as it gives birth to a new order.

---

[34]Ibid., 18–19.

The representation of God's universal powers of creativity is less developed in Paul's letters, however, than racial and familial images of procreativity. Why the apostle concentrates on more familial forms of God's creativity will be explained shortly. For the present and for the sake of comparison, though, we note how boldly this idea of universal creativity is emphasized in Philo's writings. Indeed, Philo identifies God's two most essential potencies as the creative and the kingly (ἡ μὲν ποιητική, ἡ δ' αὖ βασιλική).[35] Because God was the creator of everything, Philo says, he had the right to rule what he brought into being:

> Rather, as anyone who has approached nearest to the truth would say, the central place is held by the Father of the Universe, Who in the sacred scriptures is called "He that IS" as His proper name, while on either side of Him are the senior potencies, the nearest to Him, the creative and the kingly. The title of the former is God, since it made and ordered the All; the title of the latter is Lord, since it is the fundamental right of the maker to rule and control what He has brought into being. (*Abr.* 121)[36]

Most Jewish authors, including Paul, shared with Philo the idea that God was the personal agent who created the rationality of the universe. Judaism differed in this respect from Stoicism and certain other philosophical representatives, who located rationality more impersonally in the natural processes (laws) themselves.[37]

Sometimes Philo describes God's identity as world creator (maker) with the personal designation "father." This personal idea of fathering is the emphasis that pervades and colors Paul's images of God. As already suggested, however, Paul focuses not so much on God's generation of a

---

[35]E.g., see "maker [ποιητής] and ruler [ἡγεμών]" in Philo, *Abr.* 88; "father [πατήρ] and ruler [ἡγεμών] of all" in *Mos.* 2.88. It is more common for Philo to refer to maker (creator, father) and ruler separately than to join the two, but since both are connected to God's relationship to the whole universe, it is clear that Philo thinks of the two aspects as related integrally to God's identity as the absolute sovereign of the created order. See "Father and Maker of all [the whole/the world]" in *Abr.* 9, 58; *Mos.* 1.158; *Mos.* 2.99. See also "Father of all [the whole, i.e., the universe]" in *Abr.* 75, 121, 204; "Begetter (Parent) of all [the whole]" in *Mos.* 2.205, 209; and "uncreated Father" in *Ios.* 265. The equivalent designation, "ruler of the all [the whole/the world]" appears in *Mos.* 1.284; 2.168.

[36]Cf. Philo, *Mos.* 2.99. Philo explains that the title of the former potency is "God," since θεός ("God") derives from the verb τίθημι, which means "make" or "order" (i.e., "create"). The title of the latter potency is "Lord" (κύριος), which designates the creator's right to be master of what he brought into being.

[37]By the early Roman imperial period, however, even Stoic sources had begun to identify Zeus or some other divine agent as the personal cause of the world's universal order.

new physical order as on his procreation of a spiritual race and family. God adopted Abraham, metaphorically speaking, to father a people. But as with Paul's picture of God as creator of the universe, so too with Abraham's race, the full potential of God's creativity did not realize itself in Abraham's physical descendants, the Jews. Rather, it was only with Christ, the *true* seed and heir, that both the Jewish race and Gentile nations were able to actualize their full potential as God's people.

Despite the emphasis in Galatians on Gentile converts' superiority to Abraham's physical descendants, Paul did not really think Gentiles had preferred racial status with God. He could attribute inferior status to Jews only when they emphasized ethnic birth status and personal accomplishments in place of the status derived from dependence on God's creativity.

> For a person is not a Jew who is one outwardly, nor is true circumcision something external and physical. Rather, a person is a Jew who is one inwardly, and real circumcision is a matter of the heart—it is spiritual and not literal. Such a person receives praise not from others but from God. (Rom 2:28–29)

We should not take offense at Paul's positive comparison of Gentiles with Jews, without attending to his larger system. Philo, too, made a similar-sounding commendation of Gentile converts describing proselytes not only as equal to Jews but also as special recipients of God's affection:

> For when the Revealer [Moses] has hymned the excellences of the Self-existent [God] in this manner "God the great and powerful, who has no respect to persons, will receive no gifts and executes judgement" [cf. Deut 10:17–18], he proceeds to say for whom the judgement is executed—not for satraps and despots and men invested with power by land and sea, but for the "incomer [proselyte], for orphan and widow." For the incomer, because he has turned his kinsfolk, who in the ordinary course of things would be his sole confederates, into mortal enemies, by coming as a pilgrim to truth and the honoring of One who alone is worthy of honour, and by leaving the mythical fables and multiplicity of sovereigns, so highly honoured by the parents and grand-parents and ancestors and blood relations of this immigrant to a better home. (*Spec.* 4.177–178)[38]

Nor was Paul unique in emphasizing the importance of something other than physical birth as a basis of racial identity. Philo argued for an alternative basis of nobility:

---

[38]See also Philo, *Virt.* 103.

The proselyte . . . will be gazed at from all sides, marvelled at and held blessed by all for two things of highest excellence, that he came over to the camp of God and that he has won a prize best suited to his merits, a place in heaven firmly fixed, greater than words dare describe, while the nobly born who has falsified the sterling of his high lineage will be dragged right down and carried into Tartarus itself and profound darkness. Thus may all men seeing these examples be brought to a wiser mind and learn that God welcomes the virtue which springs from ignoble birth, that he takes no account of the roots but accepts the full-grown stem, because it has been changed from a weed into fruitfulness. (*Praem.* 152)

Although Paul can describe Christ as "the new Adam," through whose resurrection God creates a whole new creation, or "the true seed" of Abraham, through whom God fathers a spiritual race, Christ as head (heir) of the individual household is his most common emphasis. With the possible exception of Romans, where God's identity as universal creator may be the primary theme, all of Paul's letters emphasize God's character as the Father of the individual congregation. Why is this familial aspect so dominant? Paul was writing to individual congregations for whom the primary experience of God was personal and familial. The same idea was probably the most appealing to Paul as well because of his own experience of the resurrected Christ.

Moreover, it is not simply the initial act of procreating offspring that characterizes Paul's conception of God, for he is just as concerned with the nourishing and educative roles of the Father, whose headship creates a fertile environment in which family members' growth to full maturation is expected. Therefore, many of Paul's images embody not only the idea of life's generation in an initial sense but also the added idea of growth and maturation. Accordingly, Paul uses such subjects as agriculture, athletic competition, building, cultic sacrifice, and family maturation as images for growth, progress, perfection, and maturation. All share the idea of wholeness or completion. The root metaphor for all of these is Paul's idea of God as the creator.

Granted, when Paul employs images of fertility, building, and related forms of growth/completion, it is mostly in connection with the need of individual congregations to mature into the character of their life-giving Father. On the other hand, such ideas pervade all levels of Paul's idea of God as creator, and in each case Christ is the ideal paradigm of maturation and perfection. Thus, at the uppermost level, Christ is "the new Adam," through whom God creates a superior form of civilization. At the level of race, Christ is the ideal descendant and "heir" of Abraham.

In addition to these levels and types of maturation, there are other kinds of communal association. For example, Christ is depicted not only as "Lord" (κύριος) of the individual household and as political head of a vast empire, but also as priestly "Lord" of the family cult, whose members are required to be holy, pure, and perfect in their conduct toward one another and the divinity.

Moreover, the society of believers is likened politically not only to subjects of an empire but also to citizens of the city-state. Thus, when Paul compares members of the church to the different parts of the human body, he is appropriating the well-known political image of the ideal relationship among city-state citizens. For Greek political theorists, the image underscored the necessity of interdependence, respect, and mutual support for each civic and social unit within the state. The corresponding Roman idea in the late republic and the early empire is *concordia*, the social harmony that constituted the basis of an ideal state.

Because of Paul's emphasis on an enlivening form of increase, his images of progress are almost always biological rather than inanimate. His construction image is one of the few exceptions, and even in this case, the focus is more on edifying ("building up") than on the static state of a completed edifice. Aristotle's social thought included a comparable emphasis, since the teleological idea of maturation was fundamental to his conception of the political order.[39] Unlike Aristotle, however, Paul did not confine the cause of progress to natural possibilities in creation itself. Because of his experience of the resurrected Christ, he was convinced that an additional act of generativity had been required to complete creation's potential. On the other hand, it is important to recognize that he shared with Aristotle the idea that maturation was social and not individualistic. Despite Paul's emphasis on faith, he did not think of trust, as modern Westerners do, in an individualistic way.

---

[39]Aristotle, *Politics* 1.1.3–12.

Most people think they can get along perfectly well without metaphor. We have found on the contrary, that metaphor is pervasive in everyday life, not just in language but in thought and action. Our ordinary conceptual system . . . is fundamentally metaphorical in nature.

G. Lakoff and M. Johnson, *Metaphors We Live By*

2

A SURVEY OF PAUL'S USE OF ANALOGY

The fundamental importance of metaphor in Paul's theology is clear. It seems appropriate here, therefore, to survey the major images in each of his letters, especially Paul's recurring metaphors.[1] The conclusion explains how Paul's root idea of God led him to focus on specific themes and how this idea facilitated integration of a wide range of images.

PAUL'S METAPHORS AND IMAGES

The First Letter to the Thessalonians

Family Imagery. Paul's main family metaphors for God, Christ, and converts appear already at the start of 1 Thessalonians. God is the converts' and Paul's Father, Christ is Lord (or master) of God's spiritual family, and converts are mature offspring who live in imitation of Christ, their family head in 1:2–6:

---

[1] Herbert Gale, who studied analogy in Paul's letters *(The Use of Analogy)*, was interested in correlating Paul's images with his theological ideas. Unfortunately, before studying Paul's metaphors, Gale had decided what Paul's theological agenda was; and when the images did not match his expectations, he concluded they were not functional carriers of Paul's theology.

We always give thanks to God for all of you and mention you in our prayers, constantly remembering before *our God and Father* your work of faith and labor of love and steadfastness of hope in *our Lord* Jesus Christ. For we know, *brothers and sisters* beloved by God, that he has chosen you, because our message . . . came to you not in word only, but also in power and in the Holy Spirit and with full conviction; . . . And you became *imitators* of us and *of the Lord,* for in spite of persecution you received the word with joy inspired by the Holy Spirit.[2]

Paul continues to describe relations with God and converts in family terms in 1 Thess 2 but focuses on himself and his coworkers. His initial emphasis is on the childlike trust in God that he and coworkers exhibited by continuing their work in Thessalonica after shameful treatment in Philippi. The idea comes to graphic expression in 2:7: "We were like babies among you, like a nurse tenderly caring for her own [infant] children."

Scholars usually interpret the shift in metaphor, from Paul first likening himself and coworkers to infants and then to the mother of infants, as too startling to be possible.[3] The shift is no more violent, however, than the picture, in Gal 4:19, of Paul as a mother in labor pains and then, immediately afterwards, his picture of Christ being formed in the Galatians themselves. The same sudden shift from Paul's childlike

---

[2]All italics in biblical quotes in this book have been added. God is identified as "the Father" in 1:1 and as "our Father" in 1:3. By describing converts as "beloved by God" and "chosen" in 1:4, Paul also signals God's paternal relationship. Christ's special status as firstborn Son and head of the house is implied in his identity as the heavenly son who was raised from the dead in 1:10. His status is stated explicitly in 1:1, 3, 6, 8, where he is, respectively, "the lord Jesus Christ," "our lord Jesus Christ," and "the Lord." In turn, converts are Paul's spiritual "brothers and sisters" (lit. "brothers") and God's offspring in 1:4 ("beloved by God"). References to converts as "chosen" (ἐκλογή) in 1:4 and as God's "church" (ἐκκλησία) in 1:1 have ethnic and civic meanings, respectively, and do not refer to the family household. The special status associated with these ethnic and civic institutions suggests Paul likewise imagined the family as having special (freeborn) status.

[3]Thus, the NRSV translation of 1 Thess 2:7 is, "But we were *gentle* among you, like a nurse tenderly caring for her own children." The word "babies" (νήπιοι) has stronger manuscript support, however, than the word "gentle" (ἤπιοι). Writing on behalf of the editorial committee of the United Bible Societies, Bruce Metzger notes that the majority agreed that "infants" had stronger external attestation than "gentle" but only "gentle" seemed to fit the context. On the other hand, Metzger admits that a sudden shift of metaphor is characteristic of Paul and if Paul's original reading was "baby . . . mother-nurse," it would be no more startling than his shift of metaphor in Gal 4:19. See Metzger, *Textual Commentary,* 629–30.

trust in God to his own care of converts as a parent is implied in Gal 4:13–14:

> You know that it was because of a physical infirmity that I first announced the gospel to you; though my condition put you to the test, you did not scorn or despise me, but welcomed me as an angel of God, as Christ Jesus.

In both 1 Thessalonians and Galatians Paul's willingness to trust himself to converts' hospitality derived from his childlike trust in God's care. In turn, he later played the role of parent to converts.[4]

A similar shift appears only a few verses later in 1 Thess 2. While Paul was living with the Thessalonians, he worked night and day in order not to be a financial burden to them. He compares his behavior in 2:9–12 to a father's care of his children. After he left Thessalonica, however, the experience of separation was like being orphaned:

> When, for a short time, we were made orphans by being separated from you—in person, not in heart—we longed with great eagerness to see you face to face. (2:17)

Just as Paul shifted from his role as infant to nursing mother in 2:7, so too he shifts from caring father to orphaned child in 2:9–17. The image of family remains constant, but Paul sees himself and his converts in flexible roles. Thus, it is more important to grasp the idea of God implied by Paul's paradoxical combination of family images than to focus on his apparent inconsistencies.

Paul continues his use of family images in 1 Thess 3, where he tells converts that after leaving Thessalonica, he feared they would renounce their new values. Accordingly, he sent Timothy, the converts' and Paul's "brother," to encourage the community (3:1–5). At the time of writing, Timothy had returned to Paul and told him about the Thessalonians' ongoing affection. Because of his converts' continued loyalty, Paul responds in 3:8, "we now live." Thus, Paul's earlier sense of being orphaned by separation (2:17) was reversed by news about his converts ongoing life in the Spirit.

Civic, Ethnic, and Imperial Images. Paul usually describes converts with family images, but he uses several other social metaphors as well. Since Paul was a Greek-speaking Jew and a man of the broader Greco-Roman world, it is not surprising that he imagined the church at various

---

[4]See Patte's comments on Paul's simultaneous relation of childlike trust in God and his motherly care of Thessalonians (*Paul's Faith,* 140).

levels of social association. For when Aristotle defined the human animal, he said it must be identified not only as living in families but as a political being. The family was the basic unit of the state, but it was incapable by itself of activating the full human potential of its members. To accomplish this end, the family had to join with other families to form a civic society. Indeed, on the basis of the principle "The whole is prior to the part," the political order was more essential to human identity than the family because it provided the structures that made human civilization possible.[5]

Although Paul never talks about the priority of the political to the familial, he describes converts as like citizens of a city-state. Moreover, members of the church are likened to an ethnic body (race) and to subjects of an empire. In 1 Thessalonians, these ideas are more often assumed than stated. The designation for civic assembly, ἐκκλησία, *ekklēsia* ("church"), however, does appear in 1 Thess 1:1, as in the salutation of all Paul's letters. Similarly, the reference to converts as "chosen" in 1:4 is reminiscent of the Jews as God's special people (race). The following Old Testament texts illustrate Judaism's idea of election:

> Now therefore, if you obey my voice and keep my covenant, you shall be my treasured possession out of all the peoples. Indeed, the whole earth is mine, but you shall be for me a priestly kingdom and a holy nation. (Exod 19:5–6)

> For you are a people holy to the Lord your God; for the Lord your God has chosen you out of all the peoples on earth to be his people, his treasured possession. (Deut 7:6)

Paul uses still another metaphor of association in 1 Thess 2:12. After he describes his exemplary behavior and fatherly instruction in 2:10–11, we expect Paul to state in 2:12 that the purpose of such guidance was family maturation. Instead, the result is described as participation in God's glory as worthy subjects of his empire.[6] Likewise, near the end of chapter 4 Paul pictures the church as the nucleus of an empire, but his imagery is more detailed and graphic than in chapter 2. Thus in 4:16–17 Lord Jesus descends from heaven, like the emperor returning victorious from a military campaign. In 5:8 Paul extends the image to converts, who

---

[5]See Aristotle, *Politics* 1.1.3–12 and *Nicomachean Ethics* 2.

[6]See 1 Thess 2:11–12: "As you know, we dealt with each one of you like a father with his children, urging and encouraging you and pleading that you lead a life worthy of God, who calls you into his own empire and glory." I substitute "empire" for "kingdom" in the NRSV translation: see below.

are described as vigilant soldiers of their Lord who put on a "breastplate" of faith and love and whose hope of salvation is a "helmet."

Images of Purity and Piety.   At every level of the church's communal identity, Paul emphasizes its consecrated status. Thus, as a civic assembly in 1:1, it is described as "the church of the Thessalonians *in God the Father and the Lord Jesus Christ.*" Regarding the church's ethnic identity, Paul describes it in 1:4 as "beloved by God" and "chosen." When Paul says God calls converts into his *basileia* in 2:12, he intended *basileia* to have the meaning of "empire" rather than "kingdom," both because Paul regarded God's rule as universal and because he himself lived within a worldwide empire. Thus, Paul probably imagined election not only in ethnic but also in imperial terms.

Paul sometimes blurs the distinction between familial, ethnic, and civic community when he refers to the church's special, sacred nature. Thus, when he prays for God to allow him to return to converts for their instruction in 3:11–13, his primary emphasis is on converts as family members, but he assumes other forms of social association. For example, Lord Jesus is entreated to increase the Thessalonians' love not only for each other but also toward *all*. Similarly, Paul asks the Lord to strengthen converts' hearts in holiness so that they may be blameless when he arrives with *all* his saints. Even God's identity as Father seems to be enlarged by Paul's reference to him twice as "*God* and Father."

> Now may our God and Father himself and our Lord Jesus direct our way to you. And may the Lord make you increase and abound in love for one another and for all, just as we abound in love for you. And may he so strengthen your hearts in *holiness* that you may be *blameless* before our God and Father at the coming of our Lord Jesus with all his *saints*. (3:11–13)

Paul encourages the church to be holy specifically in terms of sexual morality in 4:3–7, which suggests he may have had a specific congregational problem in mind:

> For this is the will of God, your sanctification: that you abstain from fornication; that each one of you know how to control your own body in holiness and honor, not with lustful passion, like the Gentiles who do not know God; that no one wrong or exploit a brother or sister in this matter, because the Lord is an avenger in all these things, just as we have already told you beforehand and solemnly warned you. For God did not call us to impurity but in holiness.

Although Paul does not nuance his references to love in 4:9–12 with purity language when he notes that the congregation loved "brothers and sisters throughout Macedonia" and encourages it to "behave properly toward outsiders," Paul clearly assumed the church would exhibit such exemplary piety.

All of Paul's images in 5:1–11 emphasize the need to be prepared for the Lord's return.[7] He uses images of piety and virtue in 5:4–8 to describe how to be prepared. Converts are "children of *light*" and "children of the *day*" in 5:5, and correspondingly, they are exhorted to be "awake and sober" in their behavior.[8] Likewise, in their moral wakefulness, converts are compared to vigilant soldiers (5:9).

The Letter to the Galatians

Family and Extended-Family Imagery. As in 1 Thessalonians, so too in Galatians, Paul employs family images; here, however, he imagines not the single household but an extended ethnic family descended from Abraham. Since the Galatians were attracted to traditional Jewish customs, especially circumcision, Paul sought appropriate images to prove that God's people could not be defined simply by physical descent from Abraham or by adherence to law. Metaphors in Galatians are often connected; consequently, it is helpful to examine image clusters rather than individual metaphors. Since status as God's people is the fundamental issue, it is helpful to consider how the ancient Mediterranean world defined status.

Social identity (status) was determined by two factors: (i) *ascribed* status, which derived from birth into a certain family, and (ii) *achieved* status, which was won competitively in the eyes of the community. For example, a Jew was a Jew (i.e., had status as a Jew) by being Abraham's offspring. Within the community, status was then determined by birth into the priestly caste (Levi's offspring) or by descent from other noted Jewish ancestors. Note how Paul appeals to his ascribed status:

> Are they Hebrews? So am I. Are they Israelites? So am I. Are they descendants of Abraham? So am I. (2 Cor 11:21–22)

---

[7]The images derive from various spheres. E.g., in 5:2 Christ returns like a thief in the night, and his unexpected arrival is compared to the suddenness of a woman's labor pains in 5:3.

[8]Gale notes the double meaning that Paul attaches to both "day" and "night" (*The Use of Analogy*, 34–36). "Day" refers both to the day of the Lord and to the Thessalonians' spiritual enlightenment, which Paul also describes as a state of sobriety and wakefulness. "Night" refers both to the Last Judgment and, correspondingly, to a state of spiritual stupor (being in darkness, asleep and drunk). Paul complicates the image of sleep in 5:10, however, by using the image in 4:13–18 to describe death.

If anyone else has reason to be confident in the flesh, I have more: circumcised on the eighth day, a member of the people of Israel, of the tribe of Benjamin, a Hebrew born of Hebrews. (Phil 3:4–5)

I myself am an Israelite, a descendant of Abraham, a member of the tribe of Benjamin. (Rom 11:1)

Paul's identity as a Pharisee, his achieved status, was determined and measured by his fidelity to ethnic custom.

You have heard, no doubt, of my earlier life in Judaism. I was violently persecuting the church of God and was trying to destroy it. I advanced in Judaism beyond many among my people of the same age, for I was far more zealous for the traditions of my ancestors. (Gal 1:13–14)

as to the law, a Pharisee; as to zeal, a persecutor of the church; as to righteousness under the law, blameless. (Phil 3:5–6)

There was a third, alternative means of determining status, however. This was the status or honor conferred by a benefactor on a people, city, or family. Thus, the right to observe their own customs and the right, within limits, to govern members of their community were benefactions granted to the Jews by Hellenistic kings and early Roman emperors. In the same way, an urban community's civil status as city *(polis)* was granted by Greek and Roman rulers. Through manumission, a master could change his slave's social status. Although the Roman patronage system usually did not allow patricians actually to change their clients' social status, it was able to render comparable results. For patricians held the chief political and priestly offices and thus could help clients gain access to the central system of power.[9]

It is clear in Galatians that Paul's experience of God as benefactor made him realize that a special relation with God was not restricted to one particular ethnic group. "People of God" was no longer synonymous with being a Jew. Nor was Jewish birth and adherence to Moses' law an adequate basis for being God's people even for Jews. Although Paul admitted that Moses' law served a purpose for Judaism, it was incapable of effecting the maturity required to be Abraham's promised heirs. Regarding his Gentile converts, Paul shows that their status as Abraham's offspring was won not by obeying Moses' law but by a benefaction that God effected in Christ (Gal 3:1–5).

---

[9]See Brent Shaw's comments on the emperors' imperial favors *(beneficia)* in "Roman Taxation," 820–21. See also Wallace-Hadrill, "Patronage."

Abraham's own status as father was determined by his ability to trust God's promise that he would become the father of a people. His status, like that of Paul's converts, derived from his faith in God. It did not derive either from doing something to merit approval (3:6–9) or from his birth status. Paul demonstrates further in 3:15–18, through the analogy of a human will, that faith in God's promise took precedence over adherence to Jewish law. Just as a person's will could not to be annulled or altered once it was ratified, so too God's promise to Abraham could not be replaced by Moses' law, which came 430 years afterward.[10] If the law did not confirm racial status, Paul had to ask why God gave it to Moses. He explains in 3:19–22 that it was added for the express purpose of bridling offenses until the promised heir arrived, who would submit voluntarily to God.[11]

The law was not intended to replace God's promise; rather, as Paul shows with two images in 3:23–4:7, using the law as a gauge for measuring the human-divine relationship resulted in an immature relationship with God. Thus Paul compares obedience to Moses' law in 3:23–29 to children subject to a pedagogue's discipline. Similarly, he compares the Galatians' former subjection to pagan laws of nature ("elemental spirits of the world") in 4:1–7 to the status of minors under guardians.[12] The subjection in both cases was no better than slavery. Consequently, if Galatians submitted to Moses' law, their situation would be no better than when they obeyed nature's impersonal laws. Paul's repetitious use of the preposition ὑπό ("under"), both in the

---

[10]The legal practice whereby someone's will could not be altered once its stipulations had been determined and written does not agree with either Greek or Roman procedure. The person making the will could certainly change what was written. Perhaps Paul meant no one else could alter the will. The practice in Greco-Roman Egypt of writing wills and other contracts in duplicate, with the second copy written beneath the first and sealed up, was certainly intended as a deterrent to tampering. See Hans Dieter Betz's discussion of Gal 3:15 (*Galatians,* 154–55).

[11]See Betz's suggestion that this is a decidedly non-Jewish view because Judaism generally assumed the Torah was given for the purpose of effecting righteousness. Paul's view does agree with the Greco-Roman philosophical idea, however, that wise men's and philosophers' voluntary commitment to the good made them a law to themselves. See the sources cited by Betz and his general discussion of this passage (ibid., 162–80).

[12]Paul likens law to the supervisory guardian to whom the orphaned child was subject until the legal age of maturity set by the child's father. Although Paul also uses "pedagogue" in a negative sense in 1 Cor 4:15, he says the law's instruction as a pedagogue was educational, holy, and just in Rom 3:20 and 7:7–25. Human sinfulness caused it to be used in a bad way.

image of the disciplinarian and in the guardian metaphor, emphasizes that law's restraints amounted to virtual slavery.

Obeying the law could not make people Abraham's heirs. Only trusting in God's benefaction in Christ, an act like Abraham's own trust in God's promise, could provide access to God's power to make one a true offspring (cf. 3:25–29 and 4:4–7). Although Paul continues to talk about the law's inability to confirm racial honor in 3:23–4:31, the focus shifts from achieved status to birth (ascribed) status. In particular, he shows how Abraham was the converts' father.[13] Paul makes it clear that physical descent did not constitute a sufficient basis of kinship to consider oneself Abraham's heir. He argues this explicitly in 4:21–31, where Abraham's two types of offspring, one "born according to the flesh" and the other "born according to the Spirit," are contrasted. "Born according to the flesh" does not suggest sexual impropriety between Abraham and Hagar but indicates the slave girl's child was born by natural means. On the other hand, "born according to the Spirit" calls attention to the fact that, because of Sarah's sterility, Isaac's conception occurred by supernatural means. Paul's converts, just like Isaac, were Abraham's true heirs because their status as offspring was effected directly by God. Adoption was an ideal image to convey this idea because it underscored the extraordinary way in which inclusion was accomplished.

The First Letter to the Corinthians

Cultic and Household Imagery. Paul utilizes many family images in 1 Corinthians and, as in 1 Thessalonians, focuses on the single household. There is a more pronounced emphasis on the family's purity or holiness, however, than in either Galatians or 1 Thessalonians. Thus, at the beginning, Paul addresses the church as "those sanctified in Christ Jesus" and "called to be saints" (1 Cor 1:2).[14] The church was not only

---

[13]See Rom 4:11, 16–25, where Abraham is also described as the ancestor of the uncircumcised, the father of all who share his faith, and "the father of many nations."

[14]In his opening prayer of thanksgiving, Paul thanks God because the Corinthians "are not lacking in any spiritual gift" (1:7). A little later, Paul says he and the Corinthians have received the Spirit of God, not the spirit of the world, and it is for this reason the church understands the spiritual gifts bestowed by God (2:12). When this contrast between "the spirit of the world" and "the Spirit of God" are connected to other subjects in 1 Corinthians, Paul makes it clear that he sets the church off, by its morality, holiness, and purity, from "worldly" contaminants. The church occupies sacred space.

God's house; it was also his temple (see 3:9–17).[15] Similarly, the idea of the church as the fellowship of God's Son in 1:9 is identified further in 3:11 by Paul's image of Christ as the foundation of God's temple. Paul states even more specifically in 10:16–18 that participation with Christ may be compared to the Israelites' union with God's sacrificial altar:

> The cup of blessing that we bless, is it not a sharing in the blood of Christ? The bread that we break, is it not a sharing in the body of Christ? Because there is one bread, we who are many are one body, for we all partake of the one bread. Consider the people of Israel; are not those who eat the sacrifices partners in the altar?

Paul uses images of purity and sacrifice as an antidote against dissension at Corinth, for he was convinced the disagreement cited in 1:10–17 would not have occurred if the church had submitted to the purifying concord of God's Spirit: "to each is given the manifestation of the spirit for the *common* good" (12:7). Because of God's own identity as creator, Paul assumed the church's union with him would result in like order and harmony, not chaotic division. True union with God would build up and not tear down. It would result in fertility and growth, not sterility and decay. Paul illustrates the necessity of actualizing God's vivifying activity by means of three analogous images: the church as God's *harvest* (3:5–9), as God's *temple* (3:9–17), and as God's *household* (4:1–21).

The political idea of the church as *Christ's body* in 12:12–31 (see 6:12–20; 10:14–33; 11:23–34) is analogous to the church as harvest, temple, and household. Thus, just as the church's productivity derived from climatic conditions created by God, just as its stability as a building derived from the foundation laid in Christ, and just as maturation depended on its subjection to Christ's rule, so too the church's collective political status as body derived from members acting in accord with Christ's integrating Spirit. In order to preserve the church's wholeness and holiness, pictured as a "batch of dough" in 5:6–8, Paul commands the Corinthians to cleanse out the yeast that was corrupt-

---

[15]See 2 Cor 6:16–18, where Paul also refers to the church as God's temple and adds that this holy temple must be set apart from the profane:

> What agreement has the temple of God with idols? For we are the temple of the living God; as God said, "I will live in them and walk among them, and I will be their God, and they shall be my people. Therefore come out from them, and be separate from them, says the Lord, and touch nothing unclean; then I will welcome you, and I will be your father, and you shall be my sons and daughters, says the Lord Almighty."

ing the community.[16] Although the picture of yeast was not an image confined to Jewish usage, the cultic turn that Paul gives the image in 5:7 did derive from Judaism:

> Clean out the old yeast so that you may be a new batch, as you really are unleavened. For our paschal lamb, Christ, has been sacrificed.

The command, "Cleanse out the old yeast," recalls the priestly injunction to remove yeast from Jewish houses during Passover.[17] The idea of Christ as a numinous presence that required purity from those in contact with him is also emphasized in Paul's picture of sacramental union with Christ in Eucharist and baptism.[18] Paul warns the Corinthians that just as God's salvific presence did not remove Israel automatically from God's displeasure, so too the Corinthians must not desecrate Christ's Spirit or they too would suffer punishment.[19] The church's incorporation in Christ through baptism and Eucharist was not a matter of subjective identification but a new social reality. Concerning the image of the church as Christ's body, Hans Lietzmann comments, "For Paul this is not merely a comparison but a mystical truth."[20] God's people are not *like* a body; they *are* a body. Similarly, commenting on Paul's image of baptism as participation in Christ's death (see Rom 6:1–11), a death to the old self, Rudolf Bultmann suggests that something actually happened in baptism. It was an objective event, not just a subjective process of change.[21] The idea of mystical participation in one body (1 Cor 12:13), along with the image of baptism as an act of "putting

---

[16]According to Gale, the leaven is not only the corrupting influence of the incestuous man identified in 5:1–5 but the more general contaminant of malice and evil at Corinth. Moreover, since the wording in Greek of 1 Cor 5:6 and Gal 5:9 is identical, "A little yeast leavens the whole lump," Paul is probably quoting a well-known proverb. See Gale, *The Use of Analogy*, 96–97.

[17]See Exod 12:15, 19; 13:7. Paul's statement "For Christ, our paschal lamb, has been sacrificed" makes it clear the image of Passover observance was in mind. See Gale's comments on Paul's usage (*The Use of Analogy*, 98–99).

[18]Regarding the community's mystical union with Christ in the Eucharist, see 10:3–4, 6–21; 11:17–34; 12:13. Regarding the mystical union with Christ in baptism, see 10:1–2; 12:13; 15:29. Paul depicts Israel's pillar of cloud and passage through the sea as types of baptism (see 10:1–2). Moreover, God's supply of food and drink are a type of Eucharist (see 10:3–4).

[19]See 10:1–13; 11:27–34.

[20]See Lietzmann, *An die Korinther*, 62. The comment is on 12:12; the English translation is Gale's (*The Use of Analogy*, 117).

[21]Bultmann, *Theology of the New Testament*, 1:312. See a similar interpretation of Paul's mystical understanding of baptism in Lietzmann, *An die Römer*, 65, and in Dodd, *The Epistle to the Romans*, 87. Gale calls these explanations of baptism

on" Christ (Gal 3:27) and as burial of the old self, all suggest the influence of mystery cults on Paul's idea of the church as Christ's body.

In addition to these cultic images, Paul states in 1 Cor 7:12–16 that the husband or wife of an unbeliever was able, through association with Christ, to consecrate the spouse and offspring. Further, in 9:13–14, Paul suggests that just as priests shared in sacrificial offerings, so too he and Barnabas deserved to have physical needs supplied from their missionary work. Various statements in Paul's letters indicate he conceived of his ministry as a form of priestly service.[22]

Agricultural Imagery. Along with cultic purity and the household, agriculture is Paul's most frequent source of analogy in 1 Corinthians. The church is God's fertile field (3:5–9). Here Paul underscores the community's dependence on God. Just as associating with the Spirit produced holiness and just as imitating the master led to family maturation, so too union with God's sacramental climate led to spiritual harvest.[23]

Three of Paul's five images in 9:4–14 involve agricultural activity: the husbandman who plants the vineyard (9:7), the shepherd who tends the flock (9:7), and the ox that treads the grain (9:9). The common purpose of all five images was to show that Paul and Barnabas, like the participants in the activities envisaged, had the right to receive sustenance from their work. Paul could demand compensation, just as the Corinthians' spiritual freedom allowed them the right to ignore cultural convention. He refuses to take advantage of rights, however, if they caused communal problems. In the same way, the Corinthians should not take advantage of privileges that caused discord.

Agricultural images also play a very important role in Paul's discussion of resurrection, but because Paul treats the subject so extensively, we examine images of resurrection separately.

---

to attention in *The Use of Analogy,* 178–79. A particularly intriguing activity is baptism on behalf of the dead, a practice to which Paul refers in 1 Cor 15:29.

[22]He refers most explicitly to his priestly service in Rom 15:15f.:

> Nevertheless on some points I have written to you rather boldly by way of reminder, because of the grace given me by God to be a minister (λειτουργὸν) of Christ Jesus to the Gentiles in the priestly service (ἱερουργοῦντα) of the gospel of God, so that the offering of the Gentiles may be acceptable, sanctified by the Holy Spirit.

[23]In the image of the church as God's field, Paul says he planted the seed and Apollos irrigated what was planted, but it was God's climatic conditions that produced the harvest (see 1 Cor 3:5–9). That is, Paul's preaching and Apollos's instruction would not have resulted in productivity apart from God's Spirit.

Images of Resurrection. Although Paul uses various images to explain resurrection, in 15:35–50 he contrasts the resurrection body and the present body by holding up the difference between the seed and the "body" (stalk) of grain that grew from it. Apparently, the issue arose when certain Corinthians claimed there was no resurrection of the body, only immortality of the soul (see 15:12). In later correspondence, Paul rejected the idea of disembodied souls by comparing the present body to a tent that would be replaced by a heavenly house (2 Cor 5:1–3). Second Corinthians 5:4 pictures resurrection as the putting on of additional clothing. In 1 Cor 15:12–19, however, Paul rejects the idea of the soul without a body by arguing for the necessity of belief in God's power to transform the physical body. Calling Christ's resurrection "the first fruits" of the dead (15:20), Paul elaborates that just as death was mediated to humanity by means of Adam, so now in Christ all humanity is made alive (15:22–28).

In attempting to explain the nature of the resurrection body, Paul introduces the analogy of the seed (15:36–38).[24] The picture of seed as sown and the specification that "it dies," as well as the later statement that "what is sown is perishable" (15:42), suggest that being "sown" refers to burial. The larger context suggests, however, that "to be sown" does not refer to a person's actual death but to the death of an inferior mode of existence (see 15:44–49). By the example of the difference between the seed that is sown and the plant that grows from it, Paul argues that God can effect a like transformation (resurrection) already in people's present lives.[25]

Paul elaborates on the contrast between the spiritual and the physical person in 15:45–49 by means of the difference between Adam and Christ. Whereas Adam was "a man of dust" (death), Christ is "a life-giving spirit." All who are raised will bear "the image of the man of heaven" (15:49) because "flesh and blood" cannot inherit God's empire (15:50). Although the process of receiving a spiritual body is as certain as the way nature brings forth plants from seeds, neither process may be considered automatic. By stating, "God gives it a body as he has chosen" (15:38), Paul suggests that new life, both in nature and in human

---

[24]According to Gale, the seed suggests three ideas: (1) The growth that ought to follow the sowing of the seed (i.e., the stalk or plant) does not come to life unless the seed itself dies (15:36). (2) The seed that is sown ("a bare kernel") is different from its body (stalk) (15:37). (3) God gives an appropriate, and different, body to each kind of seed (15:38). See Gale, *The Use of Analogy*, 134.

[25]See Gale's explanation of 15:35–50 (ibid., 134–47).

existence, requires God's intervention. The seed analogy makes it clear
that the same power creates nature's seeming spontaneity and humanity's spiritual resurrection.[26]

Other Imagery.   In addition to family, cultic, agricultural, and resurrection metaphors in 1 Corinthians, Paul uses a number of other images. Twice he refers to the gladiatorial arena. First, in 4:9, he tells the
Corinthians that whereas they acted like kings above life's circumstances, he and the other apostles were like prisoners forced to fight
in the arena. Then in 15:30–32 he says he "fought with beasts at
Ephesus."[27] A military image is one of five images in 9:4–14 that illustrate that people engaged in a vocation deserve to have their needs
supplied by that service.[28] In this case, the soldier deserves the rations
he receives.[29]

Since Corinth was the site of the Isthmian Games, it is not accidental that Paul uses four athletic images in 9:24–27. He is discussing the
subject of eating meat sacrificed to idols, a practice especially associated
with festivals. Paul says Christians had the right, in principle, to eat meat
consecrated to a god but the practice should be avoided when it dis-
turbed other believers (8:1–13). By analogy, he and Barnabas could expect support from the church because of their vocation as apostles,
but they willingly relinquished the right for the common good (see
9:12b–18). Paul gave up his rights not only for the common good; it was
also beneficial for him. He then uses a race and a boxing match as
illustrations.

Paul's use of the image of the victorious runner (9:24) was not
evoked to encourage competition. Rather, the idea of victory called attention to the importance of the goal. Converts must devote their energy so
fully to the pursuit of their course that they would be like runners who

---

[26]See Rom 8:19–21, where Paul states that all creation would be re-created
in the manner of Christ's resurrection.

[27]Since it is unlikely that Paul actually fought in the arena, he is probably
using the image to call attention to the ferocity of his opponents.

[28]Three of the five images in 9:4–14 are illustrations of an agricultural nature (see above). The fifth image is that of temple servants and priests who receive
a share of sacrificial offerings for their service (9:13).

[29]In 1 Thessalonians Paul portrays Christ as a military leader (4:16) and
Thessalonian converts as his vigilant soldiers (5:8; see above). Moreover, Paul
uses the image of the military leader's victory procession in 2 Cor 2:14. See also 2
Cor 10:3–6, where Paul compares his labor to the waging of war. See also military
metaphors in 2 Cor 6:7; Rom 7:23; 13:12–13.

ran so as to win.[30] His further comment in 9:26 that he did not run aim-lessly or box futilely underscores the fact that success required regimen. The rigor that might be required is indicated in 9:27, where Paul says he pommeled his own body. As is often the case, Paul's actions illustrated what he expected of converts. In this connection, slavery is also used as an image, but it is less important in 1 Corinthians than in Galatians, and it functions positively rather than negatively. Thus Paul states in 9:19–23 that he made himself a slave to all humanity, for the sake of the gospel, in order to win it over to God.[31]

Paul's analogy of musical instruments in 14:6–12 shows that "speaking in tongues" must be comprehensible to be socially useful. If the bugle does not play a recognizable call, troops will not ready them-selves (14:8), and if the flute and harp do not play a distinct melody, their sound goes unappreciated (14:7). In the same way, if human language is unintelligible, it is virtually useless (14:9–11). What is true in the natural sphere is equally true in the spiritual. Success is not determined by in-comprehensible force but by the articulate power to "build up" (14:12).[32]

The Second Letter to the Corinthians

Although 2 Corinthians probably was not originally a single letter, most of it was written in response to the same problem: Jewish-Christian missionaries from outside Corinth were leading converts to question Paul's adequacy as God's representative.[33] In particular, they advocated

---

[30]See Gale's comments on this image (*The Use of Analogy,* 109–10). Al-though Paul says only one received the prize, what concerned Paul was not the prize given to the single victor. Rather, according to Lietzmann, as all the runners fully committed themselves to the contest, so too the Corinthians should pursue their course with equal vigor (see Lietzmann, *An die Korinther,* 44).

[31]See 7:17–24, where Paul encourages the Corinthians not to be concerned about changing their social and cultural status. About people who were slaves when they became converts, Paul says they are now God's freedmen. Conversely, people who were free when called are now Christ's slaves (7:21–22). Paul says his converts "were bought with a price" and, accordingly, they should not become "slaves of men" (9:23). Although the image of manumission is used, Paul implies that the Corinthians belonged to God in a way analogous to slavery.

[32]Paul has the same idea in mind in 13:1 when he says, "If I speak in the tongues of men and of angels, but have not love, I am a noisy gong or a clanging cymbal." In this case, too, if the rhetoric does not facilitate tangible, social good, it is not really effective. It is no better than the mere showiness of a noisy gong or a clanging cymbal.

[33]See Georgi's description of the opponents' perspective in *Opponents of Paul,* esp. 246–83. Regarding the composite nature of 2 Corinthians, Helmut

that Paul needed to demonstrate tangible possession of the divine Spirit, such as was evident in Moses' transfiguration (2 Cor 3:7–18) and in Jesus' miracles (cf. 3:3–4; 4:7–12; 5:16–21); this would validate Paul's own status as God's agent. In defense, Paul accused his critics of being peddlars of human wares. Far from demonstrating their divine power, these missionaries' lack of restraint and their self-glorification proved how little they understood about the momentous, eschatological nature of God's salvation revealed in Christ.

> For we do not proclaim ourselves; we proclaim Jesus Christ as Lord and ourselves as your slaves for Jesus' sake. For it is the God who said, "Let light shine out of darkness," who has shone in our hearts to give the light of the knowledge of the glory of God in the face of Jesus Christ. (4:5–6)

The phrase "Let light shine out of darkness" is a key to the imagery we will examine. Paul emphasizes God's eschatological (and paradoxical) power to bring order out of chaos, to turn defeat into victory, and to bring life out of death. It was precisely the absence of this eschatological perspective in Paul's opponents that revealed the limitations of their human idea of power.

The contrast between trust in God and confidence in outward show is reminiscent of the contrast between Abraham's offspring "according to the Spirit" and "according to the flesh" in Gal 4:21ff. In the case of 2 Corinthians, however, Paul uses fewer family images. To be sure, he refers to God as Father and to Christ as Lord (of the family) at the beginning of the letter (2 Cor 1:2–7), but there is less family imagery elsewhere.[34]

Military, Sacrificial, and Cultic Imagery. Far from succumbing to the demand that he exhibit his authority in a tangible way, Paul pictures himself as a sacrificial victim (prisoner) enroute to death in a triumphal Roman procession (2:14–16). Although the image could refer to persecution suffered in Ephesus, Paul is referring primarily to the shameful

---

Koester suggests that at the end of the first century an editor formed a single letter from fragments of five letters that Paul sent to Corinth and Achaea after he wrote 1 Corinthians. See Koester, *Early Christianity*, 126–28.

[34]Paul replaced his customary thanksgiving with a blessing in 1:3ff. because he wanted to accent his own safety rather than his converts' welfare. Not only had he been persecuted recently (see 1:8–11); he had been criticized by the Corinthians (see 1:12–2:13). Fortunately, God intervened to save Paul from both kinds of attack, and it was for this reason Paul refers to God as the "*Father* of mercies and the God of all consolation who consoles us in all our affliction" (1:3–4).

appearance he makes in the eyes of converts. Despite his humiliation, however, Paul describes the suffering as a sacrificial aroma which, "thanks be to God," was a life-giving fragrance for people being saved by his message. On the other hand, to people of limited sensibility who had not experienced God's power to resurrect and exalt the defeated, Paul gave off only the stench of death. Nonetheless, God was creating Christlike victory out of Paul's ostensible defeat.[35]

Paul's contrast of self-glorification with God's victory through Christlike submission is reminiscent of the way military and sacrificial imagery were combined by Augustus. For example, Augustus (then called Octavian) formerly had gloried in his own success, but after he defeated Antony and Cleopatra at Actium (31 BCE), he no longer gloried in personal triumph but subjected himself to the greater glory that Apollo had effected through him to heal the wounds of civil war.[36] Moreover, after returning victorious from Gaul in 13 BCE, Augustus was honored not with the typical military monument but with an Altar of Peace (Ara Pacis), which pictured him as a priest performing service on behalf of the state.

We can not say how much the public image of Augustus informed Paul's idea of Christ, but it is likely the image of priestly sacrificer and mediator of universal peace was an influence. For just as Augustus sacrificed personal triumph to the divine will and the collective good, so too selfless piety and priestly service characterized Christ as God's agent of universal reconciliation:

> All this is from God, who reconciled us to himself through Christ, and has given us the ministry of reconciliation; that is, in Christ God was reconciling the world to himself, not counting their trespasses against them, and entrusting the message of reconciliation to us. (5:18–19)

---

[35]In addition to this image, where Paul describes his ministry as an aromatic life-giving sacrifice, he uses a second cultic metaphor in 6:16–18, where he pictures converts at Corinth as God's temple, an image of the church also found in 1 Cor 3:9–15.

[36]Augustus symbolized submission to Apollo and devotion to civil harmony by building a temple to Apollo on the Palatine that emphasized the god as the patron of concord and peace. Augustus's belief that he had to restore social order and to atone for Rome's civil wars by priestly sacrifice has precedents. Both Athena and Roma, patron goddesses respectively of Athens and Rome, symbolized military vigilance on behalf of social order. Likewise, Apollo was pictured as defeating chaos and avenging piety and purity. Alexander the Great viewed himself in a similar way as a liberator, not a conqueror. See Paul Zanker's description of Augustus's piety and the public image of Augustus as chief priest of the state in *The Power of Images*, 102–34.

In addition to the image of triumphal procession in 2:14, Paul uses a second military image in 6:7, where he refers to his service on God's behalf as "weapons of righteousness." As in 2:14–16, Paul's superficial appearance is anything but that of a victor. Nonetheless, God's eschatological power exhibits itself once again as victorious:

> as servants of God we have commended ourselves in every way: through great endurance, in afflictions, hardships, calamities. We are treated as impostors, and yet are true; as unknown, and yet are well known; as dying, and see—we are alive; as punished, and yet not killed; as sorrowful, yet always rejoicing; as poor, yet making many rich; as having nothing, and yet possessing everything. (6:4, 8–10)

A third military image is used in 10:3–6, where Paul again likens his apostolic service to waging war. The purpose of the divine combat was not to destroy hostile forces but to best converts' arguments that interfered with their knowledge of God.

A fourth military image appears in 11:8, where Paul says he "robbed" other churches by accepting "support" in order to serve Corinthian converts. The verb translated "robbed" (ἐσύλησα) could refer to the plundering of an enemy. Similarly, the word translated "support" (ὀψώνιον) was used for a soldier's pay.[37]

Covenant Metaphors.   Second Corinthians 3:1–3 implies that opponents had promoted the power of their ministry over that of Paul and had accused Paul of self-commendation (see 2:17). Seizing on the idea of commendation, Paul refers to the Corinthians themselves as his letter of recommendation in 3:2–3:

> You yourselves are our letter, written on our hearts, to be known and read by all; and you show that you are a letter of Christ prepared by us, written not with ink, but with the spirit of the living God, not on tablets of stone but on tablets of human hearts.

The Corinthians could be compared to a "letter of recommendation" because they were a testimony to Paul's effective labor. Thus, by analogy with Gal 3:1ff., where Paul says the Galatians' own experience of God's Spirit proved his message was valid, Paul's and his coworkers' affection for the Corinthians was itself proof of their positive response to

---

[37]This idea is clarified in Phil 4:15ff., where Paul says converts in Philippi had supplied his needs while he worked elsewhere. In a sense, he "robbed" them because he received an allowance for which he rendered no service. See Gale, *The Use of Analogy,* 167f.

Paul's message. When Paul says, "you show that *you* are a letter from Christ," it is clear not merely that the Corinthians were written on Paul's and his coworkers' hearts; Christ was written on *their* hearts. In turn, the idea of a letter, joined with the idea of "being written on the heart," led Paul to the scriptural contrast between the Mount Sinai covenant written "on tablets of stone" and the "new covenant" written on the human heart (Jer 31:31–34; see also Ezek 11:19; 36:26).[38]

Other Images of Weakness and Impermanence. The contrast of opponents' desire for tangible power to Paul's own trust in God to work his eschatological purpose through unexpected means is implied in his image of ministry as treasure in a clay jar:

> But we have this treasure in clay jars, so that it may be made clear that this extraordinary power belongs to God and does not come from us. We are afflicted in every way, but not crushed; perplexed, but not driven to despair; persecuted, but not forsaken; struck down, but not destroyed; always carrying in the body the death of Jesus, so that the life of Jesus may also be made visible in our bodies. (2 Cor 4:7–10)

Similarly, Paul compares human existence to the impermanence of a tent in 1 Cor 5:1–2. By contrast, he describes the glory of spiritual life as a heavenly house. Beginning already in 5:2, however, Paul talks about the heavenly house as if it were a piece of clothing. The change from earthly to heavenly body is pictured in 5:4 as the act of putting on more clothing over what one is already wearing.[39]

An Agricultural Image. The image of sowing and reaping is introduced in connection with Paul's appeal for an offering for the Jerusalem church in 9:6: "the one who sows sparingly will also reap sparingly, and the one who sows bountifully will also reap bountifully."[40] The ongoing

---

[38]See Georgi's discussion of the covenant written on tablets of stone as a derogatory allusion to Paul's opponents (*Opponents of Paul,* 246–51). See also Gale, *The Use of Analogy,* 152–55.

[39]See Gale's comments on this text (*The Use of Analogy,* 155–62).

[40]The analogy is not entirely accurate because sowing much seed does not guarantee bountiful return. As the example in 1 Cor 3:5–9 indicates, such factors as climatic conditions affected the harvest's outcome. In the present usage Paul is less concerned with natural fertility, however, than with spiritual: the person who willingly gives of resources (bountiful sowing), rather than grudgingly, exhibits a spiritual productivity. When Paul adds in 2 Cor 9:13 that generosity glorifies God by submission to the gospel of Christ, Christ's own sacrificial liberality is in mind. This idea is stated explicitly in 8:9:

contrast between show and substance is implied even in this image because, as God's apostle, Paul could have demanded that the Corinthians
contribute. His opponents would certainly have claimed such a right,
but here, as in Galatians, mere subjection did not do justice to the sacrificial generosity exhibited in Christ (see 2 Cor 8:9). Paul did not concern
himself, like the opponents, with converts' money, for he wanted converts to offer their very selves as gifts to God.[41]

Family and Marriage Metaphors. Family imagery is not as common
in 2 Corinthians as in most of Paul's letters, but two images call for discussion. First, in 11:2–3, Paul describes the church's relation to Christ as
a betrothal and marriage. Whereas Christ is usually the family's "Lord"
or its firstborn Son, in this instance he is the bridegroom and converts
are his bride. Paul presents himself as the father who handles betrothal
arrangements:

> I feel a divine jealousy for you, for I promised you in marriage to one hus-
> band, to present you as a chaste virgin to Christ. But I am afraid that as the
> serpent deceived Eve by its cunning, your thoughts will be led astray from
> a sincere and pure devotion to Christ.

Although the picture of God's people as his bride or wife is not un-
common in Jewish tradition, from Paul onward Christ occupies God's
role as bridegroom and the church is the bride. In this example, Paul is
the father who protects his betrothed daughter from being lured away
from her commitment to Christ.[42] Paul's "divine jealousy" underscores
the superiority of his concern to the sectarian interests (seduction) of his
opponents.[43]

The idea of seduction may have caused Paul to turn from the image
of betrothal in 11:2 to the analogy of Eve's seduction in 11:3. On the
other hand, the image of Eve may continue the idea of purity proposed in

---

> For you know the generous act *(grace)* of our Lord Jesus Christ, that though he
> was rich, yet for your sakes he became poor so that by his poverty you might be-
> come rich.

[41]See Georgi's discussion of how Paul's request for contributions differed
from that of his opponents (*Opponents of Paul,* 241).

[42]See the comments of Victor Furnish on this passage ("2 Corinthians,"
1200). Furnish suggests the best parallel for the image in 11:1–4 is Phil 1:9–11:
the Corinthians are in danger of being seduced by opponents who would lure
them away from Paul's gospel.

[43]The period of jealously guarding the bride's purity between betrothal and
marriage refers to the period between the Corinthians' conversion and their complete union with Christ when he returns (the marriage celebration).

11:2. Since Paul had formerly talked about Christ as a "new Adam" (see 1 Cor 15:22ff., 45ff.), it is possible the image of Eve is positive as well as negative. That is, Paul desired that the church be a "new Eve" for Christ, the new Adam.[44]

The second family image appears in 2 Cor 12:14, where Paul describes himself as the father providing for the Corinthians' needs:

> Here for the third time I am ready to come to you. And I will not be a burden, for I seek not what is yours but you; for children ought not to lay up for their parents, but parents for their children.

As long as offspring were young in antiquity, parents were obliged to provide for their welfare. Paul's ongoing refusal to accept support appeared to keep the Corinthians in a state of dependency, however, and they were rightly aggravated by this refusal (see 12:15–18). Since Paul earlier refused support from Corinth (see 1 Cor 9), he chose to emphasize only one side of the obligation between parents and offspring.[45]

The Letter to the Romans

The Letter to the Romans includes most of the images surveyed in Paul's letters; several appear already in chapter 1. The election and purity of Christ's community are indicated, for example, by Paul's reference to himself and to his recipients as "called" and by his status as an apostle "set apart" for God's gospel (cf. 1:1–7). Likewise, although Paul had not founded the church at Rome and was not yet personally acquainted with

---

[44]The suggestion that Paul intended the church at Corinth to think of itself as a "new Eve" is proposed by Gale, who refers to various interpreters in support of the view (see *The Use of Analogy*, 166). See Gale's further suggestion that Paul may have based the picture of Eve's seduction not only on Gen 3 but on a rabbinical legend in which Satan is described as first appearing in the form of a serpent and later as an angel. Some credence might be given to the idea in view of the fact that in 2 Cor 11:14 Paul refers to Satan disguising himself as an "angel of light." See Gale's discussion of this in *The Use of Analogy*, 166–67.

[45]W. K. Lacey notes that the care of elderly parents was not only a moral duty in the Greek city-state but a legal obligation. Indeed procreating children to have someone care for them in old age was an often mentioned motive for parenthood and also for adoption (see Lacey, *Family*, 116–17). Similarly, Keith Bradley notes that Roman authors indicate children had material obligations as well as the duty to console parents in old age. In the case of poor freeborn and freedmen, children were trained for a trade from the age of thirteen to fourteen so that they would be able to care for parents when they were no longer able to earn a livelihood. See Bradley, *Roman Family*, 116–19.

it, he talks as if he were the father of its Gentile element. He identifies himself as the apostle responsible for bringing about all Gentile converts' Christ-like obedience, including converts at Rome (1:5–6). A few verses later, he says he often intended to visit the church to "reap some harvest" among it as well as among other Gentiles.

The images of agriculture, family, and election (purity) continue in later chapters, and other imagery is added, but Paul's contrast between creator and creature in 1:18ff. is the theme that sets the tone of the whole letter. The idea of God as creator is pervasive and is the theme that binds the whole argument together.

Household and Extended-Family Imagery. Since Paul had not founded the Roman church and was not personally acquainted with it, his family imagery tends to be less intimate than in other letters. Thus, although Jesus is referred to several times as Son in the first chapter, at first he is identified as the nationalistic Son of David (1:3–4) and not as the head of the individual family. On the other hand, by referring to addressees as God's beloved and by calling God Father (1:7), Paul indicates he also imagined Roman converts as God's family. This is indicated further by his customary word of sibling address, "brothers and sisters" (ἀδελφοί), in 1:13.[46]

Paul acknowledges his physical kinship with Jews in Romans, but this differs from his kinship with Gentile converts. Thus, while stating that his "kindred according to the flesh" had been favored historically (9:3–5), Paul nonetheless refers to Gentile converts as Abraham's offspring (4:13–18). Indeed, Paul insists that physical kinship was not enough to make one Abraham's heirs (9:6–13). Only God's divine adoption made people true offspring and heirs (8:14–17). For this reason, as in Galatians, spiritual birth is Paul's preferred image for authentic sonship in Romans (cf. 8:18–30).

Paul's reference to Christ as God's "own Son" in 8:3 (τὸν ἑαυτοῦ υἱὸν) corresponds to Israel's election as the people of God.[47] Converts were "joint heirs with Christ" (8:17), however, and Paul insists they would be "conformed to the "firstborn" Son's image (8:29). Thus, although Christ's sonship was temporally prior to that of his Gentile sib-

---

[46]See additional examples of Paul's address of the Romans as ἀδελφοί in 7:1; 8:12; 12:1.

[47]See the description of Christ's special sonship also in 8:32 (τοῦ ἰδίου υἱοῦ).

lings, they were predestined to be God's offspring in the same way that Abraham was chosen to be the father of Gentiles.[48]

Another pertinent family image is that of marriage in 7:1–6. A convert's new life in Christ is likened to a widow's second marriage. This image of Christ as husband is reminiscent of the church as bride in 2 Cor 11:2–3. Paul combines the image of marital union in 7:1–6 with chapter 6's images of slavery and freedom. He argued in 6:1–14 that because one had died to the old self governed by the law, one was free to live a new life. Now that a new basis for a relation with God and humanity was available, it was inconceivable that converts would still be subject to old sinful passions. Paul uses baptism as a graphic example of the fact that one had died and was resurrected to a new life (cf. 6:2–4). Just as the convert was buried beneath the water, so too the old self disappeared (died). Likewise, as the convert was raised out of the water, so too he/she experienced new life. Behind the mystery cult–type ritual lay the actual precedent of Christ's death and resurrection.

Paul continues to talk about the incompatibility of sin with new life in 6:15–23. The focus is no longer on death, however, but, by means of the image of slavery, on the need to obey a new master. Because God effected the freedom, the convert now belonged to God:

> Do you not know that if you present yourselves to any one as obedient slaves, you are slaves of the one whom you obey, either of sin, which leads to death, or of obedience, which leads to righteousness? But thanks be to God that you, having once been slaves of sin, have become obedient from the heart to the form of teaching to which you were entrusted, and that you, having been set free from sin, have become slaves of righteousness. (6:16–18)

There is an essential respect in which Paul's image does not fit actual slavery and even runs counter to his own view of new life. Manumission (freedom) offers a better contrast between the old and the new than the metaphor of different masters. Paul himself admits the image of slavery is unsatisfactory by saying, "I am speaking in human terms" (6:19). The unfeasibility of continuing the old life so dominated Paul's thought, however, that he used the image of the new master to underscore that impossibility.[49]

---

[48]See 9:23–26, where Paul quotes Hos 2:1 and 2:25 to confirm the view that Gentiles, who were formerly not God's people, were now the object of God's affection and his children. See also 4:16–18, where Paul quotes Gen 17:5 to confirm his view that Gentiles are Abraham's descendants as well as the Jews.

[49]The inaccuracy of Paul's description of slavery is evident in the radically different results of the two forms of slavery: one leads to death and the other ends

Having looked at baptism as a symbol of converts' death to sin (6:1–14), and at the image of slavery to a new master (6:15–23), we now come to Paul's marriage analogy in 7:1–6. Although women's status did not always improve in second marriages, this is what Paul's metaphor implies.[50] For the law of the husband in 7:2 suggests that the husband's rights enslaved the wife in the first marriage.[51] By comparing people's former slavery under sin to a young wife's subjection to her first husband, Paul was able to describe the new marriage with the resurrected Christ as a mature relationship to which the woman willingly agreed.[52]

An inconsistency in Paul's image of slavery to sin appears in the fact it was one's own death that freed one for service to a new master in 6:1–14. In the marriage metaphor, however, not the person who died was freed but the surviving marriage partner. There is a sense in which the image of one's own death and the husband's death are compatible, since the wife was a kind of double self. That is, when the husband died, she also died to the old self. In turn, the death of that relationship freed the wife for a new marriage.[53]

---

in eternal life (6:21–23). Although a slave might receive better treatment from one master than from another, the difference could hardly be so great as the contrast of death and life. Nor could the slave decide what master he would serve, in the way that Paul suggests.

[50]In traditional Greek marriage the woman was at a disadvantage in a first marriage because she had little or no say in the choice of a husband and she was usually only about sixteen whereas her husband was about thirty. In the choice of second husbands, however, widows often exercised more choice, and the age difference between wife and husband usually would not be as great. See Lacey, *Family*, 106–8. Regarding the frequency of serial marriage in antiquity, Bradley notes that many, parhaps most, men and women would anticipate at least two marriages. This was certainly true of upper-class Romans in the late republic and early empire (*Roman Family*, 129, 161–62).

[51]In certain respects a woman's relation to her husband improved in a second marriage. Since women were usually only girls when they first married, the young wife's position in relation to the husband often amounted to a state of subjection. In the case of the second marriage, however, the woman was more mature, there was less necessity to marry an older man, and often the woman's economic status had improved enough that she could negotiate more favorable marital terms than were possible for the first marriage.

[52]Paul argues as if the husband's death were the only basis for a new marriage. In fact, women could secure divorce for many reasons. Perhaps Paul had a Jewish model of marriage in mind that prohibited remarriage except in the case of the husband's death, but it is more likely the image of death to the old self, and to the law's demands, was uppermost in his mind as the reason for emphasizing the husband's death as the basis for new life.

[53]See Gale, *The Use of Analogy*, 193–94. See Gale's larger discussion of Rom 7:1–6 (pp. 190–98).

Paul refers to the new marriage in 7:4–6 as bearing "fruit for God." The union with the old husband, by contrast, aroused by the old self's passions, bore "fruit for death." Paul's convictions about the superiority of the new life in Christ controlled his use of the analogy, for it is not true that the offspring of a second marriage were necessarily superior to the offspring of a first marriage.

Regarding converts' former relation to God, Paul knew the old self was married to the law in such a way as to produce negative results. The present marriage to Christ, by contrast, enabled converts to live in a superior relation to God. This idea is complicated, however, by the fact that two levels of family imagery are operating. Christ is both husband and offspring. On the one hand, he and the convert wife bear "fruit [offspring] for God." On the other hand, Christ himself is the firstborn within a large family (8:29) and the "root of Jesse" (15:12), whose identity as heir was created by God. In the same way, converts' union with Christ enabled them to be spiritual offspring as well as "bear fruit [offspring] for God." These mixed images, though confusing to modern ears, evoked a sympathetic response from Paul's converts.

Images of God as Creator.   We can make better sense of Paul's mixture of metaphors in Romans once we recognize how they are roughly equivalent within his idea of God as creator. Thus, agricultural fertility and human procreation are analogous images from the vantage point of God's identity as creater. Similarly, liberation from slavery and resurrection from death are compatible phenomena within Paul's conception of God's absolute power. These examples do not exhaust the metaphors reviewed so far, but are sufficient for us to proceed to a more extensive study of the way God's identity as creator pervades the letter.

In 1:18–3:30 Paul shows that all humanity, Jew and Gentile alike, had fallen short of God's will. The law showed what was required, but no one obeyed its principles and God himself had to restore humanity to what he intended through the obedience effected in Christ. By appealing to the example of Abraham (ch. 4), Paul illustrates that right relation with God was effected only by God. If people assumed his status was earned, they were wrong, for Scripture says, "Abraham *believed* God, and it [Abraham's trust] was reckoned to him as righteousness." Nor was Abraham's circumcision the basis of right relation, since it only symbolized what had been already effected by God. Accordingly, Abraham's status as father did not derive from his own ability to procreate offspring but from his trust that God would make procreation possible (4:19–21). Indeed, an entirely analogous relation existed between Abraham's paternity, Christ's resurrection, and Gentiles' spiritual adoption. All three of the salvific acts were demonstrative of God's power to effect life from death. This is explicit in the paternity attributed to Abraham:

> the promise . . . [is] guaranteed to all his descendants—not only to the adherents of the law but also to those who share the faith of Abraham (for he is the father of us all, as it is written, "I have made you the father of many nations")—in the presence of the God in whom he believed, *who gives life to the dead and calls into existence the things that do not exist.* Hoping against hope, he believed that he would become "the father of many nations," according to what was said, "So numerous shall your descendants be." (4:16–18)

Thus, despite Paul's emphasis on the just condemnation of humanity for its lawlessness in 1:18ff., and the emphasis on God's impartial justification of all humanity because of its faith in 3:21ff., the primary image of God in Rom 1–4 is not lawgiver but creator.

The prevailing view of Romans is that Paul uses diatribe, a type of ancient argument, to argue polemically against Jewish forms of self-righteousness. Stanley Stowers has rightly suggested, however, that Paul argues against all forms of pretentiousness in Romans, not just Jewish arrogance.[54] Accordingly, Paul uses diatribe not to beat down a Judaizing opposition but for instructional reasons. Human pretension is condemned, but Paul's emphasis is God's power to make something out of human arrogance. Thus, in the larger argument of Romans, Paul uses righteousness and wrath as subthemes in the service of his idea of God as creator.

Various images of God in Rom 9–11 function to reconcile Israel's idea of itself as God's special people with the fact that more Gentiles than Jews were responding to God's salvation in Christ. To aggravate the situation further, God seems to have deliberately hardened Israel's heart so it would not respond. Nonetheless, God's apparent arbitrariness in favoring Gentiles may not be used to impugn God's justice because Judaism already knew descent from Abraham was an inadequate basis for being God's people. For example, both Ishmael and Isaac were Abraham's offspring, but only Isaac was chosen to be heir (9:6–9). Correspondingly, both Esau and Jacob were offspring of Isaac and were born from the same mother, but God chose Jacob even before he was born and rejected Esau (9:10–13).

---

[54]Stowers *(Diatribe)* argues that diatribe was used by philosophers and Paul for instructional rather than polemical purposes. The function of diatribe in Romans is described more fully in the following chapter.

Despite God's incomprehensible selection of Israel's forefathers and his rejection of other relatives, Judaism had no right to accuse God of partiality. It was as inappropriate to argue against God as it was for clay to argue about the use to which its potter was molding it (9:19–20). Not only does the image of potter suggest God was the creator and humanity his creation; the molding of clay evoked the image of the creator in Gen 2.[55]

God's providence as creator is conveyed by the image of the pot molded for common use, an image that anticipates the role of Judaism that Paul takes up in 11:11–13, 25–32. Israel's rejection (the fate of the common pot) was only temporary, since God did not mold it for destruction but used it to facilitate the Gentiles' salvation. In turn, God was using the Gentiles to make Judaism jealous and cause it to accept salvation in Christ, thereby exhibiting God's power to effect life, as it were, from death:

> I glorify my ministry [to Gentiles] in order to make my own people jealous, and thus save some of them. For if their rejection is the reconciliation of the world, what will their acceptance be but *life from the dead?* (11:13–15)

Paul uses two images in 11:16–32 to illustrate his belief that Jews eventually would accept God's salvation. Both suggest that all Israel would be saved because of the initial consecration of the forefathers: "If the part of the dough offered as first fruits is holy, then the whole batch is holy; and if the root is holy, then the branches also are holy" (11:16). Certain scholars propose that Paul had the idea of social solidarity in mind when he used these two images.[56] His primary emphasis, however, was that Jewish inclusion derived not from physical relation to the patriarchs but from trust in God like that exhibited in the patriarchs.[57] Thus, just as God vindicated the faith of ancestors such as Abraham, so too he would continue to justify descendants who trusted him.

---

[55]Strictly speaking, the analogy of potter and clay is not accurate. Although it is realistic to say the potter used the same clay to form vessels for menial and decorative purposes (9:21), it is inaccurate to say they were used, respectively, for destruction and mercy (9:22–24). "Vessels of wrath" and "vessels of mercy" do not describe even Paul's viewpoint, but he uses such language to underscore humanity's limited perception of God's intention. Just as Judaism thought Esau was rejected, so now it appears God rejected Israel and chose the Gentiles. This idea is based too much on a creaturely view of God.

[56]E.g., see Dodd's explanation of this idea and its application in Romans (*The Epistle to the Romans*, 178–79). See also Gale's discussion of the two analogies in 11:16–24 (*The Use of Analogy*, 205–15).

[57]According to Gale, Paul argues on two inconsistent lines: either it was the race of Israel that was heir to God's promise because of physical relation to the

Because of God's identity as creator, he could not privilege Judaism over other peoples, as Rom 9–10 and the beginning of chapter 11 show. With this idea in mind, in 11:13ff. Paul turns to warn Gentile converts about also assuming privileged status with God. On the one hand, Paul argues for God's ongoing allegiance to Judaism, by noting that it was consecrated by its forefathers' faith. He intensifies the idea that the whole batch of dough (Judaism) was made holy by the consecration of its "first fruits" (the Jewish patriarchs), by adding that an olive tree's branches were consecrated by its holy roots. On the other hand, Paul argues against Gentile converts' sense of divine privilege by applying the olive tree metaphor to them. The cultivated tree in 11:17ff. represents Judaism, carefully nurtured by God. In turn, the tree's broken-off branches are Jews who have not accepted salvation in Christ, and the new branches grafted into the trunk are Gentiles who have accepted God's salvation. Gentiles must attend to the lesson of the broken-off branches, however, because if God would not tolerate Jewish disbelief, neither will God tolerate Gentile boasting (cf. 11:17–21).

As is often true with Paul's analogies, there are also problems with the olive tree image. Although the roots of a tree determined the kind of branches that grew from its trunk, there was nothing intrinsic to the idea of roots to think of them as good, let alone holy. Thus, it was only by association with the earlier picture of dough (meal), whose first fruits were dedicated to God, that the idea of the roots' holiness arose. Moreover, certain details do not fit horticultural practice. People did not graft branches of a wild tree into a cultivated trunk, but branches of a cultivated tree into wild stock. Paul's suggestion in 11:24 that the branches that were broken off could be grafted back into the tree is entirely incompatible with horticultural practice.[58]

These inaccuracies are not to be attributed too quickly to Paul's ignorance of ancient grafting practices. It is more likely, at least in the case of grafting wild branches into a cultivated tree, that Paul's idea of God determined the elements in the analogy. That is, to call attention to God's

---

patriarchs, or the recipients of the promise were people who shared Abraham and Christ's faith, whether or not they belonged to the Jewish race (*The Use of Analogy*, 207–8).

[58]Gale was probably right in suggesting Paul adjusted natural details of the analogy to reflect his own ideas about the relation of Gentiles and Jews to the true Israel (cf. ibid., 208–15). Dodd's suggestion that Paul was unaware that the grafting of wild branches into cultivated stock was an abnormal practice is less likely. He attributes this "ignorance of nature" to Paul's limitations as an urban man (cf. *The Epistle to the Romans*, 180).

ability as creator to do something supernatural, he knowingly introduced the detail that, contrary to nature, God grafted wild branches into a cultivated tree.[59]

The Letter to the Philippians

Although Paul was incarcerated at the time of writing Philippians, he expresses joy because his imprisonment helped to spread the message about God's salvation in Christ. He thanks readers for support, financial and otherwise, and encourages them to share his Christ-like trust in God's power to overcome adversity. Because of Paul's affection for the church, it is not surprising that family images appear in the letter. Nonetheless, because of the church's interest in personal, civiclike honors, Paul had to remind it of the common good and the need for Christ-like devotion to God's values.

Purity, Sacrificial Service, and Family Imagery. Paul often addresses the converts as "brothers and sisters" (ἀδελφοί).[60] Moreover, because Epaphroditus, the church's messenger, had risked his life in service to the apostle, he is identified individually as Paul's "brother" (Phil 2:25–30). Similarly, because of Timothy's trustworthiness, he is described as "like a son" (2:19–24). Familial affection also led Paul to address converts as "beloved" (2:12). It prompted him to say they were in his heart (1:7), that he yearned for them with the affection of Christ (1:8), and that because they were his joy and crown, he loved and longed for them (4:1). An analogous affection between God and converts is indicated in the image of God as "Father" (1:2; 2:11; 4:20) and in Paul's wish that the Philippians be blameless and innocent, like "children of God" (2:15).

---

[59]The same emphasis may not be attributed to Paul's statement that God could graft broken-off branches back into the tree. If this were the case, grafting Judaism back into the tree would correspond to Paul's earlier description of the Jews' acceptance of salvation as "life from the dead" (11:15). Unfortunately, Paul suggests he considered it easier for God to graft broken branches into the tree than to graft in wild branches (11:24). It is not likely in this instance, therefore, that he intended to emphasize God's power to create life out of death.

[60]Cf. Phil 1:12; 3:1, 13, 17; 4:1, 8. Although the Greek is "brothers," the NRSV alternates in translating the designation as "brothers and sisters" and "beloved." In addition to these references, Paul twice refers to people with him as "brothers," and they are presented as spiritual siblings also of the Philippians (see 1:14; 4:21). The NRSV translates the two references, respectively, as "brothers and sisters" and "friends."

Because aspirations for personal glory were interfering with church unity, however, Paul colored family terms with sacrificial images. The church was not only Christ's household but also a locus for the sacred, similar to the Corinthian congregation being God's temple. Thus, Paul describes consecrated converts as "the saints" (τοῖς ἁγίοις) (1:1) and says they had to be "blameless and innocent, children of God without blemish in the midst of a crooked and perverse generation" (2:15). In anticipation of their Lord's return, the Philippians had to be "pure and blameless, having produced the harvest of righteousness that comes through Jesus Christ" (1:10–11). In particular, the Philippians must have Christ's mind-set and do nothing from personal ambition but look to the interests of others (2:1–8). As a priestly service on their behalf, Paul aspires to offer converts' unity with Christ as a sacrifice to God (2:12–18). He adds his own Christ-like submission to the sacrifice:

> But even if I am being poured out as a libation over the sacrifice and the of-fering of your faith, I am glad and rejoice with all of you. (2:17)[61]

The sacrificial image was made more poignant by the fact that as a prisoner, Paul feared for his life. Obedience to God might literally result in his becoming a sacrificial victim.[62] Paul calls attention to the extent of his sacrificial obedience in 3:3–11, and because it embodied Christ's Spirit, he offers it as a model to be imitated.

Paul presents his Christ-like sacrifice on behalf of the community as a contrast to social groups that sought self-glorification. First, he contrasts himself and converts with Jews, who prized physical marks of ethnicity, such as circumcision, which Paul describes as "confidence in the flesh" (3:3–4). The Philippians' devotion to God was more mature than that exhibited in Jewish circumcision, because the Gentile converts were genuinely aspiring to excise the impurities that circumcision only symbolized (3:2f.).[63]

---

[61]Paul describes the same kind of priestly service in Rom 15:15f. (see Rom 1:13f.), where converts' obedience to Christ's Spirit is also pictured as a sacrificial offering.

[62]Paul describes Epaphroditus, the Philippians' messenger, as rendering a like kind of priestly service on behalf of the community (2:25–30). For he nearly died (through illness) in the course of rendering service on the community's behalf to Paul. Paul describes the communal gift sent by Epaphroditus specifically as a sacrificial offering in 4:18.

[63]By referring to Jews as "dogs" in 3:2, Paul turns a Jewish metaphor for Gentiles on its head. For "dogs" was an image used by Jews to describe the uncivilized character of Gentiles (see Mark 7:27). By contrast, Paul argues that his Gen-

Despite Paul's explicit contrast of his Philippian converts with Jews in 3:2–11, the Philippians were not attracted to Judaism in the way that converts in Galatia were. Rather, Paul caricatures Jewish ethnicity as an oblique means of discussing comparable values of a Gentile nature that were attractive and a source of personal ambition and status in the church.

Ruler Cult, Military, and Civic Metaphors. Although we can not tell exactly what the Philippians were attracted to, they were probably seeking honors that could be won in some type of urban voluntary association. Among the likely candidates were the ruler cult and voluntary clubs modeled on the offices and administrative structure of the city-state. It is possible that military clubs, comparable to the American Legion or Veterans of Foreign Wars, were also an attraction in Philippi.[64]

Regarding the influence of the ruler cult, Philippi was a major cult center, and thus Paul was arguing specifically against the honors citizens received in devotion to the emperor, according to R. R. Brewer.[65] Since cult associations called *augustales* allowed freedmen to perform services usually restricted to magistrates, membership in the college was the greatest goal a freedman could attain.[66]

Edgar Krentz maintains, however, that some of the political terms in Philippians to which Brewer appealed as evidence of ruler cult influence could be explained better as military imagery. Not only was Philippi a

---

tile converts were more civilized than Jews because they did not rely on self-glorifying marks of physical ethnicity for status but worshiped God in spirit. Strack and Billerbeck cite rabbinical passages that show dogs were not regarded well in the ancient world (Str-B 1:722ff.). See also Lohmeyer's comment that when Luke 16:21 said, "the dogs would come and lick his [Lazarus's] sores," the intention was not to illustrate the dogs' kindness but to indicate increased misery. (See Lohmeyer, *Philipper, Kolosser, und Philemon,* 125.) Dogs prowled about in packs, feeding on refuse, snapping at each other and at the passers-by. Thus, immorality, gluttony, and other thoughtless acts led to the negative label "dog." See Gale's comments on Phil 3:2 (*The Use of Analogy,* 216–19). Paul explains further what "confidence in the flesh" means by referring in 3:4–6 to his own former pride in ethnic marks of accomplishment. He gave up all those claims to status, however, and now he placed himself singlemindedly, like Christ, in the hands of God.

[64]The idea of modeling the church on the ruler cult could be suggested by Paul's picture of Christ as world ruler (emperor) in 2:9–11. Likewise, Paul's use of political terminology in 1:27 and 3:20 could suggest converts were attracted to civiclike honors. Finally, the concentration of military imagery in 1:27–30 indicates Paul's converts could be influenced by such language.

[65]Cf. Brewer, " πολιτεύεσθε in Phil 1:27."

[66]See Zanker's comments on the attraction of the *augustales* for wealthy freedmen in *The Power of Images,* 316–23.

major site of emperor worship, it was a Roman military colony. Since
both Mark Antony and Octavian settled army veterans there, Philippi's
citizens were entitled to full citizenship in Rome, in addition to having
special civic privileges.[67] Military language is evident in Paul's description of Epaphroditus as his "fellow soldier" in 2:25, but the fullest concentration of military imagery is in 1:27–30:

> Only, live your life in a manner worthy of the gospel of Christ, so that,
> whether I come and see you or am absent and hear about you, I will know
> that you are standing firm in one spirit, striving side by side with one mind
> for the faith of the gospel, and are in no way intimidated by your oppo-
> nents. For them this is evidence of their destruction, but of your salvation.
> And this is God's doing. For he has graciously granted you the privilege
> not only of believing in Christ, but of suffering for him as well—since you
> are having the same struggle that you saw I had and now hear that I still
> have.

Krentz says Paul's advice, "standing firm in one spirit, striving side
by side," is the kind of advice a general gave his troops. Nothing was
better for soldiers than to maintain order, nothing more dangerous than
to break ranks.[68] Thus, the reference to struggle (ἀγών) in 1:30 should be
understood not as athletic effort but as battle conflict. Although Paul's
exhortation to fight together "for the faith [πίστις, *pistis*] of the gospel"
might not seem to fit the military image, Krentz shows that *pistis* referred
not only to good faith in the political arena but also to not buckling in
battle. Consequently, the following phrase, "in no way intimidated by
your opponents," refers to soldiers who held their ground and did not
turn tail under attack.[69]

Although Krentz shows that military imagery shaped Paul's rhetoric, he does not say whether or how Paul was in competition with military
clubs. The use of civic and political images in 3:17–21, however, and
Paul's demeaning tone indicate he was fearful of some group's influence.
It is equally clear the competition envisaged was not the Jewish-type values caricatured at the beginning of chapter 3.

The "enemies of the cross" in 3:18 are usually equated with the
circumcisers of 3:2, but the added description, "their god is the belly,"

---

[67]See Krentz, "Military Language and Metaphors."

[68]Cf. ibid., 114–15, 120. Krentz notes that Onasander wrote a treatise,
Strategicus (The General), at the time of Claudius, in which he described the attitude of soldiers drawn up in battle formation very much in the same manner as
that described by Paul (cf. Onasander, *Strategicus* 27).

[69]See Krentz, "Military Language and Metaphors," 124.

does not fit. Thus, Wendy J. Cotter rightly argues that the people whose "god is the belly" are not the Jews.[70] The group is described with the terms "belly" (κοιλία) and "shame" (αἰσχύνη), both of which refer to carnal excess.[71] One fact that shows the people in question were not heretical converts or a Jewish group is the absence of any argument against their teaching. Paul simply dismisses them with negative labels. What differentiates Paul from these people is not their teaching but their lifestyle. Thus, when Cotter sets these features against the backdrop of Greco-Roman city life, she concludes that Paul was indicting the conduct of members of voluntary associations.[72] These clubs, like ruler cult associations *(augustales)*, met the aspirations of freedmen and poor freeborn, who were excluded from holding official posts.[73]

Despite their claims of public service, voluntary associations had a reputation for drunkenness and carousing that sometimes led to outrageous social acts, including sedition.[74] Thus, we must ask why these clubs were so appealing to Paul's readers that he had to warn them time and again (3:18: "I have *often* told you of them") about their destructive influence. Their appeal may be implied in Paul's remark "But our citizenship is in heaven." The word translated "citizenship," πολίτευμα, *politeuma,* carries civic connotations. By using the pronoun "our" in connection with πολίτευμα, Paul implies he is using the language of civic clubs and contrasting their values with the church's superior form of citizenship. Interest in civiclike honors was so great that converts seem to have incorporated such features into the church. Paul implied this in

---

[70]See Cotter, "Our *Politeuma.*"

[71]See ibid., 92–93. Cotter notes that Koester equates the "enemies of the cross" in 3:18 with "the mutilators" of 3:2. But in order to do so, Koester must make Paul's statement "their god is the belly" refer to fanatical observance of dietary laws. Walter Schmittals's proposal that both 3:2–11 and 3:17–21 refer to libertinistic gnostics is equally problematic. He claims that "their god is the belly" is Paul's way of denouncing the gnostics' practice of eating idol meat to flaunt their freedom. Schmittals's thesis depends too much on equating "their god is the belly" people with gnosticizing groups in the Corinthian and Galatian churches— a hypothesis that is problematic even in Galatians and 1 Corinthians (see Cotter's observations, pp. 93–96).

[72]See Cotter, "Our *Politeuma,*" 95–99.

[73]The clubs also provided comaraderie for people of the same trade; they often ensured a decent burial for members; and sometimes they achieved some social recognition by organizing themselves as volunteer fire brigades. See parts 2 and 3, below.

[74]See the ancient criticisms against voluntary associations cited by Cotter ("Our *Politeuma,*" 98–100).

1:27 with the verbal form πολιτεύεσθαι when he addressed converts about their conduct: "Only live your life (πολιτεύεσθε) in a manner worthy of the gospel of Christ," that is, "Only render civic service worthy of Christ's gospel."[75]

In contrast to members of the civic clubs who were seeking public honors, Paul encourages the Philippians to be of "one spirit" and of "one mind, striving side by side for the faith of the gospel" (1:27–30). Converts should do nothing from selfishness or conceit but should look to others' interests (2:1–4). The civic ideal to be imitated is exhibited in Christ, who gave up all his status in obedience to the true source of authority and on behalf of the common good (2:5–11). As mentioned, Paul, in imitation of Christ's values, gave up all his ethnic honors (cf. 3:4–11). The true humanitarian knows conventional honors are "earthly" and selfish. Only people whose politeuma is "in heaven" are free to render true civic virtue and receive eternal honor.

Athletic Images. In addition to civic, military, imperial, ethnic, sacrificial, and family metaphors in Philippians, Paul uses two athletic images. First, in 2:16, he encourages converts to do everything without grumbling, in order that they might become blameless and that he could be proud that he "did not run in vain or labor in vain." Then, after detailing the Jewish status he gave up in imitation of Christ (3:3–11), Paul states in 3:12–14 that he forgot what lay behind and he strained forward to what lay ahead, pressing on to the goal and the heavenly prize. Both in this image and in 2:16 Paul compares his commitment to Christ to the running of a race. In the latter case, he emphasizes the single-mindedness with which an athlete ran to win the prize.

The Letter to Philemon

Slavery and Family Images. As shown in chapter 1, above, Paul gave greater weight in Philemon to the church as God's fictive family than to social convention. The social reality was that a slave had run away from his master, but Paul insists that the master consider the slave a spiritual brother, for the relation between family members in

---

[75]Franz Poland says it was common practice for voluntary clubs to adopt urban administrative structures. By regarding their clubs as civic entities in miniature, freedmen and even slaves could take pride in services rendered on behalf of the association. See Poland, *Geschichte*, 337ff. Since Philippian converts were attracted to such honors, several must have belonged to the freedman social class.

the Christian household was more important than relationships in ordinary society.[76]

Paul describes himself both at the start (v. 1) and subsequently as well (see 9, 23) as a prisoner (δέσμιος) of Christ Jesus. He implies by this means that even though he can call Philemon his "dear friend" and "co-worker," his public status as a prisoner was no better than the slavery of Onesimus. Consequently, just as Philemon could see beyond the lowly, public image of Paul, so too he ought to see his slave Onesimus in a new light. Because of Philemon's relation to Paul as "co-worker," as well as his reputation as the church's benefactor (4–7: he refreshes the hearts of the saints), Paul could request Philemon to extend comparable benefit to Onesimus as a member of the spiritual household (8–14).

Paul counted on Philemon's commitment to the counter-culture reality that God had created through the executed/exalted Jesus. Because Paul's imprisonment occurred in service to the risen Lord, he could have commanded Philemon to receive Onesimus back as a brother rather than as a slave (8–10, 15–17). On the other hand, the familial relationship between members of the new order prompted Paul, out of love, to appeal to Philemon for cooperation. Moreover, since both Philemon and Onesimus had the same spiritual father, they were spiritual brothers (cf. 16).

REFLECTIONS ON PAUL'S USE OF METAPHOR

Although Paul's major metaphors all derive from his idea of God as creator, he does not use the images in a uniform way but tailors them to fit the situation. For example, kinship images convey God's affectionate relation to members of his new creation, but whereas the fatherly relationship is expressed in terms of the individual household in Philemon and 1 Thessalonians, the focus is on extended kinship in Romans and Galatians. Moreover, in 1 Corinthians and Philippians Paul colors the family with cultic shades (sacrifice and purity).

These adaptations of kinship are creative, but Paul produces even more striking effects when he uses different levels of social association interchangeably and when he mixes different metaphorical realms. For example, in 1 Thess 2:12 Paul shifts abruptly from the picture of converts as offspring to the image of them as subjects of an empire. In 1 Cor 3:9

---

[76]See Petersen, *Rediscovering Paul*, 2–5, 22–30.

he suddenly changes his image of the church as a fertile field to picture it as a temple. Such mixture is common in Paul's letters.

The above examples show we can not think of Paul's metaphors in isolation from one another. Although individual themes were important, their congruence and interchange were determined by Paul's overarching system of belief. Therefore, we must look beyond and behind the metaphors to the radical vision of God that unites them.

Paul's Choice of Metaphors

Since Paul's metaphors derive from his idea of God as creator, nature's fertility is one of Paul's major sources of metaphor. In 1 Corinthians the church is God's fertile field, Christ is the "first fruits" from the dead, and the transition from physical to spiritual body is compared to the difference between seed that is sown and the plant that grows from it. Nature's fertility includes the human sphere as well as plant life. Accordingly, Paul says he was in labor pains with the Galatians, trying to give birth to them, and Christ was being formed in the Galatians themselves. In Romans all creation was in labor pains, groaning to give birth to God's offspring.

God is not just the source of nature's life but also the power that causes humanity to engage in activities that sustain life and enhance its growth. Consequently, Paul refers to various levels of social association that indicate God is the ultimate source of the family, extended kinship (the tribe or people), the city-state, and the empire. Although Paul assumed this about institutions in the natural order, he states it explicitly of the new spiritual order. At each level of community, Paul indicates that growth, harmony, progress, and consecration must occur.

Similarly, Paul states that family and vocational excellence must characterize life within the ideal community: fathers work night and day to care for offspring; siblings love spiritual siblings more than themselves; athletes train with such a single-minded regimen that they win the prize; and soldiers strive side by side with fellow soldiers for a single purpose.

Paul's Metaphors Point in the Same Direction

Table 1 illustrates four images: the church as a planted field, as a temple, as a family household, and as a civic body. In each case, the activities performed on behalf of the church cause (or contribute to) a positive outcome.

Table 1. Images of the Church Illustrating Growth, Maturation, Progress

Image	Actions of Paul and others related to image	God's/Christ's beneficial role	Ideal outcome
Church as planted field	Paul plants, Apollo waters	God the source of growth	harvest
Church as temple	Paul lays foundation, others build later	Christ is the foundation	A building that withstands fire
Church as family household	Paul in labor pains and feeds with milk (=mother), works night and day, provides parental guidance, offers up priestly service on family's behalf (=father), and is steward of the estate	Christ is master *(kyrios)* of house	Family members become freeborn heirs, who assume adult obligations of household
Church as civic body	Like Christ, Paul gave up his own right to personal status and self-glory to press on to heavenly prize	Christ gave up his own rights and committed himself fully to God. God appointed him universal ruler	True citizens achieve heavenly citizenship, placing no stock in self-glory but looking to others' welfare

All four images of the church assume one or another form of progression: growth to harvest; the building of a temple that will withstand fire; the maturation of family members to the adult stage of inheritance; and the performance of civic acts that enhance God and the state rather than glorify individual ambitions. All four images of the church are dynamic; even the construction metaphor emphasizes the process of building up. The emphasis is more than one of process in three cases, since Paul conceived of the progress as one of growth in the biological sense. The church as Christ's body, an image not illustrated, points in the same direction.

Therefore, Paul regarded God as the beneficial power that directs nature and society's life processes to full-term maturation. By contrast, forces that disrupt nature's productivity and the social order are not from God. Whatever causes chaos, divisiveness, and destruction is a death force and opposed to God. Fortunately, in Paul's view, God can bring order out of chaos, unity out of divisiveness, and even life out of death.

Paul uses several other metaphors involving activities that result in a progressive outcome, but they do not emphasize the biological idea of growth. It will be useful to diagram a few of these images (table 2), that are compatible with the notion of maturation and perfection in Paul's idea of God as creator.

Table 2. Images Illustrating Success through Regimen, Excellence, Focus

Image	Activity	Outcome
Athletic imagery		
Runner (1 Cor 9:24ff.)	Exercises self control (regimen, single-minded focus), does not run aimlessly	Receives the prize, the victor's wreath (cf. Gal 2:2; Phil 2:16: the running not in vain)
Runner (Phil 3:12–14)	Forgets what lies behind and presses relentlessly forward	Reaches goal and prize
Boxer (1 Cor 9:26f.)	Does not spar aimlessly but beats his own body into submission as regimen for success	Receives the prize and the wreath (implied)
Military imagery		
Soldiers (Phil 1:27ff.)	Maintain rank as single united front in battle, striving side by side and all of the same mind	Not intimidated by opponents, and this spells defeat for enemies
Soldiers (1 Thess 5:1–11)	Keep awake and sober (vigilant), and prepare for battle by putting on gear (breastplate and helmet)	Obtain victory (salvation) through their commander (Christ)
Musical instruments		
Flute and harp (1 Cor 14:7)	Do not play recognizable sounds (tunes)	People do not know (appreciate) what is played
Bugle (1 Cor 14:8)	Makes meaningless sound	Soldiers do not get ready for battle
Trumpet (1 Thess 4:16f.)	Sounds in response to commander's (Christ's) command for attack	Commander (Christ) is victorious and takes his allies to live with himself
Gong and cymbal (1 Cor 13:1)	Noisy and clanging	A meaningless din of sound (implied)

Although none of these images express biological growth, they do exhibit the positive results that issue from attention to excellence or the negative consequences of the lack thereof. Thus, Paul's emphasis on dedication in these examples, together with his concern with sanctification and blamelessness in the cultic and moral sphere, expresses a form of completion and perfection that is analogous to human maturation and nature's productivity. On occasion, as in 1 Thess 1:9–11, Paul explicitly connects the two kinds of process:

And this is my prayer, that your love may overflow more and more with knowledge and full insight to help you to determine what is best, so that in the day of Christ you may be pure and blameless, having produced the harvest of righteousness that comes through Jesus Christ for the glory and praise of God.

Paul's Cosmopolitan Idea of God

Paul's use of images to express the kinds of performance that result in success reflects the Greek idea of *aretē* (excellence). Thus, as earlier noted, Paul's idea of progress and growth is similar to emphases found in Aristotle. He also defined humans in terms of their full maturation, particularly their social and civic development, for we cannot talk about character development apart from the community that created the climate for nurturing human virtue to excellence.[77]

We need to emphasize Greco-Roman influence on Paul because there is too little recognition of the extent to which Paul and his Jewish peers were influenced by it. Sometimes, when scholars do recognize the influence of pagan culture on Judaism, they nonetheless imply that the church was more immune to these pagan forces. The improbability of the idea that the church was an uncontaminated form of Judaism is ably expressed by Jonathan Z. Smith, who cites this unexpected statement from A. D. Nock:

> When we open the Septuagint and the New Testament we find at once a strange vocabulary. . . . Such usages are the product of *an enclosed world living its own life,* a ghetto culturally and linguistically if not geographically, they belong to a literature written entirely for the initiated (italics in original).[78]

Certain scholars describe even Greek-speaking representatives such as Paul as essentially untouched by Greco-Roman culture. The following description is not unusual:

> The apostle's cultural environment was Hellenistic and his language was Greek, but his religious heritage was Hebraic. And although he used the Greek language in order to express his thoughts, the actual words and phrases that he employed suggest again and again that Hebraic presuppositions and connotations rather than the Greek may be involved.[79]

---

[77]See Aristotle, *Politics* 1.1.7–12.

[78]See Smith, *Drudgery Divine,* 70–71. Nock's statement is in "Vocabulary," 344.

[79]Gale, *The Use of Analogy,* 10.

Granted, Paul sometimes uses images that derive from Jewish tradition, and he sometimes gives pagan images a Jewish twist. When such coloring is not clearly evident, however, it seems preferable to interpret his metaphors in terms of the broader Greco-Roman context, of which Judaism was a part.

There is another reason for signaling Greco-Roman influence on Paul. The images we have surveyed show that Paul believed in God's future perfecting of his creation. This emphasis is usually described as "apocalyptic." An adjective such as "eschatological" or "teleological" is preferable, but "apocalyptic" is probably a designation that will continue to be used of Paul's theology. With this in mind, what kind of apocalyptic viewpoint did he have?

Although Beker says apocalypticism was the Jewish perspective that most influenced Paul, he himself recognizes difficulties in interpreting Paul's theology in typical apocalyptic terms. First of all, Paul modified both the imagery and the conceptuality of apocalypticism.[80] Whereas Jewish apocalypticism often emphasized God's judgment on the nations and had a nationalistic understanding of salvation, Paul emphasized the universality of God's salvation and the inclusion of Gentiles. Whereas apocalypticism usually imagined a radical disjunction between God's new creation and the present order, Paul imagined God's salvation as an enlivening of creation that facilitated its growth and maturation.

Paul's view of God's future was similar to Jesus' idea of God's kingdom. Neither believed that the initiation of God's new order depended on God's cataclysmic destruction of the old creation. For both, God's empire (or kingdom) was emerging in their own present as a reality to be seized by people who had the eyes and faith to see it. Likewise, neither believed salvation was primarily for the elite; to the contrary, both proclaimed an unexpected breadth to God's mercy.

Increasingly scholars are turning away from Schweitzer's view that Jesus expected the literal (apocalyptic) destruction of the world in the near future. According to Schweitzer, Jesus was literally wrong. God did not intervene to destroy the world. In contrast with Schweitzer's view, however, a growing number of scholars are describing Jesus as a sage whose message derived more from the Jewish wisdom tradition than from prophecy. Much of the new picture of Jesus is valid, but it is obvious Jesus was not an ordinary sage or an advocate of conventional wisdom. The most distinctive feature of his wisdom was its paradoxical character.

---

[80]See Beker, *The Triumph of God,* 19–36.

Whoever would save his life must lose it. Whoever would be first must be last. Because of God's entry into the world of human activity, everything was turned upside down. In this sense, at least, Jesus was apocalyptic. In the same way, we may talk about Paul's having an apocalyptic viewpoint, for he thought in equally paradoxical terms. A crucified criminal was resurrected and exalted. Gentile sinners were becoming God's chosen people. Thus, both Paul and Jesus stretched Jewish apocalyptic categories to accommodate a broadened experience of God's new reality.

Finally, if we continue to use "apocalyptic" as a description of Jesus and Paul's idea of God's salvation, then we need to admit that other people in the first century were apocalyptically oriented. This was certainly true for the Roman imperial cult that identified Augustus as an agent through whom a paradaiscal golden age of peace was being established across the earth. The similarities between Paul's idea of God's universal peace and the Augustan peace will be discussed in later chapters.

There are theological similarities between Paul, Philo, and Josephus that derive from broader pagan influences (see ch. 1, above). We ought to expect this from Greek-speaking Jews, who not only tried to make Judaism comprehensible to pagans but also needed to make Judaism comprehensible to their own Jewish communities. In this connection, it is hardly accidental that God would be conceived in terms that exceeded nationalistic and regional values. Thus, the ideas of God as universal creator, as world ruler, and as the divine providence who was directing the world to a purposeful end were shared by Paul, Philo, and Josephus.

In the case of Paul, however, such ideas did not derive from his natural bent as a Greek-speaking Jew. To the contrary, at one time he opposed the hellenization of Judaism and even persecuted the Hellenistic church. When he encountered the resurrected Jesus, however, his view of God expanded beyond almost all Jewish contemporaries. His ideas about Gentiles as God's chosen people certainly exceeded traditional Jewish ideas about Gentile inclusion.

3
THEOLOGICAL CONVERGENCE IN PAUL'S RHETORIC

Chapter 1 showed how Beker, Patte, and Petersen agreed that Paul's system of belief gave coherence to his letters. These scholars do not describe how Paul's various types of rhetoric combine to express such coherence. Nonetheless, Paul's various uses of rhetoric, just like his diverse spectrum of metaphors, converge in the analogous idea of God that they convey.

It must be demonstrated, of course, that Paul was actually acquainted with ancient forms of rhetoric and that he himself was capable of using rhetoric in a comprehensible way. This does not mean we should expect all of his letters to follow the same contours or to use the same literary devices. It will become clear from the following analyses that despite appreciable differences among the letters, his epistolary style is distinctive from one letter to another. More important, all of his letters reflect an analogous conception of God. First it will prove useful to talk briefly about significant differences between ancient and modern rhetoric.

We must not evaluate Paul's mode of argumentation, or any ancient author's for that matter, according to the modern Western mentality. As noted briefly in chapter 1, modern scholarly argumentation has a bias toward "eye" reasoning: we assume that a convincing argument progresses relentlessly ahead, just as the written page allows modern readers to follow a complicated sequence of ideas. Documents were written and sometimes even posted for public reading in Paul's day, but argumentation was still conceived as oral, and accordingly, authors addressed themselves more to an audience's ears than to its eyes. Even when communications were posted, they were often read publicly as well. Repetition of theme and interruption of sequence with emotive examples attended this appeal to the ear.

Since Paul's letters were read publicly by mesengers or local church leaders, oral reasoning is also important for understanding his rhetoric.[1] Nils Dahl flagged this oral aspect of Paul's letters:

> In order to follow the flow of thought in the Pauline letters, one should pay more attention to thematic statements, gradual transitions, and "ring compositions" than to . . . systematized outlines supplied by modern translations and commentaries.[2]

We may illustrate the difference in interpreting Paul's letters according to a modern or ancient understanding of rhetoric by describing the differing ways that scholars evaluate the argument of Paul's letter to the Galatians. From a modern viewpoint, the letter seems to mire down in repetition and invective. Scholars tied to a modern form of reasoning say Paul's emotion has made his rhetoric irrational and ineffective. In contrast to this viewpoint, Patte rightly argues that Paul used volatile and repetitious speech precisely at those points in the argument where something fundamentally important was at stake. The apostle evoked language that would shock the Galatians out of their lethargy and produce a different commitment. In a similar vein, Betz argues that repetition, scriptural proof-texting, and asides in Gal 3:1–4:31 were not ineffective interruptions. In order to be considered true, arguments had to correspond to the lively way in which reality was experienced, and accordingly, they needed to be punctuated with engaging examples, proverbs, and quotations.[3]

In summary, repetition, emotive language, and graphic imagery attended the oral character of Paul's letters. With these ideas in mind, we turn to a detailed study of his rhetoric.[4]

---

[1]Paul states explicitly in 1 Thess 5:27 that his letter should be read to the whole church.

[2]Dahl, "Missionary Theology," 79.

[3]Patte, *Paul's Faith,* 39–42; Betz, *Galatians,* 129, 137.

[4]Many of the ideas on rhetoric that follow are also found in White, "Apostolic Mission."

OPENING AND CLOSING CONVENTIONS
IN PAUL'S LETTERS

Introductory Observations

Several years ago, I compared Paul's use of formulaic conventions with corresponding phrases in hundreds of "nonliterary" Greek letters written on papyrus and discovered in Egypt.[5] I tried to explain how Paul's stock phrases served the same purposes that comparable formulas served in nonliterary letters. At the time of my research, a few scholars were arguing that literary letters, such as letters of instruction that philosophers sent to students, were a better resource than ordinary letters for understanding how and why Paul wrote letters. Still other scholars were emphasizing the need to understand Paul's letters in terms of classical types of argumentation that originated in the Greek city-states.

In retrospect, I realize that my analysis was overly formalistic and the choice of comparative materials too narrow, since I tried to understand Paul's rhetoric solely in terms of ordinary letters. On the other hand, my naivete was probably no worse than that of scholars who relied on the literary letter tradition or on ancient argumentative logic as *the* way to understand Paul's rhetoric.

Instead of emphasizing one form of rhetoric to the exclusion of others, it is preferable to think of Paul's various rhetorical media as serving separate but interconnected purposes. Concerning the relationship between Paul's different types of rhetoric, we may liken the rhetorical situation to the different systems of the human body we were taught to differentiate as schoolchildren.[6] There was the skeletal system, graphically presented on a large classroom stand. Then there were transparent overlays of the muscular, cardiovascular, and nervous systems, which could be flipped into place on the skeleton. Paul's letters correspond to other ancient letters in roughly the same way that we humans share common

---

[5] See White, *Body of the Greek Letter.* The designation "nonliterary" does not mean that these letters were written by uneducated people. In fact, hundreds were penned by trained chancery secretaries of the Ptolemaic bureaucracy and later by secretaries under the Roman rule of Egypt. "Nonliterary" is used as a cover label for letters not intended to be published and in contrast to "literary" letters, which were often written consciously with publication or a wider audience in mind. See White, *Light from Ancient Letters,* 5.

[6] This analogy was suggested orally by Arthur Dewey, a fellow Pauline scholar.

skeletal structures, comparable nervous systems, and so on. Although the analogy would break down if we tried to correlate types of rhetoric with specific body systems, the idea is useful as a way of understanding the respective identities and interrelationships among Paul's rhetorical systems.

To continue the analogy, the human body is always actively disposed in one or another way and never exists in a purely neutral state. In the same way, Paul always adapted his rhetoric to address issues in specific churches. Nonetheless, our focus is not on the rhetoric of Paul's individual letters but on what is analogous from one letter to another as an index of his major theological values. Strictly speaking, Dahl is correct in stating that all of Paul's letters are mixed types and that we may not identify any single epistolary type or structure that they share.[7] Nonetheless, he acknowledges an inner unity to Paul's theology that exhibits itself in recurring statements the apostle made about his converts' need to be mature by Christ's return.[8] The emphasis to which Dahl refers appears in various places in Paul's letters, but it is present in a formulaic way at the beginning and end of the letters. It is the position here that Paul's idea of God lies behind this recurring concern for converts' maturation. The following outline illustrates the formal elements of Paul's letters.

Opening

> *Address:* "Paul, an apostle of Jesus Christ, to the church of God at ____, sanctified (beloved, called, etc.) in Christ."

> *Grace greeting:* "Grace to you and peace from God our Father and the Lord Jesus Christ."

> *Thanksgiving prayer:* "I (always) thank God for (all of) you, because of ____, and I pray that God (the Lord) may make you increase (mature) in such activity that you may be pure (holy) and blameless (guiltless) in (for) the day of our Lord Jesus Christ."

Body

> *Introductory formula:* "I want you to know, brethren, that . . ." ("I/we do not want you to be ignorant, brethren, that/of . . ."). Or: "I appeal to you, brethren, that . . ."

---

[7]Dahl argued this view in "Paul's Letter to the Galatians"; see pp. 10–11. Although he does not state it so explicitly, Dahl assumes the same perspective in "Paul: A Sketch," 6–9; and in "Letter," 539–40.

[8]Dahl, "Missionary Theology," 72–73. See also "Paul: A Sketch," 9; and "Paul's Letter to the Galatians," 75.

Concluding convention:

1. Autobiographical appeal to the letter-writer's authority and Paul's expression of confidence in his recipients' willingness to comply with his instruction.

2. Identification and recommendation of Paul's apostolic messenger who carries the letter.

3. Announcement of Paul's imminent (hoped-for) visit.

4. Parenetic section: reminder of Paul's instruction, reference to Paul's/the church's conduct at the time of founding, appeal to/illustration of the example of Christ.

5. Peace wish (prayer).

Closing

Closing greetings: from third parties to recipients, or to third parties through recipients

The holy-kiss greeting

Grace blessing: "The grace of our (the) Lord Jesus Christ be with you (your spirit)."

Paul's Use of a Grace Blessing to Open and Close His Letters

Paul begins and ends his letters with the same convention, a wish for God's grace. For example, after identifying himself and coworkers as sender(s) and his correspondents as recipients in the opening address, he adapts the conventional greeting formula found in the Greek letter into the following wish for God's grace:

"Grace to you and peace from God our Father and the Lord Jesus Christ."

Correspondingly, Paul turns the customary farewell of the Greek letter into the following grace wish:

"The grace of our (the) Lord Jesus Christ be with you (your spirit)."

Although the closing grace wish lacks the concern with peace expressed in the opening and omits explicit reference to God, the wording and intent of the two conventions are quite similar.

Recognition of this repetition in the letters' opening and closing is mostly lost on modern readers, both because of the linear nature of our thinking and because of the length of Paul's letters. Paul's recipients, however, who were used to such oral touches, would have heard the repetition. The emphasis was intentional, and the pivotal location of the repetition at

the letter's very beginning and end underscored its importance. By encir-
cling his correspondence with the grace greeting and benediction, Paul
contextualized each situation with the same presupposition: it was God's
grace, effected through Christ, that created the community and, in turn,
prompted the church to address God as its founder and Father.

At an early stage in the evolution of letter writing, the opening and
closing were delivered orally. By Paul's day, however, these spoken salutations, well-wishings, and farewells were usually delivered in writing. The
following salutation and well-wishing are typical of the opening in letters
between family members and friends:

> Hermogenes to Haruotes the prophet and my dear (friend), many greetings
> [πλεῖστα χαίρειν] and continual good health [καὶ διὰ παντὸς ὑγιαίνειν].

In ordinary correspondence, the infinitive *chairein* ("greetings") was
used, as in this letter, to express the letter's initial greeting. In addition,
family letters often added a wish for the recipient's health, which was
sometimes connected directly to the greetings, as in this letter.

By using the noun *charis* ("grace") for his opening greeting, Paul
shows he was acquainted with the more familiar epistolary greeting,
chairein. By replacing the infinitive with its cognate noun, however, Paul
evokes the root meaning of *charis* as "benefit" to express religious greeting. Moreover, by stating *charis* as a fuller expression, somewhat independent of his initial address, Paul turns the greeting into a wish for
God's blessing and thereby expresses interest in his recipients' spiritual
welfare. Thus, just as his greetings are theological, so too his well-
wishing is religious. Other ancient letter writers sometimes stated that
they were praying for their recipients' welfare. On the other hand, even
when they desired aid of the god(s) in effecting well-being, the welfare
they desired was almost always of an ordinary sort and not, as in Paul,
specifically for spiritual well-being.

In the case of Paul's final grace blessing, his use of *charis* is more
than an adaptation of the conventional farewell formula. His replace-
ment of the typical farewell wish (ἔρρωσω) with *charis* is a deliberate repetition of his opening formula. Harry Gamble, describing the grace
blessing's function in the letter's closing, shows that it is neither simple
wish nor declaration. Rather, it is a blessing, and as such it incorporates
aspects of both declaration and desire. Its wish character remains intact,
even though qualified by Paul's confidence of its effectiveness.[9]

---

[9]Gamble, *Textual History,* 66–67.

It is clear from Paul's regular reference to God as Father in the initial greetings and from corresponding descriptions of recipients as God's offspring that Paul considered correspondents God's spiritual family. It is equally clear from opening and closing grace blessings that Paul considered God the source of the converts' identity as a family. Although his converts' status as God's household was already in place, the grace blessing suggests their status was still in process and not fully effected. This brings us to the function of the expressions of peace that are just inside the outermost frame, the letter's opening and closing.

The Formal Importance of Peace in Paul's Letters

In addition to opening and closing grace blessings, Paul expresses concern about his recipients' welfare with two other conventions: (1) a prayer of thanksgiving, which immediately follows the opening grace greeting, and (2) a wish of peace at the end of the letter's body. Although peace is not stated explicitly in Paul's thanksgivings, it is implied by his request that recipients be spiritually complete (at peace with God) by the time of Christ's return. Paul's emphasis on maturation in the thanksgiving echoes his wish for end-time peace at the close of the body, and taken together, they form a second ring immediately inside the letter's outermost circle of grace blessing. This double prayer and/or wish for peace expresses Paul's apprehension about his converts' ongoing status as God's people. Although the apostle says he is confident about their development, he was nevertheless convinced that maturation was necessary and that it derived from converts' ongoing receptivity to the Spirit that was mediated to the community through its Lord.

Unlike the wish for health, which was common in the opening of letters between friends and family members, thanks to a god was seldom expressed at the beginning of Greek letters. When a letter writer did offer thanks to a god, it was usually expressed as a way of informing the recipient(s) that the deity had recently secured the writer's own safety. The thanks was a way of informing friends that the writer was well at the time of writing. In contrast to this infrequent use of thanks in ordinary letters, Paul regularly offered thanks to God at the start of his letters.[10] More-

---

[10]The thanksgiving prayer appears in five of Paul's seven letters: Rom 1:8ff.; 1 Cor 1:4ff.; Phil 1:3ff.; 1 Thess 1:2ff.; Phlm 4ff. In the two letters where thanksgiving is missing, 2 Corinthians and Galatians, there are good reasons why Paul replaced thanksgiving with an alternative. In Gal 1:6ff. negative astonishment replaces thanks because Paul was unable to acknowledge the Galatians'

over, unlike ordinary letter writers, Paul did not thank God for his own deliverance from danger but acknowledged God's assistance in securing the spiritual welfare of the converts to whom he was writing.

In a classic study of Paul's thanksgiving prayers, Paul Schubert showed that Paul's thankfulness telegraphed his reason(s) for writing and anticipated key topics to be taken up in each letter's body.[11] For example, although Paul thanks God that the Corinthians were "enriched . . . in speech and knowledge of every kind" (cf. 1 Cor 1:4–5), we later learn in the letter's body that it was precisely a deficiency in the Corinthians' knowledge and speech that was causing community problems. Therefore, Paul probably intended an element of irony in his Corinthian thanksgiving. On the other hand, when Paul thanks God for the Thessalonians' "work of faith and labor of love and steadfastness of hope" (1 Thess 1:3), his thanks is quite genuine. The concrete manifestation of faith, love, and hope proved the Thessalonians' status as God's offspring.

After first identifying the specific reason for his thanks, Paul continues by praying that God would bring to completion by Christ's return the attributes and activities of converts for which he gave thanks. The converts' perfected state is described variously as resulting in harvest, blamelessness, purity, or holiness.[12]

How, therefore, in summary, do Paul's rhetorical conventions compare with those in ordinary letters? Although he never uses the ordinary wish for health at the beginning or end of his letters, it is clear his opening and concluding grace blessings serve a comparable function. Similarly, his opening thanks to God is an acknowledgment of his converts' well-being. In every case he clearly indicates, however, that he is not concerned with ordinary health but with his converts' spiritual welfare.

The wish of peace, which I say concludes the body in Paul's letters, Gamble identifies as the first item of the letter closing.[13] Rather than

---

spiritual well-being at the time of writing. In the case of 2 Cor 1:3ff., Paul's recent troubles with converts could also account for the absence of thanks. Since Paul replaced thanks with blessing, a positive convention, however, it seems more likely he wanted to praise God's deliverance of the apostle himself rather than his care of converts.

[11]See Schubert, *Pauline Thanksgivings*, 77. Although Schubert says each thanksgiving announces clearly the subject matter of the letter, he illustrates the connection between thanksgiving and letter body in an extended way only in the case of Philippians (ibid., 75–82).

[12]See Rom 1:13; 1 Cor 1:8; Phil 1:10f.; 1 Thess 3:11–13.

[13]Gamble, *Textual History*, 72.

quibble about whether the peace-wish was the last item in the body or the first convention in the closing, I wish to describe how Gamble and I agree on Paul's purpose in using the formula. I agree that although the peace-wishes fit a formal pattern and linguistic similarities exist among them, it is significant that no two are identical. Like the thanksgiving prayers, so too Paul's peace-wishes are adapted to fit their individual contexts. Like the opening and closing grace greetings and blessings, the peace-wishes conveyed actual wishes and not mere sentiment.[14]

It is clear in Paul's closing wish for peace, as much as in his grace greeting and blessing, that he adapted letter-writing conventions to serve his own purpose. His creativity is evident in the way "grace" and "peace" in the opening greeting, "Grace to you and peace" (χάρις ὑμῖν καὶ εἰρήνη), are repeated in reverse order at the close of the letter in the wish for peace and the grace blessing.[15] Despite the distinctive flavor of Paul's peace wish, he would have been readily understood by his Gentile converts because the location, content, and purpose of his wish functioned like the wish for health at the end of Greek letters.[16]

Although Gamble rightly says the function of the peace-wish is broader than the purpose it serves in individual letters, he sets it off too much from the individual context. Although the formula's location indicates it functioned as a transition to closing matters, its hinge position between closing and body indicates it also finalized the letter's message. Gamble admits that Paul adapted formulaic elements in each case to fit their context. The situational nature of the wish for peace is most obvious in the case of Gal 6:16, where Paul makes peace contingent on the alteration of the Galatians' behavior. Even in his other letters, however, the wish is nuanced by what precedes in the letter's body.[17]

Gamble is nonetheless right in saying that the function of the peace-wish was not limited to the issues taken up in each letter's body. By closing the body with a convention that played the role of a closing health wish, Paul showed that he was not concerned primarily with solv-

---

[14]See ibid., 68–71. Some scholars suggest that liturgical practice influenced Paul's use of the peace-wish, since Judaism employed peace prayers in worship and often placed them at the end of the liturgical setting. But Gamble thinks that the ordinary epistolary practice of writing peace-wishes at the close of Semitic letters is a more likely influence.

[15]See ibid., 73.

[16]Ibid., 71–72.

[17]Gamble attributes a moderately disjunctive force to Paul's use of δέ and καί (ibid., 69) in the peace-wishes, but grammatically speaking, they are as much conjunctive (i.e., connected to what precedes) as disjunctive.

ing specific problems. Individual issues were relevant only as an index of what was more important, his converts' collective harmony and development. Therefore, the fundamental purpose of the body's message, which comes to expression in its closing wish for peace, is the same as what Paul states in his prayers of thanksgiving, namely, his converts' need to be mature by Christ's return.

We need to describe more fully the closing lineaments of the body of Paul's letters in order to understand the function of the peace-wish that is the very last item of the body. In this connection, it will be helpful to explain the various ways in which ordinary people closed their letters.[18] Despite a variety of phrasing, body-concluding formulas all perform a similar purpose: they underscore or finalize the reason for writing. One spectrum of phrases that is relevant for understanding how Paul concluded the body of his letters is the spectrum of conventions writers used to persuade recipients to do something requested earlier in the letter. These conventions were used to nail down the necessity of doing what had been earlier requested. Occasionally, the letter writer conveyed his or her attitude toward the recipient as further incentive for compliance.[19]

By what he wrote at the end of his message, Paul also tried to persuade recipients to comply with requests earlier expressed in the body, and his method was more elaborate than anything one finds in ordinary Greek letters. In my view, there are five elements in his body closing convention (see the "concluding convention" in the outline of Paul's letters, page 64 above). Robert Funk identified the first three of these elements, and he noted that they conveyed various aspects of Paul's apostolic authority.[20] In ascending order of importance, Paul appealed first to his authorship of the letter; second, he referred to the authority of his messenger, who carried the letter and who interpreted it on his behalf; third, he announced the prospect of his own upcoming visit.[21]

If we limited Paul's apostolic authority to these three elements, we might conclude that he wanted converts to adhere only to his own community rules. Dahl, however, rightly challenged the idea that Paul

---

[18]Letters often did not conclude in any special way; they simply ended. Thus, the discussion that follows is based only on letters that do express one or another formulaic phrase characteristic of the end of a letter.

[19]See my description of these conventions and how they function in White, *Light from Ancient Letters,* 204–7.

[20]Funk, "Apostolic *Parousia,*" 249–68.

[21]Ibid., 258–261 (esp. 261).

thought about authority in such personal terms. He noted that Paul regularly appealed to traditional materials near the end of the letter and this
indicated his concern with broader standards.[22]

Unfortunately, ever since Martin Dibelius's 1964 study of traditional materials in the Epistle of James, scholars have tended to think
of traditional teaching (parenesis) in Paul's letters as tacked on and
not contributing anything essential to the letter's message.[23] Stanley
Stowers rightly argues, however, that parenesis has been understood too
narrowly as the stringing together of traditional precepts and exhorta-
tions in a catch-all way. There was a whole parenetic tradition that did
not limit its appeal to precepts and maxims. Parenesis included various
models of conduct, along with various modes of encouragement and dis-
suasion, and parenetic material was not rigidly confined to the end of the
letter's body.[24]

Although Paul appeals to traditional material at various points in
his letters, near the end of the letter is Paul's customary location for
bringing authoritative teaching to bear on subjects discussed earlier in
the letter. In addition to appealing to Christian instruction he previously
taught converts, Paul refers to various models they should imitate. These
paradigms include reminders of the recipients' and Paul's imitation of
Christ, along with examples of Christ's own conduct. Both the models of
behavior and the traditional teaching indicate that the pattern to be imitated is the character exhibited in Christ. Therefore, the response Paul
sought was not conformity to specific instructions but communal conformity to Christ's spirit. Consequently, we may add a fourth and fifth element to the three conventions Funk described as expressing Paul's

---

[22]Dahl, "Missionary Theology," 72–74. See also Dahl, "Paul's Letter to the
Galatians," 75.

[23]Dibelius, *James,* 2–11. Dibelius suggested that the parenetic material in Jas
1; 3:13ff.; and 4:5 consisted of maxims strung together largely or solely on the
basis of a catchword and topical association. This material seems to have no logical or specific connection with the epistolary situation itself.

[24]Stowers, *Letter Writing,* 23. In this same connection, A. J. Malherbe demonstrates that the function of 1 Thessalonians as a whole is parenetic. Whereas
many scholars interpret Paul's reminder of his missionary work with the Thessalonians (see 1 Thess 2:1–12) as evidence he is defending himself against detrac-
tors, Malherbe shows Paul used his behavior as a hortatory example that he
wanted converts to imitate (see *Paul and the Thessalonians,* 3, 46–60). Betz also
demonstrates the relevance of Paul's use of parenesis at the end of the letter's
body by noting the analogous way in which literary authors used prescriptive
kinds of language and traditional forms of authority near the end of philosophical
letters to strengthen persuasion (*Galatians,* 254).

"apostolic authority." The fourth and fifth components are, respectively, the appeal to Christlike behavior and the wish for peace that derives from conformity to such a mind-set.

In summary, the beginning and end of Paul's letters form a double ring composition. The outermost circle is formed by Paul's grace blessing and expresses Paul's desire for his recipients' spiritual welfare. The next ring is formed by the thanksgiving and the body closing convention. This inner ring specifies the means of achieving spiritual welfare and the temporal limits for its actualization. Paul identified conformity to Christ's Spirit as the church's means of achieving perfection. Christ's return marked the temporal limit allowed for such progress.

Formulas Introducing the Letter's Body and Other Letter Closing Conventions

Greco-Roman family letters often concluded with greetings to the recipient(s) from people who were with the letter writer. Paul also closed his letters with third-party greetings to recipients from people or communities who were present with him.[25] By using familial greetings, Paul emphasized the character of his communities as members of a family, and he sometimes put an even more endearing stamp on greetings by exhorting recipients, "Greet one another with a holy kiss" (1 Cor 16:20b; 2 Cor 13:12; 1 Thess 5:26).[26]

Paul also introduced the body of his letters with conventional phrases. Jack Sanders has identified these formulaic phrases as a single

---

[25]On two occasions, Paul either singles out individuals who are to be greeted by recipients (Rom 16:13–15) or requests recipients to greet "every saint in Christ Jesus" (Phil 4:21). These third-party greetings *to* people with the recipients seem to be motivated by extenuating circumstances and are not typical of Paul's closing greetings.

[26]Some scholars include the doxology as a letter closing item, but since it occurs only in Phil 4:20 and Rom 16:25–27 and since the Romans passage is disputed on textual grounds, it seems better to exclude it as a convention. Scholars also include Paul's reference to his autograph as a letter-writing convention. E.g., Paul states explicitly that he is closing the letter in his own hand in 1 Cor 16:21 and in Gal 6:11. By this means he shows he has been using a secretary up to the point he takes the pen in hand. The warning in 1 Cor 16:22, "Let anyone be accursed who has no love for the Lord," indicates Paul's signature conveyed his authority as well as his friendship. The same double nuance is found in Gal 6:11–17 and perhaps also in 1 Thess 5:26–27. As suggested above, however, Paul's assertion of personal authority belonged more naturally to the close of the body than to the letter closing.

convention, which he described as immediately following the conclusion of Paul's thanksgiving prayers.[27] Not long after Sanders's study, however, T. Y. Mullins showed that Paul was actually using two conventions, a "disclosure" formula and a phrase of request.[28] Paul used the request convention in two of his seven letters and the disclosure formula in the five others.[29]

"Disclosure" was identified as a discrete convention by the editor of P. Mert. II, 83, who says the formulaic phrase "I want you to know that . . ." (γινώσκειν σε θέλω ὅτι . . .) first appeared in P.Oxy. IV, 743 (2 BCE, line 27).[30] Paul's request formula took *parakalō* ("I entreat") as its principal verb, and Bjerkelund identified it as characteristic of Paul's entreaty both in the opening and elsewhere in his letters.[31]

LITERARY RHETORIC IN THE BODY OF PAUL'S LETTERS

Epistolary salutations, greetings, and well-wishing originated as oral conventions. Similarly, much rhetoric in Paul's theological arguments (in the letter-body) arose in oral speech. Whereas greetings and health wish formulas derived from ordinary life, however, the rhetorical conventions discussed below reverberate with the training of the academy. In Greek culture, rhetoric referred above all to public oratory. The earliest handbooks on rhetoric, such as Aristotle's *Art of Rhetoric*, arranged the principles scientifically to show what kind of oratory was ef-

---

[27]Sanders, "Transition," 348ff.

[28]Mullins, "Disclosure."

[29]The disclosure formula is found in Rom 1:13; 2 Cor 1:8; Gal 1:11; Phil 1:12; and 1 Thess 2:1. The request formula occurs in 1 Cor 1:10 and Phlm 8–10.

[30]See the comments by the editor of P.Mert. II in Rees, Bell, and Barns, *Descriptive Catalog,* 116. The convention actually appeared earlier than this in nonliterary letters, but in a slightly different form. E.g., in P.Mich. I, 6 (257 BCE), line 1, the following form appears: "I think you are not ignorant . . . that . . ." (οὐκ οἶμαι μέν σε ἀγνοεῖν . . . ὅτι . . .). Paul uses both this latter double-negative form of disclosure (Rom 1:13; 2 Cor 1:8) and the more common positive form (Gal 1:11; Phil 1:12). Although the positive form of the formula also appears in 1 Thess 2:1, Paul's use of the perfect tense constitutes an exception to his usual use of the present tense.

[31]See Bjerkelund, *Parakalo.* Paul used both the *parakalō* request and the disclosure formula for subsequent transitions within the letter body of his correspondence. In addition to the characteristically religious subjects introduced with such phrases, Paul's regular use of the vocative, *adelphoi* ("brothers and sisters"), make his use of such conventions distinctive.

fective in specific situations. Even after speeches were written down and studied as texts, orators continued to compose speeches with an ear to oral performance.

Paul's use of ring composition and other literary touches in the opening and concluding parts of his letters have been noted above. Such stylistic features surpass the conventions in ordinary letters. Paul's familiarity with literary tradition becomes even more evident, however, when we turn to the part of the letter that scholars call "theological argument." For this part of the letter, we need to turn to literary techniques that were not strictly tied to letter writing.

Scholars have noticed literary phenomena in Paul's letters for a century or more, but up to about thirty years ago they were reticent to acknowledge explicitly the elevated character of the language. The reticence is connected partly to theological biases. A specific set of theological blinders produced a restricted view of his rhetoric. Certain nineteenth-century scholars accused Paul of being the "second founder" of Christianity, the very person who turned Jesus' optimism into an emphasis on human sinfulness. In their view, this emphasis led Paul to develop a system of salvation that made Jesus into a divine Savior, and his system became the basis of the institutional church.

In protest against this negative picture of Paul, Adolf Deissmann countered with an equally naive view from the opposite direction, arguing that Paul's greatness lay precisely in the spontaneity of his religion, apart from system. As a literary corollary, Deissmann insisted that Paul wrote "real" letters and addressed real issues. Accordingly, the genre that best corresponds to Paul's hastily written letters was the ordinary Greek letter. Because each of Paul's letters was occasioned by situational needs, the collected corpus does not constitute any connected system of belief.[32] Deissmann's view won out so thoroughly that even when Bultmann showed that Paul's manner of argumentation was influenced by the ancient diatribe, he nonetheless maintained Deissmann's view that Paul's letters belonged to the lowest level of rhetorical culture, and even then he said that Paul did not imitate diatribe consciously.[33]

---

[32]See A. Deissmann, *Light from the Ancient East,* 233–42. Deissmann contrasted "real" letters with "epistles," which he described as epistolary pretenses written for a broader public and for posterity's sake. He classifies many NT letters as epistles, since they were intended from the start to address a broader public and were never written with an actual congregation or any specific problems in mind.

[33]See Bultmann, *Der Stil.*

Despite Deissmann's emphasis on Paul's artless use of language, it is clear, as shown above, that Paul skillfully adapted epistolary conventions to express his own theological emphases. Paul's use of diatribe, chiasmus, and classical modes of argumentation in the bodies of his letters is equally indicative of his literary prowess. Paul's letters evidence familiarity with philosophical imagery and with stylistic devices of a literary nature. Our discussion, however, will limit itself to three literary forms: two types of argumentation (diatribe and the use of various modes of city-state oratory) and the literary technique called chiasmus. Although these three uses of rhetoric do not appear in every letter and do not play an equally important role on the occasions where they are used, Paul's rhetoric in the letter's body served a comparable function from one letter to another.

Paul's Use of Chiasmus

As stated earlier, circularity and repetition were characteristic of Paul's rhetoric. Nonetheless, scholars usually examine the linear logic of his letters. For example, 1 Thess 2:13–16 has been interpreted as a non-Pauline insertion partly because of its similarity to 1:2–10.[34] John Hurd defends the authenticity of 2:13–16, however, precisely because of its repetitious pattern.[35] Joachim Jeremias showed how Paul repeated words, phrases, and whole sentences in reverse order according to the chiastic schema a b–b a. Indeed, in the case of Galatians, Jeremias said Paul organized most of the letter's body according to the a b–b a pattern.[36] Hurd has criticized Jeremias's view of chiasmus, however, because he conceived of it too much in terms of the reversal of a single pair of elements.[37]

---

[34]E.g., see Pearson, "I Thessalonians 2:13–16." In large part, the blatantly judgmental attitude toward the Jewish persecution of Jesus' followers in Judea sounds too polemical to have originated with Paul himself. Its tone seems to reflect the antagonism between the church and Judaism that arose after the destruction of Jerusalem in 70 CE. See also Koester, *Early Christianity*, 113.

[35]Hurd's thesis appears in "Structure of 1 Thessalonians."

[36]See Jeremias, "Chiasmus." Regarding chiasmus in Galatians, Jeremias notes that in 1:10–12 Paul identifies two criticisms of his apostleship: his gospel is κατὰ ἄνθρωπον (lit. "according to man"; 1:10–11), and it stems παρὰ ἀνθρώπου (lit. "from man"; 1:12). According to Jeremias, Paul addresses the two criticisms in reverse order (chiastically) by proving in Gal 1:13–2:21 that he did not receive his gospel "from" human agents and then by proving in Gal 3:1–4:31 that his gospel was not human in character ("according to" a human).

[37]In particular, Hurd notes that Jeremias criticized Nils Lund for identifying multiple-member chiastic structures in the New Testament and Paul. See

To return to Hurd's defense of the authenticity of 1 Thess 2:13–16 on the basis of the chiastic pattern it forms, he argues that Paul sometimes discusses one point, digresses to a second, and then returns to the original point.[38] This a–b–a pattern occurs twice in 1 Thessalonians and organizes the whole of the letter.[39] The first a–b–a pattern occurs in 1 Thess 1:2–2:16. The initial unit of the two framing *(a)* members is found in 1:2–10, and its chiastic parallel is found in 2:13–16.[40] The digression, or *b* member between the two framing parts, is found in 2:1–12. The same a–b–a structure is characteristic of 1 Thess 2:17–3:13, with 2:17–20 and 3:9–13 (the *a* members) framing 3:1–8 (the *b* member). Although the a–b–a pattern is not repeated in the letter's third section in 4:1–5:22, other chiastic features appear in the section, and we may speak loosely of 4:13–5:11 as a middle, or *b*, panel in 4:1–5:22. The subject matter of each of the three middle elements (the *b* member in the a–b–a structure) forms a thematic pattern for the whole letter. Namely, love is the subject of 2:1–12, faith the subject of 3:1–8, and hope the subject of 4:13–5:11. The same three virtues are the themes of Paul's opening prayer of thanksgiving: "remembering before our God and Father your work of faith and labor of love and steadfastness of hope in our Lord Jesus Christ" (1:3). Correspondingly, the same triadic list of virtues is expressed near the end of the letter: "Put on the breastplate of faith and love, and for a helmet the hope of salvation" (5:8).[41] According to Hurd, the three virtues were just the sort of organizing device that Paul would have carried into his epistolary pulpit.[42]

Hurd, "Structure of 1 Thessalonians," 21–22. See also Lund, *Chiasmus.* Jeremias's criticism is in "Chiasmus," 145.

[38]Hurd presents several examples of the a–b–a pattern that occur in Paul's correspondence. E.g., Paul discusses the issue of eating meat offered to idols in 1 Cor 8, then discusses his rights as an apostle in ch. 9 before returning in 10:23–11:1 to the original subject of idol meat. Similarly, Paul introduces a certain topic in 1 Cor 12, digresses to another subject in ch. 13, and then returns in ch. 14 to the original subject. See Hurd, "Paul ahead of His Time."

[39]See Hurd, "Structure of 1 Thessalonians."

[40]A fuller illustration of Hurd's thesis regarding the a–b–a structure of 1 Thess 1:2–2:16 and of 2:17–3:13 is given in White, "Apostolic Mission," 153–57.

[41]The first two intermediate members of the a–b–a structure contain the virtues of love and faith respectively and organize the body up to Paul's response to the Thessalonians' letter. The third virtue, hope, provides an appropriate eschatological note on which to end the letter as a whole.

[42]Hurd, "Structure of 1 Thessalonians," 42.

Paul's Use of Diatribe

In his famous study of diatribe, Bultmann suggested that both Paul's preaching style and his epistolary rhetoric were dialogical.[43] Stowers shows, by contrast, that diatribal oratory is actually a dominant literary influence only in Paul's letter to the Romans. Since Paul neither founded the Roman church nor had any great familiarity with it, he was obliged to adopt diatribe as a rhetorical alternative to confirm his status as an authoritative teacher. The same necessity explains Paul's extensive appeal to Scripture as a form of authority in Romans.[44] In his survey of the history of research on the diatribe, Stowers notes that New Testament and classical scholars alike have wrongly assumed that diatribe was a form of public propoganda for people on the street.[45] He shows that the actual setting of diatribe was the philosophical school, where teachers used its oratory for pedagogical purposes.

Scholars identify eight representatives of diatribal style: Teles (and Bion), Epictetus, Musonius Rufus, Dio Chrysostom, Plutarch, Maximus of Tyre, Seneca, and Philo of Alexandria.[46] These authors are identified as practitioners of diatribe on the basis of two primary criteria: (1) their use of a common body of philosophical tradition, ethical and Cynic-Stoic in nature, and (2) their common use of a dialogical form of argumentation, which exhibited certain stylistic features. Although the chief representatives are from diverse backgrounds, classicists have described

---

[43]See Bultmann, *Der Stil.* Bultmann suggests that, apart from a few epistolary conventions, Paul dictated his letters in the same style he used in preaching (p. 3).

[44]"Only in Romans is the dialogical style employed throughout the major portion of the letter's body rather than in a few isolated texts" (Stowers, *Diatribe,* 179). See Stowers's concluding comments on the role of diatribe in Romans, pp. 175–84. Regarding the idea that diatribal oratory is broadly characteristic of Paul's epistolary rhetoric, Heinrici, *Das zweite Sendschreiben,* suggested that the dialogical method in 2 Corinthians is similar to the diatribal style of Epictetus. Bultmann, *Der Stil,* suggested that stylistic features in sections of 1 Corinthians (e.g., in chs. 1, 7, 8, 14, and 15) and Galatians (e.g., in chs. 2–4) were like the diatribe, in addition to larger blocks in Romans.

[45]Stowers, *Diatribe,* 7–78.

[46]Although Teles refers to diatribal fragments of Bion, it now seems he did not include much actual Bion material. The examples of diatribe from Epictetus are all transmitted by Arrian, a student. Similarly, the diatribes of Musonius Rufus are the notes of an otherwise unknown student, Lucius. Philo is a somewhat problematic representative, since the dialogical element is largely missing in his writings.

diatribe as the oratory of street preachers.[47] In particular, diatribe is described as a means of disseminating ethical answers to troubled, uneducated masses.

Despite this blanketing description of diatribe as a form of public oratory, Epictetus's school discourses (diatribes) and Seneca's epistolary diatribes clearly do not fit this model. In fact, with the possible exception of Bion, who may not even be a representative, none of the ancient orators identified with diatribe delivered their speeches primarily in public. Apart from Philo, who is a problematic example, all spoke their diatribes in a school setting.

To the extent that diatribe's social setting has been wrongly identified, its function has been identified inaccurately. So long as one emphasized the public setting of the diatribe, its purpose was considered polemical. On the other hand, if diatribe's actual setting was the philosophical school, its censure should be considered instructional and not polemical.[48] The usual interpretation of diatribe's social setting has influenced how scholars describe diatribe's function in Paul's Letter to the Romans.

Several interpreters assume Paul used diatribe polemically in Romans to argue against Judaism and Judaizers.[49] Many of these same interpreters assume that most or all of Paul's letters were polemical and that Judaizers were always his opponents. But it is highly questionable that what connects Paul's various arguments is an external Jewish opposition. Granted, Jewish Christians of a more conservative nature probably opposed Paul from time to time, but they were not the decisive factor in determining his argumentative method. As shown, Paul's own convictions constituted the rhetorical field of meaning that shaped the way he wrote letters. Stowers's pedagogical interpretation of diatribe points in the same direction.

Just as an assumption that Paul was always engaged in polemic with Judaism is not sustainable, neither is an assumption that he remained

---

[47]Dio and Plutarch were provincial aristocrats, Epictetus had been a slave, Musonius Rufus was a Roman knight, Philo a Jewish statesman, Teles a schoolteacher, and Seneca an imperial confidant (see Stowers, *Diatribe,* 38). For a fuller description of the figures, see ibid., 48–75.

[48]Ibid., 175.

[49]E.g., Günther Bornkamm and Ernst Käsemann claim that Paul's polemic is directed at a typification of the self-righteous Jew and not at actual groups in the Roman church. See Bornkamm, "Letter to the Romans." See also Käsemann, *Romans.*

subject to Jewish influences after conversion and that Greco-Roman traditions were only mediated to him through Jewish channels. Paul's familiarity with Greek letter-writing practices alone shows the improbability of such a view. It is equally unlikely that his use of diatribal style was mediated to him only through the synagogue.[50] With such ideas in mind, we turn to a reevaluation of the rhetorical function of diatribe in Romans.

Despite Bultmann's correct identification of several stylistic features of diatribe, Stowers shows that an inadequate understanding of the social setting hindered Bultmann from bringing the genre's full lineaments into view. If Paul's preaching and epistolary style were generally diatribal in nature, why is this mode of argument sustained only in Romans? In contrast to Bultmann, Stowers says Paul's use of diatribe in Romans was an exception to his usual style. The extraordinary circumstances of his relationship to the Roman church, in comparison with churches he had founded, prompted him to use diatribe. More will be said about these circumstances shortly. For the present, here is an outline of Paul's apostrophes to fictitious interlocutors as they are identified by Stowers in Romans:

2:1–5: to the ignorant, inconsistent judge

2:17–24: to the proud but inconsistent Jewish teacher

9:19–21: to the one who questions God's judgment

11:17–24: to the "wild olive shoot," i.e., pretentious Gentile Christians

14:4, 10: to the Christian who judges fellow believers

Not only do these passages exhibit the kind of stylistic features that one finds in diatribe; all of the apostrophes have the same audience in mind and serve the same underlying purpose. Recognition of this pattern provides an explanation of the letter's purpose as a whole.

Most commentators assume Paul's imaginary audience changed between chapter 1 and chapter 2 of Romans. That is, whereas Paul censures Gentile immorality in 1:18–32, in 2:1ff. he turns his attention to

---

[50]See Meeks, *First Urban Christians*, 75–84. Meeks identifies several institutional models that were accessible to Paul, including philosophical schools, voluntary associations, and family households, as well as synagogues. Because Christian communities were an offshoot of Judaism, Meeks says the synagogue might seem the best model by which to understand Paul's idea of community. Nonetheless, the synagogue does not provide a fully adequate model to understand Paul's churches (pp. 80–81).

self-righteous and inconsistent Jews who considered themselves superior to Gentile sinners. Since many interpreters assume that Judaism was Paul's real target, they consider it appropriate that Paul's first address to a fictitious interlocutor in Romans is directed at the self-righteous Jew in 2:1–5.

In contrast to this line of interpretation, which emphasizes the discontinuity between chapters 1 and 2, a few interpreters recognize that Paul's use of πας, *pas* ("whoever you are," lit. "everyone") in 2:1 is inclusive and therefore continues the theme Paul began in chapter 1. In this case, the indictment is concerned primarily not with Jews who judged others but with human inconsistency and pretentiousness in general. Thus Paul in chapter 1 explained how Gentiles were without excuse and were punished for vices, and in chapter 2 he gives his accusation a twist and indicts everyone, even the Jew, who condemned Gentile vices but did similar things.[51] No one had any basis for boasting before God.

Therefore, the function of 2:1–5 is to emphasize the inclusiveness of the indictment in 1:18–32 for Paul's audience and to censure anyone, Jew and Gentile alike, who arrogantly presumes to be morally superior to others.[52] Thus Paul prepares the way for discussion of God's impartiality in 2:6–11.

The second apostrophe to a fictitious interlocutor appears in 2:17–24, and while it continues the theme of God's judgment begun in chapter 1, it now identifies the interlocutor explicitly as a Jew. Not even in this case, however, should Paul's apostrophe be applied exclusively to the Jew, nor should the censure be interpreted polemically. Rather, the indictment is like the teacher's stock censure of the inconsistent philosopher who was more concerned with appearance than with substance.[53] An analogy for 2:17–24 is Isocrates' statement in *Panegyricus* that a "Hellene" was less a member of the Greek race than someone who shared a common commitment to certain values.[54] Correspondingly, when Paul

---

[51]This interpretation is given by Dahl; e.g., see "Missionary Theology," 79.

[52]The inclusive delineation of the interlocutor, "whoever you are," constitutes an exception to diatribe's usual address. So, too, Paul's use of the first person plural in 2:2, "We know," is atypical. It signals the shared knowledge and commitment of Paul and his audience. Both of these features evidence Paul's intent to foster communal harmony.

[53]The priority of good character over impressive speech has a long tradition in Greek culture. E.g., Isocrates, who was well known for his rhetoric, said he took greater pleasure in his students who were respected for the character of their actions than in those who were reputed to be able speakers (cf. *Panathenaicus* 87).

[54]Isocrates, *Panegyricus* 50.

in 2:17 censures those who call themselves Jews, he makes it clear that being a Jew was something more than an ethnic matter. He states this explicitly in 2:25–29, where people who are Jews, biologically and according to external custom, are contrasted with people, Jews and Gentiles alike, who are Jews inwardly (*en tō kryptō*, lit. "in secret").[55]

The third and fourth apostrophes, in 9:19–21 and 11:17–24 respectively, continue the theme of true Jewishness. Both are responses to difficult scriptural texts. In these cases, false inferences arose in response to difficult scriptural texts rather than in rejoinder to questionable tenets in Paul's own system.[56] Paul addresses the interlocutor as *ō anthrōpe* (lit. "O human being") in 9:20, more literally than was usually the case in diatribal speech. He uses the address deliberately to accentuate the contrast between human creatureliness and divinity. This is indicated by his personification of human beings as no better than clay before God, portrayed as a potter. The issue at hand was why God apparently had rejected his own people and granted salvation to Gentiles. Why had God molded his own people into "objects of wrath" and foreigners into "objects of mercy"? Paul legitimates God's action by appealing to the equally inexplicable choice of Jacob and the rejection of Esau (9:13).[57]

On the other hand, Paul was not willing to allow God's action to remain totally mysterious. Thus, in 9:30–10:4, he gives an explanation for Israel's rejection. By not submitting to God but by placing confidence in themselves, Israelites had tried to play God. It was Israel who had rejected God as Father (creator) and not God who had rejected Israel (cf. 10:21).

Consequently, Paul's apostrophe in 9:19–24, just as in 2:1–5 and 2:17–24, is not polemical. He emphasizes not Judaism's condemnation

---

[55]For Paul, the authentic Jew is the person whose primary concern is to praise and honor God (see Rom 2:23, 29). By contrast, the person who boasts about a relationship to God and about superior knowledge of God's law and who seeks recognition on the basis of such externalities as circumcision is not a true Jew. Circumcision is spiritual (inward) and not literal.

[56]E.g., Paul's apostrophe in 9:9–21 is in response to an objection about God's partiality and arbitrariness in choosing Jacob and rejecting Esau (9:13; cf. Mal 1:2–3). And the apostrophe in 11:17–24 is in response to the false inference in 11:1 that God has rejected his people, after Paul quotes Scripture: "All day long I have held out my hands to a disobedient and contrary people" (Isa 65:1–2).

[57]See also Paul's example of the divine hardening of Pharaoh's heart (9:17; cf. Exod 9:16). In addition, Paul refers to a statement in Hosea predicting that God will take Gentiles ("Those who were not my people") and make them his "beloved" people (9:25–26; cf. Hos 2:23; 1:10). Conversely, Paul reminds his recipients that Isaiah predicted that only a remnant of the sons of Israel would be saved by God (9:27–29; cf. Isa 10:22; 1:9).

but God's impartiality, a key attribute of his identity as creator. Despite Paul's emphasis on God's impartiality, it is obvious he is not concerned with God's universality in the simple physical sense that all creatures derived from a common creator. Rather, he argues for God's impartiality in connection with God's choice of a specific race to be his people. Paul points to the precedent for this kind of creation in God's earlier choice of Isaac and Jacob (cf. 9:6–13) to be forefathers of his people. In turn, God was equally justified in making Gentiles his children.[58]

God's impartiality is demonstrated further in the apostrophe of 11:17–24, where presumptious Gentile converts are personified under the image of the wild olive shoot that had been grafted into God's cultivated tree (Judaism). The Gentile is warned not to boast, either about God's favor or about God's apparent rejection of the Jews. Just as Jewish election occurred by means of God's mercy, so too the Gentiles' status occurred only through God's intervention. Paul warns the wild olive branches that God is able both to graft excised Jewish branches back onto the tree if they repent and to cut off pretentious wild branches.

In 14:4, 10 Paul turns to his fifth and final apostrophe. Since it occurs in the middle of hortatory statements directed to Paul's epistolary audience, the distance between the imaginary interlocutor and the actual audience is not great. In this instance, the pretentious convert is censured for judging a fellow believer. Paul castigates such pretentiousness because the fellow believer is God's servant (14:4). The illegitimacy of the claim to superiority is evidenced in the fact that the person being judged is one's own spiritual sibling, created by the same Father (14:10). In summary, each of Paul's five apostrophes has the same emphasis: God's impartiality and affection for all humanity. Since God alone is creator, human pretension is inexcusable.

Just as Paul addresses possible objections to his idea of God, so too in Romans he responds to false inferences that hypothetical interlocutors might draw from his viewpoint.[59] Ordinarily in Greco-Roman diatribes, false inferences are introduced by stereotyped questions, such as

---

[58]Paul says the Gentiles both are "called" to be God's people ("children of the living God") and have attained righteousness, in 9:22–26 and 9:30 respectively. He later concludes, "There is no distinction between Jew and Greek; the same Lord is Lord of all and is generous to all who call upon him" (10:12).

[59]This is only a general description of some of the false inferences to which Paul responds in Romans.

"What then?" Although the teacher could react rhetorically in various ways, Paul usually rejects false inferences outright with the strong negative assertion "By no means!"[60] Then Paul often uses examples or scriptural quotations to refute false inferences. Thus he first rejects the inference in the question "Has God rejected his people?" with "By no means!" and then adds as proof, "I myself am an Israelite" (11:1). In this instance, he uses a personal example to deny the false conclusion. Scripture plays a major role in Paul's rejection of false conclusions in Romans (cf. 3:4, 9–18; 4:3f.; 7:7; 9:14, 19; 11:2). Indeed, he appeals to Scripture as a source of authority much more often than other diatribal authors cite authoritative traditions.

The differences between Paul's use of diatribe in Romans and its use by other ancient authors are not to be attributed to incompetence. Rather, just as in his modification of epistolary conventions, Paul adapted diatribe to serve his own agenda. We see a unity in Paul's argument in Romans from 1:18 forward: the picture of the pretentious Jew in 2:17–24 parallels the earlier censure of the foolish Gentile and, in turn, the subsequent indictment of the boastful Gentile convert. In short, Paul's censure is directed at all human pretension. Therefore, when Paul describes true Jewishness as a matter of inward essence, he is evoking the true Jew protreptically as a paradigm for all peoples.

Consequently, for Paul, true ethnic identity derived from mystical union with God. This relationship was effected through the creative power God exhibited in Christ's resurrection and in Abraham's revivified power to procreate his promised heir. The same divine power endowed converts with the potential to actualize God's character. Chapter 8, below, will explore the moral effects of converts' union with Christ, but here we limit ourselves to God's powers of creativity as the condition for such morality. God's character as creator was the organizing idea that unified both Paul's diatribe and the whole of Romans. Romans 1:16 states the theme of the letter: God's power was a source of salvation for anyone who had faith, Jew and non-Jew alike.[61]

---

[60]See Rom 3:4, 6, 31; 6:2, 15; 7:7, 13; 9:14; 11:1, 11. A modern equivalent of Paul's strong reaction is the popular expression "Hell, no!"

[61]Righteousness and wrath in 1:17–18 are subthemes of God's power as creator, rather than separate themes that call attention to God's identity as universal judge and lawgiver. Righteousness and wrath are developed in fuller form in reverse order: wrath against distortions of God's beneficial order of the universe, and God's power to redeem anyone who trusts him to create life out of death.

When we turn to Paul's letters, we find complex hortatory letters that employ various modes of persuasion. Although Paul adapted, and sometimes combined, all three forms of rhetoric, "epideictic" best describes his most fundamental reason for writing letters.[69] In particular, Paul wrote letters out of concern for the collective morality of his community's members. A similar interest in ethics made Epicureanism a letter-writing movement.[70] Unlike the Epicureans and other philosophical schools, however, Paul's pedagogical focus was on the whole community. Moreover, unlike the philosophical schools, Paul identified God, rather than the individual, as the source and motivation of development.[71]

Although Paul was as interested in ethical instruction as the moral philosophers were, his chief metaphors indicate he conceived of his communities more as a spiritual family than as a school. We may attribute this partly to traditional ideas about the Jews as God's people. On the other hand, Paul makes it clear that this familial intimacy owed more to God's salvific activity in Christ than to traditional sources of Jewish ethnicity. Nonetheless, Paul's radical concern with morality exceeds anything of a comparable nature in the fictive family units represented by Greco-Roman voluntary associations and clubs.

When we turn to Paul's use of rhetoric's three modes of persuasion, what difference does it make to say his emphasis in a letter is forensic, deliberative, or epideictic? If his emphasis was forensic, Paul would be defending his own past conduct and/or he would be accusing others of unworthy (unjust) actions. This kind of rhetoric could arise in situations such as those depicted in Galatians and 2 Corinthians, where people had maligned Paul's past actions and motives. On the other hand, if Paul's emphasis was deliberative, he would try to procure responses from his addressees that were appropriate to the specific epistolary situation.

---

[69]Stowers suggests that, generally speaking, hortatory/parenetic (epideictic) letters dominate in first- and second-century Christian letters. Forensic and deliberative rhetoric came to the fore only in fourth- and fifth-century letters from Christian bishops. See ibid., 42–43.

[70]See ibid., 42. Although the Cynic epistles are largely pseudonymous, they too were used to serve hortatory and pedagogical purposes. See Malherbe, *Cynic Epistles*, 1–34.

[71]Consequently, the classical ideal of *philophronēsis* ("friendship"), which was based on the association of social equals who were committed to common political and/or philosophical goals through their own means, was not the organizing basis for Paul's formation of communities. He emphasized the power of God's (or Christ's) divine Spirit as the source of social reform. See Malherbe, *Popular Philosophers*, 67–77.

Finally, if his emphasis was epideictic, he would encourage fidelity to basic values ("virtues") that his recipients shared.[72] Alternative interpretations of two of Paul's letters illustrate what is at issue in Paul's use of various forms of rhetoric.

In his commentary on Galatians, Betz argues that Paul felt obliged to defend himself against false charges. Formally speaking, Galatians was a forensic letter with an emphasis on Paul's defense of his past conduct with the Galatians.[73] Betz's identification of Galatians as an "apologetic letter" appears to be supported by Paul's uncharacteristic description of his apostleship in the opening address: "neither by human commission nor from human authorities, but through Jesus Christ and God the Father" (Gal 1:1). The gravity with which Paul approaches the situation is indicated by his failure in 1:2 to describe the Galatians with any positive designation other than "the churches of Galatia." Even more striking is the fact that, in place of Paul's customary thanksgiving, we find censure in 1:6–11 (the *exordium* in the apologetic speech).

Proceeding in the manner of a forensic speech, in 1:12–2:14 Paul defends himself by rehearsing how he received his commission by divine intervention and not human means (the *narratio* of the apologetic speech). Paul's supernatural commission is verified by his radical change from persecutor to advocate of God's church. Moreover, he shows that his contact with the apostles in Jerusalem was too limited and so long after conversion that they could not be the source of his gospel (1:11–12, 23; 2:2, 5, 7, 14). Paul also narrates that church leaders in Jerusalem publicly acknowledged his status as the apostle to the Gentiles. In turn, Paul shows, by means of a dispute about table fellowship at Antioch, that whereas he continued to conduct himself in accordance with the gospel, fellow Jewish Christians (including Jerusalem representatives) had acted hypocritically. In 2:15–21 (the *propositio* of the apologetic speech) Paul adduces the following proposition from the dispute at Antioch: both he and fellow Jewish converts agreed that right relation with God was no longer based on traditional Jewish observances.

Consequently, in 3:1–4:31 (the *probatio* of the apologetic speech), Paul proceeds to demonstrate that right relationship with God was effected by faith in Christ and not by observance of the law. First, Paul proves his proposition by appealing to what the Galatians themselves

---

[72]Or correlatively, Paul might use epideictic rhetoric to discourage negative characteristics ("vices") that were detrimental to the church.

[73]Betz, *Galatians,* 14–15.

could confirm from their own experience of the salvation effected in their initial response to Paul's message (3:1–5). Then he proves through scriptural illustration that right relationship with God is effected only through faith in God and not by adherence to the law. These are the main lineaments of a forensic reading of Galatians.

Contrary to Betz's forensic interpretation, Robert Hall argues that Paul's defense of himself in Galatians was less an issue than Paul's concern with an error in the Galatians' judgment that called for correction.[74] According to this interpretation, Galatians fits the deliberative form of rhetoric better than the forensic. Consequently, Hall asks, "Is the letter to the Galatians primarily concerned with defending some past action of Paul?" He argues that it is difficult to reconcile this thesis with the whole second half of Galatians (3:1–6:18), where Paul's past conduct is hardly discussed. Rather than defending himself against various accusations, Paul tries to persuade the Galatians to cleave to his viewpoint for their own spiritual well-being.[75]

Advocates both of forensic and of deliberative rhetoric assume that external social circumstances determined Paul's mode of argumentation in Galatians. On the contrary, we will not properly understand Paul's intent until we attend to the fictive reality he conceived as a possibility in God's regenerative activity through Christ. Paul was trying to persuade the Galatians, and other communities as well, of the fundamental necessity of a true relationship with God and of the authentic human community that was possible through such a relationship. Therefore, Paul intended to use rhetoric in its most honorable way. In discussing the proper function of rhetoric, Plato has Socrates state that the true rhetorician will seek to produce conviction in the soul and to do this not according to mere appearance or probability but in the service of truth and God.[76]

In a fundamental sense, epideictic rhetoric best describes Paul's intent because it sought to fix people's commitments toward or against certain values. To be sure, Paul concerns himself with the future conduct of the Galatians, as Hall suggests. But the more essential issue was the Galatians' own past experiences and how they bore upon the future as a basis of their commitment. That is, Paul concerns himself with the

---

[74]Hall, "Rhetorical Outline." See also Kennedy, *New Testament Interpretation,* 144–52.

[75]Hall, "Rhetorical Outline," 278–79.

[76]This is a summary of Plato, *Phaedrus* 276–279.

authenticity of the Galatians' former relationship with God. In this respect, Betz was right in emphasizing the significance of Paul's narration of the past, since it established what had already happened. Paul composed Galatians in such a way as to evoke the power of God's Spirit, which the Galatians had already experienced. Thus, the letter functions as a reminder of the reality encountered through the crucified one.

Although Dahl is correct that, at the level of formal description, all of Paul's letters are mixed types, still, at the level of primary intentionality, epideictic rhetoric provides the explanatory principle that best accounts for the community concord Paul advocated and presumed in every letter. This view may be illustrated further by the rhetoric of 1 Corinthians. On the one hand, Stowers concludes that the genre most determinative of 1 Corinthians is deliberative rhetoric, even though he identifies parts of the letter as epideictic.[77] On the other hand, Wilhelm Wuellner disagrees with Stowers's interpretation of the rhetorical thrust of 1 Corinthians by arguing that Paul was concerned not with what story "there was" of divisions at Corinth but with what unity "there is" in Christ, which the Corinthians had already experienced as a reality. Accordingly, Paul refused to attribute the discord to the form of community that God had created in Christ. The divisions arose not out of God's true basis of community but from human distortions of that foundation. Therefore, Paul's rhetorical goal was to reinforce God's life-giving concord as the basis of authentic community.[78]

CONCLUDING REFLECTIONS ON PAUL'S RHETORIC

This essay concludes where it began, with the idea that Paul's fundamental convictions provided an overarching coherence to his letters. Paul uses rhetoric and adopts conventional features of letters to organize his arguments. We saw that the outermost ring of Paul's letters emphasizes that God was the founder of Paul's communities. The next inner ring indicates that Paul's communities had to develop to a state of maturation by the time their Lord returned. Although Paul was concerned with specific issues, the recurring emphasis on eschatological peace in the letters' second ring shows that Paul concerned himself more with his converts' spiritual maturation than with particular problems. Corre-

---

[77]Stowers, *Letter Writing,* 108–109.

[78]See Wuellner, "Greek Rhetoric." See also "Paul's Rhetoric"; and "Epistolography and Rhetoric," 8–10

spondingly, in the case of Paul's use of diatribe in Romans and in his general preference for epideictic rhetoric, he was concerned with his converts' ongoing adherence to the spiritual values God had effected in Christ. In addition, Paul's images and metaphors underscore the need of Paul's converts to make progress toward completion or perfection. For example, Paul's images of the church as God's fertile field, as God's mature heirs, as Christ's integrated body, and as God's completed building (temple) all converged in their emphasis on the community's development (see chs. 1 and 2, above).

Consequently, all the major forms of Paul's rhetoric function in an analogous way and in the service of the same underlying idea of God. God is identified with the vivifying power of life, both to create and to nourish to full-term growth. Correlatively, Paul was convinced that he and his converts, as God's spiritual offspring, had to embody the same beneficial powers as their spiritual parent. Like Jesus, their spiritual Lord, they had to grow into the full stature of the heir who was perfectly infused with his Father's beneficial rule of the family. Like their Lord, they had to exhibit freedom from the barbarism of enslavement to individual accomplishments and honors.

With this emphasis on life-giving power in mind, part 2 discusses Greco-Roman precedents that influenced Paul's theology. We will see how Paul's ideas about God's empire, his conception of Christ as a ruler, and his ideas about the church as a community were all informed by Roman imperial culture.

PART TWO
GRECO-ROMAN INFLUENCES
ON PAUL'S IDEA OF GOD

Colossal head of Constantine with eyes looking
heavenward like Platonic ideal ruler. Head housed
in Palazzo dei Conservatori. Capitoline Museum,
Rome. Photo courtesy of Alinari/Art Resource, N.Y.

"I ain't no good any more," [Pa said]. "Spen' all my time a-thinkin' how it use' ta be. Spen' all my time thinkin' of home, an' I ain't never gonna see it no more. . . . Funny! Woman takin' over the fambly. Woman sayin' we'll do this here, an' we'll go there. An' I don' even care."

"Woman can change better'n a man," Ma said soothingly. "Woman got all her life in her arms. Man got it all in his head. Don' you mind. . . . maybe nex' year we can get a place."

"We got nothin', now," Pa said. "Comin' a long time—no work, no crops. What we gonna do then? . . . Git so I hate to think. Go diggin' back to a ol' time to keep from thinkin'. Seems like our life's over an' done."

"No, it ain't," Ma smiled. "It ain't, Pa. An' that's one more thing a woman knows. . . . Man, he lives in jerks—baby born an' a man dies, an' that's a jerk—gets a farm an' loses his farm, an' that's a jerk. Woman, it's all one flow, like a stream, little eddies, little waterfalls, but the river, it goes right on. Woman looks at it like that. We ain't gonna die out. People is goin' on—changin' a little, maybe, but goin' right on."

John Steinbeck, *The Grapes of Wrath*

4

"PEOPLE IS CHANGIN', BUT GOIN' RIGHT ON"

Political and intellectual changes crashed with such force on Mediterranean shores in the Hellenistic period that they damaged many social institutions and washed away some structures almost entirely. Social structures in the United States suffered comparable damage in the first third of this century when the stock market crashed, when drought struck our southwestern and south-central states, and when the country suffered the worst economic depression of its history. John Steinbeck's *Grapes of Wrath* describes how loss of the family farm affected hundreds of thousands of people. His novel focuses on a representative family, the Joads, and details in spellbinding terms how people were forced to change. They were no longer farmers but migrants. Eyes and minds formerly fixed on acres of fields were now fixed on narrow concrete miles that carried them to California. The disorientation was sometimes too much for fathers, the traditional family heads. Thus, mothers like Ma Joad had to take charge, and the new role of the car as the family's home gave greater status to mechanically minded offspring such as young Al Joad.

How did ancient societies adapt to altered situations like those described in Steinbeck's *Grapes of Wrath?* The changes themselves, as well as the increase in mobility resulting from such changes, led to the formation of voluntary societies as a substitute for family and to new kinds of political loyalty. Political, social, and religious changes led political theorists to advocate monarchy as superior to traditional city-state government as a solution to social problems. And Greco-Roman ruler cults came to advocate an idea of absolute sovereignty and universal empire.

CHANGING IDEAS OF DIVINITY, COSMOLOGY, AND COMMUNITY IN THE HELLENISTIC PERIOD

Luther Martin has identified three major changes in the Hellenistic era that encouraged universalism and internationalism. First, Alexander the Great's conquest of the East resulted in a vision of the whole world as city; the world of autonomous city-states was now replaced by the idea of universal empire.[1]

Second, at the same time that Alexander's conquests were modifying political ideas, a cosmological revolution was revising the idea of the natural order. Although the new cosmology was named after Ptolemy (ca. 100–178 CE), it was largely in place at the beginning of the Hellenistic era. Whereas the earlier three-storey conception of the universe imagined a flat earth in a primeval sea, domed by heaven above and an underworld below, the new scientific cosmology taught that the earth and its seas formed a sphere around which seven planetary spheres moved in a calculable order. Although Ptolemaic cosmology retained the idea of the earth as the center of the universe, the heavenly boundary now extended to a vast, invisible, and unmoving spherical shell that contained the whole system.[2]

---

[1]Cf. Martin, *Hellenistic Religions,* 4, 29.

[2]E.g., see Plato's picture of the new cosmology in the *Republic* (7.528E–530C; 10.613E–620; cf. Plato's *Gorgias* 451 C). See F. M. Cornford's extended

Third, the transformation of cosmology and politics contributed to the modification of traditional religion. The idea that both the celestial bodies and the earth were governed by rational laws was proved empirically by the way the sun caused vegetation to grow and die; by the way the waking and sleeping state of animals was governed by the alternation of night and day; and by the way the moon controlled the movement of the tides.[3] Formerly, Greeks had believed the gods intervened directly in human affairs. The gods lived on Mount Olympus, the sacred center of the world, and because Greeks dwelt in umbilical proximity to this center, they felt at home in its protecting womb. According to the new view, however, the world was no longer ruled directly by gods. The Olympian family came to be understood by philosophy as an allegorical expression of a single rational order.[4]

Formerly, city-state structures mirrored the different functions that members of the divine family performed, but with the erosion of traditional cosmology and politics, there was a corresponding erosion of the religion that supported such structures.[5] As seen below, economic developments in the classical period had anticipated changes in the Hellenistic period. The altered political situation created by Alexander's conquests, and intellectual advances such as the new cosmology, emerged out of forces that were already afoot. These forces were only given free rein, however, in the Hellenistic period.

ECONOMIC CHANGES IN THE GREEK WORLD

Eighth to Fourth Centuries BCE

The traditional basis of the Greek economy was agricultural; wealth was based on raw produce (grain and cattle) and slaves. There was little bartering and buying because the ideal was for each citizen household

---

commentary of *Timaeus* in *Plato's Cosmology*. See also Martin, *Hellenistic Religions*, 6–8; and Cotter's discussion of Ptolemaic cosmology in "Cosmology."

[3]See Michael Grant's description of Hellenistic scientific research and the drive toward realism in *From Alexander to Cleopatra*, 149–59.

[4]Cotter describes how the new cosmology led people to believe that even if the gods existed, they inhabited a realm beyond the moon that was immune to the erratic forces that affected the earth (see Cotter's description of "life beneath the moon" in "Cosmology").

[5]See Martin, *Hellenistic Religions*, 8–10.

(oikos) to be self-sufficient.[6] It is no accident that Greeks valued the hereditary farm and that household management was highly prized. Nor should it surprise us that citizenship was based on hereditary land ownership. An economic revolution began to sweep through the Greek world in the eighth century BCE, however, and the focus on self-sufficiency began to be replaced by agricultural specialization and international commerce. This reform began on islands off the western coast of Asia Minor and in coastal cities of the same region. Greek-speaking peoples who immigrated to these areas found the soil less suitable for cereal crops than for vineyards and olive trees.[7] By concentrating on olive oil and wine, along with the manufacture of textiles from local wools and the production of regional crafts, the islands and coastal cities of Asia Minor began to dominate the international market.

The economic revolution spread gradually to the mainland of Greece, especially to coastal cities that could engage in seafaring trade. Athens came to play a particularly important role because the city had been attacked and burned twice by Persia at the start of the fifth century BCE. Following the first invasion, the Athenians decided to build a navy to better defend themselves. Because of widespread fear of further invasion from Persia, the other city-states did not intervene when Athenian naval prowess upset the Greek balance of power.

Most of Greece did not pursue the struggle with Persia after the second invasion, but Athens allied itself with the islands and coastal cities of Asia Minor to remove Persian naval bases from the Aegean Sea. By systematically eliminating the bases, Athens and her allies made the sea safe for commerce, and Athens evolved into a major commercial center.[8] Economic changes created such political and social upheaval in Athens, however, that aristocratic families found their hereditary position challenged by people whose status derived from their importance in the new

---

[6]Domestic manufacture supplied not only foodstuffs but also clothing, furniture, and agricultural implements. See Rostovtzeff, *Greece*, 45ff. The following survey of economic development is largely based on Rostovtzeff (see ibid., chs. 4 and 6–12).

[7]The islands gained a reputation for sweet, fragrant wines, and the popularity of olive oil for cooking and illumination began to outstrip that of alternative oils.

[8]Although Attica's soil was not especially good for cereal crops, it was excellent for growing olive trees, and its mountain areas grew enough large timber to support shipbuilding needs. These factors encouraged Athens, the city-state center of Attica, to specialize in olive groves and vineyards and to engage in seafaring activities that supported her manufacturing interests.

economy. Both groups were challenged, in turn, by lower-class elements who made up the navy and by foreign laborers. A more democratic form of state grew up out of necessity, as a means of preserving the empire.[9]

Agricultural specialization and manufacturing growth combined to erode Athens's and many city-states' ideal of agricultural self-sufficiency. The need of grain and meat staples led to colonization, which further loosened people's ties to their hereditary farms. In the case of Athens, which turned to Macedonia and Thrace for staples and raw materials, it proved advantageous to establish a colony on the Macedonian coast. Mobility became even more widespread in Greece from the fourth century BCE onward, as colonization, ongoing civil war, and new Hellenistic kingdoms made other regions more desirable than the homeland. The city-states had simply exacted too much in life and money from citizens to hold on to their loyalty.

Changes Brought by Alexander the Great's Rule

Social turbulence in Greece at the end of the fifth century BCE worsened in the first half of the fourth century. Thus, political, economic and intellectual factors combined to encourage a new idea of society. Many political theorists believed monarchy would be a better form of government than the democratic city-state. Although intellectuals saw the advantages of monarchy, the Greek states resisted the offer of Philip II of Macedonia to lead them in a war against Persia. The states were not strong enough to withstand his compulsory unification, however, and Philip was well into finalizing plans for an attack on Persia when he was assassinated.

After Philip's son and successor, Alexander, won the confidence of his Macedonian army, he confirmed the alliance Philip had made with the Greek city-states.[10] He set about implementing his father's goals by marching out of Pella in April of 334 to invade the Persian

---

[9]Generally speaking, wherever city-states moved toward democracy, the line of development was the same. Political power passed from the monarchical clan ruler to the larger citizen body: first to a smaller body of leading families traditionally associated with the clan ruler, next to a larger group of families, whose status was no longer determined strictly by birth, and finally to all landowners. Resident aliens, serfs, and slaves continued to be excluded from citizenship.

[10]Alexander's success in stopping the advance of the Celts against Macedonian borders, his ability to put down a coalition headed by the Illyrian king, and his severe punishment of Thebes for attacking a Macedonian garrison all served as harsh lessons for any would-be opponents.

Empire. It became clear almost from the beginning, however, that, compared to Philip, Alexander regarded his role as king of Macedonia and as leader *(hēgemōn)* of the Greek allies differently. Although Philip may have appreciated Greek culture, he championed it in the service of his own emerging empire, and he remained a Macedonian at heart. By contrast, Alexander had been tutored by Aristotle and was filled with Greek ideals of human excellence *(aretē)*. Thus, he did not aspire merely to round out the borders of Macedonia like his father, or to treat the conquered as barbarians, which Greek allies would have done; rather, he imagined himself a social liberator and a creator of world empire.

Alexander was not only king of Macedonia and leader of the Greek allies; he was also the "Great King" of Asia. By founding cities in key places, such as Alexandria in Egypt, and by making improvements on existing cities, Alexander indicated he was creating an international trade route and laying the foundations of a worldwide empire. The capital of the empire would be located in the East, probably with Alexandria forming a central hub of east-west and north-south trade. The fact that two of Alexander's Macedonian successors, Ptolemy and Seleucus, founded kingdoms in the East shows they were inspired by his vision of an international and cosmopolitan empire.

UNIVERSALISM AND THE GRECO-ROMAN RULER CULT

The Greek Roots of Ruler Cult Ideology

Hero worship grew naturally out of Greek roots. Polytheistic Greeks were willing to attribute immortality posthumously to mortals who performed achievements of surpassing excellence for fellow citizens, and they formalized recognition of the benefactions in cultic worship. In theory, human heroes and gods were differentiated. Heracles was a notable example and precedent, however, of the hero who was elevated to the rank of god.[11] Although precedents existed in archaic and classical Greece for the posthumous worship of mortals, the worship of living rulers appeared only at the end of the Peloponnesian War (405 BCE) and began to be widely accepted only at the beginning of

---

[11]See Fears, "Ruler Worship," 1010.

the third century BCE.[12] The idea of absolute sovereignty and the appeal of ruler worship developed because of the intellectual and economic factors we identified earlier.[13] Citizens turned increasingly away from city-state politics and toward idealized monarchy as a solution to social ills.

Good rulers were divinized for the same reason that gods were worshiped: they were acknowledged as saviors of social order. Isocrates had such ideas of social welfare in mind when he informed Philip II (*To Philip* 116–118) that although Greeks recognized the existence of destructive forces, they were not worthy of worship but were to be conquered or driven away. Only civilizing powers were to be esteemed, imitated, and worshiped. Accordingly, he encouraged Philip to be high-minded like his ancestor Heracles, to be a civilizer and not a destroyer, and to regard all Hellas as his fatherland (*To Philip* 122–127).

The emphasis on rulers' ability to establish social harmony and to supply life's necessities was matched by comparable developments in religion. The former idea of the gods' separate roles in the divine family, which justified different levels of human responsibility within the state, was gradually replaced by the idea that the deities were similar to each other. In one way or another, the major gods all came to be associated with the power of civilization over chaos.[14] The idea of gods, goddesses,

---

[12]According to J. R. Fears, Douris of Samos said the Spartan general Lysander was "the first Greek to whom cities erected altars, offered cult sacrifice, and honored with hymns appropriate to a god" (cf. Plutarch, *Lysander* 18). Lysander's deification occurred out of gratitude for his defeat of the Athenians in 405 BCE, a defeat that restored freedom to cities under Athenian control. See Fears, "Ruler Worship," 1011. Dynastic cults to a living king appeared under Ptolemy II Philadelpus in the early third century BCE. A comparable cult was established by the Seleucid dynasty.

[13]It was not just the philosophical ideal of the king that led political theorists to espouse monarchy as an alternative to the city-state; for kings such as Dionysius I of Syracuse and Euagoras of Cyprus were better advocates of Hellenic ideals than the city-states. Moreover, Clearchus, tyrant of Heracleia and a pupil of Isocrates, encouraged subjects to worship him as a son and agent of Zeus. Likewise, Philip II had his image carried in procession along with the twelve chief gods of Macedonia. See U. Wilcken's comments on the worship of living rulers (*Alexander the Great*, 210–13).

[14]E.g., Apollo, the son of Zeus and god of radiance (the sun), was also associated with prophecy, healing and destruction, culture, and music. In short, he became the embodiment of Greek civilization. Athena, the daughter of Zeus and goddess of wisdom, prudent warfare, the arts, and industry, became the patroness of culture to Athens. Originally, Dionysus's identity was limited to fertility and to ecstatic religion. Given the importance of fertility in Greece, it is small wonder he came to have an importance approaching that of the Great Mother. Moreover, his

and heroes as benefactors became a dominant motif and the model by which Greeks glorified their own expulsion of Persia from the mainland. The repulsion of Persia, like the gods' defeat of primeval giants, became a symbol of civilization's victory over barbarism. Both were worthy of depiction on Athens's Parthenon.[15]

Although fourth-century BCE philosophers believed monarchy was the best means of solving social problems, monarchy was modeled primarily on the heroic past or on a utopian ideal, rather than on actual kingdoms. For example, Isocrates urged Philip to imitate his heroic ancestor Heracles as a benefactor. Although Xenophon chose a historical king as a model, he took liberties with the historical past. In his *Cyropaedia* he painted an idealistic portrait of Cyrus as a king whose love of his subjects could be compared to a father's concern for his children and a shepherd's beneficial care of his flocks.[16] In the *Republic* Plato described the ideal state as one in which the philosopher king kept his eyes fixed on heaven and governed the state according to a divine ideal.[17]

---

role was enlarged to include the powers of enlightenment (life and fertility) over chaos (death and sterility). Heracles's heroic exploits were interpreted increasingly as social benefits.

[15]The frieze running above the columns on the outer wall of the Parthenon showed analogous mythical combat scenes on all four sides. On the south side, Lapiths (the oldest inhabitants of Thessaly) battled centaurs; on the east, gods fought giants; on the west, Greeks fought Amazons (this symbolized the expulsion of Persia); and on the north were Trojan battle scenes. See Rostovtzeff, *Greece*, 166.

Similar comparisons between the gods and human heroism were drawn in military-funeral orations. E.g., in 434/433 BCE Plutarch said Pericles compared the Athenians who fell in battle at Samos with gods: "He declared that they had become immortal, like the gods; 'the gods themselves,' he said, 'we cannot see, but from the honors which they receive, and the blessings which they bestow, we conclude that they are immortal.' So it was, he said, with those who had given their lives for their country" (Plutarch, *Pericles* 8.6; see also Thucydides, *History* 2.35–46). See the description of funeral orations by G. Norlin (noted on Isocrates, *Panegyricus* 74).

[16]See Xenophon, *Cyropaedia* 1.6.7, 24; 8.1.44; 8.2.9; 13–14; 8.8.1. Antisthenes the Cynic also referred to Cyrus as an ideal ruler and likewise compared him to a father and a good shepherd (cf. Wilcken, *Alexander the Great*, 13–14). See also the biblical picture of Cyrus as the Lord's anointed in 2 Chron 36:23; Ezra 1:1–2; and Isa 44:28; 45:1.

[17]See the *Republic* 6.500, where Plato refers to the godlike ruler who constructs the state's constitution according to a divine pattern. Then, in 6.507–508 and in 7.540–541, the ideal ruler is described as lifting up the eyes of his/her soul to gaze on that divine reality which is taken as a pattern for the right ordering of the state.

Lysippus's sculptures of Alexander gazing toward heaven consciously recall Plato's image of the ideal ruler.[18] The eyes of Constantine in the large statuary head in the courtyard of Rome's Capitoline Museum likewise look toward heaven in imitation of Plato's ideal.

If an individual was clearly superior in virtue to other citizens, such a person had the right to rule others, according to Aristotle. Since this individual was a law unto himself, he was not subject to anyone and had the right to rule others absolutely.[19] Aristotle shared with many contemporaries the view that rulers could become gods after death through remarkable deeds of benefaction.[20] Thus, it is hardly accidental that medallions struck late in Alexander's life portray his victory over Porus as an act of surpassing excellence and picture Alexander ruling by divine will as the vice-regent of Zeus.[21]

Even a fanatical democrat such as Demosthenes had been willing to admit that the political efficiency of Philip II was superior to that of the city-state's assembly, for the king was simultaneously ruler, general, and treasurer.[22] Isocrates was acknowledging the same superiority when he informed Philip that although other men were bound by constitutional polity and were powerless to effect anything other than what due process allowed, Philip combined the power of both statesman and general.[23]

In summary, what did political theorists find appealing about monarchical rule? First, they conceived of a ruler whose primary interest was his subjects' welfare, like a father caring for his children and a

---

[18]See Fears's comments on Plato's *Republic* and on Lysippus ("Ruler Worship," 1012).

[19]Aristotle, *Politics* 3.11.12–13.

[20]Cf. Aristotle, *Nicomachean Ethics* 1145 A. See Plato's statement that the best rulers dwell in the islands of the blessed after death and that the state sets up monuments for them and offers sacrifices honoring them as divinities (*Republic* 7.540–541).

[21]See Fears, "Ruler Worship," 1012. Fears says the symbolism on the medallions does not indicate explicitly that Alexander was a god but, like the painting of Apelles that represented Alexander with a thunderbolt, it indicated he was the salvific agent of Zeus and it assumed that immortality awaited him after death because of his *aretē*.

[22]E.g., in his *Second Philippic* (cf. 3–4), Demosthenes says his fellow Athenians were foolish in acting as if they could check Philip's activities by speeches. Although they were better equipped for talking about justice, Philip was far superior in implementation. Similarly, in his *First Olynthiac* 4, Demosthenes states that because Philip was the sole director of Macedonian policy, he had an immense practical advantage over Athens in his striking ability.

[23]Isocrates, *To Philip* 14–15, 127, 140.

shepherd taking care of his flock. Second, because of the king's unilateral authority, his rule could be more efficient and nonpartisan than that of the city-state. Third, if his benefactions were substantial, there were mythical and contemporary precedents for the idea of divinization and the ruler's right to absolute rule. (Despite the view of some that the idea of Alexander's divinity originated in the East, it actually arose out of Greek ideas.)[24] Fourth, although most political theorists did not think of monarchy in international terms, the extent of Alexander's conquests, as well as the Cynics' idea of universal law and universal citizenship, provided an impetus to the idea of the universal ruler.

Alexander as Ideal Ruler

Although Alexander did not aim at the universal brotherhood that some scholars attribute to him and that Cynics advocated as an ideal, his idea of empire was more inclusive than the Panhellenism of Isocrates and Aristotle. Alexander's positive attitude toward the "barbarian" East began to exhibit itself as early as his victory at Issus. According to Arrian, after the victory Darius (the Persian king), as king of all Asia, appealed to Alexander. Alexander replied that he himself was now "Great King of Asia" and hereafter Darius must address him as such.[25] Although Alexander may not have thought well of Persians at the time, he accepted Egypt and Babylonia's offer of sovereignty and was installed as king according to their custom.[26] The Babylonian ceremony included the claim of "world

---

[24]See Wilcken, *Alexander the Great*, 210–11. Wilcken rightly notes that, with the Greeks, the dividing line between gods and men had always been fluid. As Heracles had earned a place among Olympians by his deeds, so too other mortals could merit divine honors if they performed superhuman tasks in the eyes of their contemporaries. See the examples cited by Wilcken (p. 211). See also Isocrates' comments on mortals who came to be regarded as demigods (e.g., *To Philip* 140–43).

[25]Arrian, *Anabasis of Alexander* 2.14. This was the first of two exchanges between Darius and Alexander following the battle of Issus. Alexander was asked to return Darius's mother, wife, and children, who had been captured.

[26]Alexander also began to adopt a favorable attitude toward Persian subjects following Darius's assassination. Since Persians were his subjects now and since they had formerly been the ruling element, he began to conceive of a union of Persians and Macedonians. He extended favorable treatment also to Iranians, who were a kindred race, and he probably intended his marriage to the Iranian Roxane (327 BCE) as a gesture of reconciliation. His desire to unite Macedonians and Persians, along with such kindred races as the Medes and Iranians, however, does not mean, as W. W. Tarn thought, that Alexander aimed at a universal

sovereignty," a title Alexander took quite seriously.[27] Memoranda in his archives suggest he intended to undertake a western campaign after conquest of the East and to invade Scythian territory to the north.[28] He was the prototype for Julius Caesar's idea of a worldwide empire.

In light of the absolute rule theorists attributed to the ideal monarch, along with the deification of historical fourth-century rulers, we may understand Alexander's demand for divine honors from Greek allies after his victorious return from India. He had fulfilled the very agenda that Isocrates said would secure deification for his father: the overthrow of Persia, the liberation of Greek city-states in Asia Minor, and Greek unification.[29] Despite his accomplishments, there is little or no evidence that a cult was founded to offer sacrifice to the ruler during his lifetime.[30]

It was only after Alexander's death that his generals and successors created a ruler cult dedicated to him. He was worshiped as a god by Eumenes, Lysimachus, Seleucus I Nicator, and Ptolemy I Soter, and these first successors of Alexander placed his deified portrait on their coins. Ptolemy placed his body in a sarcophagus in Alexandria and founded the state cult of Alexander. As long as the Ptolemies ruled Egypt, documents were dated by the year of the eponymous priest of Alexander, as well as by the year of the reigning king.[31]

A big step was taken in the establishment of ruler cults dedicated to the separate dynasties when Ptolemy II Philadelphus created a state cult honoring his father as "Divine Savior." When his mother, Berenice, died,

---

brotherhood of nations. Despite the respect he showed to Anatolian, Egyptian, and Semitic subjects, there is little evidence Alexander regarded them as equals. See Wilcken, *Alexander the Great,* 161–62, 208, 248–50.

[27]I agree with Wilcken that several activities of Alexander indicate he resolved to be world ruler. Although Wilcken largely bases this on Alexander's decision to conquer India, he admits that other scholars attribute the Indian campaign to nothing more than Alexander's desire to rule the Persian Empire to its fullest extent (ibid., 173–74, 224–27).

[28]Tarn argued that these memoranda were composed no earlier than 200 BCE ("Alexander's ὑπομνήματα," 1). Wilcken countered that since the memoranda go back to a first-class source, Hieronymus of Cardia, we cannot dismiss them as unreliable (*Alexander the Great,* 226). Arrian, *Anabasis of Alexander* 7.1, confirms the general lineaments of a western campaign.

[29]See Isocrates, *To Philip* 140–145.

[30]This position, with which I agree, is advocated by Fears, "Ruler Worship," 1012. On the other hand, S. R. F. Price argues that a divine cult was "offered" to Alexander in his own lifetime. Price does not state whether the cult was merely offered or was actually founded (cf. *Rituals and Power,* 26).

[31]Cf. Borza, *Alexander the Great,* 1–6.

he honored both parents in the cult as "Divine Saviors" *(theoi sōtēres)*.[32] Similarly, when his sister and consort, Arsinoë II, died, Philadelphus founded a state cult to her. Then he took the decisive step of uniting himself, in advance of death, with his deceased sister in the state cult of the *Theoi Adelphoi* ("Divine Brother and Sister"). By this act he opened the door to the ruler's deification within his or her own lifetime. From then on, Hellenistic rulers received divine honors and were worshiped in dynastic cults as soon as they performed significant acts of benefaction. Epithets such as Soter ("Savior"), Euergetes ("Benefactor"), and Epiphanes ("Self-manifestor") became common.

In addition to dynastic cults within the kingdoms, autonomous city-states began to found municipal cults to worship an individual ruler, along with their other gods, in appreciation of a specific benefit he had rendered on the city's behalf. In turn, the period of the Diadochi (Alexander's successors) gave rise to a third religious innovation within Greek cities, the worship of the divinized citizen body, Demos. Although fifth-century art and literature had personified the citizen body, just as the individual Tyche (Fortune) of certain cities was personified, the founding of cults to such entities in the third century BCE was a by-product of the ruler cult.[33]

Ruler Cult Influence on Rome and Augustus

Republican Rome had an ingrained fear of kings and a hatred for the divinization of humans. Nonetheless, ruler cult ideology exerted its influence as early as 218/217 BCE, when the cult of the Genius Publicus/Genius Populi Romani was introduced into state religion as a conscious parallel to the cult of Demos at Athens and Rhodes. In turn, Greek cities in the second century BCE began to worship the divinized Roman people (Demos) and Dea Roma in response to concrete benefits rendered by Roman governors. Although Rome established no state cult to a living mortal before Augustus, the Greek idea of conferring divine honors on rulers provided the framework for the special recognition given to generals of the late republic such as Sulla, Pompey, and Caesar.[34]

---

[32]The cult of Ptolemy and Berenice was celebrated with a great festival every four years throughout the Greek world.

[33]See the comments on municipal cults and worship of Demos in Fears, "Ruler Worship," 1013.

[34]Caesar, like Sulla and Pompey, was honored in extraordinary ways that emphasized his status as one chosen by the gods and endowed with supernatural gifts, power, and virtue. Nonetheless, he was not deified and worshiped as Divus

Although ruler worship was woven into the fabric of Roman state religion under Octavian's leadership, it had to be introduced in a modified form. Roman patricians equated ruler worship with tyranny, but by adapting ruler cult ideas to Roman sensibilities, Octavian was able to establish the very thing that had precipitated Caesar's assassination. He did not have this wisdom at the beginning but acquired it gradually through several fortuitous circumstances. As shown more fully in the following chapter, he was able to satisfy the needs of a broad spectrum of ethnic subjects while still retaining the traditional privileges of the Roman nobility. For the present, we turn to a more specific and limited explanation of his success.

Zanker argues that Octavian's acquisition of sole power in 31 BCE, after defeating Antony at Actium, marked a turning point in his career. He began to turn away from his earlier "Diadoch style" of self-glorification and resolutely toward restoration of the republic, the honoring of Roman customs, and devotion to traditional religion. The misdeeds and impiety of the civil wars had to be redeemed through sacrifice and religious piety.[35] Octavian himself provided an example of the devotion that was required to restore peace and concord to the state:

> The statues of myself in the city, whether standing or on horseback or in a quadriga, numbering eighty in all and all of silver, I had removed, and from this money I dedicated golden offerings in the Temple of Apollo, in my own name and in the names of those who had honored me with these statues. (*Res gestae* 24)

The populace sensed that peace depended on Octavian staying alive, and accordingly, they tried to force the role of monarch on him. But his new style of leadership required that he submit to the senate and respect its traditional status within the republic. Thus, in 27 BCE he officially returned control of the state, and his extended authority as temporary dictator, to the senate and people:

> For this service [the restoration] I was named *Augustus* by resolution of the senate. The doorposts of my house were officially decked out with young laurel trees, the *corona civica* [an oak wreath] was placed over the door, and in the Curia Iulia was displayed the golden shield *[clipeus virtutis]*, which the senate and the people granted me on account of my bravery, clemency, justice, and piety. (*Res gestae* 34)

Although Octavian continued to control the state through special privileges, long-term offices, and extraordinary powers granted by the

---

Julius until after his death, when he was elevated to his place among the gods of the Roman state (See ibid., 1014).

[35]See Zanker, *The Power of Images,* esp. ch. 3 (pp. 79–100).

senate, his official act of relinquishing power allowed the senate to save face and to become partners in the new state. Apart from the honorific title "Augustus," the various honors voted to Octavian in the citation above were modest and in the old Roman tradition. Octavian's new modesty and new relation to the senate as *princeps* ("leading citizen") should not be dismissed as mere pretense, because, after 27 BCE, the honors always came from others—the senate, the cities, local societies, or individuals. Even the title "Augustus" did not glorify Octavian primarily as an individual but called attention to his devotion to the state's "increase" in dignity.[36]

A recognition that rivaled "Augustus" in significance was the title "Father of His Country" *(pater patriae)*, which Augustus received in 2 BCE. He himself indicates the esteem with which he held the honor:

> In my thirteenth consulship the senate, the equestrian order and the whole people of Rome gave me the title of Father of my Country, and resolved that this should be inscribed in the porch of my house and in the Curia Julia and in the Forum Augustum below the chariot which had been set there in my honor by decree of the senate. (*Res gestae* 35)[37]

Isocrates advocated being "father of the fatherland" as an ideal when he encouraged Philip II to bring unity to the Greek city-states, and it was common for political theorists to liken the ideal ruler to a father. Moreover, the father's role as head of the household provided the ideological basis and even the terminology for the Ptolemaic state. All of Egypt was conceived as the king's estate.[38] Roman rulers also exploited the idea of

---

[36]See ibid., 90–98. Zanker states (p. 98) that *augustus* was an adjective with a range of meanings, including "stately," "dignified," and "holy." It could be connected also with the verb *augere* ("increase") and *augur,* the priest who interpreted omens. In short, "Augustus" was a brilliant choice of title because it surrounded Octavian with a number of attributes that bestowed an aura of divinity on him while not indicating kingship.

[37]When Augustus was writing his *Res gestae* (a list of his achievements) in his seventy-sixth year, he placed "Father of my Country" at the very end (sect. 35), immediately after the section noting receipt of the title "Augustus" (sect. 34). In Augustus's retrospective view, these two honors meant more than anything else. Reporting on Augustus's receipt of the honor "Father of his Country," Suetonius says Valerius Messala spoke the following on behalf of the senate:

> Caesar Augustus, I am instructed to wish you and your family good fortune and divine blessings; which amounts to wishing that our entire state will be fortunate and our country prosperous. The Senate agree with the People of Rome in saluting you as Father of your country. (*Augustus* 58)

[38]See Elliott, *A Home for the Homeless,* 170–82. Elliott details the use of the household *(oikos)* terminology: *epoikia* ("villages"), *metoikoi* and *paroikoi* ("resident

the household as a more beneficial image of power than republican structures could elicit.[39] Nonetheless, there was a significant difference in the way Julius Caesar promoted himself as "Father of His Country" and the way in which the title was willingly offered to Augustus by the senate and people of Rome.

In order to understand Augustus's success, we must take account of his willingness to respect the aristocratic ideal of the father and the patronage system that derived from it. More people depended on the Roman patrician head of the house (the *dominus* or *paterfamilias*) than was the case with the Greek father. The Greek father was certainly lord *(kyrios)* of more than wife, children, and elderly parents, since he was responsible for the household's servants and slaves. Nonetheless, the *dominus* had a large entourage of nonkin and nonservant dependents to whom he threw open his doors at dawn. For patronage was just as central to Roman identity as it was foreign to Greek. Indeed, Andrew Wallace-Hadrill argues that a Roman noble's social standing was visibly symbolized by the crowd of clients who flocked around him.[40]

Dionysius of Halicarnassus, a Greek author, praised the social usefulness of Rome's patron-client system and said it originated with Romulus. He argued that the division between patricians, who acted as priests, magistrates, judges, and patrons, and the working class (plebeians), who were farmers, craftsmen, and clients, was designed to avoid social conflict. Ruling class and ruled were held together by mutual bonds of responsibility.[41] When Rome expanded its boundaries in the late republic, however, the poor were so far away from the capital and/or so numerous that the traditional patronage system broke down. Military force and temporary dictatorships became necessary expedients for maintaining control.

Nonetheless, patricians accused popular legislators and military dictators, who alleviated plebeian needs and restored social order, of aspiring to kingship. By making themselves the equivalent of universal patrons in their distribution of public resources, such leaders were

---

aliens"), *katoikoi* ("military colonists"), *dioikētēs* (chief financial officer of Egypt), *hypoikētēs* (subordinate to *dioikētēs* but supervisor of several administrative units), *oikonomos* (administrator of a single administrative unit), etc.

[39]See ibid., 173ff. See also Elliott, "Temple versus Household," 211–40.

[40]See Wallace-Hadrill, "Patronage," 63–65.

[41]See Wallace-Hadrill's account of Dionysius's view of patronage in *Roman Antiquities* 2.9–11 (ibid., 66f.).

usurping the patricians' traditional power of patronage.[42] Thus, monarchical rule was even more threatening to the republican idea of the state than it had been for the Greek democratic states. For Rome had never pretended to offer egalitarian status to its citizens or provide direct access to the central power. Politics was mediated through representatives who reflected the state's traditional social classes, the patrician senate on the one hand and the plebs (common people) on the other hand. Although the ruling nobility grudgingly allowed the plebs a representative role, the patronage system provided an instrument whereby the nobility maintained final control.

Suetonius details how Caesar monopolized authority and thereby abused his power in the eyes of the senate:

> For not only did he accept excessive honors, such as an uninterrupted consulship, the dictatorship for life, and the censorship of public morals, as well as the forename Imperator, the surname of Father of his Country, . . . but he also allowed honors to be bestowed on him which were too great for mortal man. (*Julius* 76)

As if the specter of a sole patron were not enough threat to the republic, rumors persistently circulated that Caesar intended to move the capital to Ilium (Troy) or, like Alexander, to Alexandria.[43] Moreover, numerous actions show he believed that people's status in the state should be determined by service and not hereditary privilege.[44] These factors led to his assassination.

In contrast to Caesar, Augustus went to great lengths to restore patrician class privileges and the semblance of republican structures. For example, he restored the senate to its former numerical limit and class status by removing from its ranks hundreds of lowborn and unworthy members, who had been appointed through bribery or personal favor by Mark Antony. He discontinued the practice, required by Caesar, of publishing the senate's proceedings, revived republican customs that had

---

[42]See ibid., 68–79.

[43]See Suetonius, *Julius* 79. Suetonius notes that while Caesar was quaestor in Spain, he noticed a statue of Alexander in the temple of Hercules in Gades and, sighing with impatience at his own lack of accomplishments, asked for a discharge from present duties to pursue greater things. Subsequently, Suetonius reports, Caesar had a dream that (like Alexander) he was destined to rule the world (*Julius* 7). Regarding Caesar's egalitarian ideas, Suetonius frequently reports that the plebs were his supporters and that Caesar cared little for his soldiers' personal character so long as they performed well on duty; e.g., see ibid., 65–74.

[44]See ibid., 79.

fallen into disuse, and introduced other measures that enhanced patrician privileges.[45]

Augustus did not retain intact the traditional patronage system, which was unable to cope with the immense problems of the empire, but neither did he destroy it altogether. Instead, he made it a means of mediating his own imperial authority. He realigned the strands of the patronage network so that they all converged on himself at the center. Nonetheless, Augustus was not like a solitary spider at the center of the web, because he channeled his power through trusted aristocratic clients who acted as his "brokers" in Italy and the provinces.[46] As Wallace-Hadrill suggests, the system not only operated from the top downward (because the emperor wanted it) but simultaneously from the bottom upward. The patricians' continuing status, although dependent on Augustus, was retained and made visible by their proximity to the imperial center of power. Thus, while the senators were the emperor's potential rivals, they were also his collaborators, whom he used as his brokers of imperial power.[47]

Although the imperial patronage system appeared to privilege the traditional status of patricians, it was equally able to expand and absorb outsiders or newcomers. Even when the lower classes could not move up in the social register, the patronage system, both in the imperial period and earlier in the republic, made access to the center of power possible through patrons. In Rome, the army and the plebs had access to Augustus, just as aristocratic friends, relatives, and servile members of the household had access to him.[48] Augustus provided or created channels of access to his power also in the provinces. Thus, even though he maintained the political superiority of Rome and Italy over the provinces and officially upheld Roman class privileges, he was able to grant surrogate privileges and provide access to the center of power.

---

[45]See Suetonius, *Augustus* 35 (restoration of the senate), 36 (discontinuation of the publication of senate proceedings; cf. Suetonius, *Julius* 20), 38 and 40 (revival of customs), and 38 (introduction of measures to encourage senators' sons to gain earlier acquaintance with state affairs).

[46]See Wallace-Hadrill, "Patronage," 78–81.

[47]See ibid., 82–84. Peter Garnsey and Richard Saller note that the distribution of social goods in the emperor's patronage system was particularistic and not like the welfare systems of modern states, which distribute benefits universally to everyone of a certain economic level (*Roman Empire,* 149–50). See also Halvor Moxnes's contrast between modern bureaucracy and imperial patron-client relations in his essay, "Patron-Client Relations," 243–46.

[48]See Garnsey and Saller, *Roman Empire,* 149. See also Wallace-Hadrill, "Patronage," 72–74.

*"After the battle of Actium Augustus Caesar brought peace
to the world by land and sea."*

Livy, *History of Rome*

*"And yet if it was right to decree new and exceptional honors to anyone, he
[i.e., Augustus] was the proper person to receive them. . . . The whole habitable
world voted him no less than celestial honors. These are so well attested by temples,
gateways, vestibules, porticoes, that every city which contains magnificent works
new and old is surpassed in these by the beauty and magnitude of those
appropriated to Caesar and particularly in our own Alexandria."*

Philo, *Legatio ad Gaium*

5
THE ROMAN EMPIRE AND GOD'S EMPIRE

Although Paul was born, was reared, and spent all but the end of
his life in the Greek-speaking East, his picture of Christ as ruler is more
like the image of Augustus than like Greek or Jewish kings. Why? There
appear to be at least two reasons. First, the cult of the Roman emperor
was so universal, and it was represented in such a uniform way throughout the eastern provinces, that it was the primary model of universal rule
for Paul. Second, there are enough similarities between Rome and Judaism, in their common hesitation to glorify mortals as gods, that Paul
found the image of Augustus as religious and moral exemplar more or
less compatible with his Jewish sensibilities and his idea of Christ.

Since Paul's idea of universal rule was probably formed in response to specific imperial images found in the cities where he lived,
most of this chapter describes the Roman idea of empire and its ruler
according to the guidelines laid down in Augustus's principate. To be
sure, earlier ideas of absolute sovereignty, exhibited in Alexander and
revived under Julius Caesar and Mark Antony, were probably still alive.
Likewise, many people still believed that the individual ruler alone
could supply all that the state needed. Nonetheless, Augustus's idea of
imperial rule departed significantly from earlier Greek ideas and even

differed from the way he first imagined himself as a ruler. After establishing himself sole ruler by defeating Antony at Actium in 31 BCE, Augustus (Octavian) dedicated himself to the restoration of traditional Roman values and not to self-glory.

From the fourth century BCE on, philosophers had said virtue was the essential qualification for kingship. The ruler was the "best man" not in birth, wealth, or even military strength but in moral excellence. In the case of Rome, however, Octavian's "august" character was not determined according to Plato's Greek virtues: courage, justice, temperance, and wisdom. Romans were too practical to submit to a canon of fixed virtues. Instead, they were concerned with whatever attributes the situation required, with the emperor's ability to address problems in a practical and flexible way. Indeed, according to Wallace-Hadrill, if we want to understand Suetonius's picture of Augustus and Titus as good rulers and to grasp the basis of Pliny's panegyric of Trajan, it is better to focus on the vices that Suetonius attributes to emperors than on their virtues.[1] The worst vices were not personal in nature but were defects that harmed the state. Emperors were criticized especially when they abused the upper class, whose status, property, and safety were important republican values.[2]

With these preliminary comments in mind, this chapter examines the following aspects of the Augustan idea of empire: the earlier Roman Empire, the turning point in the redefinition of imperial rule, the nature of the Augustan program of cultural renewal, and the imperial cult in the Greek East.[3] It then turns to two aspects of Paul's idea of God's empire: its geographical limits and the emperor as a model for Christ.

THE AUGUSTAN IMPERIAL IDEAL

The Early Roman Idea of Worldwide Empire

The image of Alexander as world conqueror began to capture the Roman imagination by the late third century BCE.[4] The Romans were the first people to give Alexander the title "the Great." They had intimations of their own imperial destiny in Cornelius Scipio's defeat of Hannibal

---

[1]See Wallace-Hadrill, *Suetonius,* esp. 142–74 on virtues and vices.

[2]See ibid., 157.

[3]These aspects of the Augustan imperial ideal derive from themes discussed by Zanker, *The Power of Images.*

[4]See Wilcken, *Alexander the Great,* 277–83.

and Carthage in 202–201. Scipio's uncanny ability to be victorious led to the legend that he was the recipient of divine guidance. Later, in the time of Caesar, the Scipio legend developed further under the influence of the Alexander legend.[5]

Julius Caesar consciously adopted Alexander as his model, both for actual conquests and for campaigns he was planning at the time of his assassination. According to Plutarch, Caesar's intended campaigns would have completed a circle resulting in an empire "bounded on all sides by ocean."[6] This way of imagining universal rule corresponds to Alexander's vision of a worldwide empire.[7] In further imitation of Alexander, Caesar planned to move the capital from Rome to Alexandria (or Troy), as mentioned above.[8] The role of Egypt in Caesar's grand scheme is indicated by his sexual liaison with its ruler, Cleopatra, whom he paraded about publicly in Rome. Mark Antony's later alliance with Cleopatra must also be attributed to political ideology and not to mere sexual attraction. Antony and Cleopatra's son was named Alexander, and like Caesar, Antony had ideas of an Alexandrian empire in which fertile Egypt would play a key role.

Even if Caesar had lived longer, however, it is unlikely he could have actualized his idea of worldwide empire. As noted in chapter 4, above, his egalitarian ideas were destructive of the republican class system, and his idea of unilateral authority undercut the Roman patronage system. Just like the plan to move the capital to Alexandria, these ideas incensed Roman sensibility. This does not mean Caesar's imperial program was wholly useless. Augustus was able to implement a great deal of it, but he adapted it to a more nationalistic model. It will prove useful to illustrate the ways in which the Hellenistic ruler cult was tearing apart the fabric of state when Augustus came to power.

Alexander's Macedonian successors (the Diadochi) may not have lived up to the philosophical ideal of the monarch as a social savior, but the image of benefactor was more than rhetorical. They continued to grant special privileges to cities that had the status of *polis,* both those inside the dynastic kingdoms and independent city-states outside. Nonetheless, the glory of the city-state was overshadowed by the dynastic kingdoms. With so much emphasis on kings as the key to social

---

[5]See Koester, *Hellenistic Age,* 290.
[6]Plutarch, *Caesar* 58.2–3.
[7]See Wilcken, *Alexander the Great,* 278.
[8]See Suetonius, *Julius* 79.

stability, it was inevitable that glorification would shift from the state to individual rulers.

Because Rome was undergoing radical change in the late republic, ruler cult emphases were able to corrupt its spartan values. Overburdened by the administration of an increasingly large empire, Rome's city-state politics was doomed to extinction. Economic expansion and war spoils increased the wealth of the few and distanced them even further from growing numbers of poor. From Sulla's dictatorship onward, the disparity between rich and poor was literally mirrored in the physical appearance of Rome. Pretentious, self-contained, walled villas with marvelous vistas on the outskirts of the city were offset by vastly overcrowded neighborhoods with irregular streets and substandard apartment buildings. Rome looked nothing like the capital of a great empire.

Competing generals with private armies had given birth to brute force that rivaled and then replaced the state's power. Wracked by civil war, first between Julius Caesar and Pompey, and then between Octavian and Antony, republican deference to age, rank, and modesty gave way to exaggerated recognition of individual leaders. Roman generals performed acts that called forth plebeian honors, but the generals never attended to major city projects, such as Rome's inadequate water supply or the sewer system.

One of the earliest examples of excess is a bronze honorific statue (180–150 BCE) that depicts a Roman general as an Alexander-like prince. The statue's powerful nude physicality, a pose used for gods and heroes, glorified the general's power. The impropriety of such excess was heightened by the fact that the Roman political system required leaders to step down after a year in office. Nonetheless, yearly magistrates even in Italian towns were displaying nude and cuirassed statues of themselves with dramatically turned heads and flexed muscles. Self-glorification spread even to wealthy members of the freedmen class, such as Eurysaces the baker, who built huge tomb monuments along the roads leading out of Rome. Their self-promotion was directed at fellow craftsmen.

Despite the widespread view that Octavian veiled his desire for absolute power from the senate until he was firmly in control, the situation was actually the reverse. In 44 BCE, at the age of eighteen and as the legal (adopted) heir of Julius Caesar, Octavian's leadership was as ostentatious as the worst of earlier generals.[9] He forced public acknowledgment of his

---

[9]See Zanker's illustration of Octavian's earlier style as a general and ruler in *The Power of Images*, 33–43.

civic service on the senate and was voted an honorific equestrian statue in 43 BCE, an extravagant honor for a young man who had never held public office! Octavian obtained official recognition of Julius Caesar's divinization in 42 BCE, and after he received the honorific name of "Imperator" from the senate in 39, he began to refer to himself as *Imperator Caesar divi filius*, "Caesar, Commander, Son of the Divine." Moreover, by dropping the name Julius from his patronymic, Octavian implied he was not merely son of the divine Julius but son of the Divine, or son of God in an absolute sense.[10] A little later, coins show Octavian as *divi filius*, no longer as a Roman general but with bare chest in the pose of a god. Following his sea victory over Pompey the Younger in 36 BCE, Octavian was again represented in a nude pose on coins, this time with his right foot resting on a globe, symbolizing his all-embracing rule of land and sea. Despite his early exaggerated emphasis on special status, however, Octavian began to undergo a transformation during his struggles with Antony.

The Turning Point in Imperial Rule

In the course of Octavian's struggle with Antony for sole rule of the empire, Dionysus and Apollo became the divine patrons of Antony and Octavian respectively.[11] At first, Antony put himself forward as a protégé of Hercules, to whom his family traced its origin. His masculinity was reminiscent of portraits of Hercules and matched the way the macho soldier fraternized with his troops. When Antony came to Asia Minor after the partition of the empire among the triumvirs in 42 BCE, however, he found the figure of Dionysus, as Alexander had done, a more appealing symbol. Dionysus fit Antony's passionate nature, his love of wine, his elegant parties, and his flashy affairs with worldly women. Thus, when Antony made an alliance with Cleopatra, their Hollywood lifestyle made them the living embodiment of Dionysus and Aphrodite. As a savior, Antony symbolized liberation from life's problems by means of indulgent pleasure and the prospect of a happy future.

Octavian, by contrast, grew steadily into a different role. At first Caesar's charisma and popular appeal aided his relationship with sea-

---

[10]See the comments by Wallace-Hadrill, *Augustan Rome,* 85–86. Wallace-Hadrill notes that no standard Roman nomenclature remains in the portentous designation *Imperator Caesar divi filius.* After 27 BCE, the finishing touch was put on the title with the addition of Augustus: *Imperator Caesar divi filius Augustus.*

[11]See Zanker's discussion of the rival images adopted by Antony and Octavian in *The Power of Images,* 44–77.

soned military personnel.[12] But Caesar was also identified with tyranny and civil war. Thus, Caesar's opponents appealed to Apollo in the battle against Octavian and Antony at Philippi in 42 BCE, claiming Apollo as the protector of order and the victor over chaos (tyranny). Surprisingly, the battle's outcome showed Apollo was on the side of Octavian, Caesar's heir. Later, in the sea battle against Pompey the Younger and during the struggle with Antony, Octavian identified himself explicitly with Apollo's order and morality.

Therefore, in the *Aeneid*, Virgil depicted Octavian's battle against Antony at Actium in 31 BCE as civilization's (Rome's) war upon Asiatic barbarism. It was the forces of decency, symbolized by Apollo and Rome's traditional gods, in opposition to eastern decadence, symbolized by Egypt's animal-headed deities.[13] Following the victory over Antony, however, Octavian began to replace Apollo's image as military avenger of piety, purity, and justice with images of the god as singer, lyre player, and source of peace. Wallace-Hadrill rightly notes that Octavian was well aware that the real threat to the capital did not come from outside. Decadent Cleopatra was only a secondary danger in comparison with Rome's long history of civil war. The problem was symbolized mythically as an inherited sin, as the curse of Remus, who fell by the hand of his brother, Romulus, Rome's founder (cf. Horace, *Epodes* 7). Their sins, repeated in subsequent generations, called forth the gods' hailstorms and Tiber floods. Romans must fall to their knees and expiate their sins. Octavian saw his new role as one of devotion to the gods and of healing the wounds inflicted by civil war.[14]

The victory monuments commemorating Octavian's success at Actium reflected his change in imperial ideology. The monuments repeated a small repertoire of clear, simple images: parts of ships (rostra), mythical sea creatures, dolphins, and the figure of Victoria on the globe. There were no dramatic battle scenes of Antony and Octavian, and the monuments did not glorify Octavian directly. Likewise, the new temple to Apollo on the Palatine (28 BCE) displayed Apollo and his sister, Diana, in a marble quadriga, not Octavian in a triumphal chariot. Classical and static symbols of peace and devotion filled the sanctuary. The message was clear: the sacrilege committed against the state must be redeemed

---

[12]See Zanker's comments on Octavian's change in style (and image) of leadership, ibid., 47ff.

[13]See Virgil, *Aeneid* 8.675–729.

[14]See Wallace-Hadrill, *Augustan Rome*, 7–8.

through sacrifice and piety. The hope for lasting peace was symbolized in the seemingly endless spiral of vines growing out of tripods on the temple's marble door frames. The vegetal ornamentation symbolized Apollo's fertility, prosperity, and peace.

The new images were of a piece with Octavian's resignation of his authority to the senate and people in 27 BCE. The nobility acknowledged this as an act of piety they could support. The senate knew it needed Octavian's ongoing authority and wealth to save the empire, and thus, as suggested in chapter 4, above, it delegated special privileges and long-term offices to him that allowed him to stay in power. He took the title of *princeps,* not king, to symbolize the character of his rule. For this and like acts, Octavian was honored with the title of "Augustus" in 27 BCE by the senate and people.

Scholars have tended to interpret Octavian's resignation of power as a hollow charade. Admittedly, citizens of the *res publica* knew it was necessary that Octavian remain in command at least for a while. Nonetheless, his act of resignation showed that he submitted his own glorification to the greater glory of the state. Nor could Rome have had any illusions about returning to some past ideal. More than the Greek city-states, Rome had a living tradition constantly subject to adaptation. This *mos majorum* (custom, tradition) was neither prescriptive nor rigid but subject to interpretation and improvement. It was the principles of this heritage that Augustus vowed to preserve and improve.[15]

The Augustan Program of Cultural Renewal

Despite public signs of hopefulness after Actium, patricians remained suspicious about Augustus's true intentions. Lest there be any doubt about his values, Augustus launched an urban-renewal program such as no ruler had done before. Rome's whole outward appearance changed. Suetonius accurately claimed that whereas Augustus found Rome a city of mud brick, he left it a city of marble.[16] Virgil's picture of Carthage humming with building activity under Dido reflected Rome's own excitement under Augustus in the 20s BCE:

> Aeneas found, where lately huts had been, marvelous buildings, gateways, cobbled ways, and din of wagons. There the Tyrians were hard at work: laying courses for walls, rolling up stones to build the citadel, while others

---

[15]See Wallace-Hadrill's comments on Octavian's restoration of the state and its metamorphosis, ibid., 10–24.

[16]Suetonius, *Augustus* 28.3.

picked out building sites and plowed a boundary furrow. Laws were being enacted, magistrates and a sacred senate chosen. Here men were dredging harbors, there they laid the deep foundation of a theatre, and quarried massive pillars to enhance the future state. . . . Aeneas said: "How fortunate these are whose city walls are rising here and now!" (*Aeneid* 1.418ff.)

More important than Rome's new buildings was the vision of cultural renewal that prompted and unified Augustus's activity.[17] What was most essential in the early period may be expressed by the terms "piety" *(pietas)* and "public grandeur" *(publica magnificentia)*. In the latter part of his rule Augustus added civic reforms to his program.

Piety.   Although *pietas* refers broadly to respect for tradition, Zanker notes that, from Cato the Elder on, the dissolution of tradition was identified, above all, with neglect of the gods. Varro wrote a multivolume analysis of the need to renew devotion to the gods; it detailed all the temples, priesthoods, and practices that had been allowed to fall into disuse. He dedicated the work to Julius Caesar, hoping it would spur him to religious reform.[18] The same need for devotion was expressed by Horace:

You will remain sullied with the guilt of your fathers, Roman, until you have rebuilt the temples and restored all the ruined sanctuaries with their dark images of the gods, befouled with smoke. (Horace, *Odes* 3.6, trans. Zanker).

Although the restoration and building of many public buildings and projects were willingly shared with members of the imperial household and with other nobility, Augustus himself was the primary overseer of temples and priesthoods. Temples dedicated to the principal gods of the old republic, such as the temples to Jupiter on the Capitoline Hill, the temple of Castor and Pollux, and the temple of Concordia, were all restored (cf. Augustus, *Res gestae* 19). Octavian restored eighty-two less important temples in 28 BCE (ibid., 20). In the case of the older temples, however, old-fashioned architectural features, such as wooden roofs, terra-cotta roof tiles, and tufa columns and blocks, were simply replaced or repaired. By contrast, the new temple of Apollo on the Palatine and temples to the principal gods of the imperial house were made of white marble.

---

[17]Roger Ling says two leitmotifs pervaded Augustus's building program: extensive use of fine marble masonry with fine decorative carving, and the combination of classical Greek forms (and motifs) with traditional elements of Italian/Roman architecture. See "Roman Architecture," 1675–76.

[18]Zanker, *The Power of Images*, 102ff.

The new marble temples imitated the most impressive Greek classical style but combined it with elements of the Italian/Roman temple, such as the high podium, deep pronaos, and the steeply sloping and much decorated pediment. The best architects and artists of the East were drawn to Rome by the prospect of the fabulous undertaking.[19] The gleaming temples, built of marble from new quarries near Luna (Carrara) and often decorated with gold, literally transformed Rome. Heretofore, even buildings of the Forum had been built of coarse limestones and peppery grey tufas. By the end of Augustus's reign, however, the Forum was a forest of white columns.[20] Rome had truly become the showplace of the empire.

Even the gleaming temples were less important than the carefully thought out attention to their decoration, which was guided by an integrated set of images. The arrangements were didactic and guided by a limited number of simple symbols, which were frequently repeated and combined. For example, there were few detailed scenes because the focus was on order, traditional values, and prosperity. These were conveyed by quiet, static images of an archaic or classical style, which were combined with much repeated images of nature's fertility.

Augustus took an equally important role in the restoration of the traditional colleges of priests and revived some that had disappeared. Rather than limit their activity to specific times and places, he combined them for many religious activities, especially those associated with the principal imperial deities. Unlike Jewish priests, who belonged to a specific hereditary line, the main colleges of Roman priests consisted simply of patricians. Since political and religious status were closely entwined, the same people held both offices. Patricians gained political offices through religious service, and likewise, religious duties were secured through political office.

The importance of piety to the Augustan ideal is vividly llustrated in the Altar of Peace (Ara Pacis), completed between 13 and 9 BCE. Ostensibly the monument celebrated Augustus's victories in Gaul and his return to Rome. Nonetheless, the altar does not call attention to military victory in the manner of a triumphal arch but emphasizes the paradisaical peace that Augustus secured in his priestly service for Rome. Annual sacrifices at the Altar of Peace were entrusted to all four major priesthoods and to the vestal virgins.

---

[19]See ibid., 102–10.
[20]See Wallace-Hadrill, *Augustan Rome*, 50f.

Although the frieze on the outer wall surrounding the Altar of Peace preserves a particular moment, July 4, 13 BCE, when the returning and triumphal Augustus made sacrifice, it symbolizes the timeless peace, prosperity, and piety of Augustus's rule. The image of priestly sacrificer does not celebrate the military conqueror or the emergency savior but the emperor's role as ideal Roman and moral exemplar.[21]

The altar (still intact in Rome) is surrounded by an almost square outer wall, decorated more fully with legendary and historical scenes than any extant Augustan monument. The eastern and western sides have open doorways leading into the altar area. On the western end, the right side of the entry depicts the mythical ancestor of Rome, the Trojan hero Aeneas, with his son, Iulus, sacrificing with covered head to the Penates (the traditional family gods of every Roman household). The panel on the left side shows Aeneas's descendants and Rome's mythological founders, Romulus and Remus, suckling the she-wolf under the watchful eye of the shepherd Faustulus and the god Mars. On the eastern entrance, the panel to the right of the doorway presents the goddess Roma, divine protectress of Rome, and the panel to the left has a mother earth figure with many symbols of fertility and prosperity.

The solid north and south walls show nearly life-size processions, headed by priests and followed by members of the imperial family advancing to offer sacrifice. At the head of the procession on the southern wall is Augustus, dressed in traditional toga and with covered head, imitating the priestly pose of his ancestor Aeneas on the western wall. He is surrounded by Roman priests and followed by women of the imperial household with children at their skirts, in imitation of the theme of fertility and abundance on the eastern wall. Similarly, the procession on the northern wall is headed by priests of the major priesthoods and followed by female members of the imperial family and their children.

In addition to evidence on the Altar of Peace indicating that the performance of religious functions was Augustus's greatest duty, from the 20s BCE onward Augustus made it clear he preferred to be represented in religious pose. No longer was he the bare-breasted superhero on horseback or the cuirassed military conqueror. Rather, statues, coins, and friezes picture him primarily as *togatus capite velato* (in a toga with covered head) in the traditional pose of the priest at sacrifice (see page 123). The same image was exhibited in the East, even though it was an alien portrait of the

---

[21]See Bianchi, *Ara Pacis Augustae*, 7–29; Wallace-Hadrill, *Augustan Rome*, 70–75; Zanker, *The Power of Images*, 114–25.

ruler. The death of Lepidus, former holder of the office of *pontifex maximus* (highest priestly office of the state), opened the way for Augustus to become *pontifex maximus* in 12 BCE and to formalize his role as head of state religion (Augustus, *Res gestae* 10). Since the genius of the Roman *pater familias* (father of the family) had been worshiped in sacrificial pose in family shrines, it was understandable a fatherly ruler such as Augustus would want to be honored in the same form.

Public Grandeur. Although many of the villas with enormous atria and extensive *horti* (gardens) dotting Rome's hillsides were occupied by supporters of Augustus, he took a stand against the immorality of private luxury.[22] His relatively austere home and simple diet made a personal statement about the preferred lifestyle. Nonetheless, he would not address the differences in lifestyle between the rich and the poor by forcibly redistributing Rome's wealth. Rather, with the assistance of family members and other patricians, he set about the construction of public buildings, theaters, public baths, and parks for all of Rome, including the urban masses. For example, when Vedius Pollio died in 15 BCE and bequethed a mansion in the crowded Subura district to the emperor, Augustus entrusted the ostentatious house to Livia and Tiberius, who leveled it and replaced it with Livia's Portico, a monument for public use. The bright colonnaded area, filled with works of art, fountains, and gardens and containing a shrine to the goddess Concordia, gave residents of Subura a brief respite from their dark, crowded apartments.[23]

Much of the supervision of new public areas was delegated to Agrippa, Augustus's loyal naval commander and son-in-law. His first project was to reorganize the city's water supply. Mighty arches of new and repaired aqueducts and hundreds of fountains carried the blessings of the new rule to every dark corner of Rome. Agrippa also built an extensive public complex in Mars Field, which included the first public baths, extensive gardens, an artificial lake, the Pantheon, and the Saepta Julia, a magnificent voting place for plebs.[24]

Augustus himself completed public projects that Caesar had begun in the Forum area, the Basilica Julia and the Forum Julium. He restored

---

[22]See Fisher, "Roman Associations," 1210–11.

[23]The mansion measured roughly 375 by 245 feet, a conspicuous show of private luxury in the crowded and very poor Subura. See Zanker, *The Power of Images*, 137–39. See also Fisher, "Roman Associations," 1211.

[24]See Zanker, *The Power of Images*, 139–43. See also Fisher, "Roman Associations," 1211; and Wallace-Hadrill, *Augustan Rome*, 60.

Pompey's theater, built the new theater of Marcellus, and encouraged Balbus to build a somewhat smaller theater. Although Augustus also sponsored several public games (see Suetonius, *Augustus* 43), he was more devoted to the theater. The theater was such an important feature of classical Athens that Augustus needed it to show that Rome was the cultural center of a great empire. By embellishing the city in an extensive and coherent manner, appropriate to her role as capital, Augustus was able to enlist both the nobility and the masses in the cause. No longer did Rome's monuments reflect the jumble of individualistic buildings constructed by people seeking Hellenistic self-glorification.[25]

Civic Reforms of Augustus. One might assume Augustus's innovations would lead to problems with patricians. In fact, it was Rome's urban masses that caused him the most difficulty. They were a social element whose needs he was able to meet only near the end of his rule. Unlike Caesar and Antony, who were more willing to replace old patrician families with supporters of modest origin, Augustus was no enemy to blue blood. Indeed, he made considerable effort to preserve the old families and to make them his allies. He made a virtue out of forgiving patrician opponents and welcoming them into his camp. The doom of the nobles, as Wallace-Hadrill aptly states, was not extinction but absorption. Patricians became courtiers and brokers of imperial patronage, not victims.[26]

On the other hand, urban masses had been a tinder keg for decades, exploding periodically in times of famine, fire, and floods. From the late republic up to the late empire most of the inhabitants of overcrowded Rome were slaves or ex-slaves, many of whom were first-generation arrivals.[27] Rome's traditional means of running the city by popularly elected magistrates, who held office for a brief time and without the support of such services as a fire department, a police force, and a refuse collection service, was terribly inadequate. The poorly managed situation was aggravated by the fact that revolutionary leaders in the late republic recruited craftsmen in trade associations *(collegia)* to riot on their behalf. Thus Clodius began a political carrer in 58 BCE by enlisting the support of the *collegia*. His use of violent supporters, as well as the recruitment of

---

[25]See the comments by Wallace-Hadrill, *Augustan Rome*, 61–62. See also Zanker, *The Power of Images*, 135ff.

[26]Wallace-Hadrill, *Augustan Rome*, 29–30.

[27]See Wallace-Hadrill's discussion of the difficulties in controlling urban problems in the late republic and early empire (ibid., 43–50).

gangs, gladiators, and rural clients by Milo, Sestius, and other politicians, almost destroyed the electoral process.[28]

According to Suetonius, Julius Caesar "dissolved all guilds except those of ancient foundation" following the civil war of 49–45 BCE because the *collegia* were a threat to civic stability (*Julius* 42). Augustus also found it necessary to ban the guilds, except those of long standing and those legally approved by the state (Suetonius, *Augustus* 32). Nonetheless, the numbers of poor freeborn, freedmen, and slaves, who were either financially or legally ineligible to hold civic office, needed some basis of self-respect. It was precisely the *collegia* that supplied the identity the tradesmen desired. Unfortunately, Augustus was unwilling for decades to tap this resource and use it in his cultural program.

At first, Augustus tried to consolidate support of the city's masses, as Caesar had done, through gifts and public entertainment. He himself states that on six separate occasions between 29 and 2 BCE he distributed cash or grain to plebs, usually numbering about a quarter million (Augustus, *Res gestae* 15), but periodic games and handouts provided only a short-term solution to longstanding problems. Thus, Augustus moved away from his hands-off approach and resorted to tougher interventionism.[29]

Augustus gradually took the solving of recurring problems away from city magistrates, and he created specially trained paramilitary forces to deal with fire, floods, and urban violence. For example, after several major fires from 16 to 7 BCE, Augustus in 6 CE established a permanent fire brigade, the *vigiles*. It had seven thousand freedmen, commanded by a regular army officer, equipped with axes and buckets and the legal right to require householders to install firefighting equipment.[30]

Similarly, after several failures to deal with food shortages (i.e., in the grain supply) by the usual means, in 8 CE the distribution and acquisition of grain were placed under a military prefect and his staff.[31] Likewise, a permanent police force of three thousand men, under the command of a senior senator, was established. This body was supported

---

[28]See Fisher, "Roman Associations," 1209–10.

[29]See Wallace-Hadrill, *Augustan Rome*, 45.

[30]See ibid., 45–46.

[31]The first appointee, Turranius, who held the post for forty years, found it necessary to sail far and wide in order to aquire suffcient grain to feed the millions of inhabitants in Rome. Under the emperor Claudius major renovations were made at Rome's port city, Ostia, including an artificial harbor, which turned it into the Mediterranean grain trade's center. See ibid., 46.

by a wing of the Praetorian Guard, which was reorganized in 2 BCE so that one segment was used for crowd control at games and other public activities.[32]

Veiled togate statue of Augustus as priest.
Museo Nazionale Romano delle Terme, Rome.
Photo courtesy of Alinari/Art Resource, N.Y.

Fortunately, military force was not Augustus's only means of controlling Rome's problems. One of his most imaginative reforms was the reorganization of Rome into fourteen geographical and political regions.

---

[32]See ibid., 46–47.

The city had become a "pathless jungle," lacking any intelligible means of tracking people according to place of residence. Lack of regional division was exacerbated by the fact that the supervision of local affairs was combined with imperial matters. Augustus reorganized the duties so that senators and higher magistrates concentrated on worldwide issues, and he entrusted urban affairs to local "ward" and "neighborhood" officials.[33]

The city's fourteen *regiones* (called *rioni* in modern Rome) were broken down into 265 neighborhoods *(vici),* each of which had four annually elected masters *(vicomagistri)* and four ministers *(ministri).* The office of master was filled by leading craftsmen in each neighborhood, often freedmen, and the ministers were mostly slaves. Thus Augustus created a low-level administrative structure through which even tradesmen and slaves were given a stake in the state. The role of neighborhood officials was both political and religious because each of the 265 *vici* had priestly duties associated with neighborhood shrines. Earlier, spirits of dead ancestors (the Lares) were worshiped at the shrines, but now a togate statue of Augustus's genius was added to the cult. The construction of local altars to the Lares and to the emperor's genius by the *magistri* provided an occasion for them (and even *ministri*) to call attention to their public roles.[34] Thus, local officials combined religious and political duties in ways similar to Augustus and the patricians.[35] The manner in which Augustus wove urban freedmen and slaves into the state's fabric provides a useful model for discussing how the East was incorporated into the empire.

The Imperial Cult in the East

Although imperial-cult temples and monuments in the East deliberately imitated Greek architectural style, in one significant respect they formed a more coherent and universal image of power than those of the

---

[33]See ibid., 47.

[34]Although Augustus himself had revived the cult of the Lares and had rebuilt the principal temple of the Lares on the Velia, small local shrines were endowed by *magistri* in the neighborhoods. The Lares were originally worshiped at shrines constructed at the crossroads *(compitum)* where the boundary paths separating four farms intersected. See "Lares," *OCD,* 578. Later, crossroads shrines were located at the intersection of neighborhood streets.

[35]See Zanker's discussion of the duties of *magistri* and *ministri* in *The Power of Images,* 129–35. See also Wallace-Hadrill, *Augustan Rome,* 47–50; and Fisher, "Roman Associations," 1219–20.

Greek ruler cults. Whereas the dynastic cults had been established spo-radically in one city or another, usually for a specific reason, the imperial cult appeared everywhere, not only in autonomous city-states but in provincial centers and even in centers lacking city status. The cult was pervasive and uniform, it quickly became the most important religious cult in the East, and through it Augustus became a worldwide model of priest and benefactor.

The Imperial Cult's Pervasive and Uniform Nature.   Just as the imperial cult attached itself to local shrines of the Lares in Rome, so too in the East it attached itself to the cults and festivals of the civic gods. Wherever the cult existed as an independent entity in Greek cities, it used tradi-tional architectural features, but its temples and altars were usually larger and grander than those for traditional gods.[36] Moreover, the temples were usually located in the city's most conspicuous civic or religious center. For example, in Athens, a temple of Roma and Augustus was built on the Acropolis near the Parthenon and Erechtheum. Similarly, in Ephesus, a cult temple was located in the center of the new Upper Square. Josephus's depiction of King Herod's location of the temple of Roma and Augustus in the newly founded city of Caesarea may serve as a final example:

> In a circle round the harbor there was a continuous line of dwellings con-structed of the most polished stone, and in their midst was a mound on which there stood a temple of Caesar, visible a great way off to those sailing into the harbor, which had a statue of Rome and also one of Caesar [Au-gustus]. (*Ant.* 15.339)

From about 30 BCE, when Augustus first granted worship of him-self in the East on the condition that the goddess Roma be associated with him and that he not be named explicitly as a god, the imperial cult spread like wildfire. This chapter's epigraph from Philo of Alexandria shows that cities everywhere honored Augustus with temples and sac-rifices. The citation also indicates the cult was a constant visual reminder of the emperor's importance.

---

[36]The use of familiar architectural forms reassured Greeks of the continuity between traditional religion and the worship of the emperor. Usually the new temples were freestanding, peripteral (surrounded by a single row of columns), surrounded by colonnades, or round and with a monumental altar. By contrast, the new-style marble temple found in Rome, with its tall podium, heavy pedi-ment, and lavish decoration, appeared only in new or refounded Roman cities in the East. See Zanker, *The Power of Images*, 297f.

Whereas cities had formerly competed on the basis of their unique-
ness, now their status derived solely from recognition gained through the
imperial system of values. Although Augustus and his family rarely initi-
ated the erection of cult altars in the East, they sprang up everywhere because they provided cities a primary means of access to Augustus's
authority and status. The access to Augustus in Rome that the cult provided to foreign embassies may be compared to the modern audiences
the papacy regularly grants to pilgrims. One example illustrates how a
city's status was enhanced through its imperial cult. The city council of
Tarraco sent messengers to Augustus to inform him of a miracle associated with its cult altar, from which a palm tree grew. Although Augustus
joked about the infrequency of sacrificial fires lit on the altar that grew
the palm tree (Quintilian, *Inst.* 6.3.77), Tarraco later minted coins of the
altar and tree.

Whereas the architecture and ritual of Augustus's cult were according to the Greek style, honorific statues of the emperor and his family
imitated Roman models. This is especially clear in the case of the togate
statue with veiled head, picturing Augustus as a Roman priest. Similarly,
portraits of the emperor and his family were usually realistic. Why did
Greeks imitate these Roman models? Because Augustus and his family's
features were so well known from statues, sculptural friezes, and coin
portraits that Greeks wanted to imitate them. Familiarity with imperial
family members provided models even of the clothing and hairstyles they
favored. These styles were widely imitated throughout the empire.[37]

The Religious Importance of the Cult.   Christian scholars usually deny,
on the one hand, the political aspect of Christ's lordship and, on the
other, the religious dimension of Augustus's authority. Price rightly objects to this easy dismissal of the imperial cult as pseudoreligion.[38] Unfortunately, scholars misrepresent the opposition between Christ (the
church) and the Caesars as simply one between religion and politics.
Thus even Nock, who carefully studied religious titles in the imperial
cult (e.g., "Savior" and "New Apollo") and its ritual, biased his analysis by
arguing that whereas the ruler cult promoted homage, authentic religion
is characterized by worship.[39]

---

[37]See ibid., 301f.
[38]See Price, *Rituals and Power,* 11–22.
[39]E.g., see Nock, "Σύνναος Θεός," 236–51 (see esp. 241f.).

Price notes two other reasons scholars describe the imperial cult as political and not religious. They say that, on the one hand, it was manipulated "from above" by the state and, on the other, cities used it "from below" as a diplomatic means of enhancing their communities' status. Neither central promotion nor civic diplomacy, however, necessarily means participants did not believe the cult's religious values.[40]

Like the Greek cult of the gods, which was the model from which ruler cult ideology derived, the imperial cult represented an external power on whom the city was dependent. Thus, although Augustus represented himself as *princeps* ("leading citizen") in Rome, in the East he was not like a citizen but wielded power like a god. The emperor's exalted status was accentuated by the fact that he was now the sole recipient of ruler cult worship in eastern cities.[41]

Another aspect of Augustus's rule that differentiates him from Hellenistic kings and provides a basis for regarding imperial-cult worship as genuine religion is the worldwide peace that he established. Whereas Greek civic cults had been established in response to specific benefactions, in the case of Augustus many expressions of gratitude resulted from his general activity. For example, the assembly of the province of Asia gave the following rationale (in 9 BCE) for its desire to honor Augustus:

> The providence which divinely ordered our lives created with zeal and munificence the most perfect good for our lives by producing Augustus and filling him with virtue for the benefaction of humanity, sending us and those after us a savior who put an end to war and established all things.[42]

As a result of these factors, the imperial network that connected ruler and city was both tighter and better regulated under the Roman Empire than under Hellenistic kings. The imperial connection also certainly extended to religious service, whose continuity and vitality was assured by the important role that local elites played as priests and supporters of the imperial cult. As with the patrician class in Rome, one's upper-class status in cities of the East was enhanced by service in the imperial system.

---

[40]See Price, *Rituals and Power*, 16.

[41]See ibid., 35 and 40ff.

[42]See ibid., 54. The translation is adapted by Price from that by Lewis and Reinhold, *Roman Civilization* 2:64.

Augustus the Model: Priest and Benefactor. Despite the modern Christian reservation about identifying religion with the state, pagan priests in antiquity rarely stood outside the political order. Neither in Athens nor in Rome was there a formal division between religion and politics. As noted, the nobililty in Rome acted as both priests and politicians. The senate met on consecrated ground, and religion was integrally combined with politics.[43]

One aspect of imperial religion was the emperor's public role as priestly sacrificer. More specifically, from Augustus onward, sacrificial iconography shows that the emperor monopolized the public image of priestly power and was paraded as the example of sacrificer to all other religious officials.[44] One could hardly wish for more direct evidence of the social order's dependence on religion.

Originally, the *princeps* was expected to safeguard the integrity of Rome's traditional rituals and to perform services that would insulate Rome from the results of its own imperialism. Foreign subjects could corrupt Rome, just as Cleopatra had bewitched and contaminated Antony. The ideal was to preserve a pristine, noble center at Rome and to force subjection on the provinces. Without constant repression, however, such a distinction was doomed to failure.[45] Therefore, although Augustus retained the connection between noble status and civic/religious office, he adapted the image of imperial sacrifice so that it no longer referred specifically to Roman ritual. Rather, the symbols of Augustus as priest were general enough to evoke a form of piety and public sacrifice that could be imitated by social elites throughout the empire.[46]

After consolidating his status as *princeps* and then, in 12 BCE, his religious headship of the state through the office of *pontifex maximus,* Augustus extended the model throughout the empire. If we imagine the imperial state as a human body, the emperor was the head, whose au-

---

[43]See the comments by Beard and North, *Pagan Priests,* 1–8.

[44]See ibid., 11–13. Granted, the imperial cult was not the only kind of religious activity in the empire. There were a variety of other religions, such as the cults of Isis and Cybele. Their practice of ritual initiation, the familial worship, and the personal commitment of members to one another formed an alternative to the state's religion. Christian worship was more like these alternative religions, except in the dangerous respect that, like the imperial cult, it claimed absolute sovereignty for its lord.

[45]See Gordon, "The Veil of Power," 205–7.

[46]See ibid., 201–8.

thority and intelligence integrated the body's parts and connected the sinews so that they functioned in a harmonious manner. Nonetheless, Augustus was not the head of the body in the solitary sense of the Greek ruler. Rather, the emperor was a model of religious and civic duty that, according to the Roman patronage system, applied to all religious and civic officials. The emperor's role as example, at least for Romans, is clearly articulated by Pliny in his panegyric for Trajan: "We do not need strict rule so much as an example" (*Panegyricus* 45.6). Augustus himself stated how important exemplary practices were, and he referred to his own practices as a model to be imitated:

> By new laws passed on my proposal I brought back into use many exemplary practices of our ancestors which were disappearing in our time, and in many ways I myself transmitted exemplary practices to posterity for their imitation.[47]

The image of the *princeps* as sacrificer not only implied that elites had a duty to maintain proper relations with the gods; it also symbolized Augustus's and the elites' responsibility to human dependents. The emperor certainly controlled the patronage system, and he used civic and religious appointments to create a relation of dependence and gratitude toward himself. If he alone had played the role of priest and benefactor, however, he would have become a god in the Greek sense and would not have been able to exercise patronage through other social elites. Consequently, the patrons who held civic and priestly office provided links with Augustus's central system of power and acted as mediators between country and town and between locality and state. Civic and religious office not only confirmed one's social status in the central system but also confirmed the social inequality of clients on whose behalf the elite must render benefits. Thus, according to Richard Gordon, the relative success of the Roman imperial system, in comparison with other more violently extractive and unstable preindustrial empires, lay largely in the extension of the patronage of unequal exchange throughout the empire.[48]

---

[47]Augustus, *Res gestae* 8. Suetonious also states Augustus was conscious of his imitation of great Romans of the past and of the *princeps's* own exemplary role (*Augustus* 31, 89). See other examples of the emperor as model cited by Gordon, "The Veil of Power," 209.

[48]See Gordon, "The Veil of Power," 219–24.

THE ROMAN EMPIRE AND PAUL'S
IDEA OF GOD'S EMPIRE

Paul's idea of God's empire was clearly influenced by simply living under imperial rule. Later chapters will describe several ways in which he was affected by imperial rule; here two effects are discussed. First, his idea of God's empire was conceived in response to the physical boundaries of the Roman Empire. Second, Paul's idea of Christ was informed in some respects by the image of the emperor as ruler.

The Physical Limits of God's Empire

Several statements in Paul's letters show he regarded God's empire as encompassing the whole physical universe, much as poetic spokesmen for Augustus referred to the universality of the *princeps's* rule. For example, Paul's picture of Christ as the appointed ruler "before whom all knees would bend" certainly points to the universality of God's empire.[49] In order to illustrate the physical limits of God's empire as Paul imagined it, however, we must turn to statements that refer to his own territorial responsibility as God's apostle. Three references in Romans illustrate his sense of obligation to the Gentile world:

> I want you to know, brothers and sisters, that I have often intended to come to you (but thus far have been prevented), in order that I may reap some harvest among you as I have among the rest of the Gentiles. I am a debtor both to Greeks and to barbarians, both to the wise and to the foolish—hence my eagerness to proclaim the gospel to you also who are in Rome. (1:13–15)

> on some points I have written to you rather boldly by way of reminder, because of the grace given me by God to be a minister of Christ Jesus to the Gentiles in the priestly service of the gospel of God, so that the offering of the Gentiles may be acceptable, sanctified by the Holy Spirit. In Christ

---

[49]See Phil 2:9–11. The universality of the new empire is indicated by Paul's identification of God's new creation with God's original creation: "For it is the God who said, 'Let light shine out of darkness,' who has shone in our hearts" (2 Cor 4:6). The same universality is pictured in creation groaning in labor pains as it awaits new birth (cf. Rom 8:18–23). In 2 Cor 5:14–19 Paul states explicitly that God's reconciliation in Christ is worldwide. Not only is Christ the "firstborn within a large family" (Rom 8:28–30); he is also the new Adam, the "first fruits" of a new humanity (cf. Rom 5:12–21; 1 Cor 15:20–22). Christ's status as the new Adam is paralleled by the universality of his authority (cf. 1 Cor 15:24–28; Phil 2:9–11).

Jesus, then, I have reason to boast of my work for God. For I will not venture to speak of anything except what Christ has accomplished through me to win obedience from the Gentiles, by word and deed, by the power of signs and wonders, by the power of the Spirit of God, so that from Jerusalem and as far around as Illyricum I have fully proclaimed the good news of Christ. Thus I make it my ambition to proclaim the good news, not where Christ has already been named, so that I do not build on someone else's foundation, but as it is written, "Those who have never been told of him shall see, and those who have never heard of him shall understand." (15:15–21)

This is the reason that I have so often been hindered from coming to you. But now, with no further place for me in these regions, I desire, as I have for many years, to come to you when I go to Spain. For I hope to see you on my journey and to be sent on by you, once I have enjoyed your company for a little while. At present, however, I am going to Jerusalem in a ministry to the saints; . . . when I have completed this, . . . I will set out by way of you to Spain. (15:22–25, 28)

In the first citation, Paul says he often intended to visit Roman Christians, specifically the Gentile element of the church. As the apostle to the Gentiles, he apparently felt obliged to ensure the spiritual productivity of the whole non-Jewish world: "that I may reap some harvest among you as I have among the rest of the Gentiles." By the phrase "both to Greeks and to barbarians," Paul suggests that his obligation as Christ's messenger extends beyond Greek-speaking Gentiles. Unfortunately, he does not detail the regions he considered non-Greek.

In the second citation, Paul is more specific about his territorial responsibility as Christ's ambassador to Gentiles. He says he preached the gospel of Christ "from Jerusalem and as far around as Illyricum." He adds that he aspired not to preach the gospel where it had already been preached but to show and speak Christ to areas that had never heard about him. Since it was virtually impossible that Paul had actually preached about God's salvation in Christ throughout the arc spanned by Jerusalem to Illyricum, it is likely he is referring to the foundation of churches within the regions covered by the arc. The arc ran from the south (Jerusalem) in a westerly direction to the north (Illyricum). Since we have no evidence that Paul ever engaged in missionary work as far north as Illyricum, he is referring apparently to his belief that the influence of his Macedonian churches would extend upward into Illyricum.

Paul refers specifically to responsibilities in the East (from Jerusalem to Illyricum) as the reason he had been detained from coming to Rome and the West. But he indicates in the third citation that, after delivering a collection of money from his churches to Jerusalem, he would travel to Rome. He expresses concern about the spiritual productivity of Gentile Christians in Rome, for which he felt responsible. On the other hand, his intention to engage in missionary work in Spain was also important to his apostolic responsibility to the West. In antiquity, Spain was regarded as the western limit of the inhabited world, and consequently for Paul, a man of the eastern provinces, it may have represented the most distant boundary of civilization (at least in the West).

Thus, Paul imagined himself responsible to the Gentile world from at least as far east and south as Jerusalem to as far north as Illyricum and as far west as Spain. As extensive as Paul's missionary program was, it still falls short of the limits that Alexander the Great and Julius Caesar imagined. Paul says nothing about regions to the east of Jerusalem or about areas to the south, stretching from Egypt in the east to coastal areas of north Africa in the west. In addition to these omissions, Paul says nothing about regions in the west that were north of Rome, in Gaul and Germany. Perhaps Paul simply does not identify the full extent of his apostolic responsibility. Or he may simply have had a limited grasp of the physical extent of the inhabited world.

In any case, although Paul's idea of the regions he had to traverse was probably not influenced directly by either Alexander's or Caesar's conceptions of worldwide rule, the physical specificity of his obligation as Christ's ambassador was probably inspired by the boundaries of the Roman Empire (to the extent he was conversant with these). The physical limits for which he was accountable as apostle and the regions over which Christ must rule were imagined by Paul in the concrete terms available to him from his culture.

Paul's Image of Christ

As strange as it might seem to modern Christians, the problematic combination of Christ's divinity and humanity for the early church was analogous to Augustus's ambiguous but spectacular status as intermediary between heaven and earth. Indeed, it was precisely in Roman polytheism's and Jewish monotheism's similar apprehensions about the elevation of humans to divinity that the imperial cult and the early church found common ground. According to Wallace-Hadrill, both traditions placed their savior figure in an intermediate layer between god(s) and humans, not alongside their other god(s).[50]

---

[50]Wallace-Hadrill, *Augustan Rome,* 90.

Both traditions talk about a godlike ruler who would restore a golden-age harmony to nature and to human society. The following similarities in Isaiah, the *Sibylline Oracles,* and Virgil suggest some communication between Jewish messianism and Augustan ideology:

The people who walked in darkness have seen a great light. For a child has been born for us, a son given to us; authority rests on his shoulders; and he is named Wonderful Counselor, Mighty God, Everlasting Father, Prince of Peace. (Isa 9:2, 6)

The wolf shall live with the lamb, the leopard shall lie down with the kid, the calf and the lion and the fatling together, and a little child shall lead them. . . . The nursing child shall play over the hole of the asp, and the weaned child shall put its head on the adder's nest. (Isa 11:6–9)

The goats will come home by themselves with milk-filled udders, Nor will the cattle be in fear of great lions. . . . The serpent will perish, and the treacherous herb of poison will perish. (Virgil, *Eclogues* 4.21–25)

Rejoice, maiden, and be glad, for to you the one who created heaven and earth has given the joy of the age. He will dwell in you. You will have immortal light. Wolves and lambs will eat grass together in the mountains. Leopards will feed together with the kids. . . . Serpents and asps will sleep with babies and will not harm them, for the hand of God will be upon them. (*Sibylline Oracles* 3.785–795)

This is the man, this one, of whom so often you have heard the promise, Caesar Augustus, son of the deified, who shall bring once again an Age of Gold to Latium, to the land where Saturn reigned in early times. (Virgil, *Aeneid* 6.791–795)

These images of the ruler exceeded the traditional role of the Roman conqueror and stateman, as well as that of the Jewish nationalistic king.[51] The roles attributed to Augustus and to Christ, however, were analogous to these portrayals of a golden age. Whether or not the Augustan image of the ideal ruler was influenced directly by Isaiah, the early church and Paul's pictures of Christ were clearly influenced by the image of Augustus. For example, Paul describes Christ as having the same three salvific roles as Augustus. First, both were ideal humans who provided a model of how to devote oneself to God (the gods). In this respect, both performed a priestly service on behalf of the community. Second, because of the acts of

---

[51]See Wallace-Hadrill's suggestion that the Isaiah-like references above in Virgil may have been transmitted to the West by means of sources, such as the *Sibylline Oracles,* that Augustus exploited for his purposes. In particular, sibylline prophecies with a golden-age emphasis were stored in the new temple of Apollo on the Palatine and invoked for auspicious public occasions (cf. ibid., 91–92).

benefaction they performed, both had the right to be regarded as divine and deserving of elevation to divinity. Third, Augustus and Christ were each represented as a god made human, as a divine being who took on the temporary role of humanity to secure human salvation.[52]

Chapter 7, below, will discuss in more detail the way in which Christ's status as Lord in Paul's letters reflects dimensions of Augustus's authority. One of these forms of lordship presents Christ as the human model of piety, the person like Abraham who, against all odds, was willing to devote himself wholeheartedly to God. This is the image of priestly lordship, which sees Christ not just as sacrificial victim but as devoted sacrificer. In Phil 2:3–5 Paul exhorts his recipients to have the same priestly mind-set as Christ, looking not to their own interests but to the interests of others. In 2:14–17, Paul shows how he himself appropriated Christ's model of sacrificer:

> Do all things without murmuring or arguing . . . that I can boast on the day of Christ that I did not run in vain or labor in vain. But even if I am to be poured out as a libation over the sacrifice and the offering of your faith, I am glad and rejoice with all of you. (Phil 2:14, 16–17)

Paul presents his Gentile converts' faith as his priestly offering to God, but because he may lose his life in such duty, he describes himself as a sacrificial libation that is added to the sacrifice he offers.[53]

In addition to being the human ideal, Christ, like Augustus, is described in various ways as transcending human mortality. This is indicated most clearly in his resurrection (deification) after death. In the case of Augustus, Suetonius says supernatural signs had preceded his death, and afterward an ex-praetor took an oath that he saw the form of the emperor going up to heaven.[54] Similarly, Paul refers to several witnesses to whom Jesus appeared in a resurrected state, including himself.[55]

---

[52]See Wallace-Hadrill's discussion in *Augustan Rome*, 79–97.

[53]Elsewhere, in Rom 1:13 and 15:15–18, Paul also refers to Gentile converts' obedience (faith) as an offering and harvest that he offers up to God in priestly service. Although Paul's picture of Christ as sacrificer is not expressed so clearly as Paul's image of himself as priest, Christ is undoubtedly his model.

[54]See Suetonius, *Augustus* 97 (signs before death), 100 (deification after death).

[55]E.g., see 1 Cor 15:4–8, where Paul says Christ appeared to the following in resurrected form: Cephas (Peter), the Twelve, more than five hundred followers at one time, James, all the apostles, and, finally, Paul himself. See also Gal 1:12, 16, where Paul refers to God's revelation of the resurrected Christ to himself.

Moreover, as was often the case in godlike humans, so too in the case of Augustus and Christ, their beginning was heralded by supernatural signs. Although Paul does not record such data, Matthew's and Luke's birth stories record portents like those associated with Augustus. For example, the senate is reputed to have decreed a ban on rearing male babies in the year of Augustus's birth because of a portent indicating a Roman king had been born.[56] Similarly, Suetonius reports that Augustus's mother, Atia, had an "annunciation" dream where she learned that Apollo had impregnated her with Augustus, just as Mary learned she would give birth to a divine Son.[57]

Paul does not seem to have assimilated Christ to God in the explicit way in which Octavian was represented in his early leadership roles as Neptune, Jupiter, or various other gods. On the other hand, the later portraits of Augustus, performing functions on earth like those of Jupiter in heaven, are close to Paul's image of Christ because Paul describes Christ as the one through whom God establishes universal justice (order), peace, and liberation.[58]

It is interesting that, in his earliest letter, 1 Thessalonians (see 4:16f.), Paul's image of Christ as the general who descends with military authority is reminiscent of the early image of Octavian as a military champion. This image of Christ and his followers in conflict with external forces, however, largely disappears in Paul's later letters. For example, in the picture of warfare in 2 Cor 10:3–6 Paul employs divine weapons to overcome resistance within the community and not to destroy external enemies.

Part 3 now takes up three important elements of Paul's theology: God's identity as Father (ch. 6), Christ's identity as Lord (ch. 7), and the church as God's family and people (ch. 8).

---

[56]See Suetonius, *Augustus* 94.3; and compare this with Matthew's account of the slaughter of the innocents (Matt 2:13–18). See also Wallace-Hadrill, *Augustan Rome*, 86.

[57]See Suetonius, *Augustus* 94.4; and compare with Luke 1:26–38.

[58]See Wallace-Hadrill's description of ancient references to Augustus's role as the "Jupiter-on-earth" who establishes order like Jupiter in heaven (*Augustan Rome*, 89). In Phil 2:9–11 Paul says Christ receives the name of "Lord" to the "glory of God" and that every knee on earth (and in heaven) will submit to his rule. The benefits of Christ's rule are described as effecting God's universal justice (e.g., see Rom 3:21–31) and peace (this is regularly expressed as wishes of salutation and farewell in Paul's letters; e.g., see 1 Thess 1:1; 5:23–24; Gal 1:3–4; 6:15–16).

PART THREE
GOD OUR FATHER, CHRIST THE LORD, AND THE HOUSEHOLD OF FAITH

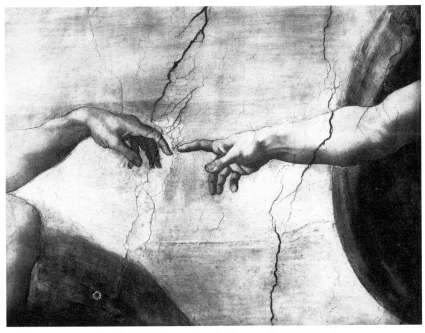

*Detail of God's creation of Adam on Sistine Chapel
ceiling by Michelangelo. Michelangelo, Sistine
Chapel. Photo courtesy of Alinari/Art Resource, N.Y.*

Rather, as anyone who has approached nearest to the truth would say, the central place is held by the Father of the Universe, who in the sacred scriptures is called He that is as his proper name, while on either side of him are the senior potencies, the nearest to him, the creative and the kingly. The title of the former is God, since it made and ordered the all; the title of the latter is Lord, since it is the fundamental right of the maker to rule and control what he has brought into being.

Philo, *De Abrahamo* 121

Thus may all men seeing these examples be brought to a wiser mind and learn that God welcomes the virtue which springs from ignoble birth, that he takes no account of the roots but accepts the full-grain stem, because it has been changed from a weed into fruitfulness.

Philo, *De praemiis et poenis* 152

6

GOD OUR FATHER

This chapter discusses two aspects of Paul's idea of God: first, under the image of creator, God's sovereignty over the whole natural order; second, under the image of Father, God's creation of individual congregations. Since Paul assumed God was the source of all life, why does he not use something like Philo's "Father and Maker of all" (see *Abr.* 121) to describe God? Why does he always use the familiar designation "our God and Father" to begin his letters and not more abstract terms?

Paul preferred "Father" to abstract designations partly because the image was attractive to converts, many of whom felt subject to impersonal powers. But for the most part, it was Paul's own conversion experience that led him to think of God in terms of personal procreative power. Although Paul had learned many things about God as a Pharisee, the idea of personal creator did not become a reality until God revealed the risen Christ to him.

The introduction of this book noted that Paul stopped persecuting Greek-speaking Jewish Christians when he realized God had vindicated a man condemned by Mosaic law. Since God himself had raised up Jesus, Paul knew Jewish law could not fully explain God's purpose. Likewise, obedience to Mosaic law could no longer form the true basis of a relationship with God. The true source of communal life was God's own power to create life from death and to bring order out of chaos.

Although Paul had experienced God's power in a personal way and although it was advantageous for rhetorical reasons to address converts as God's offspring, he certainly believed in God's universal sovereignty as creator and found ways of combining the idea with God's familiar character. Paul's dual understanding of God's nature as creator is similar to what we find in the mystery cults and the imperial cult, which also combined universal and personal power. Although devotees desired personal attention, they wanted the divine benefit to be effective. Thus, the emperor inspired confidence in his fatherly care precisely because of his worldwide rule. Likewise, suffering mystery cult divinities were effective precisely because they were empowered by the forces of nature.

Paul's combination of familiar and universal was not influenced entirely by pagan sources, however, since Judaism had claimed for centuries that the creator of the universe had chosen Israel as the special object of affection. Nonetheless, Paul heightened the Jewish idea of election to the point of scandal when he addressed Gentiles as God's children without requiring them to become Jews.[1] Before turning to the familiar aspect of God's identity as creator, however, we need to review Paul's idea of God as universal creator. There is one respect, however, in which Paul's ideas departed from Greco-Roman ideas about universal sovereignty.

The discussion of Hellenistic rulers as benefactors in chapter 4, above, and the image of Augustus as the state's priestly patron in chapter 5, indicate that we must discuss God's political authority as an aspect of his sovereignty as creator. Unlike Philo (see the citation at the head of the chapter), however, who attributed both creative and kingly powers to God, Paul attributes creativity to God but transfers God's political powers to the risen Jesus. Granted, Paul refers to God's empire *(basileia)*, but he does not designate God as king.[2] Moreover, although Paul sometimes

---

[1]Paul's idea that Gentile converts could also have a special relation with God, perhaps even favored status, is not entirely unique. Philo also talks about the special place of proselytes in the Jewish community; e.g., see *Spec.* 1.52; 4.177–178; *Virt.* 103–104; *Praem.* 152. Philo, however, assumed Gentiles would adopt Jewish customs as the basis of their status with God.

[2]E.g., the designation "kingdom [empire] of God" appears in Rom 14:17; 1 Cor 4:20; 6:9, 10; 15:24, 50; Gal 5:21; and 1 Thess 2:12. 1 Tim 1:17 refers to God as "the King of the ages," but the designation "King" is never applied to God in the seven letters most often accepted by scholars as authentic.

refs to God as Lord, he uses the title much more often for Christ. Thus, although we can not ignore the political aspect of God's sovereignty here, the next chapter takes it up more explicitly when it reviews Paul's picture of Jesus as "Christ the Lord."

GOD'S CHARACTER AS UNIVERSAL CREATOR

How Paul's Idea of Sovereignty Differed from Ruler Cult Ideology

Paul's transferral of God's political authority to Christ corresponds to imperial-cult ideas about Augustus as the divine agent through whom universal peace was inaugurated. On the other hand, God is more directly involved in effecting benefits through Christ than the gods are in Augustus's rule. To be sure, Augustus subjected himself to the golden-age concord identified with his divine patron Apollo, and his genius was worshiped in Rome only in association with the goddess Roma and the Lares. Nonetheless, he was the locus of authority in ways in which Paul never talks about Christ as ruler. Most notably, whereas Augustus was saluted as "Father of His Country" by the senate and people of Rome, Christ is never called father in any respect.[3]

Instead, like most Jewish scholars, Paul considered God the founder (Father) of communal life. Moreover, Paul regarded God as the providential sustainer of social order, and the source of nature's order.

Jewish Ideas about God's Absolute Rule of Creation

Through God's beneficial activity on its behalf, Paul demonstrates God's right to rule the world.[4] The association between benevolence and

---

[3]Augustus himself says in *Res gestae* 34 that, by universal consent, he was in complete control of the republic's affairs by his sixth and seventh consulships. As noted earlier, he adds (sect. 35) that in his thirteenth consulship he received the title of "Father of my Country" from the senate, the equestrian order, and the whole people of Rome.

[4]Like many Greco-Roman authors, Paul was convinced that injurious force was not true power. E.g., he argues in 1 Corinthians that the Corinthians' wisdom was false and powerless precisely because it caused disharmony in the community. Despite the "foolishness" and weakness of a crucified Christ, however, Paul shows in 1 Cor 3–4 how God effected communal harmony through him. The communal harmony effected by Christ demonstrates God's power (e.g., see 1 Cor 1:18–31).

right to rule has Greco-Roman roots.[5] In particular, Judaism was influenced by hellenistic philosophy's concept of the ideal ruler. As illustrated in chapters 4 and 5, above, the ruler cult had two primary articles of belief: the sovereign's right to absolute rule, and his philanthropic concern for subjects.[6]

The Sovereign's Right to Absolute Rule. Philosophy's belief in the ruler's right to absolute rule derived partly from the idea that all humanity was subject to the same universal principles. For example, Stoics believed the whole universe was alive and subject to the same rationality to which humanity was subject.[7] Although Jewish intellectuals maintained allegiance to Moses' law, many shared Stoicism's belief in the existence of universal principles. Accordingly, they tried to show how the Jewish constitution conformed to the universal laws of nature. Thus, near the beginning of his *Jewish Antiquities*, Josephus claims that Jewish law derived from Moses' knowledge that God was the Lord of the universe. Moses himself was so attuned to God's order that he was able to articulate nature's principles as specific laws:

> I must first speak briefly of him [Moses], lest any of my readers should ask how it is that so much of my work, which professes to treat of laws and historical facts, is devoted to natural philosophy [nature].[8] Be it known, then, that that sage deemed it above all necessary, for one who would order his own life aright and also legislate for others, first to study the nature of God, and then, having contemplated his works with the eye of reason, to imitate so far as possible that best of all models and endeavor to follow it. (*Ant.* 1.18–19)[9]

---

[5]E.g., see Plato's comments in book one of the *Republic*. Thrasymachus, a Sophist, argues that whatever government is in power has the right to enforce laws on its subjects: might makes right. By contrast, Socrates shows that power as such is an unreliable index of authenticity. By definition, a leader is someone who looks to the welfare of his subjects and not to personal interests. Power is genuine only if it effects beneficial results.

[6]See Georgi, *Theocracy*, viii–ix.

[7]E.g., see Cicero, *On the Nature of the Gods* 2.33–36.

[8]The word Josephus uses is not "philosophy" but "physiology," i.e., the study of the origin of the existence of the physical/natural order in the biblical account of creation.

[9]In *Against Apion* Josephus also equates Moses' laws with the principles governing the universe. Moses intended the first commandment to instill knowledge of God by God's activity in nature. The best way to worship God was to imitate God's creativity, not to make an image representing God. See *Ag. Ap.* 2.190–192.

Paul also subscribes to the idea of universal law. He argues that because God's eternal principles were clearly evident in nature, they were absolutely binding and reflected the creator's power and glory:

> Ever since the creation of the world his eternal power and divine nature, invisible though they are, have been understood and seen through the things he has made. So they are without excuse; for though they knew God, they did not honor him as God. (Rom 1:20–21)

The universality of God's law is also emphasized in the *Letter of Aristeas*.[10] Ostensibly the author is an Egyptian Greek by the name of Aristeas. Actually he is an Alexandrian Jew writing for a Greek-speaking Jewish audience to assure it of the value of its tradition. The author reports how Jewish law came to be translated into Greek by the king of Egypt (Ptolemy II), and he describes how he himself had asked the king to liberate Jews from Egyptian slavery in order to secure Jewish cooperation in the translation project. *Aristeas* justifies the Jews' liberation on the basis that they worshiped the same God as the Greeks:

> These people worship God the overseer and creator of all, whom all men worship including ourselves, O King, except that we have a different name, such as Zeus and Dis. The primitive men, consistently with this, demonstrated that the one by whom all live and are created is the master and lord of all. (*Let. Aris.* 16)

In order to present the tradition to Diaspora Jews in a defensible way, Aristeas could hardly appeal to Mosaic law in a racially specific manner. Therefore, Aristeas says it was precisely because Moses was concerned with *universal* truth that he devised laws that would surround the Jews like an iron wall. This law was intended to prevent Jews from being influenced by idolatrous perversions of the truth, such as the worship of animals and other elements of the created order.[11]

God intended even seemingly trivial prescriptions, such as those governing clean and unclean foods, to enhance authentic values. By approving domesticated and clean animals for human consumption and,

---

[10]E.g., God is described as "master and lord of all," "overseer and creator of all," and the "Most High God." There is one creation, one universal law, and God himself is "one." God's "power" is demonstrated in everything because every place on earth is filled with his sovereignty. See *Let. Aris.* 16–19; 128–132.

[11]See ibid., 128–142. The foolishness of worshiping elements of the created order, especially animals, is also emphasized in the Wisdom of Solomon, Josephus, Philo, and Paul. It was obviously a stock apologetic topic in synagogues of the Diaspora. The indictment of animal worship was equally common in hellenistic philosophy.

conversely, by forbidding wild and carnivorous animals, Moses was illustrating what wise men should imitate. They should conduct themselves like the animals they were allowed to eat. They should not achieve anything by brute force or lord it over others in the way of carnivorous animals.[12]

Moreover, Jewish intellectuals were critical of spurious forms of rule. Although earlier postexilic wisdom was not influenced directly by Greek thought, Dieter Georgi shows it was just as critical of the temple cult and its priesthood as fourth-century BCE philosophy was critical of inadequacies in the city-state.[13] Later traditions such as the Wisdom of Solomon and Joseph and Aseneth, which were acquainted with the Greek ruler cult, were also skeptical of conventional political structures. Only God's kingdom, inhabited by the virtuous, grants true peace and is worthy of the title of "world-city."[14] They spoke approvingly of Greco-Roman rule and occasionally spoke well of individual rulers, but Jewish intellectuals placed their primary confidence in God's theocracy.

God the Benevolent Ruler. The second element of ruler cult ideology was the emphasis on a ruler's benevolence.[15] The idea that all citizens should be treated with respect, in a measure appropriate to their status, was a principle that fourth-century BCE Greek theorists advocated as a means of reforming selfish interests in the declining city-state.[16] Because of the emphasis on society's collective good, both hellenistic kings and Roman emperors advocated philanthropic ideals. Philo's description of Moses' rule shows that Hellenistic Judaism subscribed to the same principles:

> For he [i.e., Moses] had set before himself one essential aim, to benefit his subjects; and, in all that he said or did, to further their interests and neglect no opportunity which would forward the common well-being. (*Mos.* 1.151)

---

[12]See *Let. Aris.* 143–149.

[13]Statements in Proverbs and Job indicate "wisdom" provided more rational and immediate access to God's presence than cultic ordinances. See Georgi, *Theocracy,* 3–6.

[14]See ibid., 7–16.

[15]Georgi notes that hellenistic philosophy considered philanthropy fundamental to authentic rule (see ibid., ix).

[16]Increasingly, the victorious party in the city-state, whether it was oligarchic or democratic, abused the weaker element. In contrast to this practice, Plato, Isocrates, and Aristotle all agreed that equal maintenance of each part and the welfare of the whole were essential to good rule.

Because intellectuals agreed that the state's collective good must be preserved, both Greek philosophers and Jewish scholars used images of the ruler that accentuated his philanthropic care for subjects. Thus the good ruler was like a physician, the pilot of a ship, the shepherd of the flock, or the manager of the household.[17] The picture of the ruler as a sage (philosopher), who embodied the state's values in his own person, was advocated in Plato's *Republic* and was an idea still timely in Philo's day:

> For it has been said, not without good reason, that states can only make progress in well-being if either kings are philosophers or philosophers are kings. But Moses will be found to have displayed, and more than displayed, combined in his single person, not only these two faculties—the kingly and the philosophical—but also three others, one of which is concerned with law-giving, the second with the high priest's office, and the last with prophecy. (*Mos.* 1.160–162)

Josephus also emphasizes the need for good social order. In fact, at the beginning of the *Jewish Antiquities*, he says history teaches us a moral: whoever heeds God's laws will prosper, but whoever disobeys them will suffer:

> The main lesson to be learnt from this history by any who cares to peruse it is that men who conform to the will of God, and do not venture to transgress laws that have been excellently laid down, prosper in all things beyond belief, and for their reward are offered by God felicity; whereas, in proportion as they depart from the strict observance of these laws, things (else) practicable become impracticable, and whatever imaginary good thing they strive to do ends in irretrievable disasters. (*Ant.* 1.14)

God's right of absolute rule derived from his providence (πρόνοια), which Josephus defines as concern for, and oversight of, human affairs.[18]

---

[17]E.g., Plato uses the physician and the pilot as leadership images in book 1 of the *Republic*. Philo refers to the shepherd's craft as appropriate training for statesmanship. By contrast, the hunting field, which made good preparation for military commanders, was inappropriate for political leaders (cf. *Ios.* 1–3; *Mos.* 2.60). Household management is put forward by Philo as an appropriate model of statesmanship, since the household was a microcosm of society (see *Ios.* 38–39; 54–55; 259; *Mos.* 2.323–324). Like Plato, Philo also uses the physician (cf. *Ios.* 62–63) and the pilot (cf. *Abr.* 83–84; 116–117) as images of the political leader.

[18]Josephus justified Judaism to a Gentile audience by deliberately replacing biblical themes such as election and covenant with Greek alternatives such as "providence." Josephus's paraphrase of biblical history assumed that God had a special relation with the Jews, but he did not stress this in a racially exclusive way. See Attridge, *Interpretation*, 78–92.

What was it about which God cared? On the basis of a speech Josephus attributes to Moses just before the crossing of the Red Sea, Harold Attridge identifies three elements. First, Moses said God's providence was directed especially toward Israel. Second, God's providence was manifest in miraculous acts that effected his salvific care. Third, Moses concluded his speech with the exhortation fully to trust God because God rewards the righteous and punishes the wicked. This third aspect is especially important because it shows that God's care of Israel was not arbitrary. It depended on Israel's or its leaders' virtue.[19]

Thus, despite God's special care of the Jews, Attridge says Josephus systematically replaces biblical covenant terms with Greco-Roman "benefactor" and "alliance" language.[20] Whereas covenantal terms were racial and exclusivistic, benefactor language conveyed God's universal character. Accordingly, in Josephus's account of Solomon's temple dedication, Solomon requested that God extend his aid to all people.[21] In addition to Josephus's benefactor language, his use of the word *symmachia* for military alliance indicates God did not bind himself automatically to a people but gave alliance in times of need, and even then only to those who deserved it. Worthiness was based on piety, not on racial identity.[22]

Thus, despite Greco-Roman influence, Josephus indicates human affairs were more directly under God's personal providence than pagan contemporaries would ever state. Although other Greco-Roman historians considered themselves servants in the service of providence, no one wrote a completely theocentric history like Josephus. Nor did other historians emphasize so much the need for a religious response *(eusebeia)* to God's providence.[23]

Like Josephus, Philo also emphasizes God's universal philanthropy. For example, in reporting Joseph's reunion with his brothers, who had sold him into slavery, it was not enough to describe Joseph's forgiveness or to reflect the biblical idea that God could effect good

---

[19]See ibid., 78ff.

[20]See Attridge's discussion of Josephus's benefactor (βοηθός) and alliance (συμμαχία) language, ibid., 78–81.

[21]For Solomon's request for aid (βοήθεια) see Josephus, *Ant.* 8.116–117. See Attridge's comments on this passage and on Josephus's use of benefactor language generally in *Interpretation,* 78–81 (esp. 81 n. 2).

[22]Attridge, *Interpretation,* 83ff.

[23]Ibid., 181–84.

from bad. Philo used the occasion to comment on God's care of the whole human race.[24]

Paul's Idea of God's Power as Universal Creator

Unlike non-Christian Jewish peers, Paul derived God's power as universal creator largely from his recent salvation in Christ. Paul believed God had exhibited his final purpose for creation in Christ's resurrection. Although the God who regenerated creation in Christ was the same artificer who created the physical universe and although the founder of the church was the same life force who fathered a people in Abraham, nonetheless Paul saw something qualitatively better about God's new community and new creation.

The importance of God's future perfection of creation for Paul will be discussed shortly, but first we illustrate God's universal sovereignty as creator, using all of Paul's authentic letters except Philemon. Whereas 1 Thessalonians and Romans provide the more general picture of God's creative identity, the Corinthian correspondence, Galatians, and Philippians convey Paul's picture of God's teleological or eschatological purpose as creator.

God's Role as Universal Life Giver. In the first three chapters of 1 Thessalonians, Paul celebrates God's spiritual creation of the Thessalonians as his children. Although the ostensible focus is on God's personal relation to the Thessalonians as Father, Paul shows that their

---

[24]See Philo, *Ios.* 240–241:

> Of my own [i.e., Joseph's] free, unbidden judgment I have voluntarily come to make my peace with you. In this I have two fellow-counsellors, my reverence for our father, . . . and the natural humanity which I feel to all men, and particularly to those of my blood. And I consider that the cause of what has happened is not you but God, who willed to use me as his servant, to administer the boons and gifts which he designs to grant to the human race in the time of their greatest need.

Philo often refers to God's love of humanity, but we may limit ourselves to one example. In explaining Abraham's migration from Chaldea to Haran, Philo describes the movement allegorically as a change in Abraham's mindset in response to God's vision of himself to Abraham:

> He (God) in his love for mankind, when the soul (Abraham) came into his presence, did not turn away his face, but came forward to meet him and revealed his nature, so far as the beholder's power of sight allowed. This is why we are told not that the sage saw God, but that God was seen by him. For it were impossible that anyone should by himself apprehend the truly existent, did not he reveal and manifest himself. (*Abr.* 79-80)

spiritual generation fit a recurring pattern that Christ, Paul, and others had previously experienced. Thus, the Thessalonians' repetition of the pattern not only confirmed their own status as divine offspring but, more important, demonstrated God's general character as parent. It will prove useful to show how Paul shaped the separate examples of spiritual generation into a single, coherent picture of God as creator.

Paul identifies God as the Thessalonians' Father in the opening greeting (1 Thess 1:1), and it is clear God's paternity was to be understood in a familial way. Paul underscores the affectionate nature of God's relation to the Thessalonians by stating *"our* God and Father" in 1:3 and by describing converts in 1:4 as "beloved" and "chosen." Just as God's power as parent was evidenced in the Thessalonians' charismatic experience of spiritual life, so too their identity as divine offspring was demonstrated in what they "became" in response to God's life-giving power:

> For we know, brothers and sisters beloved by God, that he has chosen you, because our message of the gospel came to you not in word only, but also in power and in the Holy Spirit and with full conviction. (1:4–5)

In particular, Paul thanks God because of the Thessalonians' "work of faith and labor of love and steadfastness of hope" in the Lord Jesus Christ (1:3). Thus, the Thessalonians had not merely agreed intellectually with Paul's message of salvation; they embodied concretely the virtues of faith, hope, and love in their communal life.

Paul uses two verbs, "become" and "know," repeatedly in the first two chapters to underscore the eventfulness of what happened ("became") when the Thessalonians responded positively to Paul's message of salvation. The word "know" captures the certainty with which converts experienced the importance of what had happened.[25] The Thessalonians knew something had happened to make them God's family. Moreover, as the citation below indicates, the same power that changed the Thessalonians had previously generated an analogous change in Christ and Paul. Thus, the Thessalonians participated in an enlivening reality that fit a divine pattern. The root paradigm, by means of which Paul connects and explains the separate instances, was God's resurrection of Christ from death:

> For we *know* . . . he has chosen you, because our message . . . *came* to you not in word only, but also in power and in the Holy Spirit and with full conviction; *just as you know* what kind of persons we *proved to be* among you

---

[25]The following passages illustrate Paul's repetitious use of "become" and "know" in 1 Thess 1–2: 1:4–7; 2:1–2; 2:5–8; 2:9–12.

for your sake. And you *became* imitators of us and of the Lord, for in spite of persecution you received the word with joy inspired by the Holy Spirit, so that you *became* an example to all the believers in Macedonia and in Achaia. (1:4–7, italics added)

The positive response to Paul was threatening to the Thessalonians' countrymen, who were still subject to idolatrous influence. Figuratively speaking, the Thessalonians were opposed by a negative response comparable to persecution against Christ. God's power to overcome the deathlike opposition, however, was exhibited in the joy that the Holy Spirit inspired in the Thessalonians and that raised (i.e., resurrected) them up above the persecution (see 1:6).

The following citations (with italics added for emphasis) indicate that the power that lifted the Thessalonians above their adversity also effected like consequences for Paul and his associates.

You yourselves *know* . . . our coming to you *was* not [i.e., did not *become*] in vain, but though we had already suffered . . . at Philippi, as you *know*, we had courage in our God to declare to you the gospel. (2:1–2)

As you *know* . . . we never *came* with words of flattery. But we *were [became]* gentle among you . . . So deeply do we care for you that we are determined to share with you . . . also our own selves, because you have *become* very dear to us. (2:5–8)

You *remember* [i.e., you *know*] our labor. You are witnesses . . . how pure, upright, and blameless our conduct *was [became]* toward you believers. As you *know,* we dealt with each one of you, like a father with his children, urging . . . you . . . [to] lead a life worthy of God, who calls you into his own kingdom and glory. (2:9–12)

The first citation indicates that although Paul and his associates had been mistreated immediately before coming to Thessalonica, they nonetheless had courage to proclaim God's message to the Thessalonians. Paul is not calling attention to his own courage in the face of adversity but is providing further illustration of God's power to transform negative (deathlike) circumstances.

Our emphasis on God as life giver might appear to exaggerate the similarity of the Thessalonians' and Paul's experiences with God's resurrection of Christ. Various comments of Paul clearly indicate, however, that he intended such an emphasis. For example, because he was hindered from making a return visit to Thessalonica, Paul was apprehensive and described himself as orphaned by the separation (see 2:17f.). When Timothy brought good news about his converts' ongoing faith, however, Paul was relieved of his fears (see 3:6f.). Whereas he describes separation from converts as being orphaned (i.e., a state dictated by death), he describes Timothy's good news as a state of resurrection: "For we now live" (3:8).

Likewise in 1:9–10, Paul describes the change in the Thessalonians as a movement from death to life. He states in 1:9 that they "turned to God from idols, to serve a *living* and true God." The converts had been subject not only to something false but to something lifeless. In turn, Paul emphasizes that the Thessalonians participated in the power of Christ's resurrection (regeneration), by adding in 1:10: "and to wait for his Son from heaven, whom he *raised from the dead.*"[26]

The reader may be puzzled by this use of 1 Thessalonians to illustrate God's universal role as creator, and it is true that Paul does not emphasize God's universality in 1 Thessalonians as much as God's fatherly role as creator. Nonetheless, Paul's diction implies that the God who effected spiritual creation in the church was the universal creator. The frequency with which he portrays converts' transformation as the creation of life out of death suggests Paul has God's role as universal creator in mind.[27] His description of God as the "living and true God" certainly indicates that the one who lifted the Thessalonians above adversity was the same creator who caused light to shine out of darkness (see 2 Cor 4:6).

Paul regarded God's spiritual creation as superior to the physical universe. Although Paul believed God would regenerate the whole universe, he usually emphasizes God's role as Father of the household rather than world creator. Romans departs from Paul's usual image of God, however, because Paul had not founded the church at Rome. Since Paul could not address the church as its spiritual father, he also found it more difficult to refer to God as the congregation's Father. Therefore, Paul pictures God's identity more in terms of creator and Father of the Jewish race.

As discussed in chapter 2, above, despite Paul's emphasis on God's condemnation of humanity for lawlessness in Romans, he no longer believed God's "righteousness" derived primarily from his character as lawgiver. For the theme of this letter, expressed in Rom 1:16, is not God's

---

[26]Although Paul uses "become" *(ginomai)* in 1 Thessalonians in the sense of something "occurring," the verb also has the meaning of "be born." Thus, he evokes God's intervention as a life-begetting (birth) experience for the Thessalonians as well as for Christ.

[27]The fact that Paul presents the transformation as an act of imitation, which fits a recurring pattern, assumes that the same power is at work effecting each subsequent act of divine creation.

righteousness but his "power" to effect salvation. Several images in Romans indicate that God's power to make things right issues from God's providential power as creator.

For example, Paul shows by means of God's creative activity in Abraham and Christ (see 3:21–4:25) that God was begetting whole peoples. Moreover, Christ's status as the new Adam in 5:12–21 demonstrates that God was re-creating all humanity. Only a little later, in Rom 8, Paul says that all creation was groaning in travail as it labored to be given birth (i.e., be re-created) as God's offspring.

Stowers's recent commentary on Romans supports this picture of God. For example, his reading of 3:21–4:25 differs from the traditional emphasis on the sinner's justification by faith. According to Stowers, Paul's focus in 3:21–26 was not on what humanity had to do to be saved: to have faith. Rather, the emphasis was on God's activity: God proved himself righteous by justifying Gentiles through Jesus' obedient death.[28] Correspondingly, one should not interpret the depiction of Abraham's relationship with God in Rom 4 as concerned subjectively with true faith. Rather, the focus is on "God's way of adopting whole peoples . . . by using the generative trust of Abraham and Jesus to work procreative miracles that founded new families."[29]

According to Stowers, Romans and Galatians agree that people became Abraham's descendants by incorporation into Christ, who reenacted Abraham's lineage-founding faithfulness. By different means, both Christ and Abraham exhibited God's ability to generate life (offspring) even out of death (sterility). By connecting Christ's faithfulness with Abraham's trust, Paul retained the principle of descent while subordinating it to spiritual procreation by God.[30] Although Stowers does not state explicitly that the picture of God's activity in Rom 3:21–4:25 is that of the creator rather than a lawgiver, his description implies as much.

Correspondingly, Paul's picture of the potter and the clay in 9:20–24 is a graphic image of God's character as creator. As mentioned in chapter 2, above, not only does the image of the potter evoke the idea of God as creator; the molding of clay recalls the specific picture of creation in Gen 2. The image justifies God's right as the potter to form some vessels for menial use and others for beauty (i.e., decorative use). In the context of Rom 9–11, the image justifies God's right to form Israel for menial

---

[28]Stowers, *Rereading of Romans*, 223.
[29]Ibid., 228–29.
[30]Ibid., 230.

use ("objects of wrath") and to form Gentiles for special use ("objects of mercy").

God appeared to have hardened Israel's heart because she resisted the salvation effected in Christ (see 11:1–9, 25–32). Therefore, from the human perspective, God rejected Israel arbitrarily and made its people into "objects of wrath." Conversely, it seemed God chose the Gentiles (the "objects of mercy"), on equally arbitrary grounds, to be his beloved people. Paul argues, however, that because of God's absolute sovereignty, God was only using Israel's rejection of Christ to facilitate Gentile incorporation into Abraham's stock. God's acceptance of Gentiles, in turn, was designed to make Israel jealous and cause her also to accept God's salvation in Christ. By this means God would recreate all humanity (see 11:25–32).

Thus, the image of God exhibited in Israel's apparent rejection and future acceptance derives not from God's character as judge but from God's power as creator. Paul interprets the rejection-acceptance sequence explicitly as the creator's act of bringing life out of death:

> I glorify my ministry [to Gentiles] in order to make my own people jealous, and thus save some of them. For if their rejection is the reconciliation of the world, what will their acceptance be but life from the dead! (11:13–15)

Paul's representation of Gentile converts in 11:17–24 as wild olive branches, grafted unnaturally into a cultivated tree, also exhibits God's identity as creator. For God's ability, "contrary to nature," to graft wild branches into a cultivated tree assumes that the creator's power transcends even nature's generativity.

The Future in Paul's Idea of God as Creator. Paul's use of the potter image in 9:20–24 shows that God's intention as creator will come to full fruition only in the future. The numerous images of growth, progress, and maturation discussed in chapters 1 and 2, above, illustrate the importance of teleology in Paul's idea of God. The following images illustrate the importance of the future in Paul's idea of God.

> Now if the ministry of death, chiseled in letters on stone tablets, came in glory so that the people of Israel could not gaze at Moses' face because of the glory of his face, . . . how much more will the ministry of the Spirit come in glory? . . . Since, then, we have such a hope, we act with great boldness, not like Moses, who put a veil over his face to keep the people of Israel from gazing at the end of . . . [his] glory. . . . [But] all of us, with unveiled faces, seeing the glory of the Lord . . . , are being transformed into the same image [of the Lord], from one degree of glory to another; for this comes from the Lord, the Spirit. (2 Cor 3:7–8, 12–13, 18)

Paul indicates in this citation that the new creation perfects what is immature about the present order. Although Mosaic law reflected God's glory, the spiritual ministry effected in Christ has a greater ability to actualize God's image in our being and to better approximate his glory.

Likewise, Paul's comparison of "spiritual" creation with agricultural growth in 1 Cor 15 corresponds to his image of human maturation in Galatians. In Galatians, as in 1 Cor 15, the time was ripe for full-term growth:

> heirs, as long as they are minors, are no better than slaves, though they are the owners of all the property; but they remain under guardians and trustees until the date set by the father. So with us; while we were minors, we were enslaved to the elemental spirits of the world. But when *the fullness of time* had come, God sent his Son, born of a woman, born under the law, in order to redeem those who were under the law, so that we might receive adoption as children. (Gal 4:1–5, italics added)

According to this citation, the Galatians' former subjection to impersonal astrological and natural forces, such as the moon god Men and the Great Mother Cybele, was no better than the state of children under guardians. Correspondingly, in 3:23–29, Paul says that subjection to Mosaic law was no better than a child's subjection to a disciplinarian (pedagogue). In contrast to these states of subjection, Christ's Spirit liberates us from an immature relationship with God and enables us to participate fully in his rule as mature heirs.

Besides these passages on maturation and completion in Galatians and 1–2 Corinthians is the similar, but more sweeping, statement in Rom 8, where creation itself is described as being set free from subjection to decay and enabled to obtain the glory of God's progeny. Somewhat different from the imagery of Romans, Galatians, and the Corinthian correspondence is Paul's picture of political maturation found in Philippians. In Phil 2:1–11 Paul presents Christ as the political Lord, whose obedience to God and selflessness toward humanity caused God to appoint him the ruler before whom every knee would bend, in heaven, on earth, and under the earth. As authentic subjects, converts are compared by Paul to heroic children without blemish, who shined like stars in contrast to inferior forms of communal life (2:12–18). The world's true citizens place their confidence in God's heavenly citizenship and in honor such as God bestowed on Christ.

Other passages also have a teleological thrust, but the texts discussed demonstrate sufficiently the importance of maturity and future perfection in Paul's idea of God as creator. Interpreters often call attention

to futurity in Paul's thought, but they tend to emphasize the discontinuity between the old physical world and the new spiritual order. For example, because of Paul's emphasis on the future, Beker characterizes the
apostle's belief as fundamentally apocalyptic. Although Paul does emphasize the completion of God's salvation in the future, Beker himself
finds many aspects of Jewish apocalyptic inappropriate for Paul's view of
the future (see ch. 2, above).[31]

It is equally problematic to talk about Paul's idea of the future
in strictly Jewish terms. If we describe Paul's view of the future as
apocalyptic, then we need to enlarge the designation to include comparable Greco-Roman phenomena.[32] Even the oft-cited contrast
between Greco-Roman cyclical time and Jewish linear time is an over-
simplification.[33] Whether or not Judaism was deeply attracted to the
idea of eternal recurrence, the apocalyptic formulation of the future in
terms of a paradisaical past reflects the Greek idea of return. To take
another example of pagan influence on Jewish apocalyptic, it is clear
the statue composed of four metals in Dan 2 draws on a myth, popu-
larized by Hesiod and discussed by Plato, that imagined the distant
past as a golden age that degenerated in subsequent periods.[34] The

---

[31]Beker agrees with Leander Keck ("Apocalyptic Theology") and Jörg
Baumgarten (*Paulus und die Apokalyptik*) that only a few passages in Paul are purely
apocalyptic. The characteristic language is missing, and Paul does not use Jewish
apocalypses as literary sources (see Beker, *The Triumph of God,* 19–21, 61–65).

[32]The discussions of Romans both in this chapter and in chs. 2 and 3,
above, noted that in Christ God effected both his universal judgment and his
salvific incorporation of all peoples into Abraham's stock. Paul modified the typical nationalistic separation of God's law-abiding people from Gentile "sinners"
(see also Gal 2:15). In addition to rejecting Jewish elitism, Paul modified apocalyptic's temporal demarcation of the present evil age and the salvific age to come.
For those who had eyes to see, the Spirit was already effecting "a new creation"
(see 2 Cor 5:17). Regarding these and other Pauline modifications of apoclayptic,
see Beker, *The Triumph of God,* 25ff.

[33]In an essay on Greek and Roman ideas about progress and the periodi-
zation of history, G. E. R. Lloyd challenges the overly simplified differentiation of
Jewish and Greco-Roman ideas about time. See Lloyd, "Theories," 267.

[34]Hesiod's eighth-century BCE myth about clearly defined stages of historical degeneration appears in his *Works and Days* 106–200. His account starts with a
golden age and proceeds downward through silver and bronze ages and an age of
heroes to a fifth and final age of iron. Plato appeals to the same motif about history's degeneration from a golden age in his *Statesman,* but he does not identify
five specific stages in the manner of Hesiod. Daniel's representation of pagan rulers (kingdoms) as savage animals in chs. 7 and 8 and as a monster in ch. 2 also reflects Greek influence, drawing on such Greek motifs as the representation of
Persia as monstrous and savage barbarians.

Stoic idea of the world's periodic destruction contributed further to the concept of recurring ages.[35]

According to Lloyd, there were two contrasting Greco-Roman views of decline and progress: (1) that the present was a *decline* from a golden-age past and (2) that humanity had *progressed* from a primitive state.[36] He advises us not to take either view too literally, however, because golden-age myths were often cited in a way that indicates the past was not actually superior to the present. Likewise, stories that appeal to civilization's progress often contain an equal measure of ambiguity about progress. Both perspectives provided a means of moralizing about the present.[37]

In the same way, Paul's language about apocalyptic judgment and degeneration must not be taken too literally. He certainly argues on occasion as if he believed human disobedience had corrupted a golden-age relationship with God. Thus in Gal 3:19ff. Paul interprets the introduction of Mosaic law as a necessity occasioned by human sinfulness. Similarly, he sometimes depicts salvation as a return to simple trust in God like that of Abraham, the noble father of the race (see Gal 3:1–9, 15–18; Rom 4). If we were to base Paul's view of the future only on these references, we could justly conclude he believed there was an apocalyptic disjunction between the present evil age and a pristine future (see Gal 1:4).

---

[35]The universe's periodic conflagration is more a belief of early Stoicism (i.e., up to the first half of the second century BCE) than of middle or late Stoicism. Early Stoics believed that the universe was subject to fixed rules of rationality (the *logos*) and that the philosopher should strive to live in harmony with this natural law. The overarching rationality, identified with God, manifested itself as a divine necessity (fate) and providence *(pronoia)*. Since Stoics regarded fire as most closely related to the *logos,* it was the element by which the world was consumed periodically. In due course, a new world would arise from the ashes of the old.

[36]Lloyd, "Theories." Lloyd says that the idea that humanity has degenerated from a golden past is the dominant or majority viewpoint, whereas the notion of progress from primitive beginnings is the minority view.

[37]Ibid., 265–66. To see how ancient myths were used didactically, refer to Hesiod's use of metals to represent history's decline (see n. 34, above). If Hesiod were actually resigned to the inferiority of his own fifth age, his criticism of corrupt kings would be pointless. In fact, he assumes kings can be just, and he talks optimistically about how just rulers and their peoples prosper. Plato talks in an equally ambivalent way about the superiority of the past. Although the age of Cronos was a time when the earth produced fruit without cultivation and was free of war, Plato says it lacked the civilizing conversation of philosophy and the political structures that allow humanity truly to be human (see Plato, *Statesman* 269ff.). Thus, like Hesiod, Plato was not totally nostalgic about the past.

Paul's widespread emphasis on growth and maturation, however, indicates that apocalyptic judgment was not the primary thrust of his theology. Rather, as previously suggested in chapters 1 and 2, above, the emphasis on biological growth that pervades Paul's letters indicates a very different relationship between the present and the future. A new order was coming to birth in the manner of the processes of nature, as a *continuation* of life that would issue in full-term growth. In this case, the suffering from which we are liberated is the anguish of birth, not the annihilation of physicality. Moreover, despite the noble status of Abraham as forefather, Paul did not imagine salvation as a static restoration of an Abrahamic past. Even if human sinfulness interfered with the completion of God's will, God's full purpose never existed in the past. For God did not fulfill his promise to make Abraham the father of many peoples until God effected it in Christ:

> scripture, foreseeing that God would justify the Gentiles by faith, declared the gospel beforehand to Abraham, saying, "All the Gentiles shall be blessed in you." . . . Now the promises were made to Abraham and to his offspring; it does not say, "And to offsprings," as of many; but it says, "And to your offspring," that is, to one person, who is Christ. . . . for in Christ Jesus you [Gentiles] are all children of God through faith. As many of you as were baptized into Christ have clothed yourselves with Christ. . . . And if you belong to Christ, then you are Abraham's offspring, heirs according to the promise. (Gal 3:8, 16, 26–27, 29)

Because of Paul's emphasis on growth, completion, and perfection, "teleological" is superior to "apocalyptic" as a description of Paul's view of God. If scholars prefer to call Paul an apocalyptic theologian, then we need to include the kind of positive modifications of apocalyptic that we have described as characteristic of his theology. A useful model for describing the positive relation of the past to the future is Aristotle's view that "like produces like" in nature, the parent being the "efficient" cause of that into which its progeny grew.[38] Applying this Aristotelian principle to Paul's idea of creation, we see God as the efficient cause of that into which God's spiritual offspring will grow:

> we know that the one who raised the Lord Jesus will raise us also with Jesus, and will bring us with you into his presence. . . . So we do not lose heart. Even though our outer nature is wasting away, our inner nature is being renewed day by day. For this slight momentary affliction is preparing us for an eternal weight of glory beyond all measure. (2 Cor 4:14, 16–17)

---

[38] Aristotle, *Parts of Animals,* 1.641b.23–31, 33–1.642a.1.

GOD AS FATHER OF THE FAMILY AND
FATHER OF THE RACE

This section concentrates on familial or fatherly images of God, which emphasize his parental care and affection. It begins with contemporary parallels.

The Appeal of Voluntary Guilds and the Great Mother Cult

The Great Mother: Parent and Guardian. Paul argues in Gal 3:23–29 that before Christ he had obeyed Mosaic law as the basis of his relationship with God. Similarly, he alleges in 4:1–7 that before Christ the Galatians had been subject to the "elemental spirits of the world" (i.e., forces of nature and/or astrological powers). Both cases entailed subjection to an enslaving and impersonal master.

Despite Paul's own negative estimate, neither the Galatians nor the Jews had regarded the laws they obeyed as impersonal. The Galatians probably had worshiped Cybele, the Great Mother goddess of Asia Minor, and the Jews regarded the gift of Mosaic law as evidence of God's care for the community. Thus, the image of parent was associated with the system of order that both the Jews and the Galatians venerated. Paul's negative description of Jewish law and the Galatians' former religion was colored by his own conviction that these powers had been unable to effect freedom and maturation. Since God had to intervene to effect liberation in Christ, these systems of law must have been deficient in power and benevolence. In any case, the harsh and impersonal character Paul attributes to these conceptions of law is much less true than the Stoic conception of nature's mechanical inevitability.

Since the Great Mother was widely worshiped under different names in mystery cults, it will be useful to explain her popularity. Stoics believed that a divine sympathy existed between earth and the heavenly bodies, both of which were governed by the same laws of causality. Accordingly, Stoics equated these laws with divine providence and counseled people to accept life's vicissitudes and nature's disturbances as governed by a universal wisdom and necessity too complicated for ordinary humans to comprehend.

In contrast to the Stoics, Cynics and Epicureans considered nature's lawlike inevitability to be just as enslaving as human conventions. Thus, they encouraged people simply to adopt an attitude of tranquility in the face of such impersonal necessity. Ordinary people lacked the fortitude to face nature's powers in this way, however, and therefore many interpreted these forces as parental and beneficial.

We might consider the projection of human motherhood onto nature's fertility as faulty thinking. The natural care of mothers for offspring, however, surely derived from some intrinsic and higher reality in nature itself, which was so ordered that no creatures were abandoned by the powers that enliven and nurture them.[39] Consequently, many people believed that the power controlling the physical universe was female and maternal.

As people once looked to their mothers for comfort, so too they appealed to the Great Mother as a never-failing source of aid. She was a protectress of women in childbirth, and she was reputed to maintain hearth and home, marriage and family. She was also represented as Luna, Astarte, Hecate, and Kali, the source of mysterious and nocturnal passion, of orgy and jealousy. Thus, in the case of Cybele and her young consort, Attis, the Great Mother was both the all-demanding and the devouring mistress as well as the benevolent source of life.[40]

Susan Elliott describes the role of the mountain mother goddess, whether called Cybele or by another name, as guardian of the state. In this role, the Great Mother not only was identified with nature's powers of fertility but was also regarded as guardian of the temple and city-state. In the latter capacity, the goddess played a fundamentally social role in administering justice and in maintaining communal order.[41]

The goddess's role as guardian of the state was not confined to Asia Minor; she had a comparable identity in Rome and in the Hellenistic kingdoms.[42] Granted, the role of Athena as patron goddess of Athens was conceived very differently from the role of the Great Mother as a guardian goddess. Athena was essentially an extension of the state's male rationality. The same idea of the state was also dominant in Rome in the early republic, where there was no official place for the feminine powers

---

[39]Joscelyn Godwin makes such suggestions when describing the worship of Cybele in Asia Minor. She argues that "for as long as there are mothers and children, with all their attendant concerns, so long will devotion to the Great Mother Goddess continue, whether she is called Isis, Astarte, Cybele or Mary" (*Mystery Religions,* 114).

[40]See ibid., 110–12.

[41]Elliott, "Rhetorical Strategy." Part B, esp. chs. 3 and 4, treats the Great Mother goddess's role as guardian/protectress of the state.

[42]See ibid., ch. 4, in which, among other things, Elliott discusses the geographical breadth of the Great Mother's identity as a "guardian goddess."

associated with nature. Nonetheless, when the Romans imported the Great Mother goddess from Asia Minor in 205 BCE, the dour face of the republic began to be transformed. Later, at the beginning of the imperial period, the Great Mother's protecting and sustaining role was incorporated into Augustan ideology. Since Augustus discouraged worship of Asiatic deities, however, Cybele-like aspects of guardianship and fertility were transferred to such goddesses as Roma and Tellus.[43] Augustus regarded ecstatic cults, such as those of Isis and Cybele, incompatible with Roman state religion because they appealed to people as individuals and not as Roman citizens.[44]

The Great Mother was also incorporated into state religion in the Hellenistic kingdoms. The deification of Ptolemaic queens was indicative of the movement away from a warrior state mentality. Arsinoë II, the sister-wife of Ptolemy II Philadelphus, modeled her cult explicitly on Aphrodite rather than Hera, and she identified herself with Isis, the mother goddess of Egypt.[45] There are other examples of the attraction of the Great Mother goddess as a nourishing and protecting parent deity. It will be more useful at this point, however, to turn to another representative of fictive family values, the voluntary associations in the early imperial period.

---

[43]E.g., on the eastern end of the Altar of Peace, there are two goddesses, Roma (the Athena-like military guardian of the state) and a maternal divinity associated with fecundity and growth. Although the latter goddess is probably Tellus or Ceres (goddesses of fertility), scholars do not agree on her identity. The most plausible theories are that she is either Earth (Tellus or Ceres), Venus, or Peace. In Augustan iconography divinities no longer had the shape of precise mythical figures but represented values and strengths that drew on a multiplicity of attributes. See Bianchi, *Ara Pacis Augustae,* 22–23.

[44]See Zanker, *The Power of Images,* 109. The original temple of the Great Mother (Cybele), which was erected in 205 BCE on the Palatine, burned down in 3 CE. Although Augustus refers to his reconstruction of the temple, which lay near his house (see *Res gestae* 19), he did not rebuild it in marble but only in tufa (peperino), and he relegated the cult, with its ecstatic dances and longhaired priests *(galli),* to freedmen.

[45]Sarah Pomeroy explains the contrasting devotion to Athena in classical Athens and the veneration of Isis in Ptolemaic Egypt. Although biologically female, Athena was nonetheless the patroness of rationality (wisdom) and warfare. Moreover, as a virgin goddess, "rationally" born from the head of Zeus, she was an ideal representative of the commercial and warlike interests of Athens. Isis, by contrast, shared the vicissitudes of mortal women. She too was a wife and mother, who suffered the loss of her brother-husband. Accordingly, as protectress of seafarers, marriage, childbirth, and the hearth, Isis symbolized the Ptolemaic dynasty's attempt to provide solace to immigrating and deracinated Greeks. See Pomeroy, *Women in Hellenistic Egypt,* 28–40.

The Voluntary Societies as Surrogate Families. The primary form of convivial socializing for upper-class Greeks and Romans was the dinner party.[46] The importance of eating and drinking together is indicated by the literary use of the *symposium* ("drinking together") setting for moral discussions, revelation of character types, and academic disputations.[47] Such parties were hosted by the aristocracy, however; social dining for freedmen and poor freeborn was provided by trade guild meetings and by social or religious clubs.

Despite the popularity of voluntary clubs in the imperial period, officials suspected them of sedition. As noted in chapter 5, above, the state had a good basis for mistrust, for clubs of shopkeepers and craftsmen organized in Rome in the late republic to support political causes.[48] Like Julius Caesar, Augustus was concerned about voluntary clubs, especially the trade guilds.[49] Nonetheless, he also realized they provided members with an important form of status. Class divisions prohibited successful freedmen, and even poor freeborn, from holding civic offices. On the other hand, the guilds provided structures for granting and receiving honors roughly equivalent to those derived from public office.[50] Augustus took advantage of the aspirations of guild members by reorganizing

---

[46]The one thing required for all types of parties was wine. Indeed, the most important part of the evening for Greeks was the *symposion,* which followed eating. Romans paid greater attention to the food served at dinner. Although Roman writers argued that the emphasis on civilized pleasure and social harmony was what made the Roman dinner superior to the debauchery of Greek drinking parties, Roman upper-class dinners were not only more sumptuous but often equally as riotous and dissolute as those in Greece. Cicero says that the Latin term for dinner, *convivium,* means "co-living" and thus social harmony is what matters most in Roman dinner parties. By contrast, the Greek term *symposion* indicates only drinking together (see *Letters to Friends* 9.24). Regarding the greater emphasis on food in Roman dinner parties, see Fisher, "Roman Associations," 1199.

[47]See the discussion of the Roman use of the dinner party as a literary setting in Fisher, "Roman Associations," 1199.

[48]See ibid., 1209–10.

[49]Suetonius says Augustus, like Caesar, disbanded all guilds except those of long standing and those formed for legal purposes. See Suetonius, *Augustus* 32. Ostensibly, voluntary clubs were required to have either the senate or the emperor's approval, but many voluntary associations arose in the provinces, including Paul's churches, and they did not seek formal approval (see Fisher, "Roman Associations," 1221). Fisher questions the practice of classifying many *collegia* narrowly as burial clubs. He admits, however, that decent burial was a major reason for club membership (see ibid., 1221–23).

[50]See the comments by Kloppenborg, "Edwin Hatch," 221–22. See too the statement by MacMullen, *Roman Social Relations,* 77: "What is interesting about crafts associations for our purposes is the focussing of energies on the pursuit of

formerly subversive Roman clubs into state cults, which he linked to worship of the Lares, to the goddess Roma, and to his own genius.[51]

Likewise, in Italian cities and in the provinces, Augustus encouraged the formation of *Augustales, collegia* that performed ceremonies on the emperor's behalf. Like state cults in Rome, they provided freedmen the opportunity to achieve recognition.[52] The identity such offices provided was not the only reason people sought club membership. When they moved from the country to the city, or from one city to another, kinship ties and the network of relations provided by the village or city were no longer available. The longing for family and for conventional moorings still remained, however, and because clubs provided people with a surrogate family and community, they were one of the most visible features of urban life. Even trade guilds did not exist primarily for economic benefit, since members were employers rather than employees. Rather, they gave members the civiclike honors and offices that they desired but their social class prohibited them from having in city government.

Because of the relative equality within the voluntary clubs, there was less humiliation of the type suffered by guests of inferior status at aristocratic dinner parties. Despite the social harmony denoted by *convivium,* the Roman dinner party was sometimes anything but convivial. For example, Pliny the Younger attacked the "elegant economy" by which hosts differentiated levels of friends and relegated freedmen to an even lower level. Pliny says it would have been better to serve simple fare to all, and preserve the ideal of convivial equality, than to serve luxurious fare to the few.[53]

Although voluntary *collegia* could include a mixture of classes, Nicolas Fisher says that their fellowship usually did not embrace the

---

honor rather than on economic advantage. . . . Associations resembled the whole social context they found themselves in and imitated it as best they could."

[51]See Wallace-Hadrill's explanation of how Augustus created a structure by which tradesmen could develop a sense of self-respect and civic identity (*Augustan Rome,* 47–49).

[52]Freedmen were barred from holding office as magistrates and were not allowed to serve in any official capacity on town councils. From the emperor's vantage point, the *Augustales* encouraged political and social stability and enabled him to strengthen his position as the chief source of loyalty, devotion, and patronage. See Fisher, "Roman Associations," 1220.

[53]Pliny the Younger, *Ep.* 2.6. See Fisher's discussion of Pliny ("Roman Associations," 1217). Fisher illustrates in detail the humiliation inferior guests received (pp. 1210–19). Something like the differentiation of guests described by Pliny formed the basis of Paul's criticism of the way the "Lord's supper" was being celebrated at Corinth (see 1 Cor 11:17ff.).

lowest levels of society. Women could participate in *collegia,* but mostly as spouses of members or as benefactors and patrons. Trade guilds were generally more homogeneous and prosperous, and thus more restrictive.[54]

Inns and bars functioned as clubs for people who were either too poor or lacking in status to join *collegia.* Because barmaids often offered sexual services to customers, inns and bars were the locus of promiscuous forms of urban conviviality as well as the numerous brawls. See Fisher, "Roman Associations," 1223–24. Kloppenborg cites data, on the other hand, that shows the voluntary societies embraced people of greater diversity than Fisher suggests.[55] The more inclusive clubs were usually Roman *collegia,* however, rather than Greek clubs. Roman influence also accounts for the fuller participation of slaves and women in the associations. Along with being more inclusive, the Roman *collegia* used more family designations for members.[56]

Nonetheless, Kloppenborg rightly notes that the density of family language in Paul's letters, especially the use of the fraternal root ἀδελφ- ("brother") to describe the sibling relationship of members, exceeds what one finds in other *collegia.* Paul's proposal that Philemon should regard his slave Onesimus as a "beloved brother" is especially striking. Kloppenborg concludes:

> It is here that one might locate the appeal of Pauline churches: the fictive dissolution of the obstinately vertical character of Graeco-Roman social life through the creation of a "family" that transcended such boundaries.[57]

Despite the family imagery that characterizes Paul's letters, we can not assume that all of his churches were equally inclusive. He too was

---

[54]See the comments by Fisher, "Roman Associations," 1222–23. John Kloppenborg notes that because trades clustered in the same areas of the city, their guilds also de facto were confined to specific streets or neighborhoods ("Edwin Hatch," 234 n. 78). See also MacMullen, *Roman Social Relations,* 70–74.

[55]Kloppenborg cites data from Poland, *Geschichte,* a classic study of voluntary clubs, in support of this view. Poland's data shows that the *collegia* sometimes admitted slaves as well as freeborn women. See Kloppenborg, "Edwin Hatch," 234–35.

[56]See ibid., 216, 234–35.

[57]Ibid., 238. See Kloppenborg's reference to Bömer, *Untersuchungen,* 1:172–79, who found evidence of brotherhood language in voluntary clubs that were subject to Roman influence; the extension of fraternal language to slaves, however, was virtually unattested even in Roman associations. See also Wayne Meeks's suggestion that Paul's churches included a broader spectrum of social levels than the voluntary associations (*First Urban Christians,* 79).

obliged, to some extent, to work within the limits set by the contexts in which he founded communities. This will be discussed in chapter 8.

God's Identity as Father of the Family

Although Paul's images vary from one situation to another, all of his authentic letters agree that his Gentile converts are God's spiritual offspring. As God's representative and the founder of communities, Paul likewise refers to himself as his converts' father. The following examples (with italics added for emphasis) illustrate the family relationship with converts.

> We always give thanks to God for all of you and mention you in our prayers. . . . For we know, brothers and sisters *beloved by God,* that he has chosen you, because our message of the gospel came to you not in word only, but also in power and in the Holy Spirit and with full conviction. (1 Thess 1:2, 4–5)

> Therefore, *my beloved,* just as you have always obeyed me, not only in my presence, but much more now in my absence, work out your own salvation with fear and trembling; for it is God who is at work in you, enabling you both to will and to work for his good pleasure. Do all things without murmuring and arguing, so that you may be blameless and innocent, *children of God* without blemish in the midst of a crooked and perverse generation. (Phil 2:12–15)

> I am not writing this to make you ashamed, but to admonish you as my *beloved children.* For though you might have ten thousand guardians in Christ, you do not have many fathers. Indeed, in Christ Jesus I became your *father* through the gospel. (1 Cor 4:14–15)

> For all who are led by the Spirit of God are *children of God.* For you did not receive a spirit of slavery to fall back into fear, but you have received a spirit of adoption. When we cry, *"Abba! Father!"* it is that very Spirit bearing witness with our spirit that we are *children of God,* and if children, then heirs, heirs of God and joint heirs with Christ. (Rom 8:14–17)

The affectionate nature of the relationship between converts and God is especially evident in Rom 8:15 and in Gal 4:6, where God is addressed as "Abba." An even more telling index of the importance of God's spiritual paternity is the reference to God as "Father" at the beginning of every Pauline letter.[58] Similarly, Paul regularly addresses converts as

---

[58]God is referred to explicitly as "our Father" (i.e., the Father of Paul and his recipients) in Rom 1:7; 1 Cor 1:3; Gal 1:3; Phil 1:2; and Phlm 3. God is identified in an equally personal way in 2 Cor 1:3–4 (see below). Similarly, in 1 Thess 1:1–2, he is "God the Father" and "our God and Father."

siblings, "brothers and sisters," because he and they had the same spiritual parent.[59]

The following examples (with italics added for emphasis) illustrate God's relation to converts as Father and show they became offspring precisely by means of the creativity effected through their representative head, Christ:

> Paul, . . . set apart for . . . the gospel concerning his Son, who was . . . declared to be *Son of God with power* according to the spirit of holiness *by resurrection* from the dead, Jesus Christ our Lord, *through whom* we have received grace and apostleship to bring about the obedience of faith among all the Gentiles for the sake of his name, including *yourselves* who are *called to belong to Jesus Christ.* (Rom 1:1–6)

> To the church of God that is in Corinth, to *those* who are *sanctified in Christ Jesus,* . . . I give thanks to my God always for you because of the grace of God that has been given you in Christ Jesus, . . . God is faithful; by him you were called into *the fellowship of his Son,* Jesus Christ our Lord. (1 Cor 1:2, 4, 9)

> Blessed be *the God and Father of our Lord Jesus Christ,* the Father of mercies and *the God of all consolation, who consoles us in all our affliction* . . . For just as the sufferings of Christ are abundant for us, so also our consolation is abundant through Christ. (2 Cor 1:3–5)

Because Paul and his converts' status as spiritual offspring conformed to God's paradigmatic act of generating life out of Christ's death, Christ's special status as offspring is imaged as firstborn Son, Abraham's true seed and heir according to promise.[60]

The priority of Christ's status as Son, together with the manner in which subsequent progeny conform to his status as spiritual offspring, is a subject discussed more fully in chapter 7, below. To underscore the fundamental importance, to Paul, of God's identity as Father of his converts, our study here turns to how Paul applies the idea to specific epistolary contexts.

This chapter has reviewed Paul's application of God's paternity to converts in Thessalonica, although our focus was more on God's status as creator (i.e., universal Father) than on Father. Paul's picture of his own

---

[59]The designation occurs in Rom 1:13; 7:1; 10:1; 11:25; 12:1; 15:14, 30; 16:17; 1 Cor 1:10–11, 26; 2:1; 3:1; 4:6; 7:24, 29; 10:1; 11:3; 12:1; 14:6, 20; 15:1, 50; 16:15. The address occurs with comparable frequency in the remaining letters.

[60]Paul refers to Christ as "firstborn" Son or as "first fruit(s)" of the new creation in Rom 8:29; 11:16; 1 Cor 15:20, 23. He is characterized as Abraham's true seed/heir in Rom 8:17; Gal 3:16, 19, 29; 4:6–7.

experience of God's generativity, however, is equally important in the letter. For example, in 1 Thess 2:7 Paul says that he and his associates were like "babies" (νήπιοι) in the Thessalonians' midst.[61] Although Paul might be likening the Thessalonians' receptivity toward him to a mother's care of her infants, it is more likely he is underscoring his childlike dependence on God. Only a few verses later, Paul describes his distress at being separated from the Thessalonans as a state of being "orphaned" (2:17), and when Paul sent Timothy to strengthen the Thessalonians in their persecution, he says he was "abandoned" (3:1). The first image emphasizes Paul's sense of radical trust in God, and the latter two call attention to his sense of abandonment. Nonetheless, since Timothy returned to Paul with good news about the Thessalonians, Paul writes, "We now live" (3:8). By the contrast between the new life generated by news of the Thessalonians' faith and the former sense of being orphaned/abandoned, Paul indicates God's creative power as Father revived him.

A similar picture of God as Paul's caring and protective Father is found at the start of 2 Corinthians. Describing their affliction in Asia, Paul says that although he and his associates were so utterly crushed that they felt they had received the death sentence (2 Cor 1:8–9), the affliction served the purpose of causing him to rely on God, who was able to revive even the dead. Because God delivered Paul and his associates from their peril (1:10), it is not accidental that Paul praised God a few verses earlier as the "Father of our Lord Jesus Christ" and as the "Father of mercies and the God of all consolation, who consoles us in all our affliction" (1:3–4). Thus, Paul's experience of God's power over death led him to confess God's identity as Father.

A third example of Paul's own experience of God's beneficial and creative power as Father may be illustrated from the first chapter of Philippians. Despite being incarcerated at the time of writing, Paul says the proclamation of the gospel had not been detained. In fact, his imprisonment had advanced its progress (1:12). Moreover, so far as his own fate was concerned, he claims that God would deliver him, whether he lived or died (1:19–26). The repetitious expressions of confidence and joy in the opening chapters attest to Paul's experience of God's enlivening care even in the harshest of circumstances.

---

[61]As stated in ch. 2, above, "babies" has better manuscript support than "gentle," which is almost always preferred in English translations. See also Patte's explanation of the superiority of "babies" in 1 Thess 2:7 (*Paul's Faith,* 141–42).

We now turn to a different kind of illustration of Paul's idea of God as the personal Father of converts. In his letter to Philemon, in which he encourages Philemon to be kind to a runaway slave, Onesimus, Paul pushes to an extreme limit God's power to transform situations. For he argues that the spiritual sibling relationship between Philemon and Onesimus as Paul's offspring took precedence over their secular master-slave relationship.[62] Although Paul addresses Philemon as a beloved fellow worker and partner (Phlm 1, 17), he also reminds him that he was indebted to Paul for his spiritual life (v. 19) because Paul had fathered (converted) him. Moreover, because Paul was the common spiritual father of Philemon and Onesimus, the two men were, by implication, spiritual siblings. (That God was ultimately the father who made Philemon and Onesimus brothers is understood.)

Since the primary emphasis in Romans and Galatians is on God's character as Father of the race (the extended family), treatment of paternity in these two letters appears in the next section. Paul's picture of God as Father in 1 Corinthians is treated extensively in ch. 8, below.

God's Identity as Civic Founder and Father of the Race

God, the Father of a Spiritual ("Heavenly") City. Paul twice depicts the church as a civic body in his letters, as the heavenly Jerusalem in Gal 4:26 and as a heavenly form of government *(politeuma)* in Phil 3:20. In the Galatians reference, Paul contrasts the superiority of the Jerusalem above, of which Christ's people are citizens, with the slavery to which people obedient to the earthly Jerusalem's constitution (i.e., Mosaic law) are subject (see Gal 4:21–31). Similarly, in Philippians, converts who worship in God's Spirit are described as the true circumcision, whereas people who put confidence in literal circumcision are accused of barbaric practices (Phil 3:2ff.).

Near the end of Phil 3, Paul contrasts the glory of his converts, who engaged in Christ-like activities, with the pagan inhabitants of Philippi, who wasted themselves in subjection to destructive practices (see 3:18–19) and the pursuit of self-glory. Thus, Paul argues for the superior civic character of his converts on two fronts. On the one hand, converts were more truly God's race than people who placed a premium on ostentatious marks of race such as circumcision. For God's true people worshiped him in the Spirit and put no confidence in racial exter-

---

[62]Petersen, *Rediscovering Paul,* 204–16.

nalities. On the other hand, he warns against civiclike conceptions of the community *(politeuma)*, which could degenerate into competitive destructive pride.

In Philippians, Paul apparently used Jewish circumcision as a diversionary tactic to gain access to the real target, for converts probably found it easy to support Paul's caricature of circumcision as a barbaric mutilation. With the inferiority of empty externalities established as a principle, Paul could argue more easily against something analogous, the church's attraction to civiclike honors.

Paul spends so much of his letter encouraging the Philippians to be of "one spirit" and of "one mind" and not do anything from selfishness or conceit that he obviously feared some type of destructive and selfish ambition. Consequently, he advocates adherence to Christ (the community's Lord) as the authentic model of civic virtue (see 2:1–18). Christ was the best model of a communal benefactor precisely because he subjected his own status to the true source of authority (God) and on behalf of the common good (2:5–11). In turn, Paul shows how he too, in imitation of Christ, had given up Jewish status in deference to the nobler values that derive from God (3:3–11).

Although the idea of church as God's city appears to be less important to Paul than it later would be for Augustine, the above examples indicate that Paul could imagine converts in terms of civic structures as well as a family unit. On the other hand, we should not assume, merely because Paul was Jewish, that he was disinterested in Greek and Roman civic ideas. After all, Paul grew up speaking and writing Greek in an urban center. His education surely included not only the acquisition of popular philosophical views and rhetorical skills but exposure to Greek and Roman political ideas.

In any case, the political and family spheres may not be rigidly separated, since the individual household was the fundamental political unit of the classical city-state. At an earlier stage of development, the village or town arose out of the extended family or clan *(genos)* living in a specific place.[63] But whereas clan survival depended on the right to take vengeance on any outsider who caused injury to its members, a state's

---

[63]Weaker clans or families, which sought the protection provided by a stronger clan, were often "adopted" into another extended family. Accordingly, in their formative period, city-states were ruled by aristocratic families or tyrants, who were skilled in military prowess and who were usually of noble birth. See Lacey's discussion of the role of individual family *(oikos)* units and clans (extended family units) in the formation of Greek city-states in *Family*, 21–27.

survival depended on the defense of *all* its family units. Thus, in the city-state, one clan could not be allowed to execute unilateral vengeance on other clans. Accordingly, a code of laws had to be formulated and administered to which all clans were subject.[64] Similarly, the state could not allow a stronger unit within a clan to monopolize the land of weaker family units, because the state's security depended on the ongoing independence of each household. Accordingly, city-state laws were enacted to protect individual family rights against the clan, and eventually the city replaced the clan as the extended family to which families looked for protection and to which they owed various forms of loyalty. Thus, the state became father(land) and mother(land).[65] This idea is evident in imperial ideology, which represented the emperor as "Father of His Country."

The Image of God as Founder ("Father") of the Spiritual Race. Neither the idea of the city as family nor the idea of the city's founder as father was as attractive to Paul as the idea of God as the Father of the race. Paul talked about converts more often, and in greater detail, as Abraham's offspring than as citizens. Perhaps Paul's preference for the idea of Abraham as father of the race derived, at least in the case of Romans and Galatians, from the fact that he was addressing people for whom racial incorporation was important. The importance he attaches to the analogical relationship between Abraham and Christ, as father and Son, however, indicates that the image of God as Father of the race was more important to him than the idea of God as city founder. This preference might seem to arise simply from Paul's Jewish sensibilities. It is more likely, however, that the actual correspondences Paul found between the accursed Christ and the sterile Abraham (and Sarah) formed the basis of his preference for clan (extended family) over civic imagery.

In any case, the idea of the church as an ideal city is not in competition with, but is supportive of, Paul's image of it as God's race. This is especially clear in Gal 4:26, where Paul contrasts two constitutions (i.e., the earthly and the heavenly Jerusalems) through the images of two mothers, the slave and the freeborn woman (see 4:22ff.). Similarly,

---

[64]See Lacey's discussion of the evolution of government from judgment according to individual clan customs to the unifying rule of the constitutional law of city-states, ibid., 51–54.

[65]Ibid., 53–54, 73–74.

in Phil 3:2ff. Paul talks about civic and racial status in broadly analogous terms. In particular, when he addresses recipients as "brothers and sisters" (ἀδελφοί) several times and when he cites maturation and trust as indicative of his converts' relationship to God, he clearly has in mind family images as well as civic models.[66]

The idea of God as Father of the race comes to the fore in Rom 4 and Gal 3–4, where images of Jewish communal life dominate Paul's description of converts. The primary image of God's generation of a people/race for Paul is his depiction of Abraham as symbolic head. Paul's contrast of Abraham's progeny through the slave girl Hagar and through his freeborn wife, Sarah, in Gal 4:21–31 shows that physical descent from Abraham was not by itself a sufficient basis for being his promised (i.e., spiritual) heirs.

Paul's fellow Jews would certainly have agreed that not all physical descendants of Abraham were legitimate offspring and heirs, since descendants of Ishmael, the child of the slave girl, did not have such status. Unlike most fellow Jews, however, Paul did not base Ishmael's inferior status strictly on his legal position as offspring of a slave mother. Something far more substantial than Isaac's legal status, or Ishmael's lack of it, differentiated the two offspring of Abraham and their mothers.

Ishmael's inferior status derived simply from the physicality of his generation: he was procreated by Abraham and conceived by Hagar through ordinary means. Thus, "born according to the flesh" (4:23) does not connote some sexual impropriety on the part of Abraham or Hagar but merely generation by physical means. On the other hand, Isaac's birth "through the promise" in 4:23 connotes supernatural intervention as the source of generation. Consequently, the basis of Abraham's status as father of the race through impregnation of the barren Sarah corresponds to that on which he was originally chosen to father a noble race: the promise depended solely on Abraham's ability to trust God's power to effect such paternity. Thus, both the promise and its actualization derived from the same supernatural cause, God's generativity.

Accordingly, if any Jewish claim to be Abraham's authentic heirs and God's people was based primarily on physical descent from Abraham and/or on enhancement of that status by human achievement, it

---

[66]See Paul's address of recipients as ἀδελφοί in 3:1, 13, 17; 4:1. Paul's juxtaposition of athletic victory (βραβεῖον), a civic image, with development to full maturity ("perfection") in a moral and biological sense, both a civic and a family image, shows how family and civic development are analogous in his mind (see 3:12–15).

was ill-founded. With Abraham's promised paternity and Isaac's spiritual generation in mind, we turn here to Paul's view that Christ is Abraham's one true offspring of promise and to his explanation of how Gentile converts are Christ's authentic spiritual siblings.

In Gal 3:13–14 Paul connects to Christ's crucifixion God's promise to Abraham that Abraham would be a blessing to the Gentiles:

> Christ redeemed us from the curse of the law by becoming a curse for us— for it is written, "Cursed is everyone who hangs on a tree"—in order that in Christ Jesus the blessing of Abraham might come to the Gentiles, so that we might receive the promise of the Spirit through faith.

Although Paul gradually explains this statement in what follows and precedes in Gal 3 and 4, the connection between Christ and Abraham is not entirely explicit. One thing is clear, however: the Gentiles' status as Abraham's spiritual offspring derives from the fact that God vindicated the one who was convicted and executed ("cursed") by the law. Their status as Abraham's (God's) offspring is comparable to that of Christ. In some sense, Paul conceives of Christ's crucifixion as contributing to Christ's status as the heir that God had promised Abraham, that made Abraham both the father of a people and a blessing to the Gentiles.

Immediately before this statement, Paul contrasted the threat of Mosaic law with the promised blessing to Abraham (3:6–12). Then, immediately following the statement, in 3:15–18, he identifies Jesus explicitly as the promised offspring ("seed") of Abraham who effects such a blessing. How does Abraham and Christ's typological correspondence, as father and Son, differentiate them from adherents of Mosaic law? For one thing, Paul implies that Abraham and Christ had a common trust in God's trustworthiness rather than in their own ability to satisfy God's intention. But this is only part of the correspondence. More important is the similarity of what God effected out of an analogous, shameful sterility.

The key to Abraham's status as father and Christ's status as heir (promised offspring) lies in the fact that, in both cases, God effects procreation through divine means and not by natural causation. Christ's status as Son, as well as Abraham's status as father, is unnatural and unexpected. God makes the crucified one, who is in a state of sterility and who is potentially the agent of sterility to others, the "firstborn within a large family" (Rom 8:29; cf. 1 Cor 15:20, 23). Correspondingly, the impotent Abraham procreates, and the barren Sarah conceives, the promised offspring (see Gal 4:21–31; Rom 4:16–25).

But how did God's salvific action in Abraham and Sarah, illustrated by the generation of Isaac, and Christ's role as Abraham's authentic seed correspond? Paul saw a metaphorical correspondence between the resurrection God generated out of Christ's death and the fertility procreated out of Abraham and Sarah's sterility. Thus, in Rom 4:17ff. Paul describes God's reversal of Sarah's barrenness and Abraham's impotence under the image of Christ's resurrection: "who gives life to the dead and calls into existence the things that do not exist." In turn, because of Christ's accursed state under the law, Paul regarded his crucifixion as a form of sterility. Accordingly, under the image of Sarah's fertility and Abraham's empowerment, his resurrection was metaphorically the moment of birth as Abraham's promised seed, "the firstborn within a large family" (Rom 8:29) and "the first fruits" of the promised blessing (1 Cor 15:20, 23).

Like Christ, the Gentiles attained status as Abraham's promised offspring, not based on natural descent but derived from God's procreative response to their faith. Consequently, since their identity as offspring was unnatural and spiritually generated, Paul describes adoption as the authentic form of sonship.

> But when the fullness of time had come, God sent his Son, born of a woman, born under the law, in order to redeem those who were under the law, so that we might receive adoption as children. . . . So you are no longer a slave but a child, and if a child then also an heir, through God. (Gal 4:4–5, 7; cf. Rom 8:15, 23; 9:4)

CLOSING PROSPECTIVE

The fullness of time, which resulted in the adoption of Gentiles into Abraham's progeny, was facilitated by God's appointment of Christ to be the promised heir of Abraham and the head of a new spiritual household. Consequently, Jesus' appointment (birth) as Christ is not depicted under the image of an infant or minor but of an heir with full adult authority. Regarding his political authority as Lord, we may compare his status to that of the emperor Augustus, who was the adopted and divinized son with absolute authority to rule on God's behalf. Third, as head of God's family, Jesus was authorized to act in a priestly capacity on its behalf. Through the image of the church as God's temple, in which Christ is identified as the foundation, Paul indicates that God's benefits are mediated through baptism, the Lord's Supper, and other ritual acts.

Consequently, for Paul, Christ was Lord in at least three significant respects. The examination of these spheres of Christ's rule in chapter 7, below, will show why Paul regularly refers to Christ at the beginning of his letters as "the Lord Jesus Christ." Just as "God our Father" captures the essence of Paul's idea of God, so too "Christ the Lord" embodies his conception of Christ.

He would be led into darkness, and in darkness would remain; until in some incalculable time to come the hand of God would reach down and raise him up; he, John, who having lain in darkness would no longer be himself but some other man. He would have been changed, as they said, forever; sown in dishonor, he would be raised in honor; he would have been born again.

James Baldwin, *Go Tell It on the Mountain*

7

CHRIST THE LORD

A Modern Analogy for Paul's Picture of Christ as Son

In his novel *Go Tell It on the Mountain,* James Baldwin tells the story of John Grimes, an African-American boy who does not understand why his father hates him. Although more intelligent than his younger brother and far more obedient, John is less pleasing to his father. Through a series of flashbacks, Baldwin informs readers that John was not the natural son of Gabriel Grimes but was adopted while still an infant. John's natural father committed suicide before learning his girlfriend Elizabeth was pregnant. When Gabriel Grimes first met Elizabeth and her young son, he was several years older and his first wife had already died. He proposed marriage and promised to love Elizabeth and her little Johnny, but Gabriel did not live up to his promise. Instead, he began to exaggerate the fact that Elizabeth was not married when John was born. He regarded her son as a bastard and not as his own child.

Gabriel's bad feelings toward John were aggravated by the fact that years earlier he had a dream that God would give him an anointed son like David, who would be a savior for the black race. Since Gabriel and his first wife never were able to procreate offspring, he thought the child he had with Elizabeth, whom he named Royal, would be that son. When Roy grew up a headstrong delinquent, however, Gabriel began to fear that John would become God's promised son.

Baldwin's story mirrors the biblical emphasis on God's choice of unexpected people to be his agents. Beginning with Isaac and continuing with Jacob, Joseph, David, and Solomon, God exhibited his preference for younger siblings over their older brothers. Baldwin's story does not literally fit the biblical model, since John Grimes is the older son. Nonetheless, like Paul's, Baldwin's image of divine adoption calls attention to something more important than age as the index of God's choice. Both Baldwin and Paul were responding to the biblical idea that election was determined by God and not by any human claim to status.[1]

Just as spiritual adoption is a key image for Baldwin, so too for Paul the image is essential for understanding Jesus' sonship and status as Lord, first of all because of Jesus' ignoble death. From the vantage point of Pharisaic training and Paul's perspective prior to conversion, Paul knew that Jesus' execution as a criminal made the Christian proclamation of divine sonship inconceivable. The scandal was exacerbated by the hellenistic church's claim that the one accursed according to Moses' law was God's messianic Son. Like John Grimes, Jesus had been "sown in dishonor" and had no right to be named "Royal." Thus, Christ's status, like that of John Grimes, was something God had to effect by supernatural means.

Moreover, since Christ's anointing happened in maturity, in the manner of the Davidic Messiah, adoption was a good metaphor for his sonship. For adoption in antiquity did not occur when the adoptee was young but when he was old enough to become heir of the estate and able to take over household management duties for an older, childless couple.[2]

Christ, the Recipient of God's Political Power

Chapter 6, above, suggested that God's creative and ruling potencies were, for Philo, his most essential attributes.[3] It noted that Paul has the same double emphasis, but he refers to God's creative power primar-

---

[1] We ought not forget the women whom God used to effect his purpose, e.g., the prostitute who hid Joshua's spies, Deborah the judge, Ruth, Esther, etc. Nor is it accidental that characters with these names appear in Baldwin's novel.

[2] See the description of adoption in classical Greece by Lacey in *Family*, 24–25, 40, 85–86, 88–89, 92–93.

[3] See Philo, *Abr.* 121. Philo says that the titles corresponding to the creative and kingly powers are, respectively, θεός ("God") and κύριος ("Lord"). The Greek word for "God" derives from the verb τίθημι, which means "to make" or "to order" (i.e., "to create"). See *Conf.* 137, where Philo emphasizes this etymological

ily with the image of a father and indicates that God transferred his ruling potency to Christ. This transfer is signaled in the opening greetings of Paul's letters, where he always refers to Christ as "the *Lord* Jesus Christ." Philo also could apply Greco-Roman ruler motifs to biblical figures such as Joseph and Moses, but he presents their rule in a more derivative way than Paul pictures Christ's authority. Paul's view is closer to what Judaism projected for the Messiah and to pagan ideas about the emperor's authority.

Paul's idea of Christ differed both from the Greco-Roman ruler cult and from Jewish messianic ideology in one major respect: Jesus was not anointed Lord until after his resurrection.[4] Thus, Christ did not render benefactions during his earthly life but afterwards from the divine realm, like resurrected saviors in the mystery cults. Although early Roman emperors' full divinization was also achieved after death, they ruled only during their lifetime, and benefactions already performed were the basis of their apotheosis.[5]

Therefore, despite Paul's occasional reference to Christ's preexistence and a few appeals to his earthly commands, he indicates that Christ received the name above every name ("Lord") only after resurrection (see Phil 2:5–11). Nor was Paul the only early Christian to connect political lordship to resurrection.[6] Granted, New Testament

---

derivation of God from τίθημι. In turn, κύριος is the title of God's ruling potency because it conveys the Maker's inherent right to rule what he created. The same meaning of "Lord" as legitimate authority in *Abr.* 121 is also expressed in *Decal.* 176–177, where Philo says God was the cause of good only and nothing ill. Thus, out of goodness, God issued saving commandments (i.e., Moses' law). Again, in *Mut.* 12–15, Philo says God did not reveal his proper name to Moses and Jacob (see Exod 3:14; Gen 32:29) but revealed the name and capacity of "Lord," to express his authentic power as ruler of all.

[4]E.g., Paul pairs confession of Jesus' lordship with the belief that God raised him from the dead, in Rom 10:9. Paul states explicitly in Phil 2:6–11 (see esp. 2:9–11) that God gives the name of κύριος to Christ in response to the voluntary and mortal sufferings motivated by his obedience to God.

[5]In principle, Romans would not worship living emperors in the early empire, and various sources, including Augustus himself, say he refused to accept such veneration (at least from Romans). For all practical purposes, however, he was venerated during his lifetime, and several statements in his *Res gestae* indicate he thought his benefactions warranted such recognition. E.g., he notes that on fifty-five occasions the senate decreed that thanksgivings be offered to the gods on account of his successes on land and sea (*Res gestae* 4).

[6]E.g., at the end of the Pentecost speech in Acts 2:36, Peter said of Christ: "let the entire house of Israel know with certainty that God has made him both Lord and Messiah, this Jesus whom you crucified." The connection between

authors pushed Jesus' messianic appointment back to baptism, conception, and preexistence, but pride of place belongs to the resurrection as the pivotal point when Christ began his rule. Even if this might be disputed about other authors, it could hardly be contested about Paul. Thus, Paul's presentation of Jesus as political Lord proceeds from his assumption that resurrection was the point of Christ's divine anointing and empowerment.

Other Aspects of Christ's Lordship

So far, the emphasis has been on the political aspect of Christ's sonship. Paul indicated two other respects in which Christ was Son and Lord, however: his status as head of God's household and his role as priest (and sacrifice) on behalf of the family/community. These kinds of rule were attributed to Caesar and to Augustus by Suetonius. This is not unexpected, since the imperial cult regarded the three forms of lordship as related symbiotically to one other.

Although it is artificial to separate the different aspects of Christ's lordship, there are reasons for treating Christ's political authority separately here. Paul's picture of Christ as head of the house and priestly head of the cult appears later in this chapter.

CHRIST, LORD OF GOD'S EMPIRE

Reginald Fuller says that ruler cult ideology exerted little or no influence on the church's idea of Christ as Lord and that Paul used the title "Lord" to emphasize Christ's ethical authority.[7] By contrast, James Scott says that political lordship *was* important to Paul and that Paul's idea of Christ's rule was influenced by the picture of the Davidic Messiah in 2 Sam 7.[8]

exaltation and resurrection is stated explicitly a few verses earlier in 2:29–31 and, a second time, in 2:32–35. The integral relation of Jesus' suffering and resurrection to his lordship is often assumed without using the title "Lord" *(kyrios)*. Thus, the use of Ps 8:5–7 in Heb 2:5ff. makes it clear that it is Jesus, not humanity in general, who was crowned with glory and honor because of his suffering and death. The connection between lordship and resurrection is also assumed in Matt 28:18: "all authority in heaven and on earth has been given to me." See Werner Foerster's comments in Foerster and Quell, "Lord," 1086–95.

[7] See Fuller, "Lord."
[8] See Scott, *Adoption*, 227–58.

Although Scott emphasizes the political character of Christ's lordship, he agrees with Fuller that the pagan ruler cult did not exert any major influence on Paul.[9] Much of Scott's study is useful, but though Davidic messiahship may well have exerted an influence on Paul, it is not feasible to rule out the corresponding importance of Greco-Roman models. The ruler cult was described in chapters 4 and 5, above. Here three topics are discussed: the specific use of "Lord" as a title of beneficial and legitimate rule, the use of divine adoption to legitimate a ruler's reign, and Paul's idea of Christ's political sovereignty.

Apse mosaic of Santa Pudenziana showing Christ enthroned in Jupiter-like pose flanked by apostles in togas like Roman senators. Immediately to Christ's left is Paul being crowned by a female symbol of the Gentile church, to the right Peter being crowned by a female symbol of the Jewish church. In Christ's left hand is an open book with the inscription DOMINUS CONSERVATOR ECCLESIAE PUDENTIANE ("The Lord, protector of the Church of Pudenziana"). Santa Pudenziana, Rome. Photo courtesy of Alinari/Art Resource, N.Y.

[9]Although the word Paul uses to designate adoption, υἱοθεσία, *huiothesia*, is a Greek term and although it is not in the Septuagint or other Jewish sources of the period, Scott argues that Paul's conception of the term derives from an Old Testament meaning and not from the Greek institution of adoption. See ibid., 61.

Gods and Human Rulers as Lords

When Isocrates advised Alexander's father, Philip II, to rule Greece in a humane way, he was advocating precisely the kind of rule that came to be associated with *kyrios* as a title for the true ruler. Isocrates said that power alone was not enough to legitimize rule. Greeks certainly acknowledged the existence of dark, destructive forces, but these were not to be worshiped. Only civilizing powers were to be esteemed and imitated.[10]

Foerster's study of *kyrios* adds to Isocrates' view of beneficial rule by citing other ancient sources on the subject, and he illustrates the influence of such ideology on Judaism. Despite Foerster's biased advocacy of Jewish-Christian ideas of lordship, his review is useful.[11] For example, he notes that the idea of legitimacy was attached to *kyrios* from the Greek classical period onward.[12] As early as the fourth century BCE, the designation began to be used with two applications: (i) as lawful owner of a slave in the capacity of master in charge of a household, and (ii) as legal guardian of a female relative (wife, sister, etc.).[13] In both cases, lordship was applied to someone who governed others in an authorized capacity. By contrast, arbitrariness of rule was attached to *despotēs* ("master," "despot") as a designation; the *despotēs* had virtual possession of subjects.[14]

Although Foerster argues that *kyrios* was still not used by Greeks as an unqualified epithet for God in the hellenistic period, the Septuagint's translators consistently chose *kyrios* rather than *despotēs* as a title for God to indicate that his rule was legitimate as well as absolute.[15] Perhaps Greeks had some hesitation in using *kyrios* as a designation of absolute

---

[10]See Isocrates' political advice to Philip in *To Philip* 116–117.

[11]Foerster distinguishes between East and West, as well as between Judaism, as a special type of eastern culture, and Greco-Roman culture. He argues that Judaism's idea of God's lordship was superior to any other conception in East or West. See Foerster and Quell, "Lord," 1046–58.

[12]See ibid., 1041–46. Foerster notes that the noun ὁ κύριος was formed from the adjective κύριος, which means "having power" or, more precisely, "having legal power." Thus the adjective had such meanings as "lawful," "valid," and "authorized."

[13]See ibid., 1042–43.

[14]See ibid., 1042–45.

[15]For Judaism, Foerster says the choice of *kyrios* was based on the historical fact of Israel's election. The God who liberated Israel from Egyptian bondage had the right to rule its people. Moreover, the title was also based on the fact that, as the creator, God was the legitimate Lord of all things. See ibid., 1081–82.

rule, but they were more willing to use the epithet of rulers and gods than Foerster alleges. He himself shows they often used the term for gods of specific realms, and he cites a few authors who attributed unqualified lordship to deities. For example, Pindar referred to Zeus as "Zeus, who is lord of all" (see *Isthm.* 5, 53).[16]

In contrast to Foerster, Scott says that Greco-Roman and Jewish authors alike used the designation "the lord of all" both in the religious and in the political sphere as a technical title of universal sovereignty.[17]

Christ's Divine Adoption as Lord

In his study of divine sonship in Paul's letters, Scott notes that the usual translation of *huiothesia* as "sonship" is not accurate because the term always denoted "adoption as son" and never simply sonship. On the other hand, while deriving the meaning of *huiothesia* from ordinary usage and admitting the word was not found in the Septuagint or other Jewish literature of the period, Scott insists on interpreting Paul's use of the term against an Old Testament background.[18] Paul often has Jewish models in mind, but it is inconceivable that his idea of adoption was determined entirely by Jewish antecedants.

Scott describes the Greco-Roman setting of *huiothesia* as a technical term. After sketching the evolution of adoption as an institution in Greece and Rome, he proceeds to identify the traditional Greek verbs

---

[16]Foerster says gods were referred to as "lord" from the classical era onward (ibid., 1046–58), particularly in recognition of the gods' rule of specific realms. Thus, Dio Chrysostom (*Or.* 37.11) calls Poseidon and Helios, respectively, lords of water and fire.

Regarding Foerster's illustration of absolute rule, see Foerster and Quell, "Lord," 1047–48. E.g., describing the rational order, Plato says the idea of the good was the author of all things right and beautiful and the universal "lord" of the visible world (*Republic* 7.517C). Although Foerster says that early emperors such as Augustus would not allow themselves to be called *dominus* ("lord") in the absolute sense, he admits that Augustus's public protestations were only a cover for virtually absolute rule. In fact, the word "lord" slowly but surely established itself as a title for imperial rule (see Foerster and Quell, "Lord," 1054–55, 1081–82).

[17]See Scott, *Adoption,* 131–34. E.g., he notes that Plutarch referred to Zeus as "the Lord of all" (see *Moralia* 381D) and that Osiris's birth was announced with the words "the Lord of all advances to the light" (see *Moralia* 355E). Moreover, because Fate determined the victor in battle, Demosthenes referred to the god as "the Lord of all" (see Demosthenes, *Or.* 60.21; *Funeral Speech,* 21.7). See also Josephus, *Ant.* 13.172, where Josephus alleges that, for the Essenes, Fate was the "mistress of all things."

[18]See the summary statement of Scott's thesis in *Adoption,* 267–70.

and their cognates that designate adoption.[19] The noun *huiothesia* was added to other stock terms in the hellenistic period, and it became a common designation of adoption; it was used, for example, to refer to Octavian's adoption by Julius Caesar.[20]

Scott then argues against scholars who say the Old Testament lacked the institution of adoption and against those who allege Paul's idea of adoption had to derive from some other influence.[21] It would be hard to argue against Scott's view that Israel had some rudimentary idea of adoption. What was the specific idea of divine adoption in Judaism that influenced Paul? Scott says that in four of the five times Paul uses *huiothesia,* the idea is influenced by the messianic conception of adoption described in 2 Sam 7:14 (see Gal 4:5; Rom 8:15, 23; Eph 1:5).[22] The fifth usage assumes that Judaism's status as God's adopted offspring occurred as a result of liberation from Egyptian bondage (Rom 9:4; cf. Gal 4:1–2). Scott says the exodus image also underlies Paul's other four uses of adopted sonship.[23]

The key to Scott's idea of divine adoption in Paul is his interpretation of 2 Sam 7. He says it consists of three parts: (i) King David's conversation with Nathan about building a temple for the ark of God (7:1–3); (ii) God's reaction to David's proposal, mediated through an oracle to Nathan (7:4–17); (iii) and David's prayer in response to the oracle (7:18–29). David

---

[19]Scott identifies the following six Greek verbs, along with their cognates, as the regular means of designating adoption: εἰσποιεῖν, ἐκποιεῖν, τιθέσθαι, ποεῖσθαι, υἱοποιεῖσθαι, and υἱοθετεῖν. See Scott's survey of υἱοθεσία and the Greco-Roman institution of adoption, ibid., 3–57.

[20]One of the uses of υἱοθεσία cited by Scott is taken from Nicholas of Damascus, the court historian of Herod the Great, who uses the word to refer to the adoption of Octavian that Julius Caesar decreed in his will (see ibid., 53–55).

[21]Scott argues especially against H. Donner, who defined the institution of adoption too narrowly in terms of the Roman concept of paternal authority *(patria potestas).* Donner's artificial standard virtually eliminates the possibility of any comparative study of the institution of adoption because, according to Scott, even Attic εἰσποίησις ("adoption") did not assume the fully developed Roman conception of paternity. See ibid., 62–75.

[22]See ibid., 267–70. Scott notes that the only five occurrences of υἱοθεσία in the New Testament are all in the Pauline corpus (p. 175). Whether or not Paul wrote Ephesians, Scott argues that the use of "adoption" in Eph 1:5 is quite compatible with the four remaining uses of υἱοθεσία in Paul and is equally under Paul's theological influence. He also argues for the authenticity of 2 Cor 6:14–7:1, in which the divine adoption of 2 Sam 7:14 is cited explicitly (see 2 Cor 6:18; see also Scott's interpretation, pp. 187–200, of 2 Cor 6:14–7:1).

[23]See ibid., 269.

was concerned that whereas the ark of God sat in a portable tent, he himself dwelt in a cedar "house." God's oracle put David in his place, however, because God informed David that God alone was responsible for the mobile nature of God's dwelling, God alone had brought David to power, and God alone would establish David's dynasty. The dynasty's rise to power was part of a larger divine plan that began with the exodus (7:6), continued through the Judges (7:7, 11a) and culminated in peace under David himself (7:10–11a). Accordingly, the dynasty's permanence was subordinate to Israel's status as God's adopted people.[24]

Subordinating Davidic adoption to the exodus covenant previously ratified with Israel (see 7:14, 24) required the king's divine sonship to be understood in terms of "national adoption." The same idea occurs in Psalm 89 and is expressed in terms of primogeniture: the king was made "firstborn" (Ps 89:26–27) over the people from which he was chosen (v. 19).[25]

In the Greco-Roman period, according to Scott, Judaism applied the adoption formula of 2 Sam 7:14 eschatologically either to the Messiah (4QFlor I, 11), to Israel (*Jub.* 1.24), or to both (*T. Jud.* 24.3). The Messiah's adoption is understandable in light of the expectation that the monarchy would be revived after the exile. Subordination of Davidic adoption to national adoption in 2 Sam 7, however, made its application to eschatological Israel equally understandable. For adoption of the Messiah was conceived as a special election within the people, which expected Israel to share in the sonship. Scott says Jer 30:21–22 and Ezek 34:23–24; 37:24, 27, like 2 Sam 7, anticipated the connection between Messiah and Israel, for they described the restoration as simultaneously a reinstatement of God's fatherly relationship with Israel.[26]

Scott further demonstrates how Paul's idea of adoption was influenced by the connection between messianic and national adoption presented in 2 Sam 7. First, he shows that Paul's reference to adoption in Gal 4:5 draws upon the exodus idea of adoption. Just as Israel was redeemed from Egyptian slavery at the time appointed by the Father (4:1–2), so too Paul's converts were redeemed from subjection to the "elemental spirits of the world" and became heirs, like Israel, of the Abrahamic promise (4:3–7).[27]

Although neither Israel's adoption nor the exodus are cited explicitly in 4:1–7, Scott justifies the influence of exodus typology on Gal 4 because

---

[24]See Scott's explanation of 2 Sam 7, ibid., 96–104.
[25]See ibid., 99–101.
[26]See ibid., 104–17.
[27]See ibid., 267–70.

of the liberation theme and because explicit comparisons were drawn elsewhere between the Galatians and Israel. Moreover, in Rom 9:4, Paul refers
to Israel's sonship by adoption in a list of Israel's privileges that appear to
assume exodus as the point of adoption: "They are Israelites, and to them
belong the adoption, the glory, the covenants, the giving of the law."

In addition to the exodus typology already identified, Scott argues
that the broader context of Gal 3–4 makes it clear Paul's converts were
sons and heirs only insofar as they were incorporated through baptism
(3:27) into the sonship of Christ, who was sent to redeem them (4:4–5).
Thus, in the manner of 2 Sam 7:14, 24, Christ was the messianic Son and
heir of Abraham (Gal. 3:16), whose adoption encompassed God's whole
people. Paul was influenced not only by the belief that God would redeem Israel again but by the belief that God's adoption would be effected
by means of an eschatological Messiah (see *Jub.* 12.24; *T. Jud.* 24.3;
4QFlor I, 11). Indeed, Paul cites the adoption formula of 2 Sam 7:14 explicitly in 2 Cor. 6:18.[28]

Furthermore, Scott says that Gal 4:5–6 connects divine adoption
with the indwelling Spirit, refecting the influence of "New Covenant theology" (see Hos 2:18; Jer 31:31; Ezek 34:25; 37:23, 27). Thus, whereas the
idea of adoption in Gal 4:5 does not reflect Greco-Roman usage, Gal 3–4
does presume a Jewish understanding of divine adoption. The same New
Covenant emphasis applies to the two remaining uses of *huiothesia* in
Rom 8, where Paul also connects participation in the messianic Son with
reception of the indwelling Spirit (see Rom 8:15, 23). Scott says Rom 8,
like Gal 4:5, contains elements of exodus typology and adoptive sonship
with Christ in the Abrahamic promise (cf. Rom 8:17).[29]

Finally, Scott uses the influence of 2 Sam 7:14 on Paul to protest
the view that Rom 1:3b–4 originated as a pre-Pauline creed. Ordinarily
scholars call attention to the unusual vocabulary and style of Rom
1:3b–4, as well its non-Pauline theology: Paul nowhere else refers to
Jesus' Davidic descent, and the adoptionistic language of 1:4a suppos-
edly contradicts Paul's emphasis on the Son's preexistence. According to
Scott, however, arguments from vocabulary and style are too inconclu-
sive to prove the non-Pauline nature of Rom 1:3b–4. Furthermore, it is
inaccurate to say Jesus' Davidic descent played no role in Paul's letters,

---

[28]See Scott's summary statement on the Jewish context of Paul's use of divine adoption in Gal 4:5 (4:1–7) ibid., 267–68. An earlier, fuller treatment is found
on pp. 121–86.

[29]See ibid., 268–69, for a summary of Scott's interpretation of Rom 8. The
extended treatment is on pp. 221–66.

for Rom 15:12 shows that Jesus fulfills the messianic promise of Isa 11:10, since the passage refers to Jesus as the root of Jesse.[30]

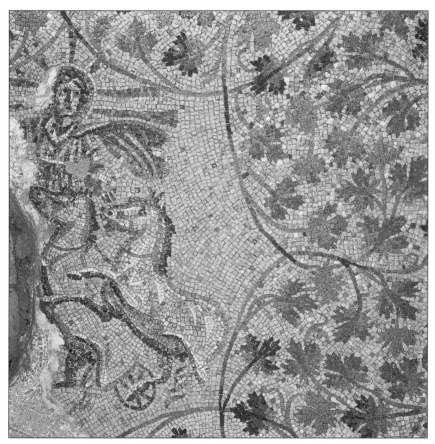

*Mosaic in cemetery under St. Peter's (Rome) picturing
Christ as Sol Invictus (sun god). Tomb of the Julii in
the necropolis under St. Peter's, Rome (Grotte Vaticane).
Photo courtesy of Scala/Art Resource, N.Y.*

Just as Jewish tradition expected the Abrahamic promise to be fulfilled in the Davidic Messiah, so too Paul's reference to Jesus as from the seed of David in Rom 1:3b presupposes the same promise-fulfillment relationship between the Abrahamic and Davidic promises of "seed." Likewise, when Paul argues in Gal 3:16 that Christ was the seed of Abraham,

---

[30]See ibid., 227–44, for Scott's interpretation of Rom 1:3b–4, which is summarized in this and the following paragraph.

he assumed Christ was David's seed. Thus, even if Paul does not refer explicitly to Jesus' Davidic sonship elsewhere, it plays a significant role in his theology.

Despite the valuable aspects of Scott's work, his emphasis on Davidic messiahship and the exodus covenant for understanding Paul comes up short. Evidence in the following section, much from Scott himself, indicates equal, if not greater, influence of pagan ideas of divine adoption on Paul's idea of Christ's identity as divine Son and Lord.

The armored statue of Augustus from the Villa of Livia at Prima Porta.
Photo courtesy of Alinari/Art Resource, N.Y.

Detail of cuirassed statue of Augustus illustrating his cosmic rule.
The sun god Sol appears in his chariot to the upper left on the
armor, the moon goddess Luna to the right, and between and
slightly above them Caelus spreads out the canopy of heaven.
Vatican Museums. Photo courtesy of Alinari/Art Resource, N.Y.

Ruler Cult Ideology and Paul's Idea of Christ's Lordship

Scott's interpretation of Jewish influence on Paul's idea of adoption is vulnerable to attack on several fronts. First of all, Davidic sonship and exodus typology, which are nationalistic, ran counter to Paul's identity as the apostle to the Gentiles. Even if we were to admit Davidic sonship and exodus typology as influences, these are not the primary themes in Paul's depiction of Christ's lordship.

Scott admits that Paul refers explicitly to Christ's Davidic sonship only in Rom 1:3–4 and 15:12. It is important, as scholars have long noted, that advocacy of Christ's political authority in Davidic terms appears only in Romans, written to a church Paul did not found and one for which a nationalistic idea of Christ was still viable. Even in this case, Paul stretches the model closer to his own idea of universality by citing scriptural references in 15:9–12 that emphasize God's inclusion of Gentiles:

> "Therefore I will confess you among the Gentiles, and sing praises to your name"; and again he says, "Rejoice, O Gentiles, with his people"; and again, "Praise the Lord, all you Gentiles, and let all the peoples praise him"; and again Isaiah says, "The root of Jesse shall come, the one who rises to rule the Gentiles; in him the Gentiles shall hope."

Even if Paul were the author of Rom 1:3–4, Scott must admit that Davidic descent does not fit his own emphasis on adoption as the key to Paul's idea of lordship. In addition, although he admits that, apart from 9:4, exodus imagery is implied and not stated, he nonetheless says Paul assumed exodus-like adoption whenever he referred to *huiothesia*. The suspect nature of this thesis may be illustrated by Gal 4:1–2, where Scott derives correspondence with the exodus from the fact that Paul talks about the Galatians' subjection to "elemental spirits of the world" (i.e., fertility and/or astrological deities). Since Paul refers simply to slavery, we can not assume he had the specific antecedent of Egyptian slavery in mind.

Paul emphasizes exodus typology very little more than Davidic imagery. It certainly is not the basis of his idea of God. Even if we were to find it was important for Paul, it would still be the case that, like Second Isaiah, he used the imagery in the service of God's universal creativity and not as a means of underscoring ethnic identity. Despite the limited use of Davidic and national (ethnic) adoption for understanding Paul, Scott's work is valuable. This is so not only because of his description of the Greco-Roman institution of adoption, or even because of the likelihood of some Davidic influence on Paul's idea of Christ, but because he identifies ideas about divine adoption in hellenistic Judaism that are compatible with Paul's understanding of Christ's lordship.

Specifically, Scott calls attention to Philo's image of Abraham as "nobly born" by divine adoption in *Sobr.* 56.[31] He also notes that Philo's

---

[31]Ibid., 88–96.

idea of God as Father-Creator and Abraham as prototypical proselyte are firmly rooted in Judaism.[32] This strand of Jewish tradition is certainly more compatible with Paul's universalism than are Davidic imagery and the exodus. The Abrahamic tradition had far greater potential for universal appeal and for a sympathetic relation to the Gentile world than either the Davidic or exodus covenant traditions, for the Old Testament tradition that Abraham would father a nation also contained the promise that all families of the earth would be blessed through him. Moreover, Abraham belonged to a mythical past, prior to the period when Jewish identity was sharpened by the constitutionality of Mosaic law. Most important, as founder of the Jewish race and as someone who had to break traditional ties to father a new people, Abraham was not himself a Jew or an adherent of prescribed Jewish practices. His identity had to be given to him by God.

Thus, it is hardly accidental that Philo and many Jewish authors said Abraham was "adopted" as God's son. Since Abraham himself was a proselyte, he functioned as a model for other would-be proselytes. Leaving family and homeland were potent symbols, even if not taken literally. The radicality of Abraham's break with his previous identity and the single-mindedness with which he turned to the one true Father made him the standard for all who aspired to nobility. As one devoted to the true Father of all, he may be described as having received from God the status of "only son," the gift of "universal sovereignty," and the civic title of "sole freeman."[33]

John Collins, in his study of Judaism in the hellenistic and imperial periods, also calls attention to the universalist tendency associated with Abraham.[34] One of the reasons Jewish authors regarded Abraham as cosmopolitan was the mobility the biblical tradition attributes to him. He had

---

[32]E.g., the emphasis on God as Father-Creator is found in Deut 32:6; Isa 43:6–7; 64:8; Jer 3:19; and Mal 2:10. The idea of Abraham as prototypical proselyte is common in Judaism, according to Scott; e.g., the ideas of Abraham as the first human to turn from polytheism to monotheism and of God as universal Father-Creator are combined in *Jub.* 11–22. See Scott, *Adoption,* 94.

[33]See Philo, *Sobr.* 56–57. See also *Abr.* 75; *Virt.* 219.

[34]See Collins, *Between Athens and Jerusalem.* Regarding the figure of Abraham in Jewish Diaspora authors of the hellenistic period, see pp. 35–46 (esp. 41–42). Regarding the reference to Abraham in Diaspora authors of the Roman period, see 204–7. At one point, while reviewing the work of Eupolemus, Collins notes that the Jewish ideals were the popular ideals of the hellenistic world. Jewish culture aspired to be first in everything beneficial to humanity. Although the primacy of Jewish identity was not abandoned, it was reconceived in terms of the common enterprise.

come from Chaldea and had lived among the Phoenicians and the Egyptians. Moreover, unlike Moses, he was not associated with ethnic law.[35]

Another aspect of Scott's study of divine adoption that is appropriate for Paul's idea of Christ's lordship is his description of Judaism's interest in Alexander the Great. It might seem incongruous to acknowledge, on the one hand, that all humanity was created by God and then to state, on the other hand, as Philo did, that Abraham was divinely "adopted." Divine adoption seems to contradict the idea of all humanity as God's offspring. Nonetheless, ancient tradition reports that Alexander had such a two-stage idea of sonship. Although Zeus was the common father of humanity, he made the noble particularly his own. This parallel with Judaism's idea of God as humanity's creator and yet as the Father who adopted Abraham is not accidental, for Judaism had a profound interest in Alexander, to the point of portraying him as a proselyte.[36]

Despite the alleged influence of the Alexander tradition on Judaism, Scott pulls back from allowing it, or the general pagan idea of the ruler's divine adoption, to have influenced Paul. Whether or not the Alexander tradition influenced Paul directly, it is likely the idea of the ruler as benefactor and savior, as well as the resultant image of the ruler as the duly authorized and adopted son of God, did influence him. Scott rightly notes the importance of divine adoption in Paul's picture of Jesus as Lord, and it is likely that the idea of the Davidic Messiah's divine anointing (adoption) influenced Paul, but it is striking that Scott denies the imperial cult's emphasis on divine adoption as an influence.

The Julio-Claudian line of emperors was literally adopted and Octavian legitimated his right to rule by explicitly appealing to his adopted status as *Imperator Caesar divi filius*, "Caesar, Commander, Son of the Divine." Moreover, as noted in chapter 5, above, by dropping Julius from the patronymic, Octavian implied he was son of God in an absolute sense and not just son of the deified Julius. The finishing touch was put on his public image when, after he received the honorary name of Augustus in 27 BCE, Octavian's full title became *Imperator Caesar divi filius Augustus*.[37]

---

[35]See ibid., 42.

[36]Although Judaism denied Alexander's claim to be the adopted son of Ammon-Zeus, Scott says his concept of divine adoptive sonship provides a hellenistic background for understanding Philo's picture of Abraham's status as God's adopted son in *Sobr.* 56. See Scott, *Adoption*, 16–18, 92, 95–96.

[37]See Zanker's illustration of Octavian's portrait and inscription on coins in *The Power of Images*, 33–37. See also Wallace-Hadrill's comments on Octavian's titles in *Augustan Rome*, 85–86.

The exchange between Jesus and the authorities reported in Mark 12:13ff., where Jesus asks to see a denarius, illustrates the breadth of familiarity with the emperor's public image. Jesus asks not only about the identity of the head on the coin but about its inscription. If the gospel authors knew about the emperor's likeness and title, Paul also knew about his status as the adopted son of God. For the emperor's image and title not only circulated on money but were displayed in portrait and relief sculptures in cult temples and on civic buildings. It is difficult to believe that Paul would have failed to take advantage of the emperor's image for his picture of Christ.

Although Paul never refers explicitly to the emperor's public image, several descriptions of Christ as Lord draw on imperial ideology. Thus, despite Paul's emphasis on Christ's humiliating submission to God, he pictures his victorious future return in 1 Thess 4:16 as the universal military ruler, like Augustus. Nor should we overlook the political nature of the hymn in Phil 2:5–11, for the name above every name that Jesus receives at his divinely adopted elevation is the title of absolute "Lord." The image of universal prostration required of subjects underscores his role as imperial ruler. He is the divine agent who can "make all things subject to himself" (Phil 3:21).

Christ's universal sovereignty is expressed as explicitly in 1 Cor 15:21–26 as in Phil 2:5–11:

> For since death came through a human being, the resurrection of the dead has also come through a human being; for as all die in Adam, so all will be made alive in Christ. But each in his own order: Christ the first fruits, then at his coming those who belong to Christ. Then comes the end, when he hands over the kingdom to God the Father, after he has destroyed every ruler and every authority and power. For he must reign until he has put all his enemies under his feet. The last enemy to be destroyed is death.

The picture of Christ as the second Adam is an even more universal image than the figure of Abraham, described as the father of all peoples (see Rom 4:16–17; Gal 3:13–14). The idea of Christ as the ruler of a new human beginning is sustained in 1 Cor 15:45–57, where, as the heavenly man, he is contrasted with the first Adam, a man of the dust. Paul announces that "flesh and blood" (i.e., the first Adam's offspring) cannot inherit God's empire.

The Adam metaphor appears again in Rom 5:12–21, where Paul emphasizes the political dimension of the image by characterizing the two Adams as types of reigning influences. The first Adam's selfish disobedience is described as resulting in a deathly tyranny. By contrast, the second Adam's obedience to God and benefaction ("free gift") for humanity constitutes a vivifying reign that leads to universal acquital and a just order. Both Rom 5:12–21 and 1 Cor 15:21–57 describe Christ's reign as effecting imperishable life.[38]

Consequently, Paul describes Christ's authority not only as absolute but also as beneficial. Like that of the ideal rulers described in chapters 4 and 5, above, Christ's warfare was of an enlightened, civilizing kind. Thus, in Gal 3:13–14, Paul says Christ liberates people from servitude to the law and simultaneously grants the benefits of freeborn inheritance promised to Abraham. Moreover, in Gal 3:28, the racial differentiation of Jew and Greek, the different social levels of slave and free, and the gender differentation of male and female are no longer indices of status under Christ's rule.[39]

Christ establishes God's just new order not by means of a code inscribed on stone but by means of his Spirit written on his subjects' hearts (2 Cor 3:1–3, 7–11; cf. Rom 3:21 ff.). Granted, the new order had constitutional principles. Paul could refer to it as "faith working through love" (Gal 5:6), because Christ's rule was concerned with the common good: "Bear one another's burdens, and in this way you will fulfill the law of Christ" (6:2). Nobility was determined by one's trust that, through Christ, God could actualize true status. Thus, like their ruler, the true citizens did not look to fellow citizens for honor and status but to God alone. For Christ's status, like that of Abraham, was based on trust in God's power as creator to make something of one's life. Like Abraham, Christ looked to the God "who gives life to the dead and calls into existence the things that do not exist" (Rom 4:17; cf. 4:13–25).

Strictly speaking, however, we have moved away from the emphasis on Christ as universal sovereign and into a description of the quality of his rule and his role as moral examplar. The same combination of political rule and priestly-moral authority is characteristic of

---

[38]1 Cor. 15:54–57 captures the radicality of Christ's victory with the following exclamation of praise:

> When this perishable body puts on imperishability, and this mortal body puts on immortality, then the saying that is written will be fulfilled: "Death has been swallowed up in victory." "Where, O death, is your victory? Where, O death, is your sting?" The sting of death is sin, and the power of sin is the law. But thanks be to God, who gives us the victory through our Lord Jesus Christ.

[39]Old constitutional standards, whether it be circumcision or uncircumcision, no longer differentiated people or counted for anything in the new order. All that now counted was the state of belonging to the "new creation" (Gal 5:6; 6:15).

Augustus's public image as ruler. These aspects of Christ's lordship are discussed next.

CHRIST, HEAD OF THE HOUSE AND PRIESTLY LORD

The rule of a household and the priestly supervision of a cult each had its identity in antiquity, and yet the two spheres of authority could have the same person as head. For instance, the head of the family presided over priestly duties in the home. Moreover, as noted in chapter 4, above, Greeks began to conceive of rulers as governing the state like a father caring for his family and estate.

Regarding this combination of political and family authority, David Verner says that political theorists had used the household code for centuries as a model of political order. Since the family was the foundational unit of the state, household management was a matter of political importance.[40] This importance is clearly exhibited in the ideological framework, as well as the terminology, of the Ptolemaic state. Egypt was conceptualized as the king's estate *(oikos)*, and household terms were used for the state's officials: the *dioikētēs* was financial "manager" of the whole estate; the *hypodioikētēs* was a "submanager" who supervised a cluster of administrative districts; and the *oikonomos* was the steward of the individual district.[41] Elliott shows that the household was equally useful for the Roman Empire, since the emperor exploited the emotional authority of the father (the *patria potestas*) and was called "Father of His Country."[42]

Roman emperors appropriated even more of the father's identity than Greek rulers by incorporating priestly responsibilities into their fatherly duties on behalf of the imperial household. Since Paul pictures Christ in all three spheres of authority as that of the emperor—political leader, beneficial head of the communal family, and priestly Lord—it is likely his idea of Christ as Lord was formed in dialogue with the emperor's public image.

---

[40]See Verner, *Household,* 7–8, 20–23. See also Balch, *Wives,* 49ff. Balch suggests that the political topos of houshold management was used as early as Plato and Aristotle and continued to be used by political theorists until the fourth century CE. In addition to Plato and Aristotle, Arius Didymus and Dionysius of Halicarnassus are identified by Balch as ancient authors who used the household management code in political discussions.

[41]See Rostovtzeff, *History,* 2:278.

[42]See Elliott, *A Home for the Homeless,* 170–82.

The aureus coin of Octavian illustrating the temple of the divinized Julius, whose apotheosis is symbolized by the star in the temple's pediment. Photo courtesy of Snark/Art Resource, N.Y.

The Emperor as Head of the Household

The Roman conception of the emperor as fatherly head of the state can be illustrated by Suetonius's *Lives of the Caesars*.[43] Although Caesar and Augustus had different visions of empire, Suetonius shows they both were concerned about the collective welfare of their subjects.

In the case of Caesar, Suetonius lists reforms in Rome that reflect his paternal concern for the state, including a more equitable form of justice that bridled the legal advantages of the rich. Caesar also reduced

---

[43]Suetonius (born about 69 CE) composed biographies of the twelve Caesars from Julius Caesar to Domitian. He wrote with a relatively high degree of objectivity, and because he was an official at the imperial court, he had access to the Caesars' public and private records. Unfortunately, Suetonius's citation of documentary material is practically nonexistent after his biography of Augustus, so it is assumed he was dismissed from his post and lost access to the imperial archives shortly after writing the life of Augustus.

the unwieldly body of statutes in the Civil Code.[44] Moreover, at the time of his assassination, he was planning several public projects in Rome: the biggest temple of Mars in the world, an enormous theatre, the establishment of public libraries, the reduction of the Civil Code to manageable proportions, and the draining of the Pomptine Marshes and Lake Fucinus. Elsewhere in Italy and in the provinces he was planning a highway that would run from the Adriatic across the Apennines to the Tiber, and he planned to cut a canal through the Isthmus of Corinth.[45]

Suetonius says that, despite several personal vices, Caesar had many extraordinary social virtues, not the least of which was his genuine dedication to dependents.[46] Nor did Caesar limit his care of citizens to the higher social classes, since he had a more egalitarian and utopian vision of the empire than his patrician peers.

According to Suetonius, Caesar modeled his political rule on an enlarged idea of household management, since he chose "Father of His Country" as the title to convey his role in the state.[47] In the Roman system of patronage, however, this and like titles were both presumptuous and threatening to republican values, for Caesar presumed to take to himself the honor of patron in such a singular and universal way that he exceeded what was appropriate. Thus, despite the positive values that Suetonius attributes to Caesar, he concludes that he deserved assassination (see *Julius* 76–79).

Nonetheless, Suetonius acknowledges that the public declaration of Caesar's deification after his death was more than a merely official decree, since it reflected public conviction. His apotheosis was confirmed by the appearance of a comet that shone for seven days running. This star was believed to be Caesar's soul, elevated to heaven (see *Julius* 88).

---

[44]See Suetonius, *Julius* 43–44. Suetonius says Caesar was also concerned with subjects outside Rome, rendering assistance to the principal cities of Italy and the provinces and aid to subject kings and provincial authorities (see ibid., 27–28).

[45]See ibid., 44.

[46]Suetonius says that Caesar was accused of the following vices: homosexual relations with the king of Bithynia, numerous affairs with women in Rome and the provinces, and incompetence in money matters (see ibid., 48–54). Despite these personal vices, Caesar had amazing endurance as a soldier and was a brilliant military strategist (see ibid., 57–70). Suetonius's description of the loyalty of Caesar's soldiers and, in turn, his devotion toward them is especially striking (e.g., see ibid., 67).

[47]See ibid., 76. Regarding Caesar's management of his household as a model of behavior, Suetonius reports that Caesar once put his baker in irons for giving him a superior bread than what was served to guests and that he executed a favorite freedman for committing adultery with a knight's wife (see ibid., 48).

In contrast to Caesar, who treated dependents with relative equality despite humble or foreign birth and who scorned republican customs favoring the upper classes, Augustus restored the traditions governing status. Whereas Caesar aspired to create a more egalitarian empire in the manner of Alexander, Augustus glorified Rome as the head of the empire.

Although Caesar intended greater social equality in the empire than Augustus was willing to grant, Augustus acted generously toward all classes, and while setting Rome's affairs in order, he also attended to the welfare of Italy and the provinces.[48] The following statement illustrates his desire to establish the state on a solid foundation:

> May it be my privilege to establish the state in a firm and secure position, and reap from that act the fruit . . . I desire; but only if I may be called the author of the best possible government, and bear with me the hope when I die that the foundations which I have laid for the state will remain unshaken. (Suetonius, *Augustus* 28)

Augustus enacted many reforms to establish social concord and order, starting with the army. He instituted a stricter discipline than Caesar, but to ensure that solders were properly rewarded for service, he established a new army treasury to pay their wages and pensions. He standardized pay and allowances by rank; he stationed the army and fleet around the empire to tactical advantage; and he deployed some soldiers as city police.[49]

Augustus increased the number of citizens in Italy by establishing twenty-eight new colonies, many of which he furnished with public buildings and revenues. In addition to receiving Latin rights (a limited citizenship for Italians outside Rome), the cities were given rights approaching those at Rome by means of a system whereby local senates could send votes to Rome for Roman elections (Suetonius, *Augustus* 46).

---

[48]Regarding Augustus's care of the various classes of Roman society, see Suetonius, *Augustus* 41. Regarding his attention to the larger population of Italy, see ibid., 46. Regarding his care for the provinces and foreign kingdoms, see ibid., 47–48.

[49]Regarding Augustus's discipline: he dismissed the Tenth Legion in disgrace because of insubordination; when cohorts gave way in battle, every tenth man in the unit was executed and the rest given inferior rations; when centurions left their posts, they were executed. After the civil wars, Augustus no longer called soldiers "comrades" but only "soldiers" because the former term was too flattering for purposes of discipline (ibid., 24–25). For the emperor's formation of an army treasury to handle the upkeep of the military establishment and for pensioning veterans, see ibid., 49. See the same section for a description of the way Augustus stationed his fleet and army around the empire.

Augustus enacted similar reforms in the provinces. Rebellious cities, such as Alexandria, were deprived of their right of self-governance, but cities destroyed by earthquake were rebuilt, others overwhelmed by debt were given financial relief, and still others that had rendered service to Rome were given Latin rights. Suetonius sums up Augustus's rule of the provincial cities and kingdoms by saying that he never failed to treat them all as integral parts of the empire (*Augustus* 47–48).

As a moral exemplar, Augustus expected as much of his own family as he required of the state. Accordingly, when he found his daughter, Julia, and a granddaughter by the same name guilty of sexual improprieties, he banished them from Rome. Likewise, he disowned Agrippa, a grandson whom he had adopted, because of his low tastes and violent temper. He referred to the two Julias and Agrippa as his "three boils."[50] Augustus's personal role as family head could be as gracious as it was strict. In addition to holding his freedmen in esteem, he merely put a slave, Cosmus, in irons who spoke about him in an insulting way, and he simply joked about a steward who hid behind him when they were charged by a wild boar.[51]

Concerning Augustus's receipt of the title "Father of His Country," it was precisely the adoption of this kind of honor as universal patron that led to Caesar's assassination. Why would Rome give to Augustus the very title it despised in Caesar? Unlike Caesar, Augustus did not take the title for himself, and more important, it was given to him only near the end of his career, after he had already rendered decades of service to the state.

Chapter 5, above, suggested that, following the defeat of Antony in 31 BCE, Augustus opposed any public image that glorified himself rather than the state. He himself states that he refused the title of "Dictator" and "would not accept any office inconsistent with the custom of our ancestors" (Augustus, *Res gestae* 5–6). Suetonius says he shrank from the title of "Lord" *(dominus)* and once, when the people did their best to force the dictatorship on him, he threw off his toga and with bare breast

---

[50]See Suetonius, *Augustus* 61–65. Suetonius records that Augustus forced a favorite freedman to take his own life because he was convicted of adultery with Roman matrons and that he broke the legs of his secretary, who had taken five hundred denarii for betraying the contents of a letter (ibid., 67).

[51]Suetonius says Augustus had temperate and simple tastes in almost everything. E.g., there was a simplicity in his furniture and household goods. He was a light eater of plain foods and a light drinker of wine (see ibid., 70–72). Despite Augustus's disciplined rule of his household, as well as his temperate tastes, he had a weakness for sexual improprieties and gambling (see ibid., 67).

begged them not to insist. Although temples could be dedicated even to proconsuls, Augustus would not accept such honors in the provinces unless they were dedicated jointly to himself and to Rome.[52]

Although he would not accept authority in the arbitrary mode of the despot, or immodestly like the master of a slave, it is nonetheless clear, both in Suetonius's biography and in Augustus's own will, that the absolute sovereignty and honor of the state belonged to him. But to show he desired public welfare rather than self-glory or personal popularity, Suetonius says that when the populace complained about the scarcity and high price of wine, Augustus rebuked them by saying, "My son-in-law Agrippa has taken good care, by building several aqueducts, that men shall not go thirsty" (*Augustus* 52).

Augustus's admirable character is evident in the freedom of speech he granted Roman citizens, even to the extent of bearing insults and lampoons against himself. Although he sometimes replied publicly to spiteful jests, he nonetheless vetoed a law that would have checked freedom of speech in Roman wills.[53]

Because of his public modesty and service to the state, Augustus was honored on multiple occasions.[54] Following the enumeration of such honors, Suetonius identifies the title "Father of His country," as the ultimate recogntion the state conferred on Augustus:

---

[52]As suggested earlier in this chapter, the title of "Lord" (whether κύριος or *dominus*) was understood as designating a master-slave relationship. Tiberius, as well as Augustus, shrank from the title (see Suetonius, *Tiberius* 27). *Dominus* was first adopted by Caligula and Domitian. From Trajan onward it was used in the sense of "Lord" or "Sire." According to Suetonius (*Augustus* 53), when the words "O just and gracious Lord!" were spoken at a farce Augustus attended, all sprang to their feet and applauded as if they were said of him. Suetonius says that Augustus checked their flattery and on the following day reproved them in an edict. Regarding Augustus's refusal to accept the title of "Dictator" and his unwillingness to accept worship dedicated only to himself, see ibid., 52.

[53]See Suetonius, *Augustus* 54–56. Regarding the proposed law that would have checked freedom of speech, J. C. Rolfe (Suetonius, 1:210, note b) notes that Romans often expressed their opinion about public men and affairs in their wills (see *Augustus* 56). In particular, he notes that in Dio Cassius (58.25) it is said that Fulcinius Trio spoke bitterly about Tiberius in his will.

[54]E.g., Suetonius said Augustus was honored by numerous senatorial decrees and by an annual two-day celebration of his birthday by the equestrian order. The populace brought yearly New Year's gifts to Augustus at the capital and, in fulfilment of a vow for his welfare, threw small coins into the Lacus Curtius (see *Augustus* 57). Augustus himself stated in *Res gestae* 4 that on fifty-five occasions the Senate decreed that thanksgivings should be offered to the gods because of his own and his legates' military victories on land and sea.

He [Valerius Messala], speaking for the whole body, said: "Good fortune . . . Augustus; for thus we feel that we are praying for lasting prosperity for our country and happiness for our city. The senate in accord with the people of Rome hails thee Father of thy Country." Then Augustus with tears in his eyes replied as follows . . . : "Having attained my highest hopes, Fathers of the Senate, what more have I to ask of the immortal gods than that I may retain this same unanimous approval of yours to the very end of my life." (*Augustus* 58)

As noted, Augustus underscores the importance of this title by listing it at the very end of his *Res gestae* as the state's ultimate honor to him.

The Emperor's Priestly Service to the State

Augustus was also portrayed as the priestly mediator of divine benefits, whose religious duty it was to preserve the order, morality, and sanctity of the state. Although Augustus's public image as priestly sacrificer was discussed extensively in chapter 5, above, the emperor's role as religious head of the state is described here further. Verner notes that Greco-Roman rulers were conceived as God's agents for the preservation not simply of the political order but of the cosmic order as well.[55] He illustrates this idea with the following citation from Plutarch:

Rulers serve God for the care and preservation of men, in order that of the glorious gifts which the gods give to men, they may distribute some and safeguard others. . . . The ruler is the image of God who orders all things. (*Moralia*, 780D–E)

Suetonius underscores this religious dimension of Augustus's rule near the beginning of his biography, where he explains how Octavian received the surname Augustus. When some Romans expressed the opinion that Octavian ought to be called Romulus as the city's second founder, Munatius Plancus proposed instead that he should be named Augustus. This was an even more honorable title than Romulus, since things consecrated by augural rites were called "august" precisely because they had the "power to increase [*auctus*] in dignity" (*Augustus* 7).

Thus, in contrast to Caesar, who tried to grasp rule by force, Augustus presented himself in the way Christ is described in Phil 2:6–7. He humbled himself voluntarily before a higher authority. It was for his piety, as well as courage, clemency, and justice, that Octavian received the name Augustus.

---

[55]See Verner, *Household*, 76.

According to Suetonius, after Augustus assumed the office of *pontifex maximus* (chief priest of the state), he increased the number and importance of the priesthoods and enlarged their allowances and privileges (*Augustus* 31). Augustus revived ancient rites that had fallen into disuse, and he publicly honored the heroic contributions of former citizens. He dedicated statues of them in triumphal garb in the two colonnades of his forum, saying the following:

> I have contrived this to lead the citizens to require me, while I live, and the rulers of later times as well, to attain the standard set by those worthies of old.[56]

This citation illustrates the essential difference between the rules of Augustus and Caesar. Whereas Caesar was disrespectful of precedent, choosing magistrates years in advance and admitting men of foreign birth to the senate, Augustus honored the past and kept republican class privileges and status unsullied by taint of foreign or servile blood.[57]

In contrast to Caesar, Augustus was sensitive to the republic's fear of monarchy, and consequently, he never formally accepted dictatorship of Rome. His official authority was no greater than other magistrates, and he would not accept any office inconsistent with ancestral custom. Although willing to pardon rebellious foreigners and to treat the provinces as integral parts of the empire, he maintained class differentiation and was reticent to admit foreigners to Roman citizenship.[58]

Furthermore, Suetonius says Augustus revived traditional dress and decorum.[59] In summary, Augustus used his priestly powers as *pontifex maximus*, just as he used his political and household-like managerial

---

[56]See Suetonius, *Augustus* 31.

[57]Regarding Caesar's presumptuousness, Suetonius says that he erected a statue of himself among the ancient Roman kings and that he took honors a mortal should have refused: he had a golden throne in the senate house and another on the tribunal; a ceremonial chariot and litter carried his statue in religious processions around the circus; he appointed a priest to his own cult; he appointed a new college of Luperci to celebrate his divinity; and he renamed the seventh month of the year July. (see *Julius* 76).

[58]Augustus's recognition of the republic's fear of monarchical rule and his own sensitivity toward such apprehension is indicated in *Res gestae* 5–6, 34. Regarding his willingness to pardon former foreign opponents, see ibid., 3. For his desire to preserve and enhance the welfare of Italians outside Rome and foreign provincials, without also elevating them to equality with Roman citizens, see Suetonius, *Augustus* 40–41, 46–48.

[59]When Suetonius refers to Augustus's revival of ancient religious rites, *Augustus* 31, he probably has the same actions in mind that Augustus mentions in *Res gestae* 8. Augustus's dedication of statues to ancient heroes is recorded in *Augustus* 31, the revival of ancient dress is mentioned in ibid., 40.

powers, for the purpose of restoring, preserving, and enhancing the
sanctity of traditional Roman law and morality.

Fourth-century sculpture of Christ as Good Shepherd.
Museo Pio Cristiano I (Vatican Museums).
Photo courtesy of Alinari/Art Resource, N.Y.

Christ, Priestly Lord and Head of the Household

Christ as Head of the Community. Paul deliberately mixes images of
Christ's military and universal status as ruler with domestic pictures of
him as Lord of God's family. This combination is so reminiscent of the
way Augustus (and other early emperors) was represented as father of the

state that Paul's similar mixture of metaphors can hardly be accidental. Paul deliberately modeled Christ's identity as Lord on comparable images of the emperor's authority.

There is this major difference, however. Whereas the emperor's political rule of the state is likened to a father's management of his estate, Christ's headship of the family is represented as like a political leader's rule of the state. That is, whereas Paul emphasizes Christ's familiar rule over the spiritual family (the church), with lesser emphasis on his rule as universal Lord, the emperor's rule of the state was likened only secondarily to household management.

In comparison with that of the emperor, there are other distinctive features of Paul's image of Christ that call for comment. Despite Christ's status as authoritative Lord of God's political order and his headship of the spiritual family, he is not called father in either capacity. God alone is the church's source of spiritual life and sustenance. Apparently, the respective spheres of Christ's and God's identities would have been muddied if Paul had mixed them. Thus, whereas God is the Father who procreates the spiritual family, the new political order and the new creation, Christ is the spiritual family's "firstborn" son, the successor and head ("heir") of the household, and the "first fruits" of the new creation.

According to strict metaphorical logic, Christ was the oldest brother, who became the family's authoritative head by virtue of being its firstborn son. But just as Paul never calls Christ father, so too he never calls him brother. Because of his singular role as spiritual head, he has the status of Lord. In this respect his image is narrower than Paul's own metaphorical identity. For just as Paul could describe himself as his converts' father, because of his role as community founder, so too he could address coverts as "brothers and sisters," since they and he had the same spiritual parent. By contrast, Christ plays a sui generis role as bridge between God and humanity, for which "Lord" is the appropriate designation.

Although Paul's image of Jesus as Son is treated in previous chapters, here is discussed the idea's relationship to his status as Lord. Paul argues in Galatians that mere physical descent was not a sufficient basis for people to regard themselves as Abraham's promised offspring. Paul clarifies his thesis in 4:21–31, where he contrasts Abraham's two offspring, the one "born according to the flesh" and the other "born according to the Spirit." Ishmael, the child of Hagar the slave girl, was procreated by natural means and thus was born according to the flesh. Isaac, by contrast, because of Sarah's sterility, was conceived by means of God's intervention and hence was born according to the Spirit.

Therefore, the basis of true generation, as illustrated by Isaac's conception, was God's own power to create life. Like Isaac's, Christ's status as Abraham's promised heir derives from the fact that God generated life once again out of a sterile situation (see 3:13). Because of Jesus' execution, which shows he was in a state of curse that could sterilize even the soil (see Deut 21:22f.), Paul saw a positive correspondence with God's transformation of Sarah's sterility. By contrast, when Paul was formerly a Pharisee, he was offended by the fact that the person who was accursed according to Deut 21:22f. was being proclaimed God's messianic Son. When Paul received an ecstatic experience of the risen Jesus, however, he had to confess the contradiction was true. Just as Isaac was born out of the shame of Sarah's sterility, so too Christ's sonship was effected out of the sterility of his crucifixion.

The same logic informs Paul's image of Jesus' special status as Son in Rom 4, but in that case, he refers to Abraham's sterility as well as to Sarah's barrenness. For example, in Rom 4:19, Paul says Abraham did not weaken in faith when he considered his impotent (i.e., "dead") body and the barrenness of Sarah's womb. Moreover, when he adds immediately afterward in 4:20 that Abraham "grew strong" in his faith, Paul indicates God enlivened Abraham's procreative ability. Abraham gave the glory to God for this life-creating power (4:20–21). Therefore, it is hardly coincidental that Paul juxtaposes God's resurrection of Jesus with the enlivening of Abraham's procreative ability in 4:24.

The paradoxical nature of Christ's status as Son is underscored in 1 Cor 1:23, where Paul admits that a crucified Christ was a stumbling block to Jews and stupidity to Greeks. Nonetheless, the truth of Christ's nobility was confirmed by the Corinthians' own increase in status as a result of God's Christ-like generation of their status. For they had not been noble, wise, or powerful when God adopted them as offspring. Rather, their nobility as offspring was modeled on that of their Lord, whose status was conferred on him by God.

Despite the decisive importance God's creativity plays in determining Christ's status as Son and Lord, Paul indicates Christ had a special attitude toward God. That is, like his forefather Abraham, Christ had a radical and unrelenting confidence in God's character as Father even in the face of death. Paul refers to this mature attitude of trust in Phil 2:5ff. as the mind of Christ, which he encourages recipients to imitate.

Paul identifies Jesus' crucifixion as an expression of radical obedience and righteousness also in Rom 5:12–21. Christ's conduct is contrasted with Adam's disobedience. The new-Adam image indicates

Christ is not only heir and head of the individual household and Abraham's promised racial seed but also the firstborn son of a new humanity. Or as Rom 8 expresses the matter, the Spirit of God who raised Jesus from the dead will set all creation free to obtain the glorious liberty of the children of God.

Christ as Priestly Lord of the Church and the Universe.   Paul's idealization of Christ as noble son and heir, whose rule effects other family members' maturation, is paralleled by his representation of Christ's priestly lordship. Paul's picture of Christ's priestly role is the precursor for the image of priest found in Hebrews. For the essence of Christ's priestly status was his willingness not to exalt himself as high priest (or political ruler, etc.) but to derive his appointment from "the one who said to him, 'You are my Son, today I have begotten you' " (Heb 5:5). Like that of Melchizedek (Gen 14:17–24), Christ's priestly status was not based on physical descent from Levi; he was heard by God because of his godly fear (5:7–9).

The superiority of Christ's priestly lordship is indicated by his location at God's right hand. Like other priests, he too was obliged to offer gifts and sacrifices to God (see 8:1ff.). But unlike the Levitical priesthood, which was obliged to continue offering sacrifices, he entered once for all into the Holy Place, taking not the blood of goats and calves but his own blood. The viewpoint of Hebrews is not that Christ, being a human, was a better sacrifice than animals. Rather, in the manner of Greco-Roman philosophical contemporaries, the true sacrifice was the submission of one's very self to God as a sacrifice. Christ's death is a graphic symbol of the radicality of his obedience. It was this same kind of sacrifice of self that Paul exhorts converts to offer in Rom 12:1:

> I appeal to you therefore, brothers and sisters, by the mercies of God, to present your bodies as a living sacrifice, holy and acceptable to God, which is your spiritual worship.

Paul also refers to Christ's sacrificial submission of self for the greater good in 2 Cor 8:9:

> For you know the generous act of our Lord Jesus Christ, that though he was rich, yet for your sakes he became poor, so that by his poverty you might become rich.

Paul refers to converts' comparable obedience as the sacrifice that he offers to God in his priestly duty as God's apostle to the Gentiles:

> Nevertheless on some points I have written to you rather boldly by way of reminder, because of the grace given me by God to be a minister of Christ

Jesus to the Gentiles in the priestly service of the gospel of God, so that the offering of the Gentiles may be acceptable, sanctified by the Holy Spirit. In Christ Jesus, then, I have reason to boast of my work for God. For I will not venture to speak of anything except what Christ has accomplished through me to win obedience from the Gentiles. (Rom 15:15–18).

Christ's priestly lordship supplied the pattern from which Paul derived his own idea of obedience as a sacrifice, as well as his belief that converts should offer their bodies as a "living sacrifice" to God. For the perfect sacrifice that Christ offered as priest (and sacrifice) is identified in Rom 3:24–25 as an "atonement by his blood." The same sacrifice of life is attributed to Christ in 4:23–25, where he is described as "handed over to death for our trespasses and . . . raised for our justification," and in 5:9–10, which states that "we were reconciled to God through the death of his Son, . . . and saved by his life."

Paul uses both Christ's "blood" and his "death" as sacrificial images that capture the extent of his obedience. Immediately after using such sacrificial language in Rom 3–5, Paul turns in 5:12ff. to the subject of Christ's obedience, which he contrasts with Adam's disobedience. He makes it clear that it was neither Christ's blood nor his death as such that effected redemption but his trust, which God vindicated. Whereas Paul describes Adam's disobedience as a sinful transgression that desecrates, he pictures Christ's obedience as a sacrificial gift (offering) that effects restoration with God.

Paul depicts the efficacy of Christ's sacrifice in 4:23–25 and 5:9f. not by means of his death alone but in terms of the death and the resurrection. He makes the same emphasis in 3:24–25, where he describes the redemption effected in Christ Jesus as a sacrifice "whom God put forward as a sacrifice of atonement by his blood, effective through faith." God's power to make something of Christ's sacrifice effects redemption, not Christ's sacrifice alone.

Paul emphasizes the purifying influence of Christ's sacrifice in 1 Cor. 15:20ff., where his resurrection is called "the first fruits" of those who have died. He illustrates the significance of Christ's sacrifice, as in Rom 5:12ff., through the contrasting consequences of Adam's and Christ's actions. In Adam all die. In Christ all are made alive. The resurrected Son is "a life-giving spirit" (1 Cor 15:45).

Thus, Paul uses numerous images to underscore Christ's efficacy as a priestly, life-preserving Lord. Because converts have been consecrated by the purifying first fruits of Christ's sacrifice, they too are filled with fruits of righteousness that may be offered to the glory and praise of God (Phil 1:10–11). Converts are sanctified (washed, blameless, sound, innocent, guiltless, justified, etc.) by the power of their priestly Lord and are made capable of approving what is excellent.[60]

All who die with Christ, an act symbolized cultically by baptism, are also resurrected with him by means of God's Spirit (see Rom 6:2; 1 Cor 12:12f.). Because of Christ's resurrection, he has dominion (lordship) even over death. Moreover, since he is the sanctifying first fruits of a new creation, all who participate in his death are also enlivened and liberated from death's power (see Rom 6:1–11). Christ's power over death is the power that is able to make all humanity—Jew or Greek, slave or free, male or female—drink from the same sacramental cup (see 1 Cor. 12:12–13; Gal. 3:28).

Therefore, the new "law of the Spirit of life in Christ Jesus" liberates humanity not only from the law of sin and death (see Rom 8:1ff.) but from all conventions that alienate people from God and from one another. The true circumcision now are those who worship God in spirit and, like Christ, put no confidence in physical marks of ethnic differentiaton:

> For a person is not a Jew who is one outwardly, nor is true circumcision something external and physical. Rather, a person is a Jew who is one inwardly, and real circumcision is a matter of the heart—it is spiritual and not literal. Such a person receives praise not from others but from God. (Rom. 2:28–29; see Phil. 3:3)

In fact, neither circumcision nor uncircumcision effects anything of consequence, but only the spiritual creation brought into being by faith in God like that of Christ (see Gal 5:6; 6:15; 1 Cor 7:19).

In summary, Christ's powers of sanctification as priestly Lord and his mastery over the household are analogous to the authority of his political rule. In each sphere of lordship, he has an authentic basis of authority. In every instance his life-giving obedience to God contrasts with the deathly influence of Adam-type disobedience.

CONCLUDING REFLECTIONS

This chapter has proposed that Paul's representation of Christ as priestly Lord, family head, and political Lord reflects emphases found in imperial-cult ideology, for these same three aspects of the emperor's

---

[60]E.g., 1 Cor. 1:2, 7; 6:9–11; Phil. 1:6; 2:14; 3:3, 20–21; 1 Thess. 3:11–13; 4:2; 5:23.

authority are advocated in ancient sources. Nonetheless, the idealized Roman emperor is clearly not the only perspective that influenced Paul's images of Christ's lordship. The Jewish-Christian idea of the Davidic Messiah also informs Paul's idea of Jesus' lordship, whether or not the influence is as great as Scott alleges. Moreover, there is a second, more likely, Jewish antecedent for Paul's idea of Christ as household master and as idealized heir, the Abrahamic tradition. In addition to these Jewish and Greco-Roman conceptions of authority, we must take account of at least one other influence, Paul's knowledge of Christ's lordship as he experienced it. This experiential knowledge caused him to modify both Jewish models and ruler cult ideology.

The beginning of this chapter noted that Paul's idea of Christ's rule differed from both Jewish and pagan ideas of authority in a significant respect: Jesus was not officially designated Christ and Lord *(kyrios)* until after his resurrection. His rule did not begin until after his apotheosis. There is a radical corollary to this idea. By announcing that Christ rules spiritually from his deified state, Paul effectively collapses the boundary separating the world of the supreme God from the sublunar sphere inhabited by humans.[61] This means the chasm that, until quite recently, had separated humanity from God is now bridged. Christ's lordship effects a restoration and harmony that exceeds even the Augustan peace. It was precisely this earth-shattering idea of salvation that Beker was trying to capture when he said that Jewish apocalyptic was the symbolic basis of Paul's theological system.[62] That is, the salvation God effected in Christ had opened up a new future for the world. Although Beker suggests that creation would only attain perfection for Paul in God's final triumph, converts who confessed Christ as Lord were already experiencing the effects of God's power of life over death.

Chapter 6, above, proposed that "teleological" was a better adjective than "apocalyptic" for describing Paul's idea of God's creativity in Christ.

---

[61]Although Paul does not use the terms "sublunar" and "supralunar," he believed in the cosmology signified by such language. E.g., immediately after differentiating "heavenly bodies" from "earthly bodies" in 1 Cor 15:40, he proceeds to differentiate the glory of the sun from the glory of the moon (15:41) and, in turn, the glory of the stars from that of the sun and the moon. Such language assumes the qualitative difference designated by "sublunar" and "supralunar." Granted, Paul did not conceptualize the two realms in a strictly material manner, in the way that certain people differentiated the terrestial and the celestial. For the creator of the physical earth was no inferior demiurge but the same being who was now creating a spiritual universe in Christ.

[62]See Beker, *The Triumph of God,* 19–21.

This suggestion brings us to another adaptation in Paul's idea of Christ's lordship. Although Paul says God has given Christ the power to subject all things to himself (e.g., see Phil 3:21), Christ is never given the Augustan status of father. God alone is Father. The following statement in 1 Cor 15:27–28 describes how Paul conceived of Christ's lordship in relation to God's identity as creator:

> For "God has put all things in subjection under his feet." But when it says, "All things are put in subjection," it is plain that this does not include the one who put all things in subjection under him. When all things are subjected to him, then the Son himself will also be subjected to the one who put all things in subjection under him, so that God may be all in all.

We know that if the earthly tent we live in is destroyed, we have a building
from God, a house not made with hands, eternal in the heavens. For in this
tent we groan, longing to be clothed with our heavenly dwelling—if indeed,
when we have taken it off we will not be found naked.

2 Cor 5:1–3

8
"A HOUSE NOT MADE WITH HANDS"

According to Banks, the family household was Paul's dominant image of the church. Paul encouraged fellowship between churches, but he nowhere indicates the church was part of a larger whole.[1] Banks is correct that Paul's converts assembled in multiple locations even in the same city and that the family was Paul's favorite image, but he goes too far when he says that Paul had no broader idea of the church than that of a series of single-family units. Meeks rightly argues that the idea of the church as a series of independent units fails to explain the unity Paul imagined between converts within a city, region, and province.[2] Likewise, Malherbe notes that Paul wrote only one letter to a city or area, assuming it would suffice for all the groups.[3]

Thus, despite the appeal of the single household as a symbol, Paul believed that his churches formed a collective identity that was broader than the family. Banks himself discusses aspects of Paul's idea of the church that point in the same direction. For example, he says Paul's regular word for community was the political designation *ekklēsia*, which, by the fifth century BCE, referred to the assembly of citizens in a

---

[1]Banks, *Community*, 31–36, 47–57. According to Banks, the fact that Paul used the word for church, *ekklēsia* ("assembly"), in the plural shows he conceptualized it as actual gatherings and not as parts of some larger communal identity.

[2]Meeks, *First Urban Christians*, 77.

[3]See Malherbe, *Social Aspects*, 79.

Greek city.[4] In light of Paul's use of the designation, one expects Banks to say something about the church as a political entity, but he says Paul used *ekklēsia* as a neutral way of referring to actual meetings. Although he rightly notes that Paul's description of the church as "in God the Father" made it different from ordinary assemblies, this hardly indicates that the term had lost its political meaning altogether.[5]

Although the family is Paul's leading image of the church, his use of other communal metaphors shows Paul regarded converts as a form of ethnic and political community in addition to a spiritual household. Thus, just as the preceding chapter confirmed various levels and kinds of lordship for Christ, so here comparable forms of communal association for Paul's converts are described through Paul's view of converts as members of a fictive family, his ethnic ideas about converts as Abraham's heirs, and his civic and imperial imagery of the church. The discussion of the household of faith is the longest because family metaphors are more common than ethnic and civic imagery in Paul and because the ancient household was fundamental to both ethnic and civic forms of social identity.

THE HOUSEHOLD OF FAITH

Real and Fictive Household in Antiquity

Although scholars often say that the ancient Greek and Roman household differed from the modern nuclear family, the comment bears repeating. The difference arises primarily not from the fact that the household was more multigenerational but from the fact that the family

---

[4]In the hellenistic and imperial periods, the term could refer to other kinds of meeting but retained its original meaning of "assembly." Hellenistic-Jewish Christians seem to have used *ekklēsia* to differentiate their gatherings from traditional Jewish assemblies. The fact that the Hellenistic Jewish word for assembly— "synagogue"—only occurs once in the New Testament confirms the church's decision to distinguish itself from the synagogue. See Banks, *Community*, 26–29.

[5]Indeed, Banks acknowledges that *ekklēsia* had a broader meaning, but he says it emerged only in later letters. E.g., in Gal 4:26–27, Paul contrasts Jerusalem with his converts, who belong to the Jerusalem above. Similarly, the Philippians had a heavenly citizenship (Phil 3:19–20). Moreover, Paul talks about converts' ethniclike status as *true* Jews (Rom 2:29) and as the *true* circumcision (Phil 3:2). See Banks, *Community*, 37–46. Since these ethnic and civic designations are not confined to the earliest letters, even in Banks's chronology, it is likely a broader view of the church informed Paul's idea of community from the beginning.

included non-kin as members. For example, the Greek citizen household *(oikos)* regularly included servants, and unusual circumstances led to incorporation of an extended-family member and/or non-kin into the family.[6] The upper-class Roman household *(familia)* not only had slaves and domestic servants but often included tenants, freedmen (former family slaves), laborers, and business associates.[7]

Bradley says that in order to understand the role of non-kin in the aristocratic Roman family, we must proceed from the fact that marriage was not a permanently binding institution. People entered marriage to maintain the patrician status of families and to preserve the social order. In addition to bearing children to perpetuate the family, the couple was expected merely to live in a state of harmony *(concordia)*.[8] When we add that public careers often took men away from Rome for extended leaves, the high incidence of divorce and remarriage is not surprising.[9]

What does marital instability have to do with the role of non-kin as family members? Since the father had legal right to offspring in divorce and was often away from home, servants regularly played parental roles. On the basis of both inscriptional and literary data, Bradley says a child's wet nurse *(nutrix)* often formed an ongoing relationship with a daughter that could last until the girl married, for she often became the child's nanny and chaperone. Male servants played a comparable role for boys (other than wet-nursing), serving as *nutritores, educatores,* and finally *paedagogi*.[10]

---

[6]E.g., when a household was childless and the head of the family was nearing retirement, he would often adopt an adult male from the extended family to become its head (Lacey, *Family,* 145–50). Similarly, when a couple had only a daughter, a male relative on the father's side of the family would marry the daughter and take over management of the household. Sometimes non-kin served such roles (pp. 139–45). Other factors also contributed to the acceptance of non-kin as family members. Before there were city-states, unrelated families in the same region sometimes banded together as protective military brotherhoods *(phrateres)* against outsiders. See Lacey's comments on the military brotherhood, pp. 26–27, 92–93. Similarly, when city-states removed the extended family's control over households, the political deme became a substitute for the extended family (pp. 84–95).

[7]Malherbe, *Social Aspects,* 69.

[8]See Bradley's illustration of the way Cicero and his friend Atticus negotiated a marriage between their siblings and exercised a supervisory role in their married life *(Roman Family,* 186–98). Unfortunately, no amount of sibling interference was able to save the marriage from eventual divorce.

[9]See ibid., 125–30.

[10]Regarding the nurse's role in the family, see ibid., 13–36. Regarding the comparable role of men as child minders, see ibid., 37–75. Aristocratic family heads sometimes entrusted even slave infants to wet nurses and nannies. Because

Although we cannot find exact parallels to the parental role played by servants in upper-class families, non-kin performed comparable roles in lower-class families. For example, Bradley notes that the words *tata* and *mamma*, roughly equivalent to "daddy" and "mommy," were widely used for non-kin. Inscriptional data indicates that in *tabernae* (inns) and poorer *insulae* (apartment buildings) adults who formed a bond with children in the apartment complexes where they lived were addressed with the affectionate family titles *tata* and *mamma*.[11]

Ancient child labor practices bring another type of surrogate parent into the picture. The nature of this non-kin relationship may be inferred from apprenticeship documents.[12] Apprentices began training about the age of twelve or thirteen, and the parent/master determined the choice of occupation. As prospective family heads, freeborn boys needed to be equipped to earn a livelihood, and until they married, earnings supplemented their parents' income. Servile children were trained to increase their worth to masters.[13]

---

the acquistion of slaves by conquest decreased after the Augustan Peace, families tried to perpetuate a new generation from within their own household (see ibid., 18–19, 26–27, and 32 n. 40). We find comparable situations in less prestigious families. Various passages in the *Metamorphoses* of Apuleius indicate that divorce and remarriage were common in the provinces. E.g., the itinerant merchant Aristomenes informs his friend Socrates that relatives at home thought Aristomenes was dead and his wife's parents wanted their daughter to remarry. Aristomenes later revealed that he had begun a new life in Thessaly with a new wife. In another incident, though the ghost of Tlepolemus visited his wife and told her not to marry his murderer, he clearly expected her to remarry. As if these remarriages were not odd enough, Apuleius says Lucius the ass was sold to a baker who married his own daughter's stepmother. See Apuleius, *Metamorphoses* 1.6, 1.9, 8.8, 9.31, 10.2; and see Bradley's discussion of the *Metamorphoses* (*Roman Family*, 173)

[11] See Bradley, *Roman Family*, 76–102.

[12] The following discussion is derived from Bradley, ibid., 103–24.

[13] The value of these contracts for a picture of nonaristocratic children's life is confirmed by Lucian, who gives an autobiographical account *(The Dream)* of how he chose a literary life over that of an artisan. Since family means were modest, Lucian's father decided his son should be apprenticed to an uncle to learn the family trade of stonemasonry. After only one day, however, in which he was beaten for breaking a slab of stone, he ran home to his mother. Later he had a vision that led him to devote his energy to culture rather than sculpture. Lucian's situation shows the need of ordinary families to put offspring to work and the severity that could attend training. The only oddity is his ability to reject the occupation. There was a reciprocal obligation between parents and offspring in antiquity. Parents should beget, rear, and train children. In turn, children should honor parents and provide them with material support, comfort, and burial in old age. See Bradley's discussion of the convention of reciprocal obligation in *Roman Family*, 116–19.

Children trained to be artisans were the elite of nonaristocratic society. Slaves and even freeborn children, if they lacked the aptitude or financial means, began work earlier, doing farming chores, working at domestic jobs, performing as entertainers (acrobats, dancers, interlude artists, mimes), etc. (One passage from the *Code of Justinian* indicates slaves were working by the age of ten, and the *Digest* suggests they could be at work by the age of five.)[14] Masters and craftsmen played parentlike roles. Like real parents, they might treat children badly, but the bond was often affectionate and caring.[15]

Social changes led to the incorporation of other non-kin into the family and to alternative forms of political identity. Even before Alexander's conquests, various developments had begun to loosen people's ties to traditional family structures.

Traditionally, city-states such as Athens allowed only families with hereditary estates to be called *oikoi* ("households") and to have citizenship rights. Families of resident aliens and other non-citizens did not qualify as households. Thus, the *oikos* was as much a political entity as a family unit. Initially, the role of land as a determinant of household and civic status deterred social changes. Since ancestral shrines and graves were located on family estates and since family and civic identity were connected to hereditary land, social and physical movement were not common.

As noted in chapters 4 and 6, above, however, various circumstances led to change in the conception of family and state. For example, since Greek colonists could not maintain old loyalties to land and family in the homeland, citizenship and household had to be defined in a more flexible way. Moreover, ongoing war between city-states, as well as new Greek kingdoms in the East, caused more and more Greeks to emigrate and to modify their hereditary traditions. Alexander and his successors' idea of a more universal state also led to alterations in the Roman conception of family and state in the early empire. For example, despite Augustus's attempt to prevent upward movement in social status, the possibility of improvement was greater for people who migrated to provincial cities than for those at home.[16]

---

[14]See *Code of Justinian* 6.43.3.1; *Digest* 7.7.6.1. See Bradley's discussion of the evidence from Roman law regarding child labor in *Roman Family*, 112–16.

[15]See the funeral inscription, cited by Bradley, in which a master craftsman says his love for the dead apprentice was greater than if he had been his own son (*Roman Family*, 116, 123 n. 75).

[16]Meeks, *First Urban Christians*, 14–25.

Portrait of Augustan-age woman from Praeneste illustrating
how Livia's public image influenced ordinary citizens.
Museo Nazionale Romano delle Terme, Rome.
Photo courtesy of Alinari/Art Resource, N.Y.

We may take the improved status of women as an example of the way social conventions were being altered by the first century CE. Pomeroy and Michael Grant both call attention to the status of hellenistic queens as an index of the changes that had occurred.[17] Improvements were not confined to royalty but also took place at lower levels. For example, the shortage of Greek women in the eastern kingdoms, especially in the early hellenistic period, enhanced women's contractual rights in marriage. Because of greater social equality between women and men in

---

[17]See Grant, *From Alexander to Cleopatra*, 194–213 and Pomeroy, *Women in Hellenistic Egypt*. Grant says the status of Hellenistic queens derived, in large part, from Macedonian precedents (see pp. 194–95). Pomeroy says it was only in the second century BCE, when Egypt was wracked by civil unrest and foreign attack, that subjects accepted the legitimacy of the Ptolemaic queens' power (see pp. 23–24).

places such as Egypt, Greek daughters began for the first time to inherit property along with their brothers, and some began to engage in business affairs.[18] Generally speaking, women in the hellenistic kingdoms were less confined to the house and freer to go about publicly.[19]

Despite such improvements, the Greek wife's status still was not equal to that of her husband, nor was it as great as her female counterpart in Rome. Women's status in imperial Rome, however, was also largely the result of recent change. During much of the republican period, the wife's status was far inferior to that of her husband, especially in marriage with *manus*. *Manus* is the Latin for hand or force (power) and, when applied to marriage, referred to the husband's absolute power over his wife. Although freed from her father's authority *(patria potestas)*, the wife became a virtual possession of her husband, who had the right to divorce her but could, at the same time, deprive her of the power to divorce him. Legally, the husband could take her life, and his authority extended to possession of her property. In principle, women could own property, but in marriage with *manus*, they transferred their property to their husbands.[20]

Various factors, including Etruscan influences, however, caused Roman women's status to improve by the early empire.[21] Verner notes that most upper-class marriages were contracted without wives being handed over to their husband's power (= *manus* type marriage) in the

---

[18]See White, "Improved Status." See also my comments on Eirene in White, *Light from Ancient Letters,* 57–61; and see Pomeroy's suggestions about women's right to own, lease, and rent land in Ptolemaic Egypt (*Women in Hellenistic Egypt,* 148–52).

[19]Pomeroy argues that neither free nor slave women were as isolated from male contact as in classical Athens. Although they were not so secluded as in Athens, tradition still seemed to discourage women from negotiating business deals with unfamiliar men. They usually appear leasing land owned by native temples or state lands, but not leasing soldiers' agricultural holdings. See Pomeroy, *Women in Hellenistic Egypt,* 148–52, 158–60; and see White, "Improved Status," 77–79.

[20]See Verner's useful explanation of the types of Roman marriage and the evolution of women's rights in the late republic and early empire (*Household,* 39–44).

[21]A colleague at Loyola University's Rome Center, Valerie Higgins, helped me see the change in Roman women's status and the role that Etruscan culture played as an influence. Regarding the superior status of women in Etruscan society, see Bonfante, "Daily Life and Afterlife." Bonfante says that no feature of Etruscan society differed so much from the Roman in the seventh to fifth centuries BCE as the position of women (see pp. 232–37). Bonfante cites statements from Livy, Ovid, and others that confirm the contrast between women in the two societies.

early empire. In these cases, the wife remained under the *patria potestas* of her father's household and retained her paternal property except for the bridal dowry. She could accumulate wealth and not be subject to the economic limitations of her husband.[22] Thus, certain ancient authors complained about women's powers of independence:

> "Why am I unwilling to marry a rich wife?" Do you ask? I am unwilling to take my wife as husband. (Martial, *Ep.* 7.12)

> There is nothing more intolerable than a wealthy woman. (Juvenal, *Sat.* 6.460)

Although Roman girls tended to become brides by their midteens, they were generally closer to the age of their husbands than Athenian women, whose husbands were often twelve to fifteen years older. Thus, as Verner rightly notes, social disparity between Roman spouses tended to be less than between husbands and wives in Athens.[23] Upper-class matrons even began to discharge public liturgies and to hold magistracies in eastern provincial cities.[24]

Sheila Dickison cites literary sources in which Romans acknowledge that their wives had greater social mobility and status than Greek women.[25] Nonetheless, Dickison admits that in Rome itself women were

---

[22]See Verner, *Household*, 39–40. Although the wife could divorce her husband in marriage without *manus,* Verner says it was with the consent of her father or guardian. Her *pater familias* could even effect a divorce against the daughter's will. Moreover, although she could hold property her husband did not control, she could dispose of it only with her guardian's consent. It is difficult to know how much the dependence on the paternal family was a real restriction, but it was not a mere formality. This is indicated by the fact that Augustan legislation granted only free women with three children or freedwomen with four exemption from guardianship control.

[23]Upper-class girls went to elementary school or were tutored privately like boys, and in the imperial period some were receiving higher education. In this respect, too, they had an advantage over Greek girls on the mainland. See ibid., 41.

[24]There is some question whether they carried out the duties themselves or held the civic offices as honorary positions. In either case, the offices were an index of their social and political status. See ibid., 51–52.

[25]See Dickison, "Women in Rome," 1319. E.g., see the following statement by Cornelius Nepos:

> For what Roman is ashamed to take his wife to a dinner party? Or whose wife is not prominent at home or not involved in society? In Greece things are far different. For neither is a wife invited to a dinner party, except of relatives, nor does she pass her life except in the inner part of the house, which is called the women's quarters, where a man is not welcome, save for a close relation. (*Lives of Famous Men,* preface 6–7)

excluded from public service of a political nature. Women certainly participated in public affairs and discharged various religious duties, but the political sphere was an arena where only men competed for civic virtue. Rule by women, such as Cleopatra, was abhorrent. Equally taboo was public speech making. The few women who pleaded legal cases were criticized as "mannish." Thus, despite exceptions, custom defined the woman's primary sphere as the home.[26] Such demarcation of male and female spheres probably lies behind Paul's treatment of women in Corinth, a Roman city.

Marble portrait of Flavian-age lady (end of first century CE) illustrating how modesty in fashion had changed from time of Augustus. Capitoline Museum, Rome. Photo courtesy of Alinari/Art Resource, N.Y.

[26]Dickison, "Women in Rome," 1319–22.

These observations on social change, along with earlier comments
on the role of non-kin as family members, provide a basis for turning to
Paul's idea of the fictive (spiritual) family and community.

Paul and the Hellenistic Tradition of Moral Instruction

E. A. Judge says that the upper-class status of Paul's sponsors, along
with his retinue of associates and his ethical emphasis, all suggest he was
a "sophist" and a founder of scholastic communities.[27] The model that
makes sense of his churches is the philosophical school, according to
this view. Paul's vocation as an artisan placed him beneath his leisured
followers, but Roman citizenship and his rabbinical training allowed him
to move among the urban elite as a teacher.[28] While agreeing that Paul
appropriated the philosophical tradition, Malherbe believes that Judge
overstates the case. The evidence does not show Paul's converts had
enough education to be considered scholastic communities.[29]

The Greek-speaking synagogue is a better model for Paul's use of the
moralist tradition because, like Paul, it emphasized divine wisdom and not
human rationality. Likewise, it concerned itself with communal ethics and
not with individual progress toward virtue. Nonetheless, Paul's adaptation
of Jewish ideas of God and community results in a hybrid form of religion
that may not finally be called a synagogue community. Paul's emphasis
on the assembly as God's family and his charismatic emphasis on
God's/Christ's Spirit as the basis of conduct indicate an intimacy of relationship that exceeds normal synagogue practice. At the same time, Paul's
teaching exceeds household instruction, and therefore, even the family
may not be taken literally as Paul's model of community.[30]

----

[27]Judge details the scholastic nature of Paul's communities most explicitly
in "Early Christians," 4–15, 125–37. Related observations appear in the following
works of Judge: *Social Pattern*; "Paul's Boasting"; and "St. Paul and Classical
Society."

[28]Judge, "Early Christians," 125–27. Malherbe rightly notes that Judge uses
"sophist" not in the pejorative sense of an unprincipled scholar, nor in the limited
sense of a professional orator, but as a general category that included both philosophers and orators (Malherbe, *Social Aspects*, 46).

[29]See Malherbe's evaluation of Judge's interpretation of Paul's converts as
scholastic communities in *Social Aspects*, 45–59.

[30]See Malherbe's illustration of Paul's creative appropriation of the moralist tradition in "Hellenistic Moralists," 278–93. Malherbe states explicitly (p. 332)
that Paul had no Jewish antecedents for his way of appropriating the moralists.
See also Meeks's comment that some other conception of community that did

When we say Paul engaged in moralist-like teaching, we must heed how it functions in his letters.[31] Without attending to nuances, we may be misled, as Judge was, in taking Paul's disavowal of rhetorical ability (2 Cor 11:6: "I may be untrained in speech") at face value rather than as an expression of irony. Moreover, to maintain that Paul's occupation as an artisan is proof that he lacked rhetorical training ignores the philosophical spectrum in antiquity.[32] Malherbe illustrates how important a familiarity with moralist rhetoric is in his interpretation of 1 Thessalonians. Whereas most scholars assume that Paul's autobiographical and antithetic style was a defense against charges of deceptive missionary work, Malherbe shows that Paul's recurring reminder of his converts' positive response to him and of his own steadfast devotion to them served a teaching function. The purpose was not to introduce new information but to emphasize the importance of what the converts already knew.[33]

Personal example was characteristic of moralist teaching.[34] Paul's recurring thankfulness in 1 Thessalonians shows that his readers were already imitating his conduct (e.g., see 1:2–10). This provided incentive for the further imitation that Paul encouraged in 1 Thess 4 and 5.[35] He

---

not derive directly from the synagogue was operative for Paul (*First Urban Christians*, 81).

[31] See Malherbe's discussion of the problematic use of parallels to explain philosophical dependence and to locate the cultural context of New Testament writings. Unfortunately, scholars approach moralists and Christian authors as if both simply gathered useful teachings, without recognizing any conceptual differences between their own views and those from whom they borrowed. Similarly, scholars seem to assume that borrowed ideas were not modified to fit the new context but were used indiscriminately. See "Hellenistic Moralists," 271–78 (esp. 275–78).

[32] See Malherbe, *Social Aspects*, 49, 55–56.

[33] See Malherbe, *Paul and the Thessalonians*, 70–71: "To the objection that it was superfluous to give precepts to people who already knew them, it was replied that exhortation is not teaching but merely engages the attention and arouses us, concentrates the memory, and keeps it from losing its grip." (See the references to Seneca, Dio Chrysostom, and Isocrates that treat the importance of reminder, p. 71 n. 29).

[34] Seneca said that the living example was superior to the spoken precept. People put more faith in their eyes than in their ears. See the examples from Seneca and other literary figures cited by Malherbe as illustrative of the importance of personal example in parenetic instruction (see "Hellenistic Moralists," 278–93; *Paul and the Thessalonians*, 52–60).

[35] See Malherbe's discussion of Paul as a paradigm for the Thessalonian community in *Paul and the Thessalonians*, 52–60.

offered himself as a model because his conduct confirmed how much he cared for converts: he supported himself (2:9); he was gentle with them, like a wet nurse suckling her own offspring (2:6–8); and he nurtured them like a father (2:11–12).

Although Paul concerned himself mostly with ethical conduct inside the church, various statements show that he also was concerned about converts' relation to the larger society. Three times in 1 Thessalonians (3:12; 4:9–12; 5:15), Paul connects love inside the community to larger social responsibility. The statement that is most useful for our purpose is found in 4:10b–12:

> But we urge you, beloved, to do so more and more, to aspire to live quietly, to mind your own affairs, and to work with your hands, as we directed you, so that you may behave properly toward outsiders and be dependent on no one.

Scholars agree that there is a connection between communal love and "working with one's hands" and, further, that Paul intended such exhortation to serve a concrete purpose. Until recently, however, most held that converts' new belief in the imminent arrival of God's kingdom caused some to become idle and these idlers became an economic drain on other members of the community. By contrast, while admitting that belief in the near end of the world could contribute to idleness, Ronald Hocks says that it should not be placed in the foreground. Paul indicates that his work precept was a regular component of his missionary teaching (4:11b: "as we directed you").[36] The motivation for such teaching may be grasped by connecting it to the two preceding items of instruction in 4:11, namely, Paul's advice that converts "aspire to live quietly" and "mind [their] own affairs." The three items served the common purpose of directing converts toward conduct that was seemly to imperial society.[37]

Malherbe argues that the expression that he translates, "to remain quiet and mind one's own business," was an apt description of the thoughtful person in the late republic and early empire who wished to withdraw from the political arena and public life. He adds, however, that not everyone approved of the kind of social quietism Paul advocated. For example, the popular view of Epicureans was that their withdrawal from

---

[36]Hocks, *Social Context,* 42f. Hocks (p. 43) appeals to Dibelius, who also maintained that nothing in the letter pointed to a definite occasion for Paul's admonition to work.

[37]Ibid., 43–44.

society evidenced public irresponsibility. Even Stoics such as Seneca were attacked when they proposed that temporary retirement prepared one for renewed public life. Plutarch said such action was irresponsible, a view confirmed by the fact that Stoics did not send many representatives into public life.[38]

In light of the criticism against philosophers who wished to pursue the contemplative life, we have to ask how Paul thought living quietly, minding one's own affairs, and working with one's hands would win the approval of "outsiders" (4:12). The key to understanding Paul, *pace* Judge, is to recognize that both he and most converts belonged to the artisan class. Although a few households belonged to upper-class society (e.g., a few families in Corinth), most male converts appear to have worked as craftsmen. Thus, in contrast to many philosophers and their students, whose social status allowed them to play a political role in society, the status of Paul's converts led to a different expectation.

Therefore, Paul was responding to criticism often aimed at Cynics who, in protesting against social conventions, were abandoning trades and taking to the streets. Fired by religious zeal perhaps, Paul's converts were also tempted to leave their trades. Aware that society regarded such people as meddlers who sponged off other people's labor, Paul cited his own practice of working with his hands as an alternative (e.g., see 2:9). He was concerned about how converts appeared to polite society because he regarded outsiders as potential insiders. Also, he shared the political view that the collective good was more important than individual rights. Thus, he had a practical concern for the effect of idleness on communal life.

Four examples from 1 Corinthians illustrate Paul's idea of the relationship of the church to society outside. For example, in 6:1–11 Paul notes that church members were going to pagan law courts to settle differences between converts. Since God's people would sit in judgment on the existing order, it was shameful that they could not settle internal differences.

Paul's advice on two of the three other issues, meat offered to idols and women's silence in assembly, might seem inconsistent with his general emphasis on freedom and equality in Christ. His instruction in these two cases, as well as in his advice on how to eat the Lord's Supper, however, was intended as a corrective to the abuse of freedom rather than as a denial of it. Insistence on personal rights probably caused all three issues

---

[38]See Plutarch, *On Stoic Self-Contradictions* 1043A–1044B.

to surface. In the case of meat offered to idols, Gerd Theissen says social stratification was creating problems. Prior to conversion, the only time poor converts ate meat was when it was distributed free at public festivals. Because the lower class identified the meat with sacrifice to one or another god, they were offended when they saw upper-class converts participating in such meals (8:7–13). By contrast, since the upper class regularly ate meat, they did not associate it specifically with sacrifice to gods. More important, they knew only the Jewish God was real, and thus it did not matter that they ate meat dedicated to gods that did not exist.[39]

Paul agreed in principle that because idols did not really exist, the upper class had the right to eat meat (8:1–6). Since "weak" siblings were tempted to revert to idolatrous practices when they saw fellow Christians at table in an idol's temple, Paul encouraged the upper class not to insist on their freedom. Indeed, a little later, Paul appears to prohibit participation in pagan cults:

> You cannot drink the cup of the Lord and the cup of demons. You cannot partake of the table of the Lord and the table of demons. (10:21)

Only a few verses later, however, Paul clearly states he does not intend to shut off communication with the outside, not even table fellowship with pagans:

> Eat whatever is sold in the meat market without raising any question on the ground of conscience, for "the earth and its fullness are the Lord's." If an unbeliever invites you to a meal and you are disposed to go, eat whatever is set before you without raising any question on the ground of conscience. But if someone says to you, "This has been offered in sacrifice," then do not eat it, out of consideration for the one who informed you, and for the sake of conscience—I mean the other's conscience, not your own. (10:25–29)

How are these inconsistencies to be reconciled? When Paul said converts could not partake of the table of the Lord and the table of demons, it seems he was referring less to literal participation in pagan cults than to the spirit in which converts engaged in activities. They were sinning against Christ when they took no thought of spiritual brethren (8:12).

Similarly, Paul accuses converts of eating the Lord's Supper in an unacceptable way (11:17–34). The Lord's Supper had degenerated into the table of demons! Christian hosts succumbed to the more unsavory

---

[39]See Theissen, *Social Setting,* 121–43.

aspect of the Roman dinner party *(convivium)* and served guests food and drink according to their social class.[40] It was this practice that led Paul to say,

> When you come together, it is not really to eat the Lord's supper. For when the time comes to eat, each of you goes ahead with your own supper, and one goes hungry and another becomes drunk. (11:20f.)

By making such discrimination between guests, hosts were profaning the Lord's body and blood (i.e., Lord's Supper) because Christ sacrificed his personal rights for others (see 11:23–34). Paul encouraged sacrifice of individual rights for building up both the church and the outside society:

> For though I am free with respect to all, I have made myself a slave to all, so that I might win more of them. To the Jews I became as a Jew, in order to win Jews. . . . To those outside the law I became as one outside the law (though I am not free from God's law but am under Christ's law) so that I might win those outside the law. To the weak I became weak, so that I might win the weak. I have become all things to all people, that I might by all means save some. (9:19–22)

Whereas Paul opposed the pagan practice of discrimination between supper guests, in the case of going to civil law courts and eating meat offered to idols he was sensitive to the public's view of the church. The same sensitivity to Roman values may lie behind Paul's injunction about the women's hair covering and their length of hair (11:2–16) and his instructions about women not speaking publicly in assembly (14:33b–36). Something like the need of the church not to be contemptuous of public appearance lies behind Paul's injunction about women's hair. Chaste clothing (e.g., the long overgarment *stola*) with veiled head, as well as modest hairstyle, may derive from the leading women of the imperial house, who were models of public decorum in the East.[41]

Paul's instruction that women should not speak publicly in church (14:33b–36) probably expresses a similar concern about women's acceptable public roles. Since Paul recognized women's right to prophesy (11:5) and since he regarded prophecy as more important than teaching (12:28–29), why else would he deny them the right to talk in assembly?

---

[40]See Murphy-O'Connor, *St. Paul's Corinth*, 158–61.

[41]See Zanker's discussion of imperial clothing and hairstyle as widely imitated models, along with illustrative portraits, in *The Power of Images*, 300–302 (see figures 131 and 253, pp. 165 and 323 respectively). See also Ramage and Ramage, *Roman Art*, 89, 136.

He admits the incongruity in 14:37, where he has to support his advice with Christ's authority: "Anyone who claims to be a prophet, or to have spiritual powers, must acknowledge that what I am writing to you is a command of the Lord."

Banks rightly notes that the command about women's silence occurred, along with speaking in tongues and the need to prophesy one at a time, in a section treating the necessity of order in worship. Apparently wives were interrupting the assembly with questions about what was being said (14:35). Thus, the injunction to "be silent" should be understood specifically with reference to questions that interrupted the assembly.[42]

Since Corinth was a Roman city, there was probably some sensitivity in the church to women engaging in debate with men. Livy illustrates the Roman concern about women in public affairs by the example of the Oppian Law. Against the advice of their husbands, women blocked streets leading to the Forum and begged the men they met to oppose the law. According to Livy, one of the consuls said,

> What sort of practice is this, of running out into the streets and blocking the roads and speaking to other women's husbands? Could you not have made the same requests, each of your own husband, at home? Or are you more attractive outside and to other women's husbands than to your own?[43]

Some women, like upper-class male counterparts, were tending to disregard convention as a result of liberation in Christ. Paul himself may have contributed initially to the emphasis on freedom. Whether or not he was a cause, Paul opposed individualism when it disrupted social order. Thus, although Paul admitted that women were equal to men "in the Lord" (1 Cor. 11:11–12), social constraints made him bridle the liberating effects.

When Paul says, "All things are lawful, but not all things are beneficial" he is introducing a principle that applied to women's rights as well as to others. He indicates this explicitly by taking up the subject of women prophesying and praying with unveiled heads immediately after explaining the principle. The following was addressed to women as well as to people eating idol meat:

---

[42]Banks says that most women had not received formal education in religious matters and yet were present for the whole meeting. This explanation is less cogent than his later suggestion that liberty was highly prized at Corinth and that wives felt free to debate matters.

[43]See Livy, *History of Rome* 34.1–2.

So, whether you eat or drink, or whatever you do, do everything for the glory of God. Give no offense to Jews or to Greeks or to the church of God, just as I try to please everyone in everything I do, not seeking my own advantage, but that of many, so that they may be saved. Be imitators of me, as I am of Christ. (10:31–11:1)

In contrast to the examples from 1 Corinthians and 1 Thessalonians, at other times Paul was apprehensive about the church's acceptance of society's values. Even in these cases, however, he was concerned about what undermined the social good. For example, as noted in chapter 6, above, Paul criticized both Judaism and pagan culture (see Phil 3) because Jewish circumcision and pagan concern for self-glory were being advocated as marks of personal honor.

Despite Paul's apparent appreciation of the social order and the moralist tradition, it is clear that, like Philo and Josephus, he derived communal identity more directly from God. The next section explains how Paul's instruction and his idea of community differed from what philosophical teachers imagined.

God's Family: "A House Not Made with Hands"

The Authenticity of the Church as God's Family. Paul did not derive his ethical ideas from the cultivation of human reason like the philosophical moralists. Nor did he advocate Stoic impassivity. Instead, because converts had a Christlike trust in God, Christ's Spirit was at work in the community, liberating members from individual ambitions and leading them to moral perfection. Prior to liberation, sin had distorted converts' capacity to reason correctly, but now God-given wisdom was causing converts to look beyond their former limited values:

For since, in *the wisdom of God,* the world did not know God through wisdom, God decided, through the foolishness of our proclamation, to save those who believe. For Jews demand signs and Greeks seek wisdom, but we proclaim Christ crucified, a stumbling block to Jews and foolishness to Gentiles, but to those who are the called, both Jews and Greeks, *Christ the power of God and the wisdom of God.* (1 Cor 1:21–24)

And this is my prayer, that your love may overflow more and more with *knowledge and full insight* to help you to determine what is best, so that in the day of Christ you may be pure and blameless, having produced the harvest of righteousness that comes through Jesus Christ for the glory and praise of God. (Phil 1:9–11)

For you know what *instructions* we gave you through the Lord Jesus. For this is the will of God, your sanctification: that you abstain from fornication. . . .

> For God did not call us to impurity but in holiness. Therefore whoever rejects this rejects not human authority but God, who also gives his Holy Spirit to you. Now concerning love of the brothers and sisters, you do not need to have anyone write to you, for you . . . have been *taught by God* to love one another. (1 Thess 4:2–3, 7–9)

These and like passages in Paul show that whereas God's wisdom is constructive and effective, human knowledge is destructive and weak. God's wisdom builds people up through communal love, holiness, and harmony, but human knowledge is divisive and competitive. Thus, in contrast to the philosopher, who said *he* came to students not only in word but also in deed, Paul says,

> *the gospel* came to you not in word only, but also in power and in the Holy Spirit and with full conviction. (1 Thess 1:5)

Paul calls attention to *God's* initiative as the true power that effects intellectual transformation.[44] Moreover, when Paul refers to himself as a model, he adds,

> You became imitators of us *and of the Lord,* for in spite of persecution you received the word with joy inspired by the Holy Spirit. (1:6)

These two passages show that the Thessalonians became imitators of Paul precisely because God's power was in his life. In turn, his power conformed typologically to a pattern that God exhibited in Christ. Christ was the perfect example of God's power to create honor out shame, even to the extent of creating life out of Jesus' death. Paul and his converts could confirm the reality of this divine power because they themselves had experienced the same transforming reality.

In the same way, Paul could appeal to the Galatians' experiential knowledge of God's paradoxical power, and he warns converts about the foolishness of seeking identity through conventional wisdom:

> You foolish Galatians! Who has bewitched you? It was before your eyes that Jesus Christ was publicly exhibited as crucified! The only thing I want to learn from you is this: Did you receive the Spirit by doing the works of the law or by believing what you heard? Are you so foolish? Having started with the Spirit, are you now ending with the flesh? Did you experience so much for nothing? (Gal 3:1–4)

In the case of the Corinthians, the attraction was not the security of Jewish law but its opposite, freedom from social convention. Paul shows

---

[44]See Malherbe, *Paul and the Thessalonians,* 58–60.

the Corinthians that, unfortunately, their wisdom had degenerated into destructive divisions:

> Now I appeal to you, brothers and sisters, by the name of our Lord Jesus Christ, that all of you be in agreement and that there be no divisions among you, but that you be united in the same mind and the same purpose. For it has been reported to me by Chloe's people that there are quarrels among you. . . . What I mean is that each of you says, "I belong to Paul," or "I belong to Apollos," or "I belong to Cephas," or "I belong to Christ." (1 Cor 1:10–13)

Paul opposes the logic of the respective theological views by pointing out their destructive consequences. If any of them had actually been valid, they would not have resulted in the strife occurring at Corinth (see 3:1–4). Once again, then, as in Galatians and 1 Thessalonians, Paul illustrates the validity of the knowledge effected through Christlike faith by means of the Corinthians' own charismatic experience of God's effectiveness. After referring to the apparent foolishness of a crucified Christ, Paul reminds his converts that, prior to conversion, not many of them were wise, not many were powerful, not many were of noble birth. Nonetheless, these very people became God's noble offspring through Christlike faith in God (1:26–31).[45]

By imitating Christ's trust in God, converts also received adoption as divine offspring (Gal 4:4–5). Thus, Paul encouraged converts to cry out in Christ's spirit, "Abba! Father!" (Gal 4:6; Rom 8:15). Despite the childlike simplicity of Christ's knowledge of God, it represented a maturity of relationship that was missing in the Corinthians' desire to justify one viewpoint over against another (1 Cor 1:10–13) and, likewise, in the Galatians' wish to base their relationship with God on slavish subjection to Mosaic law (Gal 3:1–4:11). Christ's trust in God as Father was Paul's primary metaphor both for communal wisdom and for family maturity, even if growing up into Christ's mature simplicity was not a simple matter.

Family Holiness and Love of the Brethren. Up to this point, our emphasis has been on the spiritual household's trust in God and on the beneficial and authentic effects of God's trustworthy response. This

---

[45]Likewise, regarding his own success, Paul reminds the Corinthians that he was able to convert them not because of his lofty rhetoric or bold demeanor but because his unadorned message was from God. Its power was evident in its effectiveness (2:1ff.).

aspect of communal identity derived from God's legitimate right as creator to regenerate his creation. We now turn to two other aspects of the
church's identity as God's family, its piety and its love toward family
members.

> For this is the will of God, your sanctification: that you abstain from forni-
> cation; that each one of you know how to control your own body in holi-
> ness and honor, . . . that no one wrong or exploit a brother or sister in this
> matter . . . . Now concerning love of the brothers and sisters, you do not
> need to have anyone write to you, for you yourselves have been taught by
> God to love one another. (1 Thess 4:3–4, 6, 9)

In this text, knowledge of God includes two explicit teachings:
sanctification and love of fellow Christians. Sanctification is specified as
abstaining from marital infidelity. Since Paul identifies "love of the
brothers and sisters" *(philadelphia)* as divine teaching ("taught by God"),
he was probably contrasting it with philosophical teaching about friendship. Although Stoics believed friendship was a divine gift, they taught
that it was a rational endowment that sprang from nature.[46] By contrast,
Paul made it clear two chapters earlier (see 2:1–12) that his extraordinary
gentleness was a divine gift and not something for which he could take
credit. In contrast to Epicurean ideas of friendship, which often took advantage of goodwill and caused Epicureans to be regarded as irresponsible sponges, Paul advises converts to work with their hands and not to be
a burden to others (see 4:11–12).

Therefore, love had to express itself in concrete activities. Paul advocates the same principle in Romans where, after encouraging converts
in 12:10 to love one another with brotherly affection *(philadelphia)*, he
states concretely in 12:13, "Contribute to the needs of the saints; extend
hospitality."[47] Similarly, Paul advises communal charity on three occasions in Galatians:

---

[46]Malherbe says that Paul's advice consciously differentiates the mutual
support of converts for each other from Epicurean (as well as Cynic and Stoic)
ideas about friendship. "Taught by God" sounds like a conscious rejection of
Epicurus's idea about being "self-taught." In fact, Paul may have consciously
coined *theodidaktos* (lit. "God-taught") as a term to differentiate his conception of
communal support from anthropocentric friendship. See Malherbe, *Paul and the
Thessalonians,* 99–105.

[47]It is equally clear that when Paul refers to Philemon's love toward the
Lord Jesus and the saints, he has Philemon's material support of fellow converts
in mind. This is also clear in Paul's request that Philemon not punish the runaway slave Onesimus and that Philemon allow the slave to serve Paul in imprisonment (see Phlm 13–21).

For you were called to freedom, brothers and sisters; only do not use your freedom as an opportunity for self-indulgence, but through love become slaves to one another. For the whole law is summed up in a single commandment, "You shall love your neighbor as yourself." (Gal 5:13–14)

My friends, if anyone is detected in a transgression, you who have received the Spirit should restore such a one in a spirit of gentleness. Take care that you yourselves are not tempted. Bear one another's burdens, and in this way you will fulfill the law of Christ. (Gal 6:1–2)

So let us not grow weary in doing what is right, for we will reap at harvest time, if we do not give up. So then, whenever we have an opportunity, let us work for the good of all, and especially for those of the family of faith. (Gal 6:9–10)

The same necessity of brotherly love is advised in 1 Corinthians and is heightened by Paul's specification that love of spiritual siblings is more important than one's own rights:

"All things are lawful," but not all things are beneficial. "All things are lawful," but not all things build up. Do not seek your own advantage, but that of the other. (1 Cor 10:23–24)

A statement from Philippians is a final illustration here of Paul's idea of communal love as a divine necessity:

If then there is any encouragement in Christ, any consolation from love, any sharing in the Spirit, any compassion and sympathy, make my joy complete: be of the same mind, having the same love, being in full accord and of one mind. Do nothing from selfish ambition or conceit, but in humility regard others as better than yourselves. Let each of you look not to your own interests, but to the interests of others. Let the same mind be in you that was in Christ Jesus, who . . . did not regard equality with God as something to be exploited, but emptied himself, taking the form of a slave, . . . (Phil 2:1–7)

Two of the three texts cited from Galatians state that love of neighbor is the essence of the law, described as fulfilling "the whole law" and as the "law of Christ."

Since Paul is less clear about how Christ's death shows his love for humanity than about how it is an index of Christ's trust in God, in what way does Christlike trust in God function as an ethics of brotherly love? Christ's trust in God's power as creator assumes respect for God's creation. Moreover, because of his faith in God, Christ was liberated from the hold of sinful disobedience, and he thereby became both the recipient of God's creativity and its mediator to others. Thus, all who were led by Christ's Spirit are also invigorated by the creator's life-giving power:

> To set the mind on the flesh [i.e., by false belief in self-preservation] is death, but to set the mind on the Spirit is life and peace. . . . and those who are in the flesh cannot please God. But you are not in the flesh; you are in the Spirit, since the Spirit of God dwells in you. . . . If the Spirit of him who raised Jesus from the dead dwells in you, he who raised Christ from the dead will give life to your mortal bodies also through his Spirit that dwells in you. (Rom 8:6, 8–9, 11)

Although the community was incorporated sacramentally into Christ's Spirit by dying ritually to the old self in baptism and by partaking of Christ's spirit in Eucharist, its members were still partially subject to the conditions of mortality:

> For while we are still in this tent [our mortal bodies], we groan under our burden, because we wish not to be unclothed but to be further clothed, so that what is mortal may be swallowed up by life. He who has prepared us for this very thing is God, who has given us the Spirit as a guarantee. (2 Cor 5:4–5)

Because of its partial subjection to mortality, the church must separate itself from contaminating influences. Thus, Paul advises it to be separate and holy:

> Do you not know that you are God's temple and that God's Spirit dwells in you? If anyone destroys God's temple, God will destroy that person. For God's temple is holy, and you are that temple. (1 Cor 3:16–17)

> Do not be mismatched with unbelievers. For what partnership is there between righteousness and lawlessness? . . . What agreement has the temple of God with idols? For we are the temple of the living God; as God said, "I will live in them and walk among them, and I will be their God, and they shall be my people. Therefore come out from them, and be separate from them, . . . and touch nothing unclean; . . . and I will be your father, and you shall be my sons and daughters, says the Lord Almighty." (2 Cor 6:14, 16–18)

> For you know what instructions we gave you through the Lord Jesus. For this is the will of God, your sanctification: that you abstain from fornication. (1 Thess 4:2–3)

> And this is my prayer, that your love may overflow more and more with knowledge and full insight to help you to determine what is best, so that in the day of Christ you may be pure and blameless, having produced the harvest of righteousness that comes through Jesus Christ for the glory and praise of God. (Phil 1:9–11)

Despite the church's need to be holy, paradoxically it had to participate in God's transformation of the world. Paul uses himself as the paradigm to be imitated:

> For though I am free with respect to all, I have made myself a slave to all, so that I might win more of them. To the Jews I became as a Jew, in order to win Jews. To those under the law I became as one under the law (though I myself am not under the law) so that I might win those under the law. To those outside the law I became as one outside the law (though I am not free from God's law but am under Christ's law) so that I might win those outside the law. To the weak I became weak, so that I might win the weak. I have become all things to all people, that I might by all means save some. I do it all for the sake of the gospel, so that I may share in its blessings. (1 Cor 9:19–23)

This brings us once again, then, to the importance of universal order, peace, and holiness in Paul's teaching. As the creator, God provides the spiritual means for social order, peace, and holiness. These are social principles that the church must support. On the other hand, chaotic and destructive influences must be opposed. Thus, Paul insists on the cultivation of unity and mutual good, both in the church and toward society outside:

> make my joy complete: be of *the same mind,* having *the same love,* being *in full accord* and *of one mind.* Do nothing from selfish ambition. . . . Let each of you look not to your own interests, but to the interests of others. Let the same mind be in you that was *in Christ Jesus,* who . . . emptied himself. . . . Therefore God also highly exalted him and gave him the name that is above every name, so that at the name of Jesus every knee should bend, . . . and every tongue should confess that Jesus Christ is Lord, to the glory of God the Father. (Phil 2:2–7, 9–11, italics added)

Although Paul emphasizes internal harmony, Christ's lack of selfishness results simultaneously in worldwide rule. The communal unity presently effected by Christ will become universal. This reaffirms that God's essential identity for Paul was defined by God's activity as universal creator.

ABRAHAM'S OFFSPRING ACCORDING TO PROMISE

Although Paul does not use extended-family metaphors as often as household images, it is surprising how often he does describe his churches in an ethnic sense. With the exception of Philemon, he applies Jewish terms to Gentile converts in all of his authentic letters.[48] How is

---

[48]Although the civic designation *ekklēsia* and certain images of Christ's rule show that Paul conceptualized the church as a Greco-Roman political community, his racial images show that he was also influenced by Jewish ideas of community.

this emphasis to be understood? One scholarly explanation is that conservative Jewish Christians kept trying to persuade converts to become
Jews. According to this view, external necessity forced Paul to define
Gentile converts as God's people. Unfortunately, this view does not take
seriously enough the role ethnic metaphors play in Paul's own system
of belief.[49]

Another interpretation scholars find useful is that Paul softened
Jewish requirements because he was a hellenistic Jew. In this case, it was
not conservative critics who forced Paul to justify converts as God's
people; he did it voluntarily because of Greco-Roman culture's influence. This view would be more credible if Paul had been a philosophi-
cally inclined Jew prior to conversion. Unlike Philo and Josephus,
however, Paul had not been an interpreter of Judaism in Greco-Roman
terms. He had been a Pharisee who persecuted the Greek-speaking
church specifically because of his devotion to Jewish tradition.[50]

Within Paul's former system of Pharisaic logic, Jesus had been justly
condemned by Jewish law. Therefore, since Paul had been offended by the
Christian proclamation of Jesus as the Christ and, likewise, by the Greek
church's offensive claim that Gentiles were God's people, the best explanation of Paul's transformation is that God somehow altered his former
viewpoint. This is precisely what Paul claims in his letters. He is particularly insistent in Galatians that his status as Christ's apostle came directly
from God, who revealed the resurrected Jesus to him (see Gal 1:11–17).
Thus, Paul's idea of Gentiles as God's people did not derive from Pharisaism, nor from any human influence, but from a change in perspective
caused by God himself. Indeed, all the major changes in Paul's system of
belief derive from God's revelation of the risen Jesus. As a result of that
experience, Paul came to believe that Gentiles could become God's

-----

[49]The introduction and chapter 1, above, argued that Paul's own convictions provide the best explanation of the recurring use of certain images in his letters. The following description will show that this explanation is as true for his
racial images as for his emphasis on familial metaphors.

[50]Twice Paul connects his persecution to his devotion to Jewish tradition:

> You have heard, no doubt, of my earlier life in Judaism. I was violently persecut-
> ing the church of God and was trying to destroy it. I advanced in Judaism beyond
> many among my people of the same age, for I was far more zealous for the tradi-
> tions of my ancestors. (Gal 1:13–14)

> I, too, have reason for confidence in the flesh. . . . circumcised on the eighth day, a
> member of the people of Israel, of the tribe of Benjamin, a Hebrew born of He-
> brews; as to the law, a Pharisee; as to zeal, a persecutor of the church; as to righ-
> teousness under the law, blameless. (Phil 3:4–6)

people without being Jews and that Abraham was also the father of the Gentiles.

Although zeal for Jewish tradition had led Paul to persecute the church, he was obliged to alter his view when he learned that God had exalted the crucified Jesus. Since God had vindicated a man condemned by Jewish law, Paul had to find an alternative to law as a basis of defining relationship with God. Since Paul had been a traditionalist, he had to make sense of God's resurrection of Jesus in Jewish terms.

The Jewish precedent that helped Paul to make sense of Jesus' resurrection was God's earlier dealings with Abraham, the father of the Jewish race. The most important element of the Abrahamic tradition for Paul was the promise that all nations (i.e., the Gentiles) would be blessed through his offspring. Since Gentiles were becoming God's people through the gospel's proclamation, Jesus must somehow be Abraham's promised descendant (see Gal 3:13–14, 16).

Abraham's, Christ's, and the Gentiles' analogous lack of qualification from Paul's former Pharisaic viewpoint formed the basis of their ethnic similiarity. It was precisely this idea of people generated supernaturally by God that is the key to Paul's ideas about the church as Abraham's heirs. In particular, Christ was the connecting link between Gentiles and the fulfillment of God's promise that Abraham would father many nations.

The idea that God was generating a very large family through Christ as Abraham's promised offspring is often expressed by Paul. For example, Christ's role as the promised heir who incorporates Gentiles into Abraham's lineage is stated in Gal 3:13f.:

> Christ redeemed us from the curse of the law by becoming a curse for us—for it is written, "Cursed is everyone who hangs on a tree"—in order that in Christ Jesus the blessing of Abraham might come to the Gentiles, so that we might receive the promise of the Spirit through faith.

Similarly, in Rom 8:29 Paul says, "For those whom he foreknew he also predestined to be conformed to the image of his Son, in order that he might be the firstborn within a large family."

Likewise, in Rom 4:16ff. Paul refers to Abraham as the father of many peoples (with italics added for emphasis):

> (for he is *the father of all of us,* as it is written, "I have made you *the father of many nations*")—in the presence of the God in whom he believed, who gives life to the dead and calls into existence the things that do not exist. Hoping against hope, he believed that he would become *"the father of many nations,"* according to what was said, *"So numerous shall your descendants be."*

And finally: "And the scripture, foreseeing that God would justify the Gentiles by faith, declared the gospel beforehand to Abraham, saying, 'All the Gentiles shall be blessed in you' " (Gal 3:8).

All of God's authentic people, whether Abraham, Isaac, Christ, or Gentile converts, were procreated supernaturally. Adoption was a good metaphor for describing Paul's idea of God's generation of Abraham's race.

Paul's idea of the Gentiles' procreation should not be understood too literally. On the other hand, it would be equally wrong to conceive of it too theoretically. The knowledge Gentile converts had that they were God's offspring was something they had experienced. But in what sense was their status superior to that of Abraham's physical descendants? It was not superior so long as Jews recognized that their identity derived from God and not from some natural right by birth or from personal achievement. The following statements illustrate Jews' and Gentiles' common dependence on God as the basis of their true identity.

> He [Abraham] received the sign of circumcision as a seal of the righteousness that he had by faith while he was still uncircumcised. The purpose was to make him *the ancestor of all who believe* without being circumcised and who thus have righteousness reckoned to them, and likewise the ancestor of the circumcised who are not only circumcised but who also follow the example of the faith . . . Abraham had before he was circumcised. (Rom 4:11–12)

> For this reason it [the promise] depends on faith, in order that the promise may rest on grace and be guaranteed to all his descendants, not only to the adherents of the law but also to those who share the faith of Abraham (for he is the father of all of us, as it is written, "I have made you the father of many nations")—in the presence of the God in whom he believed, who gives life to the dead and calls into existence the things that do not exist (4:16–17).[51]

---

[51]The following statements also indicate that spiritual procreation (adoption) was the basis of authentic racial identity:

> We ourselves are Jews by birth and not Gentile sinners; yet we know that a person is justified not by the works of the law but through faith in [like] Jesus Christ. (Gal 2:15–16)

> Just as Abraham "believed God, and it was reckoned to him as righteousness," so, you see, those who believe are the descendants of Abraham. (Gal 3:6–7)

> For neither circumcision nor uncircumcision is anything; but a new creation is everything! As for those who will follow this rule—peace be upon them, and mercy, and upon *the Israel of God*. (Gal 6:15–16)

> we proclaim Christ crucified, a stumbling block to Jews and foolishness to Gentiles, but to those who are the called, both Jews and Greeks, Christ the power of God and the wisdom of God. (1 Cor 1:23–24)

Despite the singular importance of God's role in fathering the race, spiritual generation required recipients to cooperate. Procreation did not occur automatically. Nor was this racial identity a static reality, for it required ongoing trust in God and spiritual maturation. Therefore, just as the church was a family whose members had to mature, so too as a race it had to make progress. In Rom 8:30 Paul says, "those whom he [God] justified he also glorified." The context of the statement shows that Paul was thinking of church members' glorification in an ethnic sense, not in the sense of individuals' perfection or of the nobilization of the individual church ("family"). Here is the fuller context, to illustrate Paul's emphasis:

> We know that all things work together for good for those who love God, who are *called* according to his purpose. For those whom he foreknew he also predestined to be conformed to the image of his Son, in order that he might be *the firstborn within a large family* [i.e., race]. And those whom he predestined he also *called;* and those whom he *called* he also justified; and those whom he justified he also glorified. (8:28–30)

This is only one of many passages where Paul applies Jewish election terms to the church.[52] Paul also refers to converts as adult offspring who inherit the blessing promised to Abraham. The idea of being set apart as a kingdom of priests (Exod 19:6) and as a people of superior morality also informs Paul's ethnic image of the church. In brief, all the major ideals identified with Judaism—election, status as Abraham's heirs, moral superiority—are applied by Paul to Gentiles. Because Paul's expectations were as rigorous as those required of Judaism, we must explain again how Paul differentiated spiritual offspring from Abraham's natural descendants.

Physical descent from Abraham, circumcision, adherence to dietary laws, and general obedience to Mosaic law were good in principle. From Paul's conversion viewpoint, however, traditional markers of racial identity became problematic when pride in descent and adherence to tradition replaced faith in God as the primary source of ethnic identity. Not only did ethnic pride interfere with building up universal community; the natural competitiveness generated by such pride could even destroy relationships within the race and family.

---

[52]Even Paul's Greek political term for the church, *ekklēsia,* is compatible with the Jewish idea of election, since it refers to the citizen element of the population that performed tasks on behalf of the larger community and whose members had superior communal status.

Unfortunately, destructive competition was not confined to Abraham's actual descendants. Cited elsewhere in this book, data in Romans, the Corinthian correspondence, Galatians, and Philippians show that the same tendencies were also undermining communal harmony in Paul's churches. He had to keep reminding converts that authentic community, like true knowledge, derived from God. Thus, Christ was the true heir precisely because, like his forefather Abraham, he did not defend his own interests but looked to the creator for his status. By this means, he became a spiritual Son who, like the Father himself, mediated benevolence to all humanity.

Converts, as well as Christ, are adult heirs of Abraham. In order to avoid Paul's sexist-sounding emphasis on offspring as "sons," the NRSV translates υἱοί, *huioi,* as "children" in Gal 4:5–7.[53] Unfortunately, this translation does not capture Paul's own contrast between immature and adult offspring. Paul uses *huios* ("son") as an image of maturity because adult sons, not daughters, were the normative model of the heir in Greek culture. Thus, Paul uses *huios* in the sense of the adult son as heir. This does not mean that Paul uses the metaphor to denigrate women's status. For only a few verses earlier in Galatians Paul stated:

> For in Christ Jesus you are all children [sons] of God through faith. As many of you as were baptized into Christ have clothed yourselves with Christ. There is no longer Jew or Greek, there is no longer slave or free, there is no longer male and female; for all of you are one in Christ Jesus. And if you belong to Christ, then you are Abraham's offspring, heirs according to the promise. (3:26–29)

Thus, *huios* is a metaphor of Christ's adult authority as Abraham's heir. In the same way, converts—whether male or female, whether Jew or Greek, whether slave or free—were also empowered to be Abraham's adult heirs. The kind of maturity that Paul intended was precisely the liberation that enabled people to transcend their sexual, racial, and social conditions within the natural order.

The essence of ethnic perfection, as well as of familial maturity, was to be free from destructive self-interest. Therefore, Paul describes spiritual offspring not only as mature but also as freeborn, as a noble race no longer enslaved to the socially conditioned limits of race, sex,

---

[53]The NRSV contrasts natural and spiritual children, rather than the different developmental stages of the same offspring.

and social level.[54] The mind controlled by human convention is a mind set on mortality:

> For those who live according to the flesh set their minds on the things of the flesh, but those who live according to the Spirit set their minds on the things of the Spirit. To set the mind on the flesh is death, but to set the mind on the Spirit is life and peace. . . . If the Spirit of him who raised Jesus from the dead dwells in you, he who raised Christ from the dead will give life to your mortal bodies also through his Spirit that dwells in you. (Rom 8:5–7, 11).

Consequently, true wisdom and true nobility spring from commitment to God's benevolent creativity as the fundamental law of the universe. Paul asserts the importance of adhering to this principle several times near the end of Galatians:

> For freedom Christ has set us free. Stand firm, therefore, and do not submit again to a yoke of slavery. . . . For through the Spirit, by faith, we eagerly wait for the hope of righteousness. For in Christ Jesus neither circumcision nor uncircumcision counts for anything; the only thing that counts is faith working through love. (Gal 5:1, 5–6)

> For you were called to freedom, brothers and sisters; only do not use your freedom as an opportunity for self-indulgence, but through love become slaves to one another. For the whole law is summed up in a single commandment, "You shall love your neighbor as yourself." If, however, you bite and devour one another, take care that you are not consumed by one another. (Gal 5:13–15)

> Now the works of the flesh are obvious: . . . strife, jealousy, anger, quarrels, dissensions, factions, . . . I am warning you, as I warned you before: those who do such things will not inherit the kingdom of God. By contrast, the fruit of the Spirit is love, joy, peace, patience, kindness, generosity, faithfulness, gentleness, and self-control. . . . And those who belong to Christ Jesus have crucified the flesh with its passions and desires. If we live by the Spirit, let us also be guided by the Spirit. (Gal 5:19–25)

> Bear one another's burdens, and in this way you will fulfill the law of Christ. (Gal 6:2)

---

[54]E.g., the following statement illustrates Paul's emphasis on the freedom of God's spiritual offspring:

> For all who are led by the Spirit of God are children of God. For you did not receive a spirit of slavery to fall back into fear, but you have received a spirit of adoption. When we cry, "Abba! Father!" it is that very Spirit bearing witness with our spirit that we are children of God, and if children, then heirs, heirs of God and joint heirs with Christ—if, in fact, we suffer with him so that we may also be glorified with him. (Rom 8:14–17)

For neither circumcision nor uncircumcision is anything, but a new creation is everything! As for those who will follow this rule—peace be upon
them, and mercy, and upon the Israel of God. (Gal 6:15–16)

These citations capture two contrasting principles of conduct. Certain people put confidence in their own achievements and thereby bite
and devour one another to get ahead. These people are enslaved to the
destructiveness of their mortality. On the other hand, people who put
their confidence in God do not engage in destructive competition but
bear each other's burdens and are servants of one another. They are a *new*
creation. They are liberated from the human destructiveness that ends in
death.

Paul describes the life-effecting spiritual principle as "the law of
Christ" (6:2). The mind or spirit he commends is the radical trust that we
find exhibited in Christ's submission to crucifixion. Paul illustrates this
principle graphically in the Christ hymn of Phil 2:5–11, but we find it
several other places in his letters. For example, in one of the above citations he says, "And those who belong to Christ Jesus have crucified the
flesh with its passions and desires" (Gal 5:24).[55]

Because of Christ's submission to God's life-effecting power, he was
made not only the head of a new household and the ruler of a new political order but also the head of a new race and a new creation. In turn, fellow heirs are characterized by the same spirit of maturity and nobility and
are thereby empowered to receive the inheritance promised to Abraham.
They too adhere to the life-effecting power of their spiritual Father. Consequently, here we find ourselves at the same place where we stood at the
end of ch. 3, above. That is, the spiritual race's maturity, inheritance, holiness, and nobility issue from the same source as its progress as a spiritual
family: God's life-effecting power of creativity. Like their divine Father, the
spiritual family and the spiritual race are engaged in life-effecting productivity, maturation, and benevolence. In the next section we will find that
the same resource accounts for the church's superior status as a civic body
and as composed of subjects of God's divine empire.

---

[55]Paul promotes the effectiveness of Christ's crucifixion faith also in the
following statement:

> We are not commending ourselves to you again, but giving you an opportunity to
> boast about us, so that you may be able to answer those who boast in outward ap-
> pearance and not in the heart. . . . For the love of Christ urges us on, because we
> are convinced that one has died for all; therefore all have died. And he died for all,
> so that those who live might live no longer for themselves, but for him who died
> and was raised for them. (2 Cor 5:12, 14–15)

HEAVENLY CITY AND DIVINE EMPIRE

Paul's Jewish background may have made family and race more attractive metaphors for the church than city-state and empire, for he describes the church as a city only twice, and though he often refers to God's empire *(basileia)*, he does not describe it in detail. Even if political images are not common in Paul's letters, however, they formed an important dimension of his idea of spiritual community, of converts as citizens of an ideal city and as the nucleus of a new empire. The principles and attributes that govern his images of the church as a family and race are equally influential in his political ideas.

"But Our Citizenship Is in Heaven"

Paul refers to the church explicitly as a civic community two times, in Phil 3:17–21 (cf. 3:20) and in Gal 4:21–31 (cf. 4:25–26). There are good reasons for arguing that Greco-Roman political ideas influenced Paul's idea of converts as a civic body. We know that political authority was an important idea for Paul, because he applies to Christ the Greco-Roman attributes of the ruler.[56] Granted, the representation of Christ in terms of the emperor is not the same as that of Christ in terms of a city-state official. Nonetheless, we know that Paul was acquainted with city politics. Since he was reared in a Greek-speaking city, he would have known how the Jewish community ruled itself and how Judaism's rule of its community was analogous to Greco-Roman citizenship rights. In both cases, self-rule was a privilege that only Rome could grant. Moreover, although all Judaism was governed by the same constitution (i.e., Mosaic law), the law was implemented city by city and not by an overarching imperial Jewish rule.

Although certain Jewish laws were distinctive, the general function of law in the community was analogous to the operation of constitutional law in the city-states. Even special terms that were applied to the Jewish community, such as *politeuma,* which Paul uses in Phil 3:20, reflect city-state *(polis)* influence. Thus, as an urban Jew and a member of the Jewish community influenced by city-state rule, Paul was acquainted with the city's civic values.

---

[56]See Paul's description of Christ's rule in Greco-Roman imperial images in ch. 7, above.

Paul's familiarity with the different social classes of the city, and with the privileges that attended each level, is reflected in his contrast between freedom and slavery and in other like images. "Freeborn" and "slave" were social distinctions that belonged to the city long before there was a Roman Empire.[57] The manner in which these designations differentiated the noble and the ignoble is implied in Paul's description of the lowly background of many Corinthian converts:

> Consider your own call, brothers and sisters: not many of you were wise by human standards, not many were powerful, not many were of noble birth. But God chose what is foolish in the world to shame the wise; God chose what is weak in the world to shame the strong; God chose what is low and despised in the world, things that are not, to reduce to nothing things that are. (1 Cor 1:26–28)

This chapter earlier suggested that, in contrast to the majority of people from the lower class, at least a segment of the Corinthian church belonged to the upper level of civic society. It was this part of the church that was scandalized by Paul's vocation as an artisan, which was regarded by the aristocracy as "slavish" work.[58] Nonetheless, as the above citation and others in 1 Corinthians indicate, Paul's idea of spiritual community led him to redefine what was noble, wise, and strong.

As argued throughout this chapter, submission to God and to communal concord was not slavish and demeaning but noble. Indeed, Paul indicates that it was the people who gloried in individual knowledge, authority, and social standing who were actually enslaved. The ignoble and immature nature of the Corinthians' emphasis on individualized knowledge is evidenced by the strife and animosity that resulted from party differences:

> I could not speak to you as spiritual people, but rather as people of the flesh, as infants in Christ. I fed you with milk, not solid food, for you were not ready for solid food. Even now you are still not ready, for you are still of the flesh. For as long as there is jealousy and quarreling among you, are you not of the flesh, and behaving according to human inclinations? (1 Cor 3:1–3)

---

[57]This chapter earlier suggested that, with rare exceptions, only freeborn inhabitants of long-standing residence (i.e., men who owned hereditary estates) could be citizens in the classical Greek city-states. Other inhabitants fell into the categories of resident alien or slave. In the Roman Empire, people were categorized as freeborn, freed (formerly a slave), resident alien, or slave.

[58]E.g., Hocks suggests that upper-class converts in Corinth would have regarded Paul's appearance as an artisan demeaning and slavish. See *Social Context*, 60.

Although Paul acknowledges different kinds and even different levels of social role within the church, he does not connect these differences to intrinsic distinctions of status. Since all members of the community are procreated by the same divine Parent, each member has comparable worth. Numerous statements in Paul's letters indicate his interest in the community's collective welfare.[59]

The distinctive nature of the church as a political body is indicated by Paul's description of it as the body of Christ. As Christ is master of the family, Lord of the empire, and promised heir of Abraham's race, so too he is its civic ruler. In the latter instance, he should not be understood literally as the "head" of the body, in the manner of Col 1:18 and Eph 1:22–23, but more broadly as the animating or guiding spirit. The following statements illustrate Paul's emphasis:

> Now there are varieties of gifts, but the same Spirit; and there are varieties of services, but the same Lord; and there are varieties of activities, but it is the same God who activates all of them in everyone. To each is given the manifestion of the Spirit for the common good. (1 Cor 12:4–7)

> For just as the body is one and has many members, and all the members of the body, though many, are one body, so it is with Christ. For in the one Spirit we were all baptized into one body—Jews or Greeks, slaves or free— and we were all made to drink of one Spirit. (12:12–13)

Paul describes the founding of the church as a civic body when he says that "we were all baptized into one body" and "were all made to drink of one Spirit." This statement refers to the sacramental acts of baptism and Eucharist, which celebrate God's community-begetting action through Christ's death and resurrection. He endows all members of the community—Jews or Greeks, slaves or free, male or female—with the same nobility of birth. Because of the nature of their founding in Christ's sacrificial death, citizenship is defined not so much in terms of privilege

---

[59]These statements from the Corinthian correspondence illustrate this interest:

> even if I boast a little too much of our authority, which the Lord gave for building you up and not for tearing you down, I will not be ashamed of it. (2 Cor 10:8)

> The cup of blessing that we bless, is it not a sharing in the blood of Christ? The bread that we break, is it not a sharing in the body of Christ? Because there is one bread, we who are many are one body, for we all partake of the one bread. (1 Cor 10:16–17)

> "All things are lawful," but not all things are beneficial. "All things are lawful," but not all things build up. Do not seek your own advantage, but that of the other. (1 Cor 10:23–24)

as in terms of service. Thus, when Paul recalls the church's union with Christ in baptism and Eucharist, he is encouraging its members to imitate the life-effecting service of Christ, which God used to found and sustain the community.

The essence of the church's character is defined by Christ's eucharistic saying: "This is my body that is for you" (1 Cor 11:24). Christ's body, symbolized under the image of broken bread, is a metaphor of his death (i.e., the broken body). The relation between Christ and the church's service, as an extension of his body, is stated explicitly in 1 Cor 10:16:

> The cup of blessing that we bless, is it not a sharing in the blood of Christ? The bread that we break, is it not a sharing in the body of Christ?

Paul appeals to the same concrete model in the description of the community as a body in Romans 12:1, 3–5:

> I appeal to you therefore, brothers and sisters, by the mercies of God, to present your bodies as a living sacrifice, holy and acceptable to God, which is your spiritual worship. . . . For by the grace given to me I say to everyone among you not to think of yourself more highly than you ought to think, but to think with sober judgment, each according to the measure of faith that God has assigned. For as in one body we have many members, and not all the members have the same function, so we, who are many, are one body in Christ, and individually we are members one of another.

Like Christ himself, the community's members have to sacrifice themselves for the collective good. It is no accident that Paul joined his request, that members present their bodies as sacrifices, to the image of the community as a body. It is precisely sacrificial service like what Christ offered that is the source of spiritual regeneration.

In the two explicit references to the church as a heavenly city in Philippians and Galatians, Paul argues that those who are led by Christ's Spirit render to the community service that is superior to that offered by ordinary citizens. In Phil 3, Paul first contrasted the church with Jews, who put confidence in such physical marks of status as circumcision, rather than in God as the authentic source of status. But as we suggested above, Paul's primary contrast was not between the church and Judaism but between the church and voluntary associations that were modeling themselves on city-state structures. In this case, Paul argues that the values of the associations, as well as the civic virtues on which they were modeled, were actually self-serving and not concerned with the collective good. By contrast, the church was led by Christ's Spirit and did not look to its own interests (cf. 2:1–4). The superiority of the spiritual constitution is verified by God's exaltation of Christ as head of the new spiritual order (cf. Phil 2:5–11). A like honor awaits members of his communal body, whose status will be confirmed when its political head returns:

> But our citizenship is in heaven, and it is from there that we are expecting a Savior, the *Lord* Jesus Christ. He will transform *the body of our humiliation* that it may be conformed to *the body of his glory*, by the power that also enables him to make all things subject to himself. (3:20–21, italics added)

Although Paul does not engage in a detailed comparison with civic structures, when he represents the church as a heavenly city in Galatians, his idea of the city is similar to the description of spiritual citizenship in Philippians. In Galatians, Paul contrasts the church as a civic entity with Jerusalem, and he argues that whereas inhabitants of Jerusalem live under an enslaving constitution, his converts are freeborn citizens of the Jerusalem above. The context makes it clear that the contrast is between people who put confidence in birth status or personal achievement and other people who look only to God for their status. As earlier stated in this chapter, God liberates people from the conventional constraints of race, sex, and social class. This is strongly emphasized in Galatians:

> For you were called to freedom, brothers and sisters; only do not use your freedom as an opportunity for self-indulgence, but through love become slaves to one another. For the whole law is summed up in a single commandment, "You shall love your neighbor as yourself." (Gal 5:13)

Paul's athletic imagery also reflects the influence of city life (rather than racial or familial life), and there are other urban influences on his idea of community, but the above examples indicate clearly enough that Paul could conceive of the church as a form of spiritual citizenship.

"God . . . Calls You into His Own Kingdom and Glory" (1 Thess 2:12)

Although Paul sometimes described the resurrected Jesus as if he were David's messianic successor, his emphasis was nonetheless on Christ as ruler of both Gentiles and Jews. Thus, it is highly unlikely he had a strictly ethnic idea of the state in mind. Although there were smaller temple states and kingdoms, a kingdom was not really an important political entity in the imperial rule of Rome. For these reasons, and others to be identified, it is likely the Roman Empire is the primary model that informs Paul's idea of the *basileia* of God. Thus, Paul's appropriation of the Greek title "Lord" and his use of imperial images to describe Christ suggest he modified Jewish messianic ideas in the direction of imperial ideology.

Perhaps the similiarity between the Roman Empire and Paul's idea of God's new order accounts for his lack of specificity in describing God's empire, over which Christ is appointed ruler. It would have been foolish to describe too concretely a political order that would replace the existing empire. Moreover, since the spiritual empire would become a full-blown entity only in the future, perhaps Paul was not able to be more explicit about its contours. Although Paul does not present detailed lineaments of the empire, he clearly indicates the universal extent of Christ's rule:

> Then comes the end, when he [Christ] hands over the kingdom [empire] to God the Father, after he has destroyed every ruler and every authority and power. For he must reign until he has put all his enemies under his feet. The last enemy to be destroyed is death. For "God has put all things in subjection under his feet." (1 Cor 15:24–27)

> Therefore God also highly exalted him and gave him the name that is above every name, so that at the name of Jesus every knee should bend, in heaven and on earth and under the earth, and every tongue should confess that Jesus Christ is Lord, to the glory of God the Father. (Phil 2:9–11)

These and like statements indicate that God had appointed Christ to rule not only the inhabited earth but the universe as well.[60] As noted in chapter 7, above, emperors were regarded as divine agents who preserved not only earthly peace but the universal order as well. Paul presents Christ as a military leader who, like the Roman emperor, establishes universal justice:

> And so all Israel will be saved; as it is written, "Out of Zion will come the Deliverer; he will banish ungodliness from Jacob." "And this is my covenant with them, when I take away their sins." (Rom 11:26–27)

> For the Lord himself, with a cry of command, with the archangel's call and with the sound of God's trumpet, will descend from heaven, and the dead in Christ will rise first. Then we who are alive, who are left, will be caught up in the clouds together with them to meet the Lord in the air; and so we will be with the Lord forever. (1 Thess 4:16–17)

> For all of us must appear before the judgment seat of Christ, so that each may receive recompense for what has been done in the body, whether good or evil. (2 Cor 5:10)

---

[60]Statements in 1 Cor 8:5f. and 2 Cor 2:14–16; 5:10, 16f. also refer to Christ's status as universal Lord.

Paul also refers to Christ's spiritual subjects as his military comrades in arms:

> Let us then lay aside the works of darkness and put on the armor of light; let us live honorably as in the day, not in reveling and drunkenness. (Rom 13:12f.)

> But since we belong to the day, let us be sober, and put on the breastplate of faith and love, and for a helmet the hope of salvation. For God has destined us not for wrath but for obtaining salvation through our Lord Jesus Christ. (1 Thess 5:8f.)

> Indeed, we live as human beings, but we do not wage war according to human standards; for the weapons of our warfare are not merely human, but they have divine power to destroy strongholds. We destroy arguments and every proud obstacle raised up against the knowledge of God, and we take every thought captive to obey Christ. We are ready to punish every disobedience when your obedience is complete. (2 Cor 10:3–6)

These citations show that Christ's military prowess, as in the case of Athena (Minerva), Hercules, and Apollo, is a metaphor for the conquest of social discord. Thus, despite Paul's occasional emphasis on God's vengeance, his primary emphasis is that Christ's and his comrades' warfare is constructive and educative. Accordingly, Paul states in 2 Cor 10:4f., "We destroy arguments and every proud obstacle raised up against the knowledge of God." Similarly, in the 1 Thessalonians citation, Paul says, "God has destined us not for wrath but for obtaining salvation."

As in Paul's other forms of social association, so here too he expects Christ's imperial subjects to have a superior morality, holiness, and knowledge. The parallel to progress and maturation in the family and race is also expressed with reference to Christ's subjects and, unexpectedly, with the same image of inheritance (with italics added for emphasis):

> Do you not know that wrongdoers will not *inherit the kingdom of God?* Do not be deceived! Fornicators, idolators, adulterers, . . . none of these will *inherit the kingdom of God,* And this is what some of you used to be. But you were washed, you were sanctified, you were justified in the name of the Lord Jesus Christ and in the Spirit of our God. (1 Cor 6:9–11)

> Now the works of the flesh are obvious: fornication, impurity, . . . enmities, strife, jealousy, anger, quarrels, dissensions, factions. . . . I am warning you, as I warned you before: those who do such things will not *inherit the kingdom of God.* (Gal 5:19–21)

The key to understanding Paul's use of the image of inheritance for subjects of an empire is identified in Romans:

> For the promise that he would *inherit the world* did not come to Abraham or to his descendants through the law but through the righteousness of faith. If it is the adherents of the law who are to be the heirs, faith is null and the promise is void. . . . For this reason it depends on faith, in order that the promise may rest on grace and be guaranteed to all his descendants, not only to the adherents of the law but also to those who share the faith of Abraham (for he is the father of all of us, as it is written, "I have made you the father of many nations"). (Rom 4:13–14, 16–17, italics added)

This statement indicates that Paul did not think merely that *some* Gentiles would be incorporated into Abraham's stock; he believed God was reconciling the whole world to himself in Christ. Thus, he believed that the special relation with God as Father that his converts had experienced would extend to all humanity. All would participate in the fulfillment of the promised blessing to Abraham. In this sense, then, the application of the metaphor of inheritance to the church as composed of Christ's subjects was not so illogical as it first appears.

Christ's universal authority has the same basis as his rule of the family and his status as promised heir: God's life-effecting power. In turn, Christ's subjects likewise became emissaries of God's spirit of reconciliation (with italics added):

> For *the love of Christ urges us on,* because we are convinced that one has died for all. . . . And he died for all, so that those who live might live no longer for themselves, but for him who died and was raised for them. From now on, therefore, we regard no one from a human point of view; even though we once knew Christ from a human point of view, we know him no longer in that way. So if anyone is in Christ, there is a new creation: everything old has passed away; see, everything has become new! All this is from God, who reconciled us to himself through Christ, and *has given us the ministry of reconciliation;* that is, in Christ God was reconciling the world to himself. (2 Cor 5:14–19)

Paul expresses Christ's absolute defeat of the forces that would harm his subjects:

> Who will bring any charge against God's elect? It is God who justifies. Who is to condemn? It is Christ Jesus, who died, yes, who was raised, who is at the right hand of God, who indeed intercedes for us. Who will separate us from the love of Christ? Will hardship, or distress, or persecution? . . . No, in all these things we are more than conquerors through him who loved us. For I am convinced that neither death, nor life, nor angels, nor rulers, . . . nor anything else in all creation, will be able to separate us from the love of God in Christ Jesus our Lord. (Rom 8:33–35, 37–39)

Paul's political images—the church as city and empire—agree with other communal metaphors of the church. All assume the spiritual community's self-giving service to God and creation. This service, in every case, is modeled on Christ's sacrificial service, and he exhibits in his resurrection the reward of authentic service.

In light of Paul's emphasis on the church as the bearer of God's grace, not only to members of the community itself but also to pagan humanity, it is no accident that Augustine developed his idea of the church as a nuclear city within the larger world-city. Paul's idea of the church's civic character was surely an influence.

CONCLUDING REFLECTIONS

Paul conceived of the church at many levels of community. Nonetheless, whether imagined under the image of the single family or that of the nucleus of an empire, the church must express self-giving affection for its spiritual members' welfare. Nor does Paul limit the expectation of service to members of the spiritual community. For he believed all Jews and Gentiles would eventually confess God as Father and Christ as Lord. Paul's belief in God's (and Christ's) universal community arose from his idea of God as creator. The same creator who generated the physical universe was now effecting its spiritual maturation. Paul connected God's new creation to his original activity as world creator.

> For we do not proclaim ourselves; we proclaim Jesus Christ as Lord and ourselves as your slaves for Jesus' sake. For it is the God who said, "Let light shine out of darkness," who has shone in our hearts to give the light of the knowledge of the glory of God in the face of Jesus Christ. (2 Cor 4:5–6)

> For the creation waits with eager longing for the revealing of the children of God; for the creation was subjected to futility, not of its own will but by the will of the one who subjected it, in hope that the creation itself will be set free from its bondage to decay and will obtain the freedom of the glory of the children of God. We know that the whole creation has been groaning in labor pains until now; and not only the creation, but we ourselves, who have the first fruits of the Spirit, groan inwardly while we wait for adoption, the redemption of our bodies. (Rom 8:19–23)

The idea that God's salvation will issue in universal community may be illustrated by one image, Paul's representation of Christ as a new Adam. All the negative influence that emanated from Adam's original disobedience is removed by Christ's obedience, which Paul conceives as issuing in a new (regenerated) humanity.[61]

---

[61]See Paul's extended contrast between Adam and Christ in Rom 5:12–21 and in 1 Cor 15:21–28, 45–51.

HALIE'S VOICE: Tilden was right about the corn you know. I've never seen such corn. . . . Tall as a man already. . . . Carrots too. Potatoes. Peas. It's like a paradise out there, Dodge. You oughta' take a look. A miracle. I've never seen it like this. Maybe the rain did something. Maybe it was the rain. . . . You can't force a thing to grow. . . . You just gotta wait til it pops up out of the ground. Tiny little shoot. Tiny little white shoot. All hairy and fragile. Strong though. Strong enough to break the earth even. . . . Maybe it's the sun. Maybe that's it. Maybe it's the sun.

Sam Shepherd, *Buried Child* (act 3)

EPILOGUE

Something remains to be said about modern parallels to Paul's perspective. Problematic in the scholarly interpretation of Paul is that Paul's viewpoint is often explained with designations such as "justification by faith." Such an emphasis is wrong on at least two fronts. First, Paul's language is more graphic and metaphorical than this kind of abstract formulation. Second, the focus on "justification," as well as the allied emphasis on "Judaizers" as *the* cause of the apostle's perspective, fails to capture Paul's most essential idea of God. He no longer thought of God as a lawgiver and judge, even if God were a forgiving lawgiver.

As a result of Paul's own mystical experience, he used "sensible" images to convince Gentile converts of the gracious nature of God's creative potency. Jonathan Edwards's suggestions about the proper mode of speaking about God are quite analogous to Paul's use of metaphors:

> The duty of singing praises to God seems to be appointed wholly to excite and express religious affections. No other reason can be assigned why we should express ourselves to God in verse, rather than in prose, and do it with music, but only, that such is our nature and frame, that these things have a tendency to move our affections.

> The same thing appears in the nature and design of the sacraments. . . . God, considering our frame, hath not only appointed that we should be told of the great things of the gospel, and of the redemption of Christ, and instructed in them by his Word; but also that they should be, as it were,

exhibited to our view, in sensible representations, in the sacraments, the more to affect us with them.[1]

These citations from Edwards's mid-eighteenth century *Treatise Concerning Religious Affections* show that religious certainty is demonstrated not through abstract proofs but by affective symbols. Thus, regarding *how* Paul spoke about God, Edwards understood his perspective better than most modern interpreters.

In addition to recognizing the importance of affective language for interpreting Paul, we must also acknowledge the equal importance, to him, of God's powers of generativity. On this front, as well as in Edwards's emphasis on how to talk about God, we have modern representatives who provide useful parallels to Paul. The works of three authors come to mind.

Sam Shepherd's play *Buried Child*, cited as the epigraph of this epilogue, tells the story of a seriously dysfunctional family. Dodge, the father, has for all practical purposes already died. He lies sleeping or drunk on a couch night and day. Halie, the mother, lives in a bygone and romantic youth, carrying on an affair with an Episcopal priest. Tilden, one of the family's two grown sons, is living at home like a retarded child. Another son, although not at home, is bitter about growing up with less athletic talent than his brother. His sense of physical inferiority is exaggerated by the absence of a leg, which he lost in an accident.

By the third act, we learn what triggered the abnormal behavior of three of the four family members. Sometime in the past, everything had gone wrong for Tilden, who had been a high-school athletic hero. Although the details are not spelled out, we learn that his marriage failed and that he got into trouble out of state. He returned home and had an incestuous affair with his mother, whom he impregnated. A few weeks after the mother (Halie) delivered the child, his father (Dodge) killed the infant and buried it in a field behind the house. Dodge indicates that this was when problems came to a head:

> See, we were a well established family once. . . . All the boys were grown. The farm was producing enough milk to fill Lake Michigan twice over. . . . Then Halie got pregnant again. Outa' the middle a' nowhere, she got pregnant. . . . We had enough boys already. In fact, we hadn't been sleepin' in the same bed for about six years. . . .
>
> I killed it. I drowned it. Just like the runt of a litter. Just drowned it.[2]

---

[1] Edwards, *A Treatise*, 115.
[2] Shepard, *Buried Child*, 58f.

In spite of the family's psychological death and its inability to relate meaningfully to one another, uncultivated fields suddenly began to produce voluntarily a bumper crop of vegetables. Tilden, to the surprise and aggravation of Dodge, kept carrying in vegetables from unplanted fields. It is difficult to know exactly what Shepherd intended by the paradoxical juxtaposition of family sterility and agricultural harvest, but one thing is clear. Despite family members' psychological death, nature's fertility continues.

We well might ask, "What does this dysfunctional family have to do with St. Paul's theology?" Sam Shepherd would probably say "Nothing!" Nonetheless, there is an important lesson to be learned from his play. Just as nature has the uncanny power to turn death into fertility, so, too, Paul shows that God has the power to bring life out of death, particularly the power to transform bad social situations.

A second popular work has useful material for illustrating Paul's theological perspective—John Steinbeck's *Grapes of Wrath*. Steinbeck's novel talks about Oklahoma farmers who, because of dust bowl conditions, were uprooted from their farms and livelihood. Unprepared for the life of migrant workers, husbands and fathers such as Pa Joad were not able to lead families to a new life. Nonetheless, wives and mothers such as Ma Joad and mechanically minded offspring such as young Al Joad were able to negotiate the change. Thus, as in Shepherd's play, life broke through seemingly uncultivated soil. Although the regeneration depicted by Steinbeck and Shepherd is striking, it nonetheless reflects nature's power. Likewise, through the analogy of nature's potency, Paul evokes God's powers of social renewal.

Another, more modern work, James Baldwin's novel *Go Tell It on the Mountain,* also illustrates Paul's perspective. Although Baldwin mentions St. Paul in his novel, he nowhere indicates that the apostle is *the* theological model he is applying to modern social issues. Nonetheless, no biblical precedent or author seems to fit his viewpoint as exactly as does Paul. Indeed, Baldwin may well capture the spirit of Paul better than any other modern author.

In Baldwin's novel, Johnny Grimes was badly treated by Gabriel Grimes because he was not Gabriel's natural offspring. Gabriel feared the illegitimate Johnny, rather than his own natural offspring, would be the special, chosen child of God. In fact, this was what happened, even though Johnny himself fought against the spiritual generation that made him God's agent.

Physical and intellectual similarities between Johnny Grimes and Baldwin himself are certainly intended, but John is more than a cipher for Baldwin's own intellectual success in the white man's world. Johnny is a representative of the African-American race, just as, for Paul, God's resurrection of a man condemned under the law signals the adoption of "lawless" Gentiles into the people of God. In both situations—of Christ and the Gentiles—Paul had to acknowledge that God's authentic offspring were determined neither by natural birth status nor by conventionally recognized markers of social identity. Through spiritual adoption, the Gentile was God's legitimate offspring and Abraham's heir just as much as the Jew. Correspondingly, in the case of James Baldwin, his own striking power of words, along with comparable power showered on numerous other African-American leaders (male and female), shows that God's true children are those whom God adopts for his purpose rather than those who are socially favored in the eyes of American culture.

In the last analysis, whether depicted in Baldwin's novel or in Paul's letters, our status with God is something that lies outside our own ability to effect. After all, we are mortals and God is creator. But if we offer our creaturehood and mortality back to God, in the willingness to be spent in his service to others, God can raise us up, as he raised up Christ, to be his own true heirs of creativity and life.

> "You remember Jesus," Elisha said. "You keep your mind on Jesus. He went that way—up the steep side of the mountain—and He was carrying the cross, and didn't nobody help Him. He went that way for us. He carried that cross for us."
>
> "But He was the Son of God," said John, "and He knew it."
>
> "He knew it," said Elisha, "because He was willing to pay the price. Don't you know it, Johnny? Ain't you willing to pay the price?"[3]

---

[3]Baldwin, *Go Tell It on the Mountain*, 21.

SHORT TITLES LIST

Attridge, *Interpretation*
  Attridge, Harold W. *The Interpretation of Biblical History in the An-tiquitates Judaicae of Flavius Josephus.* HDR 7. Missoula, Mont.: Scholars Press, 1976.
Balch, *Wives*
  Balch, David. *Let Wives Be Submissive: The Domestic Code in I Peter.* SBLDS 26. Chico, Calif.: Scholars Press, 1981.
Baldwin, *Go Tell It on the Mountain*
  Baldwin, James. *Go Tell It on the Mountain.* 1952–1953. Repr., New York: Dell, 1985.
Banks, *Community*
  Banks, Robert. *Paul's Idea of Community.* Rev. ed.. Peabody, Mass.: Hendrickson, 1994.
Baumgarten, *Paulus und die Apokalyptik*
  Baumgarten, Jörg. *Paulus und die Apokalyptik.* Neukirchen-Vluyn: Neukirchener, 1975.
Beard and North, *Pagan Priests*
  Beard, Mary, and John North, eds. *Pagan Priests: Religion and Power in the Ancient World.* London: Duckworth, 1990.
Beker, *The Triumph of God*
  Beker, J. Christiaan. *The Triumph of God.* Philadelphia: Fortress, 1990.
Betz, *Galatians*
  Betz, Hans Dieter. *Galatians: A Commentary on Paul's Letter to the Churches in Galatia.* Hermeneia. Philadelphia: Fortress, 1979.
Bianchi, *Ara Pacis Augustae*
  Bianchi, Emanuela, *Ara Pacis Augustae.* Trans. Isobel Butters Caleffi. Rome: Fratelli Palombi, 1994.

Bjerkelund, *Parakalo*
Bjerkelund, C. J. *Parakalo: Form, Funktion, und Sinn der Parakalo-Sätze in den paulinischen Briefen*. Oslo: Universitetsforlaget, 1967.

Bömer, *Untersuchungen*
Bömer, F. *Untersuchungen über die Religion der Sklaven in Griechenland und Rom*. 4 vols. Mainz: Akademie der Wissenschaften und der Literatur, 1958–1963.

Bonfante, "Daily Life and Afterlife"
Bonfante, Larissa. "Daily Life and Afterlife." Pages 232–78 in *Etruscan Life and Afterlife*. Detroit: Wayne State University Press, 1986.

Bornkamm, "Letter to the Romans"
Bornkamm, Günther. "The Letter to the Romans as Paul's Last Will and Testament." Pages 16–28 in *The Romans Debate: Revised and Expanded Edition*. Ed. Karl Donfried. Peabody, Mass.: Hendrickson, 1991.

Borza, *Alexander the Great*
Borza, Eugene N., ed. *The Impact of Alexander the Great*. Hinsdale, Ill.: Dryden, 1974.

Bradley, *Roman Family*
Bradley, Keith R. *Discovering the Roman Family: Studies in Roman Social History*. New York: Oxford University Press, 1991.

Brewer, "πολιτεύεσθε in Phil 1:27"
Brewer, R. R. "The Meaning of πολιτεύεσθε in Phil 1:27." *JBL* 73 (1954): 76–83.

Bultmann, *Der Stil*
Bultmann, Rudolf. *Der Stil der paulinischen Predigt und die kynish-stoische Diatribe*. FRLANT 13. Göttingen: Vandenhoeck & Ruprecht, 1910.

Bultmann, *Theology of the New Testament*
Bultmann, Rudolf. *The Theology of the New Testament*. Trans. K. Grobel. 2 vols. New York: Scribner's, 1951, 1955.

Cole, "Greek Cults"
Cole, Susan G. "Greek Cults." *CAMGR* 2:887–908.

Collins, *Between Athens and Jerusalem*
Collins, John. *Between Athens and Jerusalem: Jewish Identity in the Hellenistic Diaspora*. New York: Crossroad, 1983.

Cornford, *Plato's Cosmology*
Cornford, Francis M. *Plato's Cosmology: The Timaeus of Plato Translated with a Running Commentary*. New York: Harcourt, Brace, 1937.

Cotter, "Cosmology"
Cotter, Wendy J. "Cosmology and the Jesus Miracles." Pages 118–31 in *Whose Historical Jesus?* Ed. W. E. Arnal and M. Desjardins. Waterloo: Wilfrid Laurier University Press, 1997.

Cotter, "Our *Politeuma*"
    Cotter, Wendy J. "Our *Politeuma* Is in Heaven: The Meaning of Philippians 3:17–21." Pages 92–104 in *Origins and Method: Towards a New Understanding of Judaism and Christianity*. Ed. Bradley H. McLean. Sheffield: Sheffield Academic Press, 1993.
Dahl, "Letter"
    Dahl, Nils A. "Letter." *IDBSup* 538–40.
Dahl, "Missionary Theology"
    Dahl, Nils A. "Missionary Theology in the Epistle to the Romans." Pages 70–94 in *Studies in Paul: Theology for the Early Christian Mission*. Ed. N. A. Dahl. Minneapolis: Augsburg, 1977.
Dahl, "Paul: A Sketch"
    Dahl, Nils A. "Paul: A Sketch." Pages 1–21 in *Studies in Paul: Theology for the Early Christian Mission*. Ed. N. A. Dahl. Minneapolis: Augsburg, 1977.
Dahl, "Paul's Letter to the Galatians"
    Dahl, Nils A. "Paul's Letter to the Galatians: Epistolary Genre, Content, Structure." Paper presented at the annual meeting of the SBL. Chicago, Nov. 8–11, 1973.
Deissmann, *Light from the Ancient East*
    Deissmann, Adolf. *Light from the Ancient East*. Trans. L. R. M. Strachan. 1922. Repr., Peabody, Mass.: Hendrickson, 1995.
Dibelius, *James*
    Dibelius, Martin. *James: A Commentary on the Epistle of James*. Rev. H. Greeven. Trans. M. A. Williams. Hermeneia. Philadelphia: Fortress, 1976.
Dickison, "Women in Rome"
    Dickison, Sheila K. "Women in Rome." *CAMGR* 3:1319–32.
Dodd, *The Epistle to the Romans*
    Dodd, Charles H. *The Epistle of Paul to the Romans*. MNTC. 1932. Repr., London: Hodder & Stoughton, 1954.
Edwards, *A Treatise*
    Edwards, Jonathan. *A Treatise Concerning Religious Affections in Three Parts*. Ed. John E. Smith. New Haven: Yale University Press, 1959.
Elliott, *A Home for the Homeless*
    Elliott, John H. *A Home for the Homeless*. Philadelphia: Fortress, 1981.
Elliott, "Temple versus Household"
    Elliott, John H. "Temple versus Household in Luke–Acts." Pages 211–40 in *The Social World of Luke–Acts*. Ed. J. Neyrey. Peabody, Mass.: Hendrickson, 1991.

Elliott, "Rhetorical Strategy"
Elliott, Susan M. "The Rhetorical Strategy of Paul's Letter to the Galatians in Its Anatolian Cultic Context." Ph.D. diss., Loyola University of Chicago, 1997.

Farnell and Rose, "Mystery"
Farnell, L. R., and H. J. Rose. "Mystery." Pages 45–49 in vol. 16 of *Encyclopaedia Britannica*. William Benton: Chicago, 1958.

Fears, "Ruler Worship"
Fears, Rufus J. "Ruler Worship." *CAMGR* 2:1009–25.

Fernandez, *Persuasions and Performances*
Fernandez, James W. *Persuasions and Performances: The Play of Tropes in Culture*. Bloomington: Indiana University Press, 1986.

Fisher, "Roman Associations"
Fisher, Nicholas R. E. "Roman Associations, Dinner Parties, and Clubs." *CAMGR* 2:1199–1225.

Foerster and Quell, "Lord"
Foerster, Werner, and Gottfried Quell. "Κύριος" ("Lord"). *TDNT* 3:1039–95

Fuller, "Lord"
Fuller, Reginald H. "Lord." *HBD* 573–74.

Funk, "Apostolic Parousia"
Funk, Robert W. "The Apostolic Parousia: Form and Significance." Pages 249–68 in *Christian History and Interpretation: Studies Presented to John Knox*. Ed. W. R. Farmer, C. F. D. Moule, and R. R. Niebuhr. Cambridge: Cambridge University Press, 1967.

Furnish, "2 Corinthians"
Furnish, Victor. "2 Corinthians." *HBC* 1190–1203.

Gale, *The Use of Analogy*
Gale, Herbert M. *The Use of Analogy in the Letters of Paul*. Philadelphia: Westminster, 1964.

Gamble, *Textual History*
Gamble, Harry Jr. *The Textual History of the Letter to the Romans: A Study in Textual and Literary Criticism*. Grand Rapids: Eerdmans, 1977.

Garnsey and Saller, *Roman Empire*
Garnsey, Peter, and Richard P. Saller. *The Roman Empire: Economy, Society, and Culture*. Berkeley: University of California Press, 1987.

Georgi, *Opponents of Paul*
Georgi, Dieter. *The Opponents of Paul in Second Corinthians*. Philadelphia: Fortress, 1986.

Georgi, *Theocracy*
> Georgi, Dieter. *Theocracy in Paul's Praxis and Theology.* Minneapolis: Fortress, 1991.

Godwin, *Mystery Religions*
> Godwin, Joscelyn. *Mystery Religions in the Ancient World.* San Francisco: Harper & Row, 1981.

Gordon, Richard, "The Veil of Power"
> Gordon, Richard. "The Veil of Power: emperors, sacrificers and benefactors." Pages 199–231 in *Pagan Priests: Religion and Power in the Ancient World.* Ed. Mary Beard and John North. London: Duckworth, 1990.

Grant, *From Alexander to Cleopatra*
> Grant, Michael. *From Alexander to Cleopatra.* New York: Collier Books, 1982.

Hall, "Rhetorical Outline"
> Hall, Robert G. "The Rhetorical Outline for Galatians: A Reconsideration." JBL 106 (1987): 277–87.

Heinrici, *Das zweite Sendschreiben*
> Heinrici, C. F. Georg. *Das zweite Sendschreiben des Apostel Paulus an die Korinther.* Göttingen: Vandenhoeck & Ruprecht, 1890.

Hocks, *Social Context*
> Hocks, Ronald F. *The Social Context of Paul's Ministry: Tentmaking and Apostleship.* Philadelphia: Fortress, 1980.

Hurd, "Paul ahead of His Time"
> Hurd, John C., Jr. "Paul ahead of His Time: 1 Thess. 2:13–16." Pages 31–33 in *Paul and the Gospels.* Vol. 1 of *Anti-Judaism in Early Christianity.* Ed. P. Richardson with D. Granskou. Waterloo: Wilfrid Laurier University Press, 1986.

Hurd, "Structure of 1 Thessalonians"
> Hurd, John C., Jr. "Concerning the Structure of 1 Thessalonians." Paper presented at the annual meeting of the SBL. Los Angeles, Sept. 1–5, 1972.

Jeremias, "Chiasmus"
> Jeremias, Joachim. "Chiasmus in den Paulusbriefen." *ZNW* 49 (1958): 145–56.

Judge, "Early Christians"
> Judge, E. A. "The Early Christians as a Scholastic Community." *JRH* 1 (1960–1961): 1–8, 124–37.

Judge, "Paul's Boasting"
  Judge, E. A. "Paul's Boasting in Relation to Contemporary Professional Practice." *ABR* 16 (1968): 37–50.
Judge, "St. Paul and Classical Society"
  Judge, E. A. "St. Paul and Classical Society." *JAC* 15 (1972): 19–36.
Judge, *Social Pattern*
  Judge, E. A. *The Social Pattern of Christian Groups in the First Century.* London: Tyndale, 1960.
Käsemann, *Romans*
  Käsemann, Ernst. *Commentary on Romans.* Grand Rapids: Eerdmans, 1980.
Keck, "Apocalyptic Theology"
  Keck, Leander. "Paul and Apocalyptic Theology." *Int* 38 (1984): 229–41.
Kennedy, *New Testament Interpretation*
  Kennedy, George A. *New Testament Interpretation through Rhetorical Criticism.* Chapel Hill: University of North Carolina Press, 1984.
Kloppenborg, "Edwin Hatch"
  Kloppenborg, John. "Edwin Hatch, Churches, and *Collegia.*" Pages 212–38 in *Origins and Method: Towards a New Understanding of Judaism and Christianity.* Ed. Bradley H. McLean. Sheffield: Sheffield Academic Press, 1993.
Knox, *Life of Paul*
  Knox, John. *Chapters in a Life of Paul.* Ed. Douglas R. A. Hare. Rev. ed. Macon, Ga.: Mercer University Press, 1987.
Koester, *Early Christianity*
  Koester, Helmut. *History and Literature of Early Christianity.* Vol. 2 of *Introduction to the New Testament.* 2 vols. New York: Walter de Gruyter, 1982.
Koester, *Hellenistic Age*
  Koester, Helmut. *History, Culture, and Religion of the Hellenistic Age.* Vol. 1 of *Introduction to the New Testament.* 2 vols. New York: Walter de Gruyter, 1982.
Krentz, "Military Language and Metaphors"
  Krentz, Edgar. "Military Language and Metaphors in Philippians." Pages 105–27 in *Origins and Method: Towards a New Understanding of Judaism and Christianity.* Ed. Bradley H. McLean. Sheffield: Sheffield Academic Press, 1993.
Lacey, *Family*
  Lacey, W. K. *The Family in Classical Greece.* Repr., Ithaca, N.Y.: Cornell University Press, 1989.

Lakoff and Johnson, *Metaphors*
> Lakoff, George, and Mark Johnson. *Metaphors We Live By.* Chicago: University of Chicago Press, 1980.

Lewis and Reinhold, *Roman Civilization*
> Lewis, Naphtali, and Meyer Reinhold, eds. *Roman Civilization: Selected Readings.* 2 vols. 3d ed. New York: Columbia University Press, 1990.

Lietzmann, *An die Korinther*
> Lietzmann, Hans. *An die Korinther.* Expanded by W. G. Kümmel. 4th ed. HNT 9. Tübingen: J. C. B. Mohr [Paul Siebeck], 1949.

Lietzmann, *An die Römer*
> Lietzmann, Hans. *An die Römer.* 4th ed. HNT 8. Tübingen: J. C. B. Mohr [Paul Siebeck], 1933.

Ling, "Roman Architecture"
> Ling, Roger, "Roman Architecture." *CAMGR* 3:1671–90.

Lloyd, "Theories"
> Lloyd, G. E. R. "Theories of Progress and Evolution." *CAMGR* 1:265–75.

Lohmeyer, *Philipper, Kolosser, und Philemon*
> Lohmeyer, Ernst. *Die Briefe an die Philipper, an die Kolosser, und an Philemon.* Göttingen: Vandenhoeck & Ruprecht, 1954.

Luedemann, *Paul, Apostle to the Gentiles*
> Luedemann, Gerd. *Paul, Apostle to the Gentiles: Studies in Chronology.* Trans. F. S. Jones. Philadelphia: Fortress, 1984.

Lund, *Chiasmus*
> Lund, Nils W. *Chiasmus in the New Testament: A Study in the Form and Function of Chiastic Structures.* 1942 ed. Repr., Peabody, Mass.: Hendrickson, 1992.

MacMullen, *Roman Social Relations*
> MacMullen, Ramsay. *Roman Social Relations.* New Haven: Yale University Press, 1974.

Malherbe, *Ancient Epistolary Theorists*
> Malherbe, Abraham J. *Ancient Epistolary Theorists.* Atlanta, Ga.: Scholars Press, 1988.

Malherbe, *Cynic Epistles*
> Malherbe, Abraham J. *The Cynic Epistles: A Study Edition.* Missoula, Mont.: Scholars Press, 1977.

Malherbe, "Hellenistic Moralists"
> Malherbe, Abraham J. "Hellenistic Moralists and the New Testament." *ANRW* 26:1, 267–333.

Malherbe, *Paul and the Thessalonians*
Malherbe, Abraham J. *Paul and the Thessalonians: The Philosophic Tradition of Pastoral Care.*Philadelphia: Fortress, 1987.
Malherbe, *Popular Philosophers*
Malherbe, Abraham J. *Paul and the Popular Philosophers.* Minneapolis: Fortress, 1989.
Malherbe, *Social Aspects*
Malherbe, Abraham J. *Social Aspects of Early Christianity.* Baton Rouge: Louisiana State University Press, 1977.
Martin, *Hellenistic Religions*
Martin, Luther H. *Hellenistic Religions: An Introduction.* New York: Oxford University Press, 1987.
Meeks, Wayne A. *First Urban Christians*
Meeks, Wayne A. *The First Urban Christians: The Social World of the Apostle Paul.* New Haven: Yale University Press, 1983.
Metzger, *Textual Commentary*
Metzger, Bruce M. *A Textual Commentary on the Greek New Testament.* New York: United Bible Societies,1971.
Moxnes, "Patron-Client Relations"
Moxnes, Halvor. "Patron-Client Relations and the New Community in Luke–Acts." Pages 241–68 in *The Social World of Luke–Acts.* Ed. J. Neyrey. Peabody, Mass.: Hendrickson, 1991.
Mullins, "Disclosure"
Mullins, Terence Y. "Disclosure: A Literary Form in the New Testament." *NovT* 7 (1964): 44–50.
Murphy-O'Connor, *St. Paul's Corinth*
Murphy-O'Connor, Jerome. *St. Paul's Corinth: Texts and Archaeology.* Wilmington, Del.: Michael Glazier, 1983.
Nock, "Σύνναος Θεός"
Nock, Arthur Darby. "Σύνναος Θεός." Pages 202–51 in vol. 1 of *Arthur Darby Nock: Essays on Religion and the Ancient World.* Ed. Zeph Stewart. 2 vols. Corrected reprint of 1972 edition. New York: Oxford University Press, 1986.
Nock, "Vocabulary"
Nock, Arthur Darby. "The Vocabulary of the New Testament." Pages 341–47 in vol. 1 of *Arthur Darby Nock: Essays on Religion and the Ancient World.* Ed. Zeph Stewart. 2 vols. Corrected reprint of 1972 edition. New York: Oxford University Press, 1986.
Patte, *Paul's Faith*
Patte, Daniel. *Paul's Faith and the Power of the Gospel.* Philadelphia: Fortress, 1983.

Pearson, "1 Thessalonians 2:13–16"
    Pearson, Birger A. "1 Thessalonians 2:13–16: A Deutero-Pauline Interpolation." *HTR* 64 (1971): 79–94.
Petersen, *Rediscovering Paul*
    Petersen, Norman. *Rediscovering Paul: Philemon and the Sociology of Paul's Narrative World.* Philadelphia: Fortress, 1985.
Poland, *Geschichte*
    Poland, Franz. *Geschichte des griechischen Vereinswesens.* 1909. Repr., Leipzig: Zentral-Antiquariat der DDR, 1967.
Pomeroy, *Women in Hellenistic Egypt*
    Pomeroy, Sarah B. *Women in Hellenistic Egypt: From Alexander to Cleopatra.* New York: Schocken, 1984.
Price, *Rituals and Power*
    Price, S. R. F. *Rituals and Power: The Roman Imperial Cult in Asia Minor.* London: Cambridge University Press, 1984.
Ramage and Ramage, *Roman Art*
    Ramage, Nancy H., and Andrew Ramage. *Roman Art: Romulus to Constantine.* New York: Abrams, 1991.
Rees, Bell, and Barns, *Descriptive Catalog*
    Rees, B. R., H. I. Bell, and J. W. B. Barns, eds. *A Descriptive Catalogue of the Greek Papyri in the Collection of Wilfred Merton.* Vol. 2 (= P.Mert. II). Dublin: Hodges Figgis, 1959.
Riddle, *Paul, Man of Conflict*
    Riddle, Donald W. *Paul, Man of Conflict.* New York: Abingdon-Cokesbury, 1940.
Rostovtzeff, *Greece*
    Rostovtzeff, Michael. *Greece.* Ed. Elias J. Bickermann. Trans. J. D. Duff. New York: Oxford University Press, 1963.
Rostovtzeff, *History*
    Rostovtzeff, Michael. *The Social and Economic History of the Hellenistic World.* Ed. P. M. Fraser. 3 vols. 2d rev. ed. Oxford: Oxford University Press, 1957.
Rowlingson, "The Jerusalem Conference"
    Rowlingson, Donald T. "The Jerusalem Conference and Jesus' Nazareth Visit: A Study in Pauline Chronology." *JBL* 71 (1952): 69–74.
Sanders, "Transition"
    Sanders, Jack. "The Transition from Opening Epistolary Thanksgiving to Body in the Letters of the Pauline Corpus." *JBL* 81 (1962): 348–62.
Schubert, *Pauline Thanksgivings*
    Schubert, Paul. *Form and Function of the Pauline Thanksgivings.* BZNW 20. Berlin: Töpelmann, 1939.

Scott, *Adoption*
  Scott, James M. *Adoption as Sons of God: An Exegetical Investigation into the Background of* υἱοθησία *in the Pauline Corpus*. Tübingen: J. C. B. Mohr [Paul Siebeck], 1992.
Shaw, "Roman Taxation"
  Shaw, Brent D. "Roman Taxation." *CAMGR* 2:809–27.
Shepard, *Buried Child*
  Shepard, Sam. *Buried Child: A Play in Three Acts*. New York: Dramatists Play Service, 1979.
Smith, *Drudgery Divine*
  Smith, Jonathan Z. *Drudgery Divine: On the Comparison of Early Christianities and the Religions of Late Antiquity*. Chicago: University of Chicago Press, 1990.
Stendahl, "The Apostle Paul"
  Stendahl, Krister. "The Apostle Paul and the Introspective Conscience of the West," *HTR* 56 (1963): 199–215. Repr. pages 78–96 in *Paul among Jews and Gentiles and Other Essays*. Philadelphia: Fortress, 1976.
Stowers, *Diatribe*
  Stowers, Stanley K. *The Diatribe and Paul's Letter to the Romans*. SBLDS 57. Chico, Calif.: Scholars Press, 1981.
Stowers, *Letter Writing*
  Stowers, Stanley K. *Letter Writing in Greco-Roman Antiquity*. Philadelphia: Westminster, 1986.
Stowers, *Rereading of Romans*
  Stowers, Stanley K. *A Rereading of Romans: Justice, Jews, and Gentiles*. New Haven: Yale University Press, 1994.
Suggs, "Paul's Macedonian Ministry"
  Suggs, M. Jack. "Concerning the Date of Paul's Macedonian Ministry." *NovT* 4 (1960): 60–68.
Tarn, "Alexander's ὑπομνήματα"
  Tarn, W. W. "Alexander's ὑπομνήματα and the 'World-Kingdom.'" *JHS* 41 (1921): 1–17.
Theissen, *Social Setting*
  Theissen, Gerd. *The Social Setting of Pauline Christianity: Essays on Corinth*. Trans. John Schütz. Philadelphia: Fortress, 1982.
Tomson, *Halakha in the Letters of the Apostle*
  Tomson, Peter. *Halakha in the Letters of the Apostle to the Gentiles*. Vol. 1 of *Paul and the Jewish Law*. Minneapolis: Fortress, 1991.

Verner, *Household*
> Verner, David C. *The Household of God: The Social World of the Pastoral Epistles*. SBLDS 71. Chico, Calif.: Scholars Press, 1983.

Wallace-Hadrill, *Augustan Rome*
> Wallace-Hadrill, Andrew. *Augustan Rome*. London: Bristol Classical Press, 1993.

Wallace-Hadrill, "Patronage"
> Wallace-Hadrill, Andrew, ed. "Patronage in Roman Society: From Republic to Empire." Pages 63–87 in *Patronage in Ancient Society*. New York: Routledge, 1989.

Wallace-Hadrill, *Suetonius*
> Wallace-Hadrill, Andrew. *Suetonius: The Scholar and His Caesars*. London: Duckworth, 1983.

White, "Apostolic Mission"
> White, John L. "Apostolic Mission and Apostolic Message: Congruence in Paul's Epistolary Rhetoric, Structure, and Imagery." Pages 145–61 in *Origins and Method: Towards a New Understanding of Judaism and Christianity*. Ed. Bradley H. McLean. Sheffield: Sheffield Academic Press, 1993.

White, *Body of the Greek Letter*
> White, John L. *The Form and Function of the Body of the Greek Letter: A Study of the Letter-Body in the Non-Literary Papyri and in Paul the Apostle*. SBLDS 2. 2d ed., corrected. Missoula, Mont.: Scholars, 1972.

White, "Improved Status"
> White, John L. "The Improved Status of Greek Women in the Hellenistic Period. *BR* 29 (1994): 62–79.

White, *Light from Ancient Letters*
> White, John L. *Light from Ancient Letters*. Philadelphia: Fortress, 1986.

Wilcken, *Alexander the Great*
> Wilcken, Ulrich. *Alexander the Great*. Trans. G. C. Richards. 1931. Repr., New York: Norton, 1967.

Wuellner, "Epistolography and Rhetoric"
> Wuellner, Wilhelm. "Epistolography and Rhetoric in 1 Corinthians." Paper presented at the annual meeting of the SNTS. Cambridge, England, Aug. 8–12, 1988.

Wuellner, "Greek Rhetoric"
> Wuellner, Wilhelm. "Greek Rhetoric and Pauline Argumentation." Pages 177–88 in *Early Christian Literature and the Classical Intellectual*

Tradition. Ed. W. R. Schoedel and R. L. Wilken. Paris: Beauchesne, 1979.

Wuellner, "Paul's Rhetoric"
  Wuellner, Wilhelm. "Paul's Rhetoric of Argumentation in Romans: An Alternative to the Donfried-Karris Debate over Romans." *CBQ* 38 (1976): 330–51.

Zanker, *The Power of Images*
  Zanker, Paul. *The Power of Images in the Age of Augustus.* Trans. Alan Shapiro. Ann Arbor: University of Michigan Press, 1988.

ANCIENT WORKS CITED

The Apostolic Fathers. Trans. K. Lake. 2 vols. Loeb Classical Library. Cambridge, Mass.: Harvard University Press, 1976–1985.

Apuleius. *Metamorphoses.* Trans. J. Arthur Hanson. 2 vols. Loeb Classical Library. Cambridge: Harvard University Press, 1989.

Aristotle. *Aristotle in Twenty-three Volumes.*Trans. H. Rackham et al. 23 vols. Loeb Classical Library. Cambridge, Mass.: Harvard University Press; London: W. Heinemann, 1926–1962. Rev. ed. 1952.

Arrian. *Arrian.* Rev. text and translation with new introd., notes, and appendixes by P. A. Brunt. 2 vols. Loeb Classical Library. Cambridge, Mass.: Harvard University Press, 1976–1983.

Augustus. *Res gestae divi Augusti: The Achievements of the Divine Augustus.*Introduction and commentary by P. A. Brunt and J. M. Moore. London: Oxford University Press, 1967.

Cicero, Marcus Tullius. *Cicero in Twenty-eight Volumes.* Trans. H. Rackham, W. Glynn Williams, et al. 28 vols. Loeb Classical Library. Cambridge, Mass., Harvard University Press, [1913–] 1972.

Curtius, Quintus. *History of Alexander.* Trans. John C. Rolfe. 2 vols. Loeb Classical Library. 1946. Repr., Cambridge: Harvard University Press, 1962.

Demosthenes. *Funeral Speech, Erotic Essay, Exordia, and Letters* Trans. Norman W. DeWitt and Norman J. DeWitt. 7 vols. Loeb Classical Library. Cambridge, Mass., Harvard University Press, 1949.

Dio Cassius. *Roman History* (books 56–60). Trans. Earnest Cary. Loeb Classical Library. 1924. Repr., Cambridge: Harvard University Press, 1961.

Dio Chrysostom. *Dio Chrysostom.* Trans. J. W. Cohoon and H. L. Crosby. 5 vols. Loeb Classical Library. Cambridge, Mass.: Harvard University Press, 1932–1951.

Diodorus Siculus. *Universal History.* Trans. C. Bradford Welles. Loeb Classical Library. Cambridge: Harvard University Press, 1963.

Dionysus of Halicarnassus, *The Critical Essays* (= "Art of Rhetoric"). Trans. Stephen Usher. 2 vols. Loeb Classical Library. Cambridge: Harvard University Press, 1974.

Hesiod. *Works and Days.* Trans. Hugh G. Evelyn-White. Loeb Classical Library. Cambridge: Harvard University Press, 1967.

Horace. *Odes and Epodes.* Trans. C. E. Bennett. Loeb Classical Library. 1914. Repr., Cambridge: Harvard University Press, 1978.

Isocrates. *Isocrates.* Trans. G. Norlin et al. 3 vols. Loeb Classical Library. London, W. Heinemann, Ltd., 1928–1945.

Josephus, Flavius. *Josephus.* Trans. H. St. J. Thackery, R. Marcus, A. Wikgren, et al. 10 vols. Loeb Classical Library. Cambridge, Mass.: Harvard University Press, 1926–1965.

Juvenal. *Juvenal and Persius.* Trans. G. G. Ramsay. Loeb Classical Library. London: W. Heinemann, 1928.

Letter of Aristeas. Pages 83–122 in vol. 2 of *The Apocrypha and Pseudepigrapha of the Old Testament.* Ed. R. H. Charles et al. 2 vols. 1913. Repr., Oxford: Oxford University Press, 1967.

Livy. *Livy.* Trans. B. O. Foster, F. G. Moore, E. T. Sage, et al. 14 vols. Loeb Classical Library. London. W. Heinemann, 1951–1963.

Lucian of Samosata. *Lucian.* Trans. A. M. Harmon, K. Kilburn, M. D. Macleod. 8 vols. Loeb Classical Library. Cambridge, Mass.: Harvard University Press, 1936–1967.

Martial. *Epigrams.* Ed. and trans. D. R. Shackleton Bailey. 3 vols. Loeb Classical Library. Cambridge, Mass.: Harvard University Press, 1933.

Nepos, Cornelius. *Lives of Famous Men (De viris illustribus).* Trans. Gareth Schmeling. Lawrence, Kans.: Coronado, 1971.

Philo of Alexandria. *Philo.* Trans. F. H. Colson, G. H. Whitaker, et al. 10 vols. and 2 supplementary vols. Loeb Classical Library. Cambridge, Mass.: Harvard University Press, 1922–1962.

Pindar. *The Odes of Pindar.* Trans. Richmond Lattimore. Chicago: University of Chicago Press, 1947.

Plato. *Plato, with an English Translation.* Trans. H. N. Fowler, R. G. Bury, et al. 10 vols. Loeb Classical Library. Cambridge, Mass.: Harvard University Press, 1914–1929.

Pliny the Younger. *Letters and Panegyricus.* Trans. Betty Radice. 2 vols. Loeb Classical Library. Cambridge, Mass.: Harvard University Press, 1975–1989.

Plutarch. *Plutarch's Lives.* Trans. B. Perrin. 11 vols. Loeb Classical Library. Cambridge, Mass.: Harvard University, 1917–1951.

Quintilian. *The* Instituto oratoria *of Quintilian.* Trans. H. E. Butler. 4 vols. Loeb Classical Library. London. W. Heinemann, 1921–1922.

Sallust. *Sallust.* Trans. (rev.) J. C. Rolfe. Loeb Classical Library. Cambridge, Mass.: Harvard University Press, 1965.

Suetonius. *The Twelve Caesars.* Trans. Robert Graves. Rev. Michael Grant. New York: Penguin, 1989.

Tacitus, Cornelius. *Dialogus, Agricola, Germania.* Trans. W. Peterson. Loeb Classical Library. London: W. Heinemann, 1932.

Tertullian. *Prescriptions against Heretics.* Pages 31–64 in *Early Latin Theology.* Trans. and ed. S. L. Greenslade. LCC 5. Philadelphia: Westminster, 1956.

Thucydides. *Thucydides.* Trans. S. Smith. 8 vols. Loeb Classical Library. London: W. Heinemann, 1919–1923.

Virgil. *The Aeneid.* Trans. Robert Fitzgerald. 1981. Repr., New York: Random House, 1990.

_____ . *Eclogues.* Trans. J. W. Mackail. New York: Random House, 1950.

Xenophon. *Cyropaedia.* Trans. Walter Miller. 2 vols. Loeb Classical Library. 1914. Repr., Cambridge: Harvard University Press, 1968.

INDEX OF MODERN AUTHORS

INDEX OF ANCIENT SOURCES